THE LIFE OF HENRY DRUMMOND

THE LIFE

OF

HENRY DRUMMOND

BY

GEORGE ADAM SMITH

WITH PORTRAIT

NEW YORK
DOUBLEDAY & McCLURE COMPANY
1898

Norwood Press
J. S. Cushing & Co. — Berwick & Smith
Norwood Mass. U.S.A.

To His Mother

PREFACE

In the preparation of this volume I have received generous help from many friends, who have placed at my disposal their memories of Henry Drummond and their collections of his letters; or who have further assisted by their counsel on points of difficulty, and by their careful revision of several of the chapters. I am especially indebted to Mr. James Drummond, who arranged his brother's papers and furnished many details of information.

As to the letters which are quoted in the volume, I have to explain that the names of those to whom they were addressed have been given, for the most part, only where this was rendered necessary by the allusions which the letters contain.

In a life so crowded with interests and activities, some facts have doubtless been overlooked. A few of these, which appeared too late to be put in their proper chapters, have been gathered together in an Appendix.

In the quoted material the *round* marks of parenthesis and their contents belong to the original; what is enclosed in *square* brackets has been added.

COILLEBHROCHAIN, PERTHSHIRE,
September, 1898.

CONTENTS

ix

CHAPTER IX

CHAPTER XIX

APPENDIX I

APPENDIX II

'. . . By a fine gentleman, I mean a man completely qualified as well for the service and good, as for the ornament and delight, of society. When I consider the frame of mind peculiar to a gentleman, I suppose it graced with all the dignity and elevation of spirit that human nature is capable of. To this I would have joined a clear understanding, a reason free from prejudice, a steady judgment, and an extensive knowledge. When I think of the heart of a gentleman, I imagine it firm and intrepid, void of all inordinate passions, and full of tenderness, compassion, and benevolence. When I view the fine gentleman with regard to his manners, methinks I see him modest without bashfulness, frank and affable without impertinence, obliging and complaisant without servility, cheerful and in good humour without noise. These amiable qualities are not easily obtained, neither are there many men that have a genius to excel this way. A finished gentleman is perhaps the most uncommon of all the great characters in life. Besides the natural endowments with which this distinguished man is to be born, he must run through a long series of education. Before he makes his appearance and shines in the world, he must be principled in religion, instructed in all the moral virtues, and led through the whole course of the polite arts and sciences. He should be no stranger to courts and to camps; he must travel to open his mind, to enlarge his views, to learn the policies and interests of foreign states as well as to fashion and polish himself and to get clear of national prejudices, of which every country has its share. To all these more essential improvements he must not forget to add the fashionable ornaments of life, such as are the languages and the bodily exercises most in vogue; neither would I have him think even dress itself beneath his notice.'

CHAPTER I

AS WE KNEW HIM

IT is now eighteen months since Henry Drummond died — time enough for the fading of those fond extravagances into which fresh grief will weave a dead friend's qualities.   And yet, I suppose, there are hundreds of men and women, who are still sure — and will always be sure — that his was the most Christlike life they ever knew.   In that belief they are fortified not only by the record of the great influence which God gave him over men, for such is sometimes misleading; but by the testimony of those who worked at his side while he wielded it; and by the evidence of the friends who knew him longest and who were most intimately acquainted with the growth of his character.

In his brief life we saw him pass through two of the greatest trials to which character can be exposed. We watched him, our fellow-student and not yet twenty-three, surprised by a sudden and a fierce fame. Crowds of men and women in all the great cities of our land hung upon his lips, innumerable lives opened their secrets to him, and made him aware of his power over them.   When his first book was published, he, being then about thirty-three, found another world at his feet; the great of the land thronged him; his social opportunities were boundless ; and he was urged by the chief statesman of our time to a political career. This is the kind of trial which one has seen wither some of the finest characters, and distract others from

the simplicity and resolution of their youth.   He
passed through it unscathed: it neither warped his
spirit nor turned him from his accepted vocation as a
teacher of religion.

Again, in the end of his life, he was plunged to the
opposite extreme.   For two long years he not only
suffered weakness and excruciating pain, but what
must have been more trying to a spirit like his,
accustomed all his manhood to be giving, helping,
and leading, he became absolutely dependent upon
others.   This also he bore unspoiled, and we who had
known him from the beginning found him at the end
the same humble, unselfish, and cheerful friend whom
we loved when we sat together on the benches at
college.

Perhaps the most conspicuous service which Henry
Drummond rendered to his generation was to show
them a Christianity which was perfectly natural.   You
met him somewhere, a graceful, well-dressed gentleman, tall and lithe, with a swing in his walk and a
brightness on his face, who seemed to carry no cares,
and to know neither presumption nor timidity.   You
spoke and found him keen for any of a hundred
interests.   He fished, he shot, he skated as few can,
he played cricket; he would go any distance to see
a fire or a football match.   He had a new story, a
new puzzle, or a new joke every time he met you.
Was it on the street?   He drew you to watch two
message boys meet, grin, knock each other's hats off,
lay down their baskets and enjoy a friendly chaffer of
marbles.   Was it in the train?   He had dredged from
the bookstall every paper and magazine that was
new to him; or he would read you a fresh tale of his
favourite, Bret Harte.   ' Had you seen the *Apostle of
the Tules;* or Frederic Harrison's article in the *Nine-*

teenth Century on " Ruskin as a Master of English Prose," or Q's *Conspiracy aboard the Midas,* or the " Badminton " *Cricket?* ' If it was a rainy afternoon in a country house, he described a new game, and in five minutes everybody was in the thick of it. If it was a children's party, they clamoured for his sleight-of-hand. He smoked, he played billiards ; lounging in the sun, he could be the laziest man you ever saw.

If you were alone with him, he was sure to find out what interested you and listen by the hour. The keen brown eyes got at your heart, and you felt you could speak your best to them. Sometimes you would remember that he was Drummond the evangelist, Drummond the author of books which measured their circulation by scores of thousands. Yet there was no assumption of superiority nor any ambition to gain influence — nothing but the interest of one healthy human being in another. If the talk slipped among deeper things, he was as untroubled and as unforced as before ; there was never a glimpse of a phylactery nor a smudge of unction about his religion. He was one of the purest, most unselfish, most reverent souls you ever knew, but you would not have called him saint. The name he went by among younger men was ' The Prince'; there was a distinction and a radiance upon him that compelled the title.

That he had ' a genius for friendship ' goes without saying, for he was rich in the humility, the patience, and the powers of trust which such a genius implies. Yet his love had, too, the rarer and more strenuous temper which requires ' the common aspiration,' is jealous for a friend's growth, and has the nerve to criticise. It is the measure of what he felt friendship to be that he has defined religion in the terms of it.

With such gifts, his friendship came to many men and women — women, to all of whom his chivalry and to some his gratitude and admiration were among the most beautiful features of his character. There was but one thing, which any of his friends could have felt as a want — others respected it as the height and crown of his friendship — and that was this.

The longer you knew him, the fact which most impressed you was that he seldom talked about him-self, and no matter how deep the talk might go, never about that inner self which for praise or for sympathy is in many men so clamant, and in all more or less perceptible. Through the radiance of his presence and the familiarity of his talk there sometimes stole out, upon those who were becoming his friends, the sense of a great loneliness and silence behind, as when you catch a snow-peak across the summer fragrance and music of a Swiss meadow. For he always kept silence concerning his own religious struggles. He never asked even his most intimate friends for sym-pathy nor seemed to carry any wound, however slight, that needed their fingers for its healing.

Now many people, seeing his enjoyment of life and apparent freedom from struggle, — seeing also that spontaneousness of virtue which distinguished him, — have judged that it was easy for the man to be good. He appeared to have few cares in life and no sorrows; till near the end he never, except in Africa, suffered a day's illness, and had certainly less drudgery than falls to most men of his strength and gifts. So they were apt to take his religion to be mere sunshine and the effect of an unclouded sky. They classed him among those who are born good, who are good in their blood.

We may admit that, by his birth, Henry Drummond did inherit virtue. Few men who have done good in

the world have not been born to the capacity for it.
It takes more than one generation to make a consummate individual, and the life that leaps upon the world
like a cataract is often fed from some remote and
lonely tarn of which the world never hears the name.
Henry Drummond's forbears were men who lived a
clean and honest life in the open air, who thought
seriously, and had a conscience of service to the community. As he inherited from one of them his quick
eye for analogies between the physical and the spiritual laws of God, so it was his parents and grand-
parents who earned for him some at least of the ease
and winsomeness of his piety.

But such good fortune exempts no man from a share
of that discipline and temptation without which neither
character is achieved, nor influence over others. Our
friend knew nothing of poverty or of friendlessness;
till his last illness he never suffered pain ; and death
did not enter his family till he was thirty-six. And,
as we have said, he was seldom overworked. Yet at
twenty-two he had laid upon him the responsibility
of one of the greatest religious movements of our time,
and when that was over there followed a period of
uncertainty about his future vocation of which he
wrote: 'I do not know what affliction is, but a strange
thought comes to me sometimes that " waiting " has
the same kind of effect upon one that affliction has.'
Nor can we believe that he was spared those fiercer
contests which every son of man has to endure upon
the battle-field of his own heart. No one who heard
his addresses upon Temptation and Sin can doubt that
he spoke them from experience. We shall find one
record, which he has left behind, of his sense of sin
and of the awful peril of character.

We must look, then, for the secret of his freedom

from himself in other directions, and I think we find
it in two conspicuous features of his life and teaching.

The first of these was his absorbed interest in
others — an interest natural to his unselfish temper,
but trained and fed by the opportunities of the great
mission of his youth, which made him the confidant
of so many hundreds of other lives. He had learned
the secret of St. Paul — *not to look upon his own
things, but also upon the things of others* — that sov-
ereign way of escape from the self-absorption and
panic which temptation so often breeds in the best of
characters. No man felt temptation more fiercely, or
from the pressure of it has sent up cries of keener
agony, than St. Paul, who buffeted his own body and
kept it under. But how did he rise above the despair?
By remembering that *temptation is common to man*,
by throwing his heart upon the fight which men were
everywhere waging about him, and by forgetting his
own fears and temptations in interest and sympathy
for others. Such souls are engrossed spectators of
the drama of life; they are purged by its pity, and
ennobled by the contemplation of its issues. But a
great sense of honour, too, is bred within them, as
they spring shoulder to shoulder with so many struggling comrades — a sense of honour that lifts them
free of the baser temptations — and they are too interested in the fate of their fellows, and too busy with
the salvation of others, to brood or grow morbid about
themselves. Of such was our friend.

But Drummond had been taught another secret of
the Apostle. St. Paul everywhere links our life in
Christ to the great cosmic processes. *For by Him
were all things created, that are in heaven, and that
are in earth, visible and invisible; all things were created by Him and for Him . . . and ye are complete*

in Him who is the head of every principle and potency.
To Henry Drummond Christianity was the crown of
the evolution of the whole universe. The drama
which absorbed him is upon a stage infinitely wider
than the moral life of man. The soul in its battle
against evil, in its service for Christ, is no accident
nor exception, thrown upon a world all hostile to its
feeble spirit. But the forces it represents are the
primal forces of the Universe; the great laws which
modern science has unveiled sweeping through life
from the beginning work upon the side of the man
who seeks the things that are above. I think it is
in this belief, informed by a wide knowledge of science, but still more indebted to an original vision of
nature, that, at least in part, we find the secret of the
serenity, the healthy objectiveness, and the courage
of Henry Drummond's faith.

It was certainly on such grounds that in the prime
of his teaching he sought to win the reason of men
for religion. This was always his first aim. He had
an ill-will — one might say a horror — at rousing the
emotions before he had secured the conviction of
the intellect. I do not mean that he was a logician,
for his logic — witness the introduction to his first
book — was often his weak point. But he always
began by the presentation of facts, by the unfolding
of laws, and trust in these and obedience to them was,
in his teaching, religion. He felt that they lay open
to the common sense and natural conscience of man.
Those were blind or fools who did not follow them.
Yet he never thought of these laws as impersonal, for
the greatest were love and the will that men should
be holy, and he spoke of their power and of their
tenderness as they who sing, *Underneath are the
everlasting arms.* He had an open vision of love

wrought into the very foundation of the world; all
along the evolution of life he saw that the will of
God was our sanctification.

In these two, then, his interest in other men and
his trust in the great laws of the universe, we find
the double secret of that detachment — that distance
from self at which he always seemed to stand.

But we should greatly mistake the man and his
teaching if we did not perceive that the source and
the return of all his interest in men and of all his
trust in God was Jesus Christ.   Of this his own
words are most eloquent : —

> ' The power to set the heart right, to renew the
> springs of action, comes from Christ.   The sense
> of the infinite worth of the single soul, and the
> recoverableness of a man at his worst, are the
> gifts of Christ.
> ' The freedom from guilt, the forgiveness of sins,
> come from Christ's cross; the hope of immor-
> tality springs from Christ's grave.   Personal
> conversion means for life a personal religion, a
> personal trust in God, a personal debt to Christ,
> a personal dedication to His cause.   These,
> brought about how you will, are supreme things
> to aim at, supreme losses if they are missed.'

That was the conclusion of all his doctrine.   There
was no word of Christ's more often upon his lips than
this : *'Abide in Me and I in you, for without Me ye
can do nothing.'*

The preceding paragraphs have passed imperceptibly from the man himself to his teaching.   And this
is right, for with Henry Drummond the two were one.
So far as it be possible in any human being, in him

they were without contradiction or discrepancy.   He
never talked beyond his experience; in action he
never seemed to fall behind his faith.   Mr. Moody,
who has had as much opportunity as perhaps any man
of our generation in the study of character, especially
among religious people, has said: 'No words of mine
can better describe his life or character than those in
which he has presented to us *The Greatest Thing
in the World*.   Some men take an occasional journey
into the thirteenth of First Corinthians, but Henry
Drummond was a man who lived there constantly,
appropriating its blessings and exemplifying its teachings.   As you read what he terms the analysis of
love, you find that all its ingredients were interwoven
into his daily life, making him one of the most lov-
able men I have ever known.   Was it courtesy you
looked for, he was a perfect gentleman.   Was it kindness, he was always preferring another.   Was it humility, he was simple and not courting favour.   It could
be said of him truthfully, as it was said of the early
apostles, "that men took knowledge of him that he
had been with Jesus."   Nor was this love and kindness
only shown to those who were close friends.   His face
was an index to his inner life.   It was genial and
kind, and made him, like his Master, a favourite with
children. . . .   Never have I known a man who, in
my opinion, lived nearer the Master or sought to do
His will more fully.'[1]   And again: 'No man has ever
been with me for any length of time that I did not
see something that was unlike Christ, and I often see
it in myself, but not in Henry Drummond.   All the
time we were together he was a Christlike man and
often a rebuke to me.'[2]

[1] *Record of Christian Work*, May, 1897, p. 129.
[2] Letter to the Rev. James Stalker, D.D.

With this testimony let us take that of Sir Archibald Geikie, D.C.L., F.R.S., the Director-General of the Geological Survey of the United Kingdom. When he became the first Professor of Geology in Edinburgh, Drummond was his first student. They travelled together in Great Britain, and on a geological expedition to the Rocky Mountains,[1] and in later years they met at intervals. Sir Archibald had therefore every opportunity of judging his friend's character, and this is what he writes of him. It is in continuation of some reminiscences which will be quoted later: —

'In later years, having resigned my Professorship for an appointment in London, I met him much more seldom. But he came to see me from time to time, always the same gentle and kindly being. His success never spoiled him in the very least degree. It was no small matter to be able to preserve his simplicity and frankness amidst so much that might have fostered vanity and insincerity in a less noble nature than his. I have never met with a man in whom transparent integrity, high moral purpose, sweetness of disposition, and exuberant helpfulness were more happily combined with wide culture, poetic imagination, and scientific sympathies than they were in Henry Drummond. Most deeply do I grieve over his early death.'

Now there was one portion of Christ's spirit and Christ's burden which those who observed Henry Drummond only in his cheerful intercourse with men, upon the ways of the world, would perhaps deem it impossible that he should have shared. His first religious ministry was neither of books, nor of public speech. As we shall see, soon after he had read to his fellow-students his paper on 'Spiritual Diagnosis,' in which he blamed the lack of personal dealing as the

[1] See below, chap. vii.

great fault of the organised religion of his time, he was
drawn to work in the inquiry rooms of the Revival
of 1873-75. And in these he dealt, face to face, with
hundreds of men and women at the crises of their lives.
When that work was over, his experience, his fidelity,
and his sympathy continued to be about him, as it
were, the walls of a quiet and healing confessional,
into which wounded men and women crept from the
world, dared

'To unlock the heart and let it speak' —

dared to tell him the worst about themselves. It is
safe to say that no man in our generation can have
heard confession more constantly than Drummond
did. And this responsibility about which he was ever
as silent as about his own inner struggles was a heavy
burden and a sore grief to him. If some of the letters
he received be specimens of the confidence poured
into his ears, we can understand him saying, as he
did to one friend: 'Such tales of woe I've heard in
Moody's inquiry room that I have felt I must go and
change my very clothes after the contact;' or to another, when he had come from talking privately with
some students: 'Oh, I am sick with the sins of these
men! How can God bear it!' And yet it is surely
proof of the purity of the man and of the power of the
gospel he believed in that, thus knowing the human
heart, and bearing the full burden of men's sins, he
should nevertheless have believed (to use his own
words) 'in the recoverableness of a man at his worst,'
and have carried with him wherever he went the air
of health and of victory.

To such love and such experience there naturally
came an influence of the widest and most penetrating
kind. Very few men in our day can have touched the

springs of so many lives.   Like all his friends, I knew
that hundreds of men and women had gone to him,
and by him had been inspired with new hope of
their betterment and new faith in God.   But even
then I was prepared neither for the quality nor for
the extent of influence which his correspondence reveals.   First by his addresses and his conversation,
and then with the vastly increased range which his
books gave him, he attracted to himself the doubting
and the sinful hearts of his generation.   It must be
left to the other chapters of this biography to illustrate
the breadth and variety of the power both of himself
and of his teaching.   But here it may be affirmed with
all sobriety that his influence was like nothing so much
as the influence of one of the greater mediæval saints
— who yet worked in a smaller world than he and with
a language which travelled more slowly.   Men and
women sought him who were of every rank of life and
of almost every nation under the sun.   They turned
instinctively to him, not for counsel merely, but for
the good news of God and for the inspiration which
men seek only from the purest and most loving of
their kind.   He was prophet and he was priest to
hosts of individuals.   Upon the strength of his personality or (if they did not know him) of the *spirit*
of his writings, they accepted the weakest of his logic,
the most patent of his fallacies.   They claimed from
him the solution of every problem.   They brought
him alike their mental and their physical troubles.
Surest test of a man's love and holiness, they believed
in his prayers as a remedy for their diseases and a
sure mediation between their sinful souls and God.
It is with a certain hesitation that one asserts so much
as this, yet the evidence in his correspondence is indubitable ; and as the members of some great Churches

are taught to direct their prayers to the famous saints of Christendom, so untaught and naturally, as we shall see, more than one have since his death found themselves praying to Henry Drummond.

To write an adequate life of such a man is of course an impossibility; a friend has said it would be 'like writing the history of a fragrance.' One can describe and make assertions about his influence, but those can hardly appreciate who did not know himself. Indeed, this volume would never have been undertaken — both because of its difficulty, and because of what undoubtedly would have been his own wishes on the point — had it not become clear to his relatives and friends that the life of one who exercised a saving influence on thousands of people all over the world would, in the absence of an authorised biography, be attempted by persons who, however feelingly they might write, could convey only a fragmentary knowledge of their subject.

Nor can his biographer hope to satisfy his intimate friends, men and women of all stages of religious experience, of many schools of thought, and of all ranks and callings in life, to whom his sympathy and versatility, as well as the pure liberty of his healthy spirit, must necessarily have shown very different aspects of his character and opinions. For such, all that a biographer can do is to provide pegs, on which they may hang, and perhaps render somewhat more stable and balanced, their own private portraits of their friend.

One thing is obvious. So much of Drummond's best work was done, so to speak, 'in the confessional,' upon many who are still alive, and some of whom are well known to their fellow-countrymen, that it is impossible to describe it except with a reserve which may appear to deprive the picture of life. But, although among his papers material exists for narratives of sin, and even of crime, of moral struggle, of conversion and of Christian service, of the most thrilling interest, it is the duty of his biographer to imitate his own reticence, even at the risk of disguising the depth and the reality of his influence.

But the biographer of Henry Drummond can at least describe the influences which moulded him, trace the growth of his character and the development of his opinions, and give a record of the actual work he did, and of the movements which he started or enforced. Among the first of these the religious movement in Great Britain from 1873 to 1875 stands supreme, and deserves the most thorough treatment. The history of this has never been written. The present generation do not know how large it was, and with what results upon the life of our nation. As for Drummond, it made him the man he was in his prime : in his expertness in dealing with men, in his power as a speaker, nay, even in some principles of his faith, he is inexplicable without it. So a long chapter will be devoted to the movement and to his share in it.

As to the growth or change of his opinions, that also it is needful to trace in detail, not only that we may do justice to himself, but because certain of the lines of that growth follow some of the most interesting religious and intellectual developments of our time. Here was a young man trained in an evangelical family, and in the school of the older orthodoxy, who consecrated his youth to the service of Christ, and never all his life lost his faith in Christ as his Lord and Saviour, or in Christ's Divinity, or in the power of His Atonement, but who grew away from many of the doctrines which, when he was young, were still regarded by the Churches as equally well assured and indispensable to the creed of a Christian: such as, for instance, belief in the literal inspiration and equal divinity of all parts of the Bible. In his later life Drummond so explicitly avowed his adherence to an interpretation of Scripture very different from this, that it is not only right that the latter should be described in his own words (hence the large extracts in chap. x. of this volume), but that also the narrower positions from which he started on his career should be set plainly before us. For this reason I have recounted some of the opinions of his student days with a greater fulness than their intrinsic importance would warrant. The story of his growth from them may be of use to the many students whom the Biblical criticism of our time has brought face to face with similar facts, problems, and issues.

Parallel to this change in his views of Scripture and contributory to it, is the very interesting growth of the influence wrought upon his religious opinions by physical science and that discovery of natural laws in which his generation has been so active. But besides these two developments there is a third, which is also characteristic of our time. To Drummond, in his youth, religion was an affair of the individual; he was impatient (if such a temper could, at any time, be imputed to him) with the new attempts in Scotland and England to emphasise its social character. It is true he never bated by one jot his insistence upon the personal origin of all religion; yet he so greatly extended his sympathy and his experience, he so developed the civic conscience, as to become one of the principal exponents in our day of the social duties of religion. Thus his career is typical of the influence upon the older Christian orthodoxy of the three great intellectual movements of our time — historical criticism, physical science, and socialism (in the broad and unsectarian meaning of that much-abused term).

Again, Henry Drummond was a traveller, with keen powers of observation, a scientific training, and a great sympathy with human life on its lowest levels and outside edges. He visited the Far West of America at a time when Indian wars were still common and the white man was represented only by soldiers, hunters, and miners of gold. He visited Central Africa at a time when the only white men there were missionaries and a few traders, and of that region he made practically the first detailed scientific examination. He visited the New Hebrides, when the effects of Christianity upon the savages of these islands were beginning to be obvious; he bought clubs and poisoned spears from men who were still cannibals; he worshipped with those who had been cannibals and were now members of his own church. Of these travels it is only of the second that he has published an account. Yet his notes of the others are often as interesting and always as careful. I have thought it right, therefore, to incorporate in this life of him a transcription of these notes, and to supply from his African diary so much of scientific or other human interest as has not appeared in his *Tropical Africa*. It was in Africa that he made his only original contributions to science, and in justice to these it seems right to give, in greater detail than his modesty allowed to appear in his volume, his observations of the geology of the African continent.

Finally, Henry Drummond was a writer of books, which brought him no little fame in the world. This biography is written by one of a circle of life-long friends, and with their affections upon its words; yet it was among them that some of his books received the most severe criticism, and therefore I have deemed it not inconsistent with the spirit of the biography to introduce an adverse judgment upon the substance of one of his volumes. As to the style in which all are written, if the saying be anywhere true that the style is the man, it is true here. The even and limpid pages of his books are the expression of his equable and transparent temper. And as we have seen that his character was the outcome of a genuine discipline, so we shall find evidence that his style was the fruit of hard labour and an unsparing will.

But all these talents and experiences were only parts of a rare and radiant whole, of which any biography, however fully it may record them, can with them all offer only an imperfect reflection. So complete a life happens but once in a generation. ' It is no very uncommon thing,' says the writer whose words are prefixed to this chapter,[1] 'it is no very uncommon thing in the world to meet with men of probity; there are likewise a great many men of honour to be found. Men of courage, men of sense, and men of letters are frequent; but a true fine gentleman is what one seldom sees. He is properly a compound of the various good qualities that embellish mankind. As the great poet animates all the different parts of learning by the force of his genius, and irradiates all the compass of his knowledge by the lustre and brightness of his imagination, so all the great and solid perfections of life appear in the finished gentleman, with a beautiful gloss and varnish; everything he says or does is accompanied with a manner, or rather a charm, that draws the admiration and good-will of every beholder.'

[1] Sir Richard Steele in the *Guardian*, No. 34.

C

CHAPTER II

SCHOOL AND COLLEGE

HENRY DRUMMOND came of a family resident for some generations near the town of Stirling. His great-grandfather was portioner of the lands of Benthead, Bannockburn. His grandfather, William Drummond, was a land surveyor and afterwards a nurseryman at Coneypark. He appears to have been a man who thought for himself on matters of religion. It was among some notes of his, upon resemblances between the laws of nature and those of the spiritual life, that his grandson, after the publication of *Natural Law in the Spiritual World*, discovered a remarkable anticipation of the main thesis of that volume.[1] William Drummond had eleven sons. Of these Henry, who was the father of our Henry, became head of the firm of William Drummond & Sons, seedsmen and nurserymen at Stirling and Dublin. One of his brothers and partners, David, resided at Dublin. Another was Peter, who established the Agricultural Museum in Stirling, and withdrew from the firm in order to give his energies to the Stirling Tract Enterprise, of which he was the founder.

Mr. Henry Drummond, senior, was a man of great worth. ' He was fifty years of age before he taught in a Sabbath-school or opened his lips in public on religion,' but from that time onwards he was in the front of every good cause in Stirling. He was a

[1] *See* p. 153.

18

Justice of the Peace, President of the Young Men's Christian Association, chairman or director of most of the philanthropic institutions of the town, and an elder in the Free North Church, under the ministry of the Rev. Dr. Beith. He founded, and for many years conducted, a Sunday-school at Cambusbarron in the neighbourhood of his home. 'He could play on an audience of children as a man plays on an instrument.' His discipline was strict, but he had his children's confidence. By his contemporaries he was implicitly trusted for his probity in business, his fast friendship, and his sagacious counsel. To the end of a long life his character remained fresh and winsome. He died on January 1, 1888.

Mr. Drummond married Miss Jane Blackwood of Kilmarnock. She had a brother, James Blackwood, of Gillsburn, whose attainments in science deserve some notice here, partly for their own worth, and partly because of their resemblance to the qualities and pursuits of his distinguished nephew. 'While still a youth he became proficient in chemistry and geology, and constructed a camera obscura, microscope, and telescope. Stands, tubes, and lenses were all fashioned by himself. He was one of the earliest makers of daguerreotypes in Scotland. In later years he devoted himself to the study of petrology, the science of the constituents of rocks, and became, next to his friend, the late Professor Heddle of St. Andrews, the chief authority on that subject in Scotland. How many will remember an evening spent with him at Gillsburn, when the grand microscope was brought out and Mr. Blackwood showed slices of rock ground till they were transparent. How instructive it was to hear him explain "the perpetual motion slides," in which there are cavities filled with fluid and tiny air

globules that move to vibrations in the earth so slight
that our senses cannot perceive them!'[1]   Mr. Blackwood was a genial and enthusiastic man, with the
power of inspiring young people both in the study
of science and in some forms of religious service.
Like his nephew he possessed the gift of mesmerism.
Henry, when he was young, met this uncle twice or
thrice every year, but was not directly influenced by
him.   The striking resemblances, both of gifts and
interests, must be put down to heredity.

Mr. and Mrs. Drummond had four sons: James,
Henry, Frederick, who died young, and Patrick; and
two daughters, Agnes and Jessie.   Henry was born
in Stirling on August 17, 1851.   His father's house
was then No. 1 Park Place, the house next to Glenelm, which afterwards became the family home, and
is still the residence of his mother.   The houses stand
on the southern side of the King's Park and look
across to the Rock and Castle.   The park was the
children's playground.   James and Henry were sent
first to a ladies' school, and, when Henry was six or
seven, to the High School of Stirling, where he remained till he was twelve.

At that time the High, or Grammar, Schools of
Scotland were of various quality.   Those of the larger
towns received boys from nine to eleven, and sent
them to the university at sixteen or seventeen.   They
gave a fair education in classics, English, history,
mathematics, and the rudiments of French and German.   Boys meant for business took a course of book-
keeping, but natural science was almost wholly ignored.
Some of the schools of the smaller towns competed
successfully with those of the larger in preparation
for the university; but others, taking boys at six or

---

[1] Abridged from a notice of Mr. Blackwood by the Rev. D. Landsborough.

seven, dismissed them at twelve or thirteen to business
or to the more advanced schools, with a few exceptions
whom they prepared for college.   There was no general system.   Till 1859 the universities had not an entrance examination in Arts, and afterwards one only
for the shortened curriculum of three, instead of four,
years.   The quality of the school depended on the
character of the headmaster, and varied greatly from
place to place and from time to time.   At the close
of the session, a university professor might be invited
to examine, sometimes orally, sometimes in writing,
but the examinations were often loose.

The school discipline did not extend beyond the
classes.   Preparation was done at home, and a boy's
habits of study largely depended on his guardians.   In
many a humble home in Scotland, after the day's work
was done, the tired parents, or an aunt or a big sister,
would bravely attack the Latin grammar, and carry
their boy through his daily preparation.   When Scotland's debt to her parish and burgh schoolmasters is
being celebrated, I love to think of those even more
heroic sacrifices of the home.   They were given without parade or the feeling that there was anything big
about them; they were unknown to all but those for
whom they were performed, and even by them they
were often forgotten.

Nor in the early sixties was a boy's play organised
for him as it so largely is to-day.   Yet there was little
danger of loafing.   A day-school boy lives in no
vacuum; at home, in the streets, and in the country
around there are a hundred healthy interests of which
boarding-schools know little.   In Henry's time boys
had their rounders, 'Dully,' a rough cricket, and a
primitive football; 'Cavey,' 'Scots and English,'
'Thieves and Police,' 'Corners,' 'Bullyable', and other

running games; sham fights and sieges, all hard and
healthy sports. The long Saturday, free from school
discipline, and often from the discipline of home, has
always made for good in the life of a Scottish boy.
It develops his independence, teaches him to plan his
time, and takes him upon long and healthy adventures.
Henry enjoyed his Saturday freedom even at the
boarding-school in Crieff, and on a visit there many
years afterwards, out of a grateful memory of what it
had been to himself, he impressed on the headmaster
its indispensableness to the character of the boys.
There was, let it be said again, practically no loafing.
Those who held aloof from sports were laughed or
pommelled into a share of them. 'G and A,' says
Drummond in a letter to his brother, 'are by no
means so spoony as formerly, but still at times they
try their old plans — walks and so forth.' It was a
breezy, healthy life, and not the least part of its health
was the way the 'town's school' brought all classes of
the 'town's bairns' into rivalry, both of work and
play. Among Drummond's mates was a miner's son,
William Durham, who carried everything before him
at Stirling, and died at the close of a brilliant career
in Edinburgh University. He was the original of the
'Lad of Pairts' in the story by 'Ian Maclaren,' who
himself joined Stirling High School a few months
before Drummond left it for Crieff. Drummond also
remembered there the original of 'Bumbee Willie.'

The boys were made to write essays. They found
their way to the Macfarlane Free Library, and in that
dingy place hunted up their subjects in the few en-
cyclopædias — chiefly the *Penny* and the *Britannica*.
Their own reading was mainly in Ballantyne's stories
or Beadle's 'American Library' of sixpenny books,
published monthly in orange covers — Red Indian

tales, with white hunters for their heroes. About half a dozen of the older boys formed a ' United Book Club,' to which each contributed a weekly penny, and a cousin with more pocket-money than the rest made up the deficiencies. This bought periodicals like the *Boys' Magazine* and the *Boys' Journal*, which, in those days before rubber stamps were invented, were marked ' U. B. C.' with a stamp carved out of 'caum.'[1]

In school the English class was always opened with prayer. Every Monday morning a verse of a Psalm was repeated and a chapter read, and every Friday morning a question was asked from the Catechism. ' We envied the Episcopalians their freedom from the Catechism.'

Mr. Drummond did not send his children to a Sabbath-school, but on Sunday they gathered to sing hymns, and were catechised and formally addressed by their father. They went twice to church.

' Henry was more prominent in the playground than in the class. I[2] think of him most of all in the English department. Under its distinguished teacher, Mr. Young,[3] two objects received special attention, — reading aloud and grammar, analysis and composition. Henry was a beautiful reader, and more than once obtained the reading prize. I think the skill which was then developed largely helped to make him the speaker he subsequently became.' He was a rapid learner, but volatile, careless of hours, and often late for meals. Yet his family remember how through his boyhood this was the most serious fault for which he was ever rebuked. One of his hobbies was collecting eggs. His sense of bargaining was always very

[1] Soft slate or shale.
[2] The Rev. John H. M'Culloch, now of North Leith.
[3] ' Mr. Young was an old white-haired man with fine manners, who taught English with much dignity and impressiveness.' — REV. T. CRERAR.

strong, and his pockets were even fuller than those of
other boys with knives, pencils, and marbles. 'He
took a foremost place in the playground, where he was
ready for any game; there he began that acquaintance
with his fellows, and that personal influence upon
them, which so distinguished his years of manhood.'[1]
He took to cricket with enthusiasm, and some skill;
both at Stirling and at Crieff he kept wickets for the
eleven. But fishing was his favourite sport — his first
rod a bamboo cane with a string at the end of it. His
brother says: 'He was a better fisher than I, but when
I caught my first trout he was more jubilant than if it
had been his own.' Even as a boy he cast a very
pretty line. He could swim, but not well. On summer Saturdays, with other boys, he went far up a burn
among the hills behind his home, caught trout, lit a
fire, scraped some poached turnips with tinkers' scraps,
and bathed and cooked alternately the livelong day.
Around these high excursions lay one of the most
glorious landscapes even in Scotland — the Rock
and its Castle, the links of Forth, Bannockburn, the
Ochils, and to the northwest, the first great Bens:
Lomond, Venue, Ledi, and Voirlich. He has not
written of what all this was to him, and you could
seldom have told from his conversation that he was a
'Son of the Rock.' But after he had seen most of the
world, whenever he came back to Stirling he would
take his old walk round the Castle and say to his
brother, 'Man, there's no place like this — no place
like Scotland!'

'He was not more than averagely popular among
his contemporaries, and had hardly any intimate
friends, but bigger boys were fond of giving him
things, and he was a great favourite with men.' His

1 From reminiscences by Rev. J. H. M'Culloch.

interest in fishing was partly the cause of this. But even in childhood he must have had some distinction which caught an experienced eye, and there were occasions on which he took the lead of other children and impressed himself on older people, always, as witnesses testify, without any self-consciousness. The Rev. James Robertson, a famous preacher to children, was holding a service for all the Sabbath-schools of the town in Erskine United Presbyterian Church. ' The Free North School was the last to arrive, and the church being already crowded, one class was arranged on the pulpit stairs, and Henry and two other boys were taken into the pulpit itself. Mr. Robertson began his sermon by saying that the Bible is like a tree, each book a branch, each chapter a twig, and each verse a leaf. "My text is on the thirty-ninth branch, the third twig, and the seventeenth leaf. Try and find it for me." Almost immediately Henry slipped from behind him and said, "Malachi third and seventeen."—"Right, my boy; now take my place and read it out." Then from the pulpit came the silvery voice: "*And they shall be Mine, saith the Lord of Hosts, in that day when I make up My jewels.*" Mr. Robertson laid his hand on the boy's head and said: "Well done. I hope one day you will be a minister." ' [1]

With this picture we may take another, which we owe to the good fortune that John Watson came to Stirling High School shortly before Henry left it for Crieff : —

' It was in the King's Park more than thirty years ago that I first saw Drummond, and on our first meeting he produced the same effect upon me that he did all his after life. The sun was going down behind Ben Lomond, in the happy summer time, touching with gold the grey old castle, deepen-

---

[1] From reminiscences by Mr. Fotheringham.

ing the green upon the belt of trees which fringed the eastern side of the park, and filling the park itself with soft,
mellow light.   A cricket match between two schools had
been going on all day and was coming to an end, and I had
gone out to see the result, being a new arrival in Stirling
and full of curiosity.   The two lads at the wickets were in
striking contrast — one heavy, stockish, and determined, who
slogged powerfully and had scored well for his side; the other
nimble, alert, graceful, who had a pretty but uncertain play.
The slogger was forcing the running in order to make up
a heavy leeway, and compelled his partner to run once
too often.   "It's all right and you fellows are not to cry
shame," — this was what he said as he joined his friends, —
"Buchanan is playing A 1, and that hit ought to have been
a four; I messed the running."   It was good form, of course,
and what any decent lad would want to say, but there was an
accent of gaiety and a certain air which was very taking.
Against that group of clumsy, unformed, awkward Scots
lads, this bright, straight, living figure stood out in relief, and
as he moved about the field my eyes followed him, and in my
boyish and dull mind I had a sense that he was a type by
himself, a visitor of finer breed than those among whom he
moved.   By and by he mounted a friend's pony and galloped
along the racecourse in the park till one saw only a speck
of white in the sunlight, and still I watched in wonder and
fascination — only a boy of thirteen or so, and dull — till he
came back, in time to cheer the slogger who had pulled off
the match with three runs to spare — and carried his bat.

'"Well played, old chap," the pure, clear, joyous note rang
out on the evening air; "finest thing you've ever done,"
while the strong-armed, heavy-faced slogger stood still and
looked at him in admiration, and made amends.   "I say,
Drummond, it was my blame you were run out. . . ."
Drummond was his name, and some one said "Henry."   So
I first saw my friend.

'What impressed me that pleasant evening in the days of
long ago I can now identify.   It was the lad's distinction, an
inherent quality of appearance and manner of character and
soul which marked him and made him solitary.'

When Henry was twelve, James and he were sent to Morison's Academy at Crieff. They boarded with the rector, Mr. Ogilvie, one of a band of able brothers who have done noble service for education in Scotland. After two years James entered his father's business, but Henry stayed on to prepare for the university. A series of letters to James and his parents record the details of a very happy life. He begins German and learns chess and whist. Mr. Ogilvie introduces a weekly lecture on Natural Philosophy, and an air-pump and electrical apparatus are purchased to the excitement of the school. The football club gets its first Rugby ball and proper goals. There is fishing in the Turret, and skating on the loch of Ochtertyre. The boys rehearse for theatricals; Henry is to be a lady. Christy ministrels are coming, but Henry has seen from the Stirling paper that the troupe is not a good one, and dissuades the rector from taking the school to see them! And so on. These letters are charming, but their charm cannot be conveyed in quotations. They are written with some promise of his later style — subject to frequent misspellings. There is much shrewdness and humour in describing his masters and schoolmates, an independent judgment, which is adverse, of a tract sent him from home, a touch of sarcasm when he has succeeded to his older brother's topcoat and congratulates the latter on his new one, a healthy power of chaff, a bit of boyish brutality in reporting that ' J. has typhous (*sic*) fever; poor fellow, it will weaken him sadly, but he needed something of that kind to tame him,' and just one touch of priggishness. Throughout there beats a strong sympathy with all at home, and a very pretty desire that father, mother, brothers, and sisters should each have some pleasure. The habit thus formed was retained.

Till the end Drummond almost never missed writing his mother so that she should get a letter every Saturday night.

I have presented these details of Henry Drummond's early years, not because I deem them singular, but because this natural boyhood, eagerly enjoyed, was the secret of his life-long sympathy with boys, and of his wonderful influence over them. To the end he preserved the vivid memory, which only the pure in heart preserve, of what he himself had been as a boy: at what queer angles he had seen the world; what had interested and what had tempted him; what he had understood in the religion he was taught and what he silently dropped. That religion was evangelical Christianity of a doctrinal form, strict in its adherence to a somewhat dry routine of preaching and teaching, but not gloomy nor ascetic, for it forbade no amusements, allowed the boys to lead an athletic life, to play chess and whist, to learn dancing, and as they grew older to go to dancing parties. The boys were patriotic, as boys could not help being who lived under Stirling Castle, and public-spirited, for Mr. Drummond's large share in social movements interested and did not weary his children. If the area of religious experience was denominational, this involved no bitterness, but merely an ignorance of the works of other Churches, which, Henry once naïvely told me, was the source to him afterwards of the most delightful surprises at the great amount of good in the world.

From his home discipline Henry carried away a neatness and punctuality that lasted all his days. His schoolmates have emphasised the unselfishness of the boy, and unselfishness was the note of his life to the end. But the most beautiful thing which the letters reveal is the full confidence between parents and children, so that the latters' own powers of judgment were fostered, and their humour had free play. It is a healthy home where the old and the young folk have the same jokes.

In July, 1866, Henry left Crieff with prizes for Latin and English, and for an essay on 'War and Peace.' In October, being fifteen years of age, very small, and haunted by a fear that he would not grow, he matriculated at Edinburgh University. During the first session he lodged with two older students, Crerar and Carmichael, who superintended his studies. He was still the boy, and it is amusing to see how his habits of chaffering and exchange were developed. He haunted the auction rooms of Edinburgh, and made bargains which would have been great if he had had any use for the articles — two guitars which he did learn to play,[1] and other instruments which he did not learn. He advertised his 'eggs in exchange for money or a telescope,' and was pestered by a dealer 'with offers of articles enough to fill a pawnshop.' He went to look over the wall of Pitt Street Gymnasium and take stock of the new velocipedes. ' I do not know what to think of them. They are as light as a feather, and look rather startling ('Did you see *Punch's* cartoon, "Riding upon Nawthin'?'"), and go at a great pace, but appear to oscillate and *waggle* in what I should think was a rather unpleasant manner. However, I daresay the "By-Cyclones" were all greenhorns. It takes a few lessons before you become expert, which is a great blessing, as it would prevent everybody asking "to try it" if any of us ever have one. The Parisian kind are being advertised on all hands. I saw a genuine one,

---

[1] ' "What do you want with two?" we said in our proud seniority. "Oh, I can sell one of them for the price of the two," which, however, he never did. He got ribbon about the guitar, and pirouetted, twanging it right musically and heartily.' — REV. T. CRERAR.

a beauty, price £8. They have them dearer. An
Edinburgh firm, I believe, are making them much
cheaper — and with an improved drag, a most ingenious and easily worked thing — some say £2 10s.
Sho! I cannot get at the truth. One could easily
make one if a pattern were given.' So he kept his
eyes open to everything that would interest his
brother at Stirling. He had, too, a pretty tact and
sympathy with the varied sorts of folk among whom
he was thrown for the next four years. He explains
why he cannot offend his fellow-lodgers by introducing
to the common table (at his father's suggestion and
expense) more than his proper share of dainties. He
appreciates his landladies, humorously describes their
babies to his mother, and gives a genial account of
the many characters which the pilgrim from lodging
to lodging constantly encounters.[1]

In the first year of Arts at Edinburgh University
in those days there was much on which one looks
back now with considerable amusement. The students were either boys or bearded men, fresh from
the plough and the workshop. In classics and mathematics the junior classes were below the standard of
the senior forms in the High Schools. They worked
through several Latin and Greek authors, not the
most difficult, did a heap of prose exercises, and
learned several books of Euclid with a little algebra.
The freshmen carried large oak sticks to class, cut and

---

[1] The Rev. T. Crerar sends the following reminiscence from Drummond's first
year in lodgings: 'Once the two older students (Carmichael and I) sampled too
well before he returned a lot of toffee that had been sent to him. He expressed no
sorrow, though toffee was sweet at that time, and the seniors felt remorse at the
result of their preying on his good nature. But a morning or two after he had his
revenge. He rushed into our room, saying, "Some one died of cholera in that
bed, perhaps in the very sheets you are lying in." We rose in horror and dismay.
Then he pointed the finger and retreated. The death had happened eight years
before! The toffee was avenged.'

bludgeoned the desks, snowballed the traffic on the
South Bridge, and by general subscription in copper
paid their ringleaders' fines, both to the University and
the Police authorities. They formed a debating society, the Philomathic, which the older societies scorned
as juvenile and as rustic and vulgar, nicknamed 'the
Pheelomawthic.' Its ambitions were not mean. Besides the usual historical questions to which schoolboys devote themselves, it determined week by week
the rank of the great stars of literature and solved the
most abstruse economic problems; but it was also
practical, reviewing once a year the policy of the Government. In Drummond's time it disposed of the Irish
Church, decided against the education of women, reformed the Game Laws, and drew up a new programme
of the Arts curriculum. But it grew most passionate
upon its own constitution and upon points of order.
Then its eloquence blew vast and was beaten into the
desks with the oak sticks.

Partly through a dislike of classics, Henry took an
erratic course through Arts. The first year, 1866-67,
he had Senior Humanity under Professor Sellar and
English with Professor Masson. The second year he
took Junior Greek with Professor Blackie, Logic and
Metaphysics with Professor Fraser, and Junior Mathematics with Professor Kelland; and the third year
Second Mathematics and Natural Philosophy with
Professor Tait. It was under Professor Tait that
Drummond first woke up to something more than
the performance of routine, and his notebooks have
full transcripts of the lectures with diagrams of the ex-
periments. Yet he only gained the fourteenth place in
a class of one hundred and fifty. In the spring of 1869
he passed the examination in mathematics and physics
for the degree of M.A. In his fourth session he took

Senior Greek, Senior Humanity for the second time, and Moral Philosophy with Professor Calderwood. His essays for the latter were on the 'Reliability of Consciousness,' 'The Moral Faculty,' and 'The Dictum of Comte: that causes are inacessible, we must therefore substitute the Study of Laws.' They are pretty good, but betray an amusing tendency to revert to the subject of animal magnetism, with which Drummond was beginning to be fascinated. In April, 1870, he closed his Arts course by passing the degree examinations in Mental Philosophy. 'I had never courage,' he wrote, 'to attempt the classical department of the M.A.' During his divinity course he came back to the University for Botany, Chemistry, Zoölogy, in which he took second place with seventy-six per cent., and Geology, in which he won the class medal. But, although he tried twice, he failed to pass the first part of the Bachelor of Science examination and left the University without a degree. To one of his more successful friends he wrote: 'J. W. addresses me "two-thirds M.A." I wish the University was liberal enough to reward a martyr like myself with its precious degree upon credit, and I am almost inclined to petition the Senate to that effect.'

Meanwhile Drummond had put himself under another discipline, in which it is possible to see the development of his later powers, chiefly his powers of observation and his style of writing English. At the beginning of his second session he attended a meeting of the Philomathic Society and was proposed as a member, — against his will, he says, but nevertheless there and then he made his first speech, — an undergrown boy of sixteen with auburn hair, a bonny fresh face, and keen eyes. His first essay, on 'Novels and Novel-reading,' followed in two months. 'It was not an utter failure and the old hands praised it,' he wrote to his mother, to whom alone of all his correspondents he repeats any praise that he has heard of himself.   In 1868 some members of the Society started, in monthly manuscript, 'The Philomathic, a Literary Magazine conducted by a few of the Alumni of Edinburgh University.' It lived for eight months. Drummond was the editor, and contributed in January, 1869, an essay on 'Mesmerism and Animal Magnetism.' This is an enthusiastic defence of the sincerity and usefulness of a movement then under much ridicule.   It asserts as indubitable the evidence of the ability of one man's will to induce certain states in others. 'How probable this is in a reasonable universe! The Creator cannot have isolated men from each other nor shut each up in his own prison body.   In the human body he has engrafted a life-giving, communicable, and curative power! . . .   Mesmerism has been proved to be a better anæsthetic than chloroform. . . . With such serious and beneficial results its practice for amusement ought to be seriously condemned. . . . Mesmerism must prevail; only in its infancy, it will some day be recognised as Nature's universal curative agent,' and so forth.   The usual pleas on behalf of a process which had not (at least in this country) obtained the attention from scientific authorities which it has since gained are advanced with force and clearness.   But the interest of the paper lies in the fact that Drummond himself had practised upon others the power of mesmerism.

'It was at that time,' writes the Rev. J. H. M'Culloch, 'that he developed an aptitude for what was then known as electro-biology. The student who shared rooms with me proved a capital subject and Drummond could do anything he

D

liked with him without giving offence. Once I remember
being in the University reading-room when this student came
in, walked up to where I was sitting, and without a word took
his watch off the chain and handed it to me. I looked up
and saw at once what was what. I asked him what he had
been about, and he told me that Drummond had been prac-
tising on him. I told him that he should ask him for his watch,
and then when I found that he had no recollection of having
given it to me, I handed it back to him and told him that this
sort of thing should come to an end.'

Why Drummond gave up this practice I do not
exactly know. I have heard that it was because he
was once startled by the unforeseen length to which
his influence had gone upon another student, though
the latter at the time it was exercised was living at a
distance from him. So much for the paper on 'Animal
Magnetism.' Drummond also contributed to the debates in the Philomathic, speaking against the Irish
Church and in favour of the education of women, the
latter on the grounds of the 'awful crime of leaving any
mind untrained and of the terribly unintellectual state
of the average girl of the period!'

He had begun to form a library and to read for himself. He bought some books at auctions. He has read,
he says, Channing's works, some of Ruskin's and of
Robertson's of Brighton, Lamb's Essays, Shenstone
and Cowley, Lowell and the American humourists. He
must have read largely in poetry, chiefly in Cowley,
Pope, Byron, and Lowell, for his papers of this time
have many unhackneyed quotations from all of these.
He had fallen under the spell of Ruskin. At the
election of Lord Rector of the University in 1868 he
canvassed for him, as against the political candidates,
Mr. Robert Lowe and Lord Advocate Moncrieff.

But the best proof of how rapidly Drummond was
educating himself in argument and style appears from

two papers and a little bundle of notes for a third. In 1870 he delivered his valedictory address as President of the Philomathic, and after expounding the advantages of debate, contrasted the lecture, conversation, and reading as a means of gaining knowledge. 'The lecture,' he says, 'is the best means. If it has fallen into disrepute in our day, that is because there are no good lecturers. The advantage of public teaching lies in the sympathy which it creates. A lecturer, however, should not be conversational. He is as much out of place as a lecturing conversationalist.' 'The matter of a lecture is the pedantry of conversation.' He passes on to reading: 'Books are the great delusion of the present age. We find them everywhere. Nature is mocked and put in the background.' 'A good book is as valuable as a good friend, but he who has too many books, like him who has too many friends, is sure to be led away by some of them.' 'Most neglect the great end of reading. The thing sought is not what you will get in an author, but what the author will enable you to find in yourself. Unreflective minds possess thoughts as a jug does water, only by containing them; if pebbles be dropped in the water, if the thought of another plunges in among our own, the contents brim over and we discover in ourselves sentiments and ideas which, apart from certain external conditions of development, had never been formed, and the mind had been left in perpetual slumber.' 'The great danger of reading is superficiality. Many read far too much.'

The second of the papers mentioned above was one of several sent about this time (1870, when he was not nineteen) to the editors of magazines and returned by them. This one was offered to *Cassell's Magazine*. It is entitled 'The Abuse of the Adjective.'

After a couple of pages against slang, 'by the introduction
of which our language is losing its solid, classic grandeur and
becoming enfeebled and diluted with a wretched levity,' he
goes on to speak of 'an internal enemy, a more subtle because
less apparent danger, the indiscriminate use of adjectives.'
'Adjectives have become cosmopolitan.   Immensity, minute-
ness, rotundity, profundity, astronomy, gastronomy, emotions,
monkeys, feelings, frying-pans, mountains, mouse-traps, trees,
toothpicks, sunsets, and sewing-machines are all qualified in
turn by exactly the same set of adjectives. . . .   Appropri-
ateness of meaning seems utterly lost sight of, and all are
used promiscuously, apparently with but one object, to add
strength to an otherwise insipid observation.   In short, the
prevailing opinion and province of an adjective seems to be
"A big word, having no special significance of its own,
employed to give force and liveliness to a sentence consisting otherwise of plain, common-sense words."   That delicacy of expression is sacrificed to elaboration, and exactness
of description to sonorousness, further appears from the
increased use of qualifying Adverbs, as well as from the fre-
quency with which the Superlative degree is employed. . . .
Not the least dangerous quality of this manner of expression
is its infectiousness.   It runs through a community like an epi-
demic and its opponents take to it in self-defence. . . .   Mild
language does not do at all.   Every man is a braggart.   The
desire to say a strong thing has grown almost irresistible, and
truth becomes sacrificed to strength and impressibility (*sic*).'
'Those most addicted to the habit are Ladies. . . .   Our
Ladies, in conversation at least, are no longer the Gentle
Sex.   They have grown in their ideas masculine, and in their
expression of them barbarous.   When the voice of Beauty
is heard it speaks in uncouth tones.   But professional men,
who ought to be free of the habit, have also succumbed.
Some men have a notion that this manner of "piling on" the
adjective constitutes raciness.   When the conversation is
flippant *in se* it is not so extremely objectionable.   Truly, if
we talk nonsense, we ought to talk it well, *i.e.* well nonsensi-
cally.   But what we complain of is that a deal of sense is in
the language of nonsense. . . .   Language should be subordinate to thought, not thought to language. . . .   Com-

monplace people are deluded by the habit. They mistake
the half-dozen really good thoughts which every fool possesses for the revelation of the hidden glory of a great mind.
But so far from serving any utilitarian purpose the habit of
multiplying adjectives really makes a sentence less impressive than if simple words had been used.   There is a natural
tendency to suspect insincerity whenever the language is
extraordinary enough to suggest strain or effort on the part
of the author.' The paper then illustrates from ballads,
children's stories, and the Bible the simplicity of the greatest
literature, and closes with the practical exhortation : 'If the
danger be pointed out, there is surely no reasonable individual who would not sacrifice any slight gratification it may
afford him for the sake of the issues at stake, the corruption
versus the preservation of the English language.'

The bundle of notes referred to were in preparation for an article in the *Stirling Observer* upon
Alva Glen — Drummond's earliest published writing.
They reveal a keen sense of beauty and an extraordinary care in sketching natural facts.   Every
boulder in the glen, every turn of the banks, every
twist and cascade in the burn, the geological formations, the colouring of the rocks, the fragrances of the
wood, the sounds of human industry that penetrate
to the furthest corners, the features of the sky-line,
the distant prospects, are all noted in a series of rapid
impressive clauses that succeed in making a stranger
to the scene feel as if he were viewing it.[1]

I have quoted all this, not so much for its own sake,
though a deal of it is very clever, but because it shows
how diligently and how sanely Drummond prepared
the clear and brilliant style for which he afterwards
became famous.   There is no evidence in any of his

[1] There exists, too, a curious paper entitled 'Treason among the Tombs,' due to
a visit to Glasnevin Cemetery, Dublin, and the sight of monuments to Irishmen
shot or hung during the Fenian rebellion. He is shocked by the open defiance
of Great Britain which the inscriptions record, and makes a number of sound
remarks upon the problems of British government in Ireland.

essays at this time of an original capacity of thought;
but there is abundant proof of unusually keen powers
of observation, of a fine and healthy taste in letters,
and of distinct powers of illustration and interpretation — all of them exercised with a sanity and maturity not less than remarkable from a boy of just
over eighteen years of age. 'One thing,' writes Mr.
M'Culloch, 'which struck me at college was the fashion in which Drummond laid himself out in a quiet
way thoroughly to know how those around him looked
at things. He had the faculty of putting himself *en
rapport* with everybody. Everybody liked him, too,
because he was never inquisitorial. He gained the
confidence of others almost without their knowing it,
and they were glad they had been so frank with him.
This, too, became a characteristic in that larger world
where he ultimately found his vocation.'

During his University course Drummond had shot
up into a tall man, graceful when at rest, and moving
with a litheness and a spring that were all his own.
A fellow-student[1] thus remembers him: 'He often
stood in a thoughtful manner, or sauntered about the
northeast corner of the college quadrangle between
classes. He generally wore a tall hat, and had long
auburn hair. Though I fain would have spoken to
him, his ethereal appearance and great grace and
refinement seemed to forbid an approach to one who
appeared different from the majority of the students.
He was generally alone. Indeed, his apparent loneliness first drew my attention to him. He seemed to
have no companions as the other students had, but
was only one of them, handsome, bright, and silent.
He struck me as one possessed by great thoughts,
which were polarising in his mind and giving a happy
expression to his face.'

[1] Now Dr. H. M. Church of Edinburgh.

CHAPTER III

PREPARATION FOR THE MINISTRY

'DURING his Arts curriculum Henry Drummond formed no plans for his future, beyond some thought of finding his way into the Divinity Hall of the Free Church of Scotland.'[1]

To this there was much to dispose him, and he had already passed through some religious experience. In his last illness he told Professor Simpson that 'when he was twelve he had a great work going through Bonar's *God's Way of Peace*, but thinks it did him harm.' While he was a student, he attended some mission services at Cambusbarron. He was profoundly impressed by the addresses he heard, and soon after told his father that he wished to enter the ministry.[2] In Edinburgh he shared his lodgings with several divinity students; and in Stirling he met many ministers and evangelists, among them Dr. Binnie of the Reformed Presbyterian Church, to whose kindness in counsel he afterwards looked back with gratitude.

The first notice of his intentions occurs in a letter to a fellow-student of date April, 1870. 'Are you not sorry to leave the University? I feel it very much. Altho' I intend to enter the Church Hall next winter, it is still a degeneracy to go

[1] From recollections by the Rev. J. H. M'Culloch.

[2] From recollections by Mr. Fotheringham. The Cambusbarron Mission was in charge of the Rev. Alexander Macdonald, now of Ardclach; and the special services were conducted by Mr. Stephen Burrows, now evangelist at Naples.

from an ancient University to a nameless college! Happily I shall still be a student. I have now to commence the pleasant study of Hebrew, and have the prospect of being plucked in that particular branch at the F. C. Board Examination in July. Fortunately I know the alphabet from the 119th Psalm!' On May 15th he began Hebrew by himself, and soon after made a literal translation of some of the Psalms. On July 26th he passed the Board.

In the summer he had taken a tutorship in a family in Kincardineshire and he there spent his nineteenth birthday — his first from home. It cast him into a train of serious reflection.

'May I never be too hardened to let these annual milestones sweep by unwept for! In looking back on my past years I see nothing but an unbroken change of Mercies. Few lives have been as happy as mine. The rod of affliction may conquer many, but if I am subdued at all I have been "killed with kindness"— unmerited, unrequited, unsolicited, unexampled kindness. "What can I render unto God for all His gifts to me?" Alas! I have rendered nothing, nothing but evil. The only misery I have endured has been of my own creation — the confusion of face for my own iniquity, the mournings for sins that were past, and the consciousness of my own guilt before God. For days I have felt ashamed to look up to Him and too wicked to approach His footstool. I believe I have discovered by my own sad experience the true meaning and justice of His attributes, "Longsuffering," "Plenteous in Mercy," etc. O that these humiliating periods of darkness were at an end! I think I can honestly

say that the chief desire of my heart is to be reconciled unto God and to feel the light of His
countenance *always* upon me. As honestly, I
think, I can say that God in His great goodness
has given me little care for the things of the
world. I have been enabled to see the extreme
littleness of the world in comparison with the
great Hereafter [so] that the temptations of the
former seem as nothing to the attractions of
the latter, and I cannot be too thankful that I
have been thus spared being whirled into the vor-
tex of the cares of this life and the deceitfulness
of riches. This may sound like vainglory, but I
am far too deep in the abyss of sin to deceive
myself in that respect. I say it not boastfully but
in fear and trembling, with deep humiliation that
all these mercies have made me little better than
if I had them not.'

This religious crisis happened to Drummond in the
form which we should have expected from his upbring-
ing. He had inherited a pure and healthy nature. He
had been kept from the grosser sins of youth and he was
always patient and unselfish. But with the religious
doctrines of Evangelicalism there had also come to
him a very sensitive moral temper. The Evangelical
movement had many defects, which in his younger
days Henry shared and which we shall see him un-
learning; but when, as in his case, sincerity was the
atmosphere of the home in which its doctrines were
taught, it succeeded in creating in the children a tender and scrupulous conscience, and by urging them
to the consideration above all of their personal relation to a just and merciful God, it strongly developed
the sense, while they were still young, of their individ-

ual responsibility. To have felt the awful peril of one's own character; to have wakened into the wonder of God's patience with one's unworthy life; to have known in one's own experience the power of man's soul to turn and repent — these are the essentials of religious experience and the indispensable apprenticeship of a religious teacher. It is not necessary that every man should violently break into this sense of God's grace, out of the intoxication of some vicious passion or from the weariness and despair of a long habit of evil. Pure minds like Henry Drummond's will feel as powerfully the accumulated memories — an avalanche of them loosened perhaps by some gentle touch — of a lifetime of God's common mercies and of His daily patience with their wilful ways. For this is a wonder, of which every day deepens the awe to their sensitive hearts. Once when talking of 'sudden conversions' I asked Drummond whether he had passed through one. 'No,' he said, after thinking for a little, 'I cannot say I did.'[1] 'But,' he added, 'I have seen too many ever to doubt their reality.'

Drummond was thoroughly sane. With the deep seriousness of his nature there mingled a strong humour and an equally strong joy in sport, of which his letters of this summer bear many signs. He had a great deal of fishing, and with jubilation over his first grilse he fills of his brief diary nearly as much as he gives to the spiritual reflections I have quoted. In October we have an instance of his fun. Before beginning his divinity course he had to be examined by the Presbytery of Stirling. This is a right which the Presbyteries of the Church have jealously maintained over the theological students within their bounds.

---

[1] Compare Dr. Stalker's testimony below, p. 70.

But, except in the matter of personal religion, the students have always resented this superintendence; and justly, for their competence in scholarship and theology is so far secured by the General Assembly's Examination Board. Hebrew — unfortunately for those who teach it — is not regarded by the average man as indispensable to the preacher, and the paradigms of its grammar are especially irksome to men who have already toiled through a university course. In the beginning of October Drummond wrote a friend: 'J. W. and I passed the Presbytery exam. yesterday with much *éclat*. We took the precaution beforehand to hide the Presbytery's Hebrew Bible in the coal-scuttle; so we got no examination in Hebrew.'

In November Drummond entered New College, Edinburgh, the youngest of twenty-five or thirty students who formed the First Year. The divinity course of the Free Church of Scotland occupies four winter sessions, and thus at New College there are always some hundred regular students of the Church, besides twenty or thirty others from America, Ireland, and the Reformed Churches of the Continent of Europe. Among a hundred men studying for the same profession there is bound to be closer fellowship than among the far larger number of students and the more scattered interests of the Arts course; and during Drummond's time at New College this bond was further strengthened by the institution of a common dinner-table. Given a certain proportion of able men, the atmosphere of the College was always genial and stimulating. One remembers not only greater maturity, but more buoyancy, more humour, and more *camaraderie* than in the University.

When Drummond entered, Robertson Smith had

just left. Andrew Harper, now Professor of Hebrew at Melbourne, and David Patrick (now editor of *Chambers's Encyclopædia*) were in their third year. W. G. Elmslie, afterwards Professor of Hebrew in the Presbyterian College of London, was in his second year, and during Drummond's time Smith, Harper, and Elmslie were in succession Dr. Davidson's assistants. In his own year were James Stalker, John Watson, and two other of his intimate friends : A. S. Paterson, who died in 1875, at Uitenhage, in South Africa, and John F. Ewing, who did such noble work in Melbourne before his early death there in 1890. Two years after Drummond there came up to the New College Peter Thomson, of whose great abilities we must speak later; and D. M. Ross, the assistant to the Professor of Logic in the University. The mutual part of their education the students transacted chiefly in the Theological Society, which met on Friday evenings. Drummond must have had some reputation as a speaker, for, although the youngest man in College, he was asked, in the absence of the student appointed, to lead off the negative side of a debate, 'Ought the government to provide for the teaching of the Bible in schools ?' He also spoke for the affirmative of the debate, 'Ought the Church to introduce an order of lay evangelists?' and in his letters home he makes more of this speech than of the other. The College Missionary Society met on Saturday mornings to hear addresses, and to arrange the conduct of a college mission in a district, then somewhere in the neighbourhood of the Cowgate. One of the students was missionary-in-charge, and others helped him with the meetings and taught in the Sabbath-school. In this work Drummond took his share with great heart. The families he visited were in Covenant Close.

The First Year's classes were Junior Hebrew under Dr. Davidson, Apologetics with Dr. Blaikie, Natural Science with Dr. Duns, and a short course of lectures on Evangelistic Theology from the famous Indian missionary, Dr. Duff. Dr. Duff, then in extreme old age, had preserved much of the fire and volume of speech which in their prime had swept through Scotland and carried public opinion on Missions to the pitch of enthusiasm. And still his reverend figure moved through the college, an object of awe to young men who knew nothing of his earlier triumphs. But the six weeks allowed for his subject were all too few for the scale on which he planned his lectures and for the enormous mass of details that he threw into them. He had two parallel courses, both magnificent torsos. One, on the History of Missions, began with the eternal decrees and broke off with the early Church. Another, on Hindoo Theology, did not seem to our bewildered minds even to arrive on the margin of history. Little wonder that so rich and fiery a brain blazed out in indignation upon the indifference of young men who had neither the theological power nor the apostolic fervour of their teacher. We could not follow the incarnations of Vishnu, nor rouse our interest in the patriarchs before Abraham. 'How many gods have the Hindoos, Mr. ——?' Dr. Duff asked a luckless student of Drummond's year. The student kicked Drummond, who sat next to him and who whispered, 'I don't know, about twenty-five, I think.' 'Twenty-five!' shouted the student, gaily. 'Twenty-five, Mr. ——! Twenty-five! Twenty-five million of millions!' There were not many of the Edinburgh students who gave themselves to foreign missions. We sorely tried the great missionary's heart. Nothing could have been kinder or more

unselfish than his treatment of us ; he was very zealous
to interest each man in India.   Drummond shared the
common apathy.   Besides, his mind was not of the
order that was carried away by romance or by the enthusiasm of others.   He needed the touch with the
concrete, and this he got years afterwards on his
travels in Africa and the East, with the result that
among all testimonies to foreign missions in the last
half-century none are more thorough or more sincere
than his.[1]

It was to Natural Science that Drummond chiefly
devoted himself at New College, and he easily carried
off the first prize.   But his note-books proved that
he worked hard both at Hebrew and Apologetics.
Besides the grammar, Dr. Davidson then gave to the
First Year a few lectures introductory to the Higher
Criticism of the Pentateuch.   It was by such lectures
that Dr. Davidson started in the early seventies the
great movement of Old Testament study which has
characterised Scottish theology during the last thirty
years.   He did not then take his students beyond the
positions reached by Ewald ; but that was sufficient to
break up the mechanical ideas of inspiration which
then prevailed in the churches, while with the teacher's
own wonderful insight into the spiritual meaning of
Scripture it made the student's own use of his Bible
more rational and lively, and laid upon a sounder basis
the proof of a real revelation in the Old Testament.
Drummond took very full notes of Dr. Davidson's lectures.   In the class of Apologetics he chose for the
statutory homily which he had to deliver, ' The Six
Days of Creation,' a subject which combined his interest in the Old Testament and his knowledge of Natural

[1] Later than his course Dr. Carstairs Douglas pleaded with him to go to China,
and impressed him much, but nothing came of this.

Science, while a year later he wrote for the class of Systematic Theology an essay on 'The Doctrine of Creation.' He treated this under two heads, the Creation of Matter and the Creation of the World. Under the former he held the question of the Eternity of Matter to be insoluble. Under the latter he put the question whether the world as explained by Modern Science was irreconcilable with the Scriptural statement of Creation? Certain scientific schools undoubtedly demand 'Matter without a Maker, Intelligence with Law but no Liberty, and Life with Liberty but no Responsibility.' The most glorious attribute of their 'deity' is physical necessity, and his highest principle of action utilitarianism. But granted that Natural Selection and Evolution are facts, they are not irreconcilable with the belief that God has created and sustains the world. On the contrary 'this belief can allow them a very prominent place,' but on the distinct understanding that this place has been previously assigned them by God, and that they are under His supervision and care. Looked at from this point of view, the principle of Natural Selection becomes a real and beautiful acquisition to Natural Theology, and Mr. Darwin's work on *The Origin of Species* may be regarded as perhaps the most important contribution to the Literature of Apologetics which the nineteenth century has produced. The same year Drummond delivered to some Society an address upon Evolution. He affirmed the principle of Development as an eternal principle, the emphasis upon which 'has been the century's noblest contribution to Theology'; but he criticised Darwin's enunciation of it on three points: 'He ignores the existence of a personal God, denies God's sovereignty, and denies the existence of design in the Universe.' These notes of college essays, juvenile and crude, are of interest as the first steps of Drummond's mind towards the work of his later years.

But at this stage Drummond did not see how to apply the principle of development to the origins of Scripture and the story of Revelation. In an essay which he wrote for the class of Apologetics, he asks: 'How can development explain the Bible? The stages of development are missing. There is an impassable gulf between the Bible and the rest of Hebrew literature. . . . The Old Testament is infinitely above the religions of the peoples who surrounded Israel.' It has 'no cumbrous ritual, doubtful morals, nor mythical elements.' 'Theoretically its religion is not only an anomaly to the Hebrew nature, but to human nature.' The one sound element in this part of his paper is the emphasis which he lays upon the 'inability of the Jew to reach unaided by Divine help the highest doctrines of his religion, for in so many cases those ran counter to even his best natural ideals and expectations.' For all the rest Drummond as yet stood upon the ground of the older orthodoxy, with its doctrine of literal inspiration, and its blind belief in the absolutely divine character of everything in the Hebrew Scriptures. Blind indeed, else how could he, or that older orthodoxy in general, have believed that there are no links of development between the Old Testament and the religions from the midst of which it sprang, or that in the Old Testament itself there are 'no cumbrous ritual, doubtful morals, nor mythical elements'?

This college essay is of interest to us, as indicating the grounds on which Drummond stood during his first great mission, but which he afterwards abandoned for others, not less evangelical nor less capable of defending a true revelation in Scripture, but more

rational and more in accordance with the facts of
Scripture itself. At the very point at which a theological student is most disposed to be sceptical — the
close of his first session in theology — Drummond accepted orthodox Christianity, not after any passionate
struggle towards the contrary, nor with any strength
of original thought, but upon a full knowledge of the
issues, and after serious consideration. The absence
of all trace of revolt is characteristic. Drummond
never appears to have passed through a crisis of that
kind, or, if he did, it was of the mildest kind; and
when the symptoms appeared in younger men, he
treated them as temporary. He called them 'measles.'
And the effect is seen in all his teaching, as well as in
the limitation of his influence on certain classes of
minds. To Drummond the Christian experience of
faith was one not so much of struggle as of growth.
One is sometimes impatient with his beautiful way of
putting this.[1] But he expounded as he himself had
experienced. His temperament was the artistic, which
is sensitive to whatever is lovely and of good report,
and which does not struggle against what is hostile and
superfluous, but simply ignores it, as Drummond did
with certain doctrines upon which at first he laid such
emphasis. But he had the artistic temperament with
two additions — a most unselfish consideration for the
beliefs and prejudices of older people, and a most
warm moral sense. 'I cannot conceive' (he writes in
the last of the essays we have quoted) 'of such a thing
as the moderate punishment of sin, for "every sin
deserves God's wrath and curse to all eternity."' This,
though in the words of the Catechism, was no mere
echo of the religious school in which he had been
brought up, but the cry of his own heart. Sin, wrong-

---

[1] See farther on, *Natural Law in the Spiritual World,* in chap. iv.

E.

doing, self-indulgence, were the only subjects upon which, to the end of his life, we ever heard hot words from him.

The sessions at New College, 1871–72 and 1872–73, were occupied with the regular classes,—Senior Hebrew, New Testament Exegesis, Systematic Theology, and Church History. In March, 1872, Drummond wrote a paper on 'The Person of Christ: His Divinity sketched from Certain Aspects of Atonement.' He continued to take part in the debates of the Theological Society, of which, in 1873, he was elected one of the three Presidents, along with Stalker and Paterson. He also taught a class of boys in the Sabbath-school of the College Mission. He was anxious to fill up the long evenings with study, but found many distractions. His reading included Ruskin, George Eliot, Carlyle, especially *Sartor Resartus*, much poetry, and *The Eclipse of Faith*, in appreciation of which he came to hard words with a fellow-student. In the summer of 1871 he went to Ireland, and wrote the account of political feeling referred to in the last chapter. He had much fishing and a walking tour in the Highlands. Everything is vividly described, and his letters are full of humour. It was during these two sessions that he took the Science classes at the University, to which reference has been made. Professor Archibald Geikie offered him a geological tutorship in November, 1872.

At the close of his third session, in April, 1873, Drummond did what a number of Scottish divinity students do every year — went to a German university for the summer semester. Their favourite resorts used to be Berlin, where Dillmann and Dorner were; Halle, so long as Tholuck was alive; Erlangen, while Delitzsch and Hoffmann were there; Göttingen, both be-

fore and after Ewald's death; and Tübingen, where,
though Baur had died some years before, Beck was
still lecturing, and succeeding to a great measure of
Tholuck's influence, Weizsäcker taught the New Testament, the great Sanscrit scholar, Roth, gave a course
on the 'General History of Religions,' and Wilhelm
Pressel, most learned and most genial of Pfarrers,
opened his Pfarrhaus at Wankheim to all Scottish
students and introduced them to the German language and German theology. Drummond chose
Tübingen, and went there with John Ewing and
D. M. Ross. I do not know which classes he
attended. More important was the general life and
atmosphere of the place, and this he enjoyed to the
full.

Who does not that goes to Tübingen straight from
a Scottish winter? The glory of the southern spring
and summer; the first sight of vineyards and the first
tramp through a real forest; the mediæval castles and
churches, Urach and Lichtenstein, Hohenzollern and
Bebenhausen, the hospitality and 'gemüthlichkeit' of
the Swabians; the genuine piety, with other forms and
larger liberties than Scottish religion has allowed itself;
the social side of the students' life, their 'kneipes,' their
music, and their duels; the first impressions of the
thoroughness of German scholarship, and of the depth
of German thinking; the gradual mastery of the great
language, and the entrance upon the vast new literature
— with all these it is not wonderful that so many of
us at Tübingen should have wakened for the first time
to what Nature is, and even found there, in a sense,
the second birth of our intellect. Henry saw a number
of duels, was welcomed by a Verein, took a long Whit-
suntide tramp through the Black Forest with three of
its members, and so haunted the Wankheim Pfarr-

haus and won the Pfarrer's heart, that when they met, some years later, in Princes Street, Edinburgh, the old gentleman rushed at him and kissed him on both cheeks. Altogether, he made a great impression on the Tübingen people, as he did everywhere, by his sunniness and his sympathy; and to some of us who followed him three years after, it was enough of a passport to the friendship of the men and women most worth knowing in Tübingen, that we were friends of ' Heinrich Droomond.'

To his Sisters

'TÜBINGEN, May 28.

' You will hear that I am going my tour with three German students. As they know little or no English, I shall have great chances of picking up the language, but I find that one has really to rely almost entirely on home work, for it is perfectly astonishing how little one really learns by conversation. You get into the trick of ringing the changes on a few sentences and phrases, and one is apt to think one knows far more than one really does. I find it is no joke getting up a language; the myriad words and shades of meaning are almost appalling. The accent in Tübingen is a fearful dialect, which Berliners cannot understand at all, at least when the peasants speak. I have the satisfaction of picking up Hoch-Deutsch, and quite steering clear of the patois. I have got to know an authoress in Tübingen, a very famous lady [probably Frau Ottilie Wildermuth, authoress of the charming *Bilder aus Schwabenland*], and she has invited me to her house as often as I like to come to

supper on Tuesday evenings. I shall not be
slow to avail myself of her kindness.

'P.S. Hechingen. Thursday morning. *En route*
for Schwarzwald. Morning rather misty. Country
splendid.'

On his return from ,Germany, Drummond resolved
to postpone his fourth session at New College for a
year or two, in order to give himself to the study of
Natural Science, and to regular Mission work. He
retained, however, his position as President of the
Theological Society, and read an essay before it on
'Spiritual Diagnosis.' He had, as yet, practically
no experience of religious work among adults; yet the
essay enumerated the principles, and laid down the
methods upon which, beginning from this very month
onwards, he conducted all his wonderful ministry to
men. I did not know of the existence of the paper
till too late to quote it here; but Dr. Stalker sends
me the following recollection, and I add some echoes
of it from the criticism, delivered at the time it was
read by Mr. Barnetson, now Free Church minister of
Roslin: —

'In the Theological Society, near the commencement of the session 1873–74, he electrified us with
an essay on Spiritual Diagnosis, the thread of which
I still perfectly remember. He contrasted the clinical
work of a medical student with the total absence of
any direct dealing with men in a theological curriculum, and maintained that a minister can do far more
good by "buttonholing" individuals, than by preaching
sermons. The essay was understood to be purely
speculative, and as yet there was no word in Edinburgh of Mr. Moody's coming; but, within a month,

Mr. Moody had arrived, and in his meetings Henry was putting his speculations into practice.'

'Gentlemen, the paper now read in your hearing is a brilliant one in many respects. There is an earnestness of purpose and a definiteness of aim, which are manifest at the outset, and never flag throughout. He is in hot haste to let us know what he means. After emphasising our Lord's dealing with individuals, he says: "We know well enough how to move the masses, how to draw a crowd around us . . . how to flash and storm in passion, how to work in the appeal at the right moment, how to play upon all the figures of Rhetoric in succession, and how to throw in a calm, when no one expects but every one wants it. Every one knows this or can know it easily, but to draw souls one by one and take from them the secret of their lives, to talk them clear out of themselves, to read them off like a page of print, to pervade them with your own spiritual essence and make them transparent, *this* is the spiritual diagnosis which is so difficult to acquire and so hard to practise." "The scientific treatment of the power of spiritual discernment" is the felt want which the paper expresses; this power exercised upon another for his good is what the essayist understands by "spiritual diagnosis." The lack of such a science he laments, and at the same time shows that there is a reason in the nature of things why this should be. He brings forward evidence—from Solomon, Plato, Addison, and other writers—for the reality of the spiritual life. To get the variety of its workings and interworkings reduced to scientific classification is the great task before pastoral theology, which, if achieved, would supply the missing link between college training and practical work. The variety of phenomena in the spiritual life he finds to be no bar to a spiritual science, inasmuch as there are equally numberless phenomena in the sciences of chemistry and biology.   But there is a difficulty in the *nature* of the facts to be dealt with.   The *need* for such a science he finds in seeking to guide an awakened sinner to Christ.   How to direct such an one, how to note the changing experiences and their precise import — for this we have no education.   The mere skeleton of the soul's state at different stages is all that many have to guide them in the delicate task of ministering to a mind distressed, and it is quite insufficient.   The *dangers* arising from this want of due acquaintance with the subject are next dealt with, and a warning is deduced: " To avoid the Didactic and practise the Attractive must be the rule." The unsatisfactory basis on which spiritual diagnosis rests is then adverted to — " it rests at present upon mere individual impression."   It has no philosophic basis, which is a matter of profound regret, since the scientific method could be so easily applied to it.   And the paper concludes with an estimate of this power as seen in the Puritans, whose humanity he reckons not to have abounded with the milk of human kindness, and also with an axiom for spiritual diagnosis : " Tenderness and courtesy are requisite to approach the heart, without which the heart is approached only to be shocked." '

In these recollections two of Drummond's characteristics are very evident, — his sense of law and of definite order in all religious experience, and the insistence upon tenderness and courtesy, of which qualities he was himself one of the most perfect examples this generation has seen, — and it was these which gave him his wonderful power over the individual.

The same week he started operations as missionary

in the Riego Street Mission of Free St. Cuthbert's
Church, then under the collegiate ministry of Sir
Henry Moncrieff, Bart., and Mr. Gavin Anderson. He
opened with this appointment the second of his brief
diaries, in which he records ' his first public appearance, Mr. Anderson having asked him to take the
concluding prayer at the congregational prayer-meeting. The first time I ever faced an audience, sensa-
tions not remarkable. When my turn came I trembled
on standing up — considerably all through. Tremour
in voice. I should think not perceived; mind kept perfectly clear and cool. Voice seemed not my own, but
a new voice. Have no possible idea how it sounded.
Prayer was simple and to the point. It was outlined
in thought during the afternoon — a sentence or two
were written, but then not all remembered at the
time.'

' I was more than satisfied with the result. *Of
course there was nothing of my doing in it.*' Two
years before this he had found that he spoke much
more powerfully extempore than when he wrote
out his speeches beforehand, and this is confirmed
by his friend Mr. M'Culloch. But the experience
never betrayed him into laxity of preparation. For
his meetings in Riego Street, attended at first by
only a dozen people, he wrote out his prayers very
carefully, and prepared full notes for his addresses.
' To-night held my first prayer-meeting. There were
ten women and two men present, all the right class.
Address — what shall I say? I think it must have
been very poor, particularly as to the delivery. Was
not the least nervous, but did not know exactly where
to look. People listened attentively — very. One
woman (like a servant) put me out rather by laughing, I suppose at the crudities of my attempt. It

certainly was crude. It closed with a bang, *i.e.* an abrupt collapse ! '

So the diary itself closes. The following week a religious movement began in Edinburgh and spread over the country, which caught up the stammering evangelist to a higher platform and gave him his first extraordinary influence and fame among men.

CHAPTER IV

THE GREAT MISSION. 1873-1875

TOWARDS the end of the summer of 1873, two Americans landed at Liverpool with the purpose of holding religious meetings in the large cities of England. To quote their bills, one of them preached, and the other sang, the Gospel. The singer was the younger of the two, thirty-four years of age, with a strong baritone voice, and he sang sitting at an American organ, upon which he accompanied himself. The one who preached was about thirty-seven, short, thick-set, with a heavy jaw and a strong American accent. Their names were American, with the usual middle initial — Dwight L. Moody, the preacher, and Ira D. Sankey, the singer.

In their own country the men had already given proofs of power, and their personal record was unstained. But they came to England with no fame and hardly any credentials. Their methods were strange and aggressive, the season of the year unsuitable, and in their attempt upon Liverpool they failed. They moved to York and found as little sympathy there. So they went on to Newcastle and Sunderland, where at last, after a few weeks, large meetings were gathered and thoroughly roused. Many men and women, but especially men, were convinced of sin, and professed faith in Jesus Christ as their Saviour. The news spread across the country.

The Rev. John Kelman of Leith, who had heard

of the work from his brother in Sunderland, visited
the meetings both there and at Newcastle.   By what
he witnessed he was convinced of the real power of
the movement, and at the close of a service at Walker
he gave the evangelists an invitation to Scotland.
About the same time similar proposals reached them
from Mr. Hood Wilson of Edinburgh and from Dundee.   Mr. Kelman strongly advised them to begin in
Edinburgh, as from there the whole of Scotland could
be most easily reached.   To this Mr. Moody agreed,
and Mr. Kelman returned to form a committee and
prepare the way.[1]   For the next six weeks there were
daily gatherings for prayer, and on Sunday, the 23d
of November, the Edinburgh mission was opened with
a very crowded meeting in the Music Hall, at which Mr.
Moody was too ill to speak.   The meeting on Monday
was in the Barclay Church, and Mr. Sankey's organ having been broken, he did not sing.   With these inauspi-
cious beginnings, the week-day meetings were at first
but fairly large.   Only a few of the leading ministers
were present; many refused to intimate the mission,
and it was with difficulty that Mr. Sankey's harmonium
was admitted, even into some of the churches previously
granted for meetings.   Every week, however, the tide
rose, and by Christmas began to flow in volume.   On
New Year's Eve, a crowded watch-meeting was attended
not only by many ministers, but by a still larger number of the leading laymen of the town.   Members
of all the Protestant denominations professed themselves quickened.   The prejudices of those who for
years had resisted every attempt to introduce instrumental music into public worship were overcome, and

---

[1] Mr. Kelman acted as secretary of the Edinburgh committee.   Moody wrote
to Drummond some years afterwards: 'My love to Kelman; I never think of the
work in Edinburgh without thinking of him.'

they lustily sang with Mr. Sankey and his organ. The most respected leaders of religion spoke from the evangelist's platforms, helped in the inquiry rooms, and instructed the young converts. Professor Cairns, Professors Charteris and Calderwood of the University, Professors Blaikie and Rainy of New College, Dr. Andrew Thomson, Mr. Hood Wilson, and Dr. Horatius Bonar; Dr. Andrew Bonar and Dr. Marshall Lang from Glasgow; Mr. George Cullen, Mr. M'Murtrie of St. Bernard's and Mr. Wilson of Tolbooth, Mr. William Arnot, Mr. James Robertson, Mr. John Morgan, Mr. Whyte of Free St. George's, Mr. Knox Talon of the Episcopal Church, Lord Polwarth, Sheriff Campbell, Mr. James Balfour, Mr. William and Mr. David Dickson, Mr. Brown Douglas, Mr. David M'Laren, and a number of lawyers, doctors, and merchants gave their assistance. On all sides the fire spread. Hundreds of converts were gathered from the careless and formal members of the Church, as well as from among people who never went' to church. In contrast to most congregations, the number of men at the meetings equalled and sometimes exceeded that of the women. It was possible to fill one church after another with young men, and to see in each a hundred rise to confess that they had been converted by God's Word. And the work became a general subject of discussion, sometimes hostile, but always serious, among all classes of society.

The secret of all this lay open. The evangelists themselves were obviously men of sincerity and power. They made mistakes. Mr. Moody said some rash things, as a foreigner could not help doing, and many crude ones, as an uneducated man must. While some of his addresses were powerful, others were very poor. But these faults soon sank from sight in the deep impression of a true zeal to win men for a better life, and to pour fresh power into the routine of Christian work. Men felt themselves in presence of a Power, towards whom their obligations and opportunities were not to be weakened by any defect in its human instruments. And as time went on the sincerity and strength of the latter became more apparent. The evangelists were practical, they were sane, and they grew more sane under the influence of the men who gathered to their help. Mr. Moody suffered no fools, and every symptom of the hysteria which often breaks out in such movements was promptly suppressed. The preaching won Scotsmen's hearts by its loyalty to the Bible and its expository character. Next to Mr. Moody's passion for proclaiming the gospel was his zeal for instruction. He believed in the Bible class, and like some other recent movements in Scotland, the revival of Bible classes and of the religious instruction of youth owes not a little to his example. But his practical spirit reached farther. His gospel, which had its centre in the Atonement, was the gospel of an Incarnate Saviour: no mere voice, but hands and feet, with heart and brains behind, to cleanse the cities of their foulness, organise the helpless and neglected, succour the fallen, and gather the friendless into families. We have forgotten how often Mr. Moody enforced the civic duties of our faith. Yet read again his addresses and articles of the time, and you will believe that in the seventies there was no preacher more civic or more practical among us. He reawakened in Scotland not a few echoes of Chalmers; and to read him again is to be filled with surprise that in the country of Chalmers so few of Moody's followers should have sustained the more liberal keynotes which he struck for them! Again, Mr. Moody

was no schismatic: just because he was so practical he
was loyal to the churches. Hardly educated himself,
he emphasised the education of the ministry. He
never strove for applause by criticism of the average
clergyman, nor for laughter by jeers at him. He knew,
as some of his present successors do not seem wise
enough to know, that it is not your passing evangelist,
however brilliant, who reaches the drifting and sunken
of our cities, but the parish minister and city missionary. But the chief features of the movement were its
prayerfulness and its ethical temper. Those who took
most part in it knew how it lived by prayer, earnest,
simple, and direct. The theology was stiff, some might
say mechanical, but it was never abstract. To use a
good old word, it was thoroughly experimental, and
busied with the actual life of men.

Over the town and neighbourhood a number of
meetings were addressed by ministers and elderly laymen of position in Edinburgh. It was after the evangelists had been at work for some time, when their
gospel was well known, there were large numbers of
inquirers, and the emphasis of every speaker was very
properly laid upon 'decision for Christ.' In their natural anxiety to make this duty appear as simple as
possible, some of these speakers laboriously succeeded
in exhausting it of all reality, and shut up their hearers
to the baldest travesty of faith that was ever presented
to hungry men. A young man who had not heard
Moody, but who was awakened and anxious, listened
for several evenings to these speakers. He saw them
whittle away one after another of the essentials of
faith, and call him to a reception of salvation in which
there was neither conscience nor love, nor any awe.
In their extremity they likened the acceptance of
Christ to the taking of a five-pound note offered you

for nothing, or of a glass of water, or of an orange!
The veil grew thinner and thinner between his eyes
and the mystery which was beyond, till at last, at the
touch of one of their grotesque parables, it tore, and —
there was nothing behind.　Religion turned out to be
a big confidence trick.　In this feeling he attended a
meeting conducted by Mr. Moody himself.　The crowd
was enormous.　The sight of two thousand men, all
of them serious, most of them anxious, plunged him
into real life again.　The words of the hymns he heard
were poor, and the music little better, but the mystical
power came back with them, and he found himself
worshipping.　Mr. Moody began to speak with that
Yankee accent in which, except when it is boasting of
its country, you seldom fail to feel the edge of the real.
There was an occasional exaggeration, but some
humour fell and swept the address clean of every
appearance of unreality.　Mr. Moody spoke of the
peril of life, of the ghastly hunger of the soul without
God, of conscience, and of guilt; then with passion
and with tenderness of God's love, and of the Saviour
Christ, who is among us to-day as surely as on the
shores of Galilee, or by the Pool of Bethesda.　Hundreds of men stood up in silent witness that they had
found salvation, and the young man knew what they
had found.　He did not stay behind with them, but
he went away feeling that God was in the meeting,
very clear what Christ could save him from, and conscious that it was at the peril of his manhood if he
refused to follow Him.

　　The movement spread over Scotland.　Messrs.
Moody and Sankey spent the spring of 1874 in Glasgow and other towns in the west.　Everything happened that had happened in Edinburgh, but on a
larger scale.　In Greenock, from three to four thousand

persons heard the gospel daily; there were meetings of two and three thousand every Sunday morning at nine. In Glasgow, the Crystal Palace, as it was then called, a building of glass, was crowded night after night with five thousand people, and still many were turned from the doors; it was nine times filled in six days. There would be from fifty to two hundred inquirers after every meeting. The body of the church or hall would be occupied by groups of men and women, all anxious, and many weeping, while ministers and their friends spoke to them of Christ. Then those who 'accepted Him' would be asked to stand up, and often all did so. The custom was to reserve every Monday evening for a meeting of converts. At the last one in Glasgow there were thirty-five hundred present. From all parts of Scotland visitors attended the meetings in Edinburgh and Glasgow, and deputations were sent from these centres over the country. So, when the evangelists went to other towns, they found their way prepared, and in some cases the results were even more rapid than they had been in either of the capitals. Stirling, Perth, Dundee, Aberdeen, Inverness, and towns to the east and north of it, Oban, Campbeltown, and Rothesay were all visited during the summer and autumn of 1874. Nor did the work diminish in a district when the evangelists passed on. In Edinburgh it was said that the results rather increased after their farewell meeting. The converts were organised: twelve hundred, who gave their names in Edinburgh, were visited every fortnight for the next two years! This careful supervision, attempted also in other places, had the best effect on the churches, in which the number of young communicants was largely increased. Ministers themselves were quickened. Although some, it is true, were

tempted to become sensational and others to rely on
the Spirit, without seeking to deserve His aids by
their own study and prayer, preaching upon the whole
was stronger and more fresh than it had been, and
new heart was put into congregational routine. In
1874, Mr. M'Murtrie — and this is but one among
many testimonies — wrote that he had 'never known
so happy a winter as last, during the whole course of
his ministry.' Dr. Cairns wrote that 'the revival had
made very hopeful the whole future of the Bible class
in Scotland.'

But the power spread beyond the congregations,
and one of the most striking features of the movement
was the social and philanthropic work which it stimulated. Like all religious revivals[1] this one had its
origin among the well-to-do classes, and at first offered
some ground for the sneers at bourgeois religion
which were cast upon it. But Mr. Moody, who had
the true imagination of the city, and the power to
bring up before others the vision of its wants, inspired
the Christians of Glasgow to attempt missions to the
criminal classes and the relief of the friendless. The
lodging-houses were visited and every haunt of va-
grants about the brick-kilns upon the South Side and
elsewhere. Temperance work was organised, and
although there were, as always in that work, very
many disappointments, a considerable number of poor
drunkards were befriended and reformed. A huge
tent was raised on the Green, and afterwards replaced
by a hall, which became the scene of a Sabbath morning breakfast to the poor, and the centre of a great deal of
other philanthropic activity. New interest was roused
in industrial schools, and on the advice of Sheriff Watson, a veteran in this line of education, an industrial

[1] Thorold Rogers, *Lectures on the Economic Interpretation of History.*

F

feeding school was established for ill-fed or ill-clad children. At Saltcoats a house was bought and furnished for orphans; new impulses were given to the Orphan Homes of Scotland, founded in 1871 by Mr. Quarrier, who, with his fellow-workers among the poor of Glasgow, had given inestimable assistance to Mr. Moody's mission. A boarding-house was opened in Glasgow for young women. Mr. Moody gave great attention to Young Men's Christian Associations, and at the height of the movement secured very large subscriptions for their foundation or expansion. He felt strongly that they[1] had been conducted upon methods which were either too vague or too narrow, and that for their success 'clear and liberal views were needed.' He defined their aim — to promote the spiritual instincts and look after the temporal wants of young men. Each 'ought to be a nursery of Christian character, a most efficient evangelistic agency, a centre of social meeting, and a means of furthering the progress of young men in the general pursuits of life.' But along with 'liberality in your aims you must have thoroughness in details. The spiritual must be distinctly dominant. Do not, however, put the association in place of the Church; it is a handmaid of the Church and a feeder of the Church. For every man it must find some work,' and 'use every particle of power in the young convert.' Again, we may express the wish that the manly and liberal views of the evangelist had been carried out by *all* the institutions which he did so much to invigorate.[2]

---

[1] See a letter by him in *Times of Blessing*, vol. i. p. 4.

[2] Another effect of the movement ought to be recorded in Edinburgh and at other places, both in England and Scotland. Some Episcopalian ministers heartily coöperated with the evangelists. But in this denomination more good appears to have been done by special missions and conferences by their own clergy in the wake of Messrs. Moody and Sankey. There were very successful missions in

How Henry Drummond was drawn into this great movement I have not been able to trace with exactness. Soon after he began his mission in Riego Street[1] he asked a fellow-student if he had heard of the two Americans who were evangelising at Newcastle, and with the date of their arrival in Edinburgh the diary of his own work stops short, as if he had been suddenly carried off upon some larger stream. Two New College men who had attended one of the early gatherings in Edinburgh, and had stayed behind to see the novel inquiry meetings, then exciting much jealousy, were asked by Mr. Moody to assist, and refused. When they returned to their lodging they felt some shame at their inability to speak of their Lord to anxious men who were seeking Him, and after prayer together they resolved to offer themselves for the work. To Drummond's own mind this suspected feature of the movement must have appeared its most promising element. Here was the very factor which he had missed in the organisation of the Church, and for which, only that month, he had been pleading in his essay to the Theological Society. We can understand how his keen mind watched the movement, and in spite of this prejudice in its favour, found at first not a little to repel him. He was curiously different from the two men with whom he was to become so intimate a colleague, — not in theology, nor in zeal to win his fellow-men for Christ, but in those other things that by the bitter irony of our life separate us from each other far more cruelly than even the divisions of religion do. His accent, his style, his tastes, were at the other pole from those of the evangelists. His

Edinburgh, conducted by Mr. Pigou, vicar of Doncaster, and Father Benson ; in Brighton, by Mr. Hay Aitken ; in Leeds, London, and elsewhere.

[1] See pp. 55–56.

speech was quiet and restrained, — an excited preacher
was always a wonder to him, — he had a perilous
sense of humour, and I do not think that he ever
really cared for large public meetings. Nor did the
social possibilities of the movement attract him: at
this time he had not the civic conscience. But from
the first he felt Mr. Moody's sincerity, and the practical
wisdom of the new methods. The aim at the individual, the endeavour to rouse and secure him — this was
what he had missed in ordinary church methods and
now found. The inquiry meetings bridged the gap
between preacher and hearer, and brought them
together, man to man, before God. On his side Mr.
Moody was feeling the need of a young man to take
charge of the meetings for young men, and it is a
tribute to his insight that he chose one whose style
and tastes were so different from his own. At first
Drummond was employed, like other students, only in
the inquiry room. 'Often he was to be seen going
home through the streets after a meeting with a man
in whose arm his own was linked. He wore round
his shoulders, or rather his head, a tartan plaid, green
and black, in which I always see him yet when I recall
those days. The figure was extremely picturesque.

'The next stage was that of addressing meetings,
which came about in this way. As the marvellous
work developed in Edinburgh, the news, of course,
flew in every direction; and requests came pouring in
from all parts of the country for speakers to come and
describe it. These were dealt with, in the first place,
by the committee who had charge of Mr. Moody's
meetings, but as the students of New College had
gone into the movement nearly in a body, a few of us
shaped ourselves into an informal committee to receive
the applications and send out deputations. Of course

the descriptions of what was going on in Edinburgh were combined with evangelistic addresses; and the flame of revival burst out in one place after another — north, south, east, and west.

'This went on for months, and Drummond was in the thick of it all the time. I still remember vividly some of his deputation work. The sympathy of young men had been very visible in Edinburgh, but it was in Glasgow that the first very remarkable meeting for this class was held, and the feature to which reference has just been made was conspicuously stamped on the movement. The meeting is still remembered in Glasgow, and in religious circles throughout Scotland, as "the hundred-and-one night." It took place in Ewing Place Congregational Church, which was filled with young men. Mr. Moody had sent to Edinburgh for a deputation of students, and Stewart, Miller (now of the Bridge of Allan), Gordon (Vienna), Brown (Glasgow), Henry, and I went. Mr. Moody did not speak at all himself; but Dr. Cairns of Berwick delivered a powerful address on Immortality; then the students spoke one after another; and Dr. H. J. Wilson wound up. As the meeting proceeded, the spiritual power was such as I have never experienced on any other occasion; and when Mr. Moody, at the close, ordered the front seats to be cleared, and invited those who wished to be prayed for to occupy the vacant pews, a hundred and one came forward. As the evangelist pleaded, and that solemn stream began to gather from every corner of the church, the sense of Divine power became overwhelming, and I remember quite well turning round on the platform and hiding my face in my hands, unable to look on the scene any more. Yet all was perfectly quiet, and the hundred and one were men of intelligence and character, who were not carried away with excitement, but moved by the force of conviction.   I do not remember anything remarkable in Henry's speaking that night; the address which told most was, I think, that of Frank Gordon, whose speaking was characterised by a wonderful pathos and passion.   When we six went back to the hotel, we sat very late discussing the remarkable scene we had just witnessed.   Some one started the question whether it is usual to remember the date and the incidents of one's own conversion.   At such a moment it was easy to be confidential, and it turned out that we were equally divided, three remembering the circumstances in which their spiritual life began, and three not. Henry was, I think, among the latter.   Each of us possesses an interleaved Testament, beautifully bound in morocco, as a memorial of that night; and each book contains the signatures and mottoes of all six. These Testaments were Henry's idea, and he presented them to the rest.   His own copy went with him through his subsequent evangelistic wanderings, and was worn to rags.

'On another occasion I remember that Henry and I set off together to fulfil two engagements without having decided to which place each was to go.   We talked the matter over as the train carried us up the Highland line, but at last we tossed for it.   I went to Inverness and he, I think, to Nairn or Elgin.   As matters turned out, this decision was very important; for, where he went, there was such a blessing that he felt called to devote himself more absolutely to the work; and he used to speak of this occasion as one of the turning-points by which his subsequent work was determined.'   Others remember that Mr. Moody himself was in Elgin, and to Drummond's surprise opened the door to him when he arrived there.

It was, in fact, because of what he heard or saw of this work in Elgin that Mr. Moody sent Drummond to Sunderland — the first instance of his policy of setting Drummond to continue the work among young men at places which Mr. Sankey and he had visited. Stewart either went with Drummond or joined him a few days later, but 'the work immediately developed to such an extent that he telegraphed for help. I[1] sent Ewing,[2] who up to that point had kept out of the movement, but was instantly caught by its spirit and soon proved one of the most powerful workers. In subsequent years we used to chaff Ewing by telling with what fear and trembling I had sent him, and how aghast Henry was when he heard who was coming to be his coadjutor. Even at the time, in spite of the solemnity of the supernatural forces in the midst of which we felt ourselves, there was a great deal of high spirits in our intercourse.' The deputation went for three days and stayed a fortnight, with still less hope of getting away, for the work grew past all belief and spread to the neighbouring towns. In answer to urgent invitations the three young Scotsmen visited Newcastle, South Shields, Bishop Auckland, Hartlepool, Morpeth, and Hexham. Sunderland appears to have been fairly aroused by the mission. The work began as elsewhere among the middle classes, and spread to the working-men. All denominations took part in it. Members of the Society of Friends were among the hardest workers, but all the Nonconformist ministers gave their help, and the three young men found themselves at the head of a large and influential organisation which they had to superintend from day to day, besides con-

---

[1] Rev. James Stalker.
[2] Rev. John F. Ewing, afterwards of Toorak.

ducting the services and the meetings with inquirers.
It must have been a tremendous ordeal, both mental
and moral.   Ewing used to speak of it as the greatest
month of his life.   But there appears to have been no
excitement, and the large daily gatherings for prayer
were conducted with deep earnestness.   The results
were very manifest: the after-meetings were large,
very many members of church-going families were
moved to a real decision to follow Christ, and numbers of young men, who had not been to any church
for months and years, professed themselves converted.
The tiny Young Men's Association rose to a membership of four hundred, and a year or two afterwards the
work done among them was declared to be permanent
and still spreading.   In the end a thousand persons in
Sunderland alone gave in their names as converts.
Parents were so stirred that arrangements were made
to extend the public services to children; and in this
delicate work — the propriety of which Drummond
afterwards questioned, believing with justice that religion comes to a child most naturally through its home,
— some amount of real good was done, in spite of the
artificial and premature 'experiences' that such a
movement always forces.   In his weekly letters to his
father and mother Drummond tells the following
story: —

'SUNDERLAND, April 24, 1874.

'. . . You see I am still here and do not know when
we are to get away.   Requests are pouring in on
us from all quarters and the work is just as deep
as it could be.   We have three meetings each
night, one exclusively for young men.   Generally
there are about a hundred inquirers in all every
night, and as most of these come to the light before
leaving you may imagine the wonderful nature of

the work going on around us. We got Ewing to help us yesterday, but my health is just as good as ever. We are kept at it from morning till night. Schools, infirmaries, poorhouses, etc., have all to be addressed, and the work has got in among several of the public institutions. Yesterday we had an "all day" meeting for inquirers. The young men's meetings have been a marvellous success and have done an amount of good which the countryside will feel the influence of for generations. They are going out in bands to work the neighbourhood, and as there is a dense colliery population they may do a great deal of good. I am living in a very quiet family, and although you might think there is a deal of excitement going on, I seem to be spared it all and live as quietly as if I were at Killin. . . . Next week we shall run in to Newcastle occasionally to meetings there, but one of us will always be left here.'

'HARTLEPOOL, May 6, 1874.

' The people here have been very pressing for some of us to run down and hold a couple of meetings, and I made up my mind to comply while the other two went to Newcastle, where I join them to-morrow. The Sunderland work would take a week even to sketch, and it seems to have reached all classes and all ages. Among the schools it seems to have broken out with force, and we could spend another month among them with great profit. On Sunday I had an enormous children's meeting and a hundred and fifty remained to an after-meeting. In the evening we had the Victoria Hall crammed (with adults) and a very large number entered the inquiry room at the close. On Monday evening we had a farewell meeting with the young converts. There was a large church full and it was one of the happiest meetings I was ever at. The general impression in Sunderland is that the work is just beginning, and although we have left the place, I expect we shall have to go back again. To give you an idea of the work in Sunderland I may say that upwards of *three hundred* names were given in *at the young men's meeting alone* of young men who had professed to have been converted during the three weeks of the meetings. One minister of a small chapel stated after the first fortnight that *forty* had been converted already out of his little flock. To me the whole matter seems an unreal dream. It is impossible to realise it. I suppose it was never meant we should. Hartlepool is a little chilly after Sunderland. . . . The whole countryside is ripe here, and I do not really know when this English tour of ours is to end.'

'SUNDERLAND, May 12, 1874.

'I am leading a very wandering life. . . . Our hands are very full here. We have applications from all quarters to go to work. Our present duty, however, is to stay in Sunderland. We have given it a rest this week and are working Newcastle and Bishop Auckland, but next week we are to have a great week of meetings here for all classes, and a special one each night for young men only and probably another one for children. The work among children has been most wonderful, and we have visited Sabbath and Day Schools. As you can guess, we started with but a very meagre stock of material, and have got on wonderfully. I should much like, however, to have a few of those American *Sabbath School Messengers*, as my stock of illustrations is worn absolutely threadbare. If you come across anything nice you might also send it, and A. might join in the hunt. I am really anxious about this, and I hope you will manage to send a few scraps before many posts are passed. . . . On Monday we had another converts' meeting — a large church full. The Sunday evening meeting has become quite an institution in the town, and is having an extraordinary influence on all classes. There are always three thousand or four thousand present and we have always a large prayer-meeting.'

'HEXHAM, June 9, 1874.

' I got here on Saturday evening after a good week at Sunderland. We worked two meetings each night, but the one was six miles off so that we only had one each to attend to. The results were most satisfactory. I think there would be about a hundred in each place — I cannot say exactly converted, but under very deep impression. One night I spent at Morpeth and had a very nice meeting. On Sunday I had no less than three meetings here, all very interesting. They were just about to close the meetings which have been going on for some weeks. They thought the thing was getting played out, but they seem to have taken a fresh start, and the meetings this week have been the biggest they have ever had. Half the audience last night were church people. . . . If the work had been bad I should have been with you to-morrow, but I see now it will not do to break off. You know every night counts. As to my health, I think I am stronger than ever. There could not be a more healthy place than this, and I take the whole day in the woods and hills. I am engaged all week at Shields, but on Saturday I could get free for a few days and we might have a ramble together.'

'SOUTH SHIELDS, June 26, 1874.

' The work here has been steady. Results not like Sunderland exactly, but I think we ought to be very well satisfied. I am pressed to stay and will probably be either here or in the neighbourhood.'

From another place, the same month.

' . . . I had got thus far when a long interruption occurred. The gentleman with whom I am living opened up his whole past history to me — a very chequered one it has been — and I think our visit will be the means of doing him some good. I could not stop his yarn, as I saw something perhaps was to come of it. This is a specimen of the kind of private work which we have to do in *every house* we stay at, with scarcely an exception.'

Meetings of three and four thousand, daily addresses to hundreds of young men, a constant confessional, crowds of anxious inquirers, urgent invitations from all quarters, the success of the work obviously dependent upon his presence, ministers and leading laymen in many towns looking to him as their chief, the sense (right or wrong) that the Christianity of the next generation in these places might largely be determined by the work he had charge of — conceive of all this falling to a man not quite twenty-three! It might well seem to him ' an unreal dream.' Yet there is abundant evidence in his letters that he did not lose his

head nor suffer his natural spirit to be warped. He
kept his interest in the common affairs of home,
wrote about his younger brother's egg-collecting, and
looked forward as eagerly as any school-boy to a holiday
with his mother. From outside testimony, he seems
to have depreciated rather than exaggerated the results
of the work. He remained shrewd and sensible; and
it was already noticed of him that, as in all his later
years, he never betrayed, either on or off the platform,
one secret of the many hundreds that must have been
confided to him by those who sought his counsel and
inspiration. The Sunderland Mission made Drummond a man. He won from it not only the power of
organising and leading his fellow-men, but that insight
into character, that knowledge of life on its lowest as
on its highest levels, that power of interest in every
individual he met, which so brilliantly distinguished
him, and in later years made us who were his friends
feel as if his experience and his sympathy were
exhaustless.

When Messrs. Moody and Sankey closed their Scottish Mission at Rothesay in the beginning of September, they passed over to Belfast, where they stayed for
five weeks. Here the same huge meetings, the same
large number of inquirers and of converts, followed
their work as in Scotland. When they moved to
Londonderry they sent for Drummond (who had spent
his holidays fishing and evangelising in Orkney and
Shetland) to continue the work in Belfast; and, with
his friend James Stalker, he began to address meetings
there about the 8th of October. When the mission
opened in Dublin he moved to Derry, and carried on
the work alone for some weeks. He had been at
home for part of the autumn, and his people had urged
him to resume his theological studies the next winter

session.   In the following letter he gives evidence not
only of his resolution to abide by the mission so long
as it should need him, but of that clearness of percep-
tion as to what his own proper work was, and that
quiet power of overcoming all influence to the contrary, which was so marked a feature of his character.

'LONDONDERRY, Oct. 19, 1874.

'. . . Just a few lines from the seat of war to tell
you how things are going on.   The enemy is falling by hundreds.   I think Derry beats any work
I have been in by a great deal.   The first meeting
almost overwhelmed me.   Moody was here for
four days, and, leaving on Thursday morning, sent
me to keep up the meetings.   The place was first
roused thoroughly, and no more.   When I came
I found the biggest church here filled to the last
seat.   I think it was one of the most impressive
meetings I have seen.   The inquiry meetings were
far bigger than any they had had — amongst them
seventy young men.   On Saturday we had a converts' meeting.   Last night another evangelistic
meeting; the church crowded to the pulpit stairs
half an hour before the time.   There were more
than three hundred anxious. Of course I cannot go
to Dublin for some time.   I have just telegraphed
to Moody.   I feel the responsibility of the work
here is very great.   Being sent here by Moody,
and being the only worker, I have full swing of
the entire work.   It is far too much for me, and I
am almost frightened when I think of it.   One
very fine feature of the movement here is the hold
it has taken amongst the young men.   I believe
there were one hundred and fifty (young men
alone) anxious last night, and about one hundred

have already decided before that, and were at the converts' meeting on Saturday.

' I suppose I am fairly engaged now to follow Moody all winter, and take his young men's meetings. I cannot help thinking more and more every day that this is the work God has planned for me this session. Why I should have such a tremendous privilege is the only mystery to me. I do not believe there has ever been such an opportunity for work in the history of the Church. Moody says if the young men's meeting can be kept up in every town, he believes there will be ten thousand young men converted before the winter is over. What a tremendous thought! In the light of all this, I cannot help thinking, as I have said, that the path I have chosen for the next months is the path which God has lit up for me. I was very uncomfortable when I was at home last — you all seemed so much against it, and I felt it more than you think. But now I feel I *must* go onward, the pointing of the Finger has grown plainer and less unmistakable than ever. I feel as if I dared not draw back. I wish you could all see it too.'

To Dublin the evangelists went with some trepidation. One correspondent warned them of failure in a truly Hibernian style : ' I have seen so many of these revivals, and they all end worse than they were before they began ! ' Their first meeting in the Exhibition Palace was reckoned at ten thousand ; and although for some time after that the work went more slowly than any since the Edinburgh Mission, it ultimately reached even greater dimensions than the evangelists had yet experienced. This increase was partly due to the hearty coöperation, for the first time in the history of the movement, of the Episcopalian clergy, while the daily press chronicled the meetings with a fulness never displayed elsewhere. ' Men of all the Church parties attended the meetings. Three of the Bishops have been at them; and one of these, the Bishop of Kilmore, has warmly commended " the wonderful work in Dublin" while presiding over his Synod. The Bishop of Derry at the reopening of York Minster said that " in Scotland and Ireland a strong fervour had been awakened, and hundreds and thousands had been made earnest by a single voice singing the Gospel of Jesus Christ." The Rev. Lord Plunket, while " not personally relishing all the accompaniments of their teaching," blessed God " for the good which is being done by our American visitors," and rejoiced " that Christ is being preached, and souls are being saved." Many Roman Catholics frequented the meetings. Although the evangelists were working for the first time in a population the majority of which was Catholic, they made so great an impression of the real good they were doing that one Catholic newspaper, *The Nation*, severely rebuked another for abusing them, and bade them Godspeed. This impression could never have been secured had Mr. Moody used controversy or denunciation, but these he wisely avoided.' [1]

There was unity among Christians. In the first week of December a Convention was held, for which the railway companies offered tickets from all parts of Ireland. On the Tuesday an ' all day ' meeting was attended by fifteen thousand people in the Exhibition Palace, and there were nearly one thousand ministers present, in seats reserved for them. The topics chosen

---

[1] The above details are from letters to *The Times of Blessing* in November, 1874, by Dr. Fleming Stevenson.

were 'Praise and Thanksgiving,' 'How to reach the Masses,' and 'How to fill Ireland with the Gospel.' These were introduced by two Episcopalians and a Presbyterian, and discussed by ministers of other communions. Mr. Moody himself spoke on Sectarianism. 'God had vouchsafed a blessed unity. Woe to the unhappy person who should break it! Yet it would be broken if there was proselytism. The cry is, "Come out! Come out from a sect!" But where? Into another sect! The spirit that is always proselytising is from Satan. I say, *Stay in*. If you have a minister that preaches Christ, stand by him. You will get nothing but trouble and pride by leaving him. There are people who consider that denouncing churches and finding fault with ministers is "bearing testimony." These people will "bear testimony" for years, and that is all Christ gets from them. I warn you, beware of trying to get people away from the folds where they have been fed. The moment we begin to lift up our little party or our Church, then the Spirit of God seems to leave and there is no more conversion.'

Drummond came to Dublin for a meeting of men on Sunday, November 8th. There were nearly three thousand present, and at the close a large number of inquirers. On December 3d Dr. Fleming Stevenson writes : —

'For some time past another large meeting had been conducted in the Metropolitan Hall at the same hour as the evening inquiry meeting, and yet the attendance at both has increased. It is exclusively for young men, and is conducted by Mr. Henry Drummond, who was urgently entreated to leave work of the same kind at Derry that he might come up to this. At first it seemed harder to deal with them and less impression was made than elsewhere ; but that is all past, and probably there are nowhere more striking instances of the grace of God.'

G

Drummond himself said at Manchester that during
four weeks of young men's meetings in Dublin from
ten to fifty were converted every night, that in one
business place alone there had been seventy-five converts, and that altogether hundreds had sent in their
names as converts. To judge from the letters he
afterwards received from Dublin, these were mainly
artisans, shopmen, and clerks. Some of them were
quite uneducated; the first result of their conversion
to Christ was usually a strong passion to learn to read.
One poor fellow who had taught himself in a few
months after his conversion writes: 'Since you left
Dublin I had had such a creatin [?] Happeytite longing for the knowledge of the Holy Bible.' But this
is the only grotesque testimony out of many.

Messrs. Moody and Sankey opened their mission
in Manchester on a dark Sunday of drenching rain.[1]
Yet they gathered a meeting of two thousand workers
at eight in the morning and two other meetings later
in the day, for which the Free Trade and Oxford halls
were required. They stayed in Manchester a month.
On New Year's Eve they began in Sheffield, on
January 17th in Birmingham, and on February 5th
in Liverpool. In all three towns the same features
marked their work as in Dublin, Belfast, Glasgow,
and Edinburgh: enormous meetings from the very
start, at first small, ultimately large, numbers of converts, the quickening of church life, and a very widespread interest among the general population. They
had gatherings of Christian workers at eight on Sunday
mornings, from two to four thousand in number. The
historic halls of the cities — the Free Trade, the Bingley,
the Albert — were crammed on Sunday evenings, and,
in spite of overflow meetings, the streets around were

[1] November 29th.

filled in the rain and the darkness with crowds singing hymns.   In Liverpool a wooden hall was erected to seat eight thousand.   Though the Church of England clergy generally refused to act on the executive com- mittee, and in one or two places withdrew altogether from the work because some of its prominent supporters took part at the same time in Liberation meetings, a group of them were always found on Mr. Moody's plat- form, and, in Sheffield and Liverpool especially, they assisted with prayers and addresses.   Practically all the Nonconformist ministers gave help, at their head MacLaren of Manchester and Dale of Birmingham.

Through all these cities Drummond followed the evangelists with his meetings for young men, and (except in Sheffield) with the usual breadth, depth, and permanent results of his influence.   The fol- lowing extracts from his letters show this, as well as the many anxieties which now began to try him.   The letters are mostly to his mother.

'MANCHESTER, Friday, Dec. ?

' The work here is very fair, perhaps not so enthu- siastic as in some places, but what can be done in a fortnight with six hundred thousand people. My department is not yet in full working order. The young men have never been reached yet in any numbers, but we shall make an extra effort next week and try to get them moved.   There is not so much unity among the ministers as one would like to see, and the Church party have had a feud with the other ministers which cannot be broken up in a day.   The enclosed card is to be left by Christian workers in *every* house in Manchester before the New Year, a gigantic undertaking !   I think it will do great good, not the actual card exactly, but it will give the hundreds of workers an introduction to thousands of people. I do not expect to make many friends here. You know when the work is not boiling hot, there is always a good deal of jealousy of strangers arriving upon the scene, and I daresay some of the ministers who are only lukewarm would rather I had kept myself to myself. Moody had——, the evangelist from ——, to help in the general work, and there was such a row about it that he had to send him away in three days! However, I am in better odour and will not get the sack whatever happens.'

'MANCHESTER, Dec. 31, 1874.

'A Happy New Year — my first from home. It seems strange to be absent at this time, and I am sure to have a fit of melancholics before to-morrow finishes. . . . There was a great scene at the station, all the bigwigs in Manchester down to see Moody off. I shall have to hold the fort here for some time yet. The prospects of work are not very cheering, and unless they get better in a week, I shall strike my tent and march for headquarters at Sheffield. . . . The cold has been intense. There has been so much ice that we have got tired of skating; and now there is not much time for it.'

'MANCHESTER, Wednesday, Jan. 6, 1875.

'I never met a finer set of men — the best Committee by far Moody ever had. . . . My work here has been a little up-hill. The young men have never been touched by Moody, and the Y.M.C.A. has its hands full of district work elsewhere and cannot work with us. I have had to develop a new set of workers, and beat up a

new meeting. I am glad to say, the work is
steadily growing every night and I think it will
be a centre of real good immediately. However,
it will no sooner be up to working power, than
I shall have to leave for Sheffield. . . . I was
offered a church (here) the other day—a splendid
new Presbyterian church! I need not say that I
have declined with thanks.'

'SHEFFIELD, Friday, January 8th.

'You will perceive from my changed address that
I am once more " stalking through the land " as
Daniel's band says. A telegram most unexpected
yesterday, at noon, from Moody brought me off in a
great hurry-scurry to Sheffield. I could not help
it. " Come to Sheffield at three to-day. I have a
great men's meeting for you to-night," so the
message ran, and of course I had just to leave
all and run too. I suppose it was for the best,
though I was real sorry to leave my little Manchester meeting, which hard labour had worked
up after much discouragement to a really good
work. It has been growing in interest and power
every night and was coming to be a great success
at last. However, I daresay I may be back tó it
for a day or two next week. Of course, it is a
much smaller thing than the work here. On
Wednesday night I suppose my audience would
count about three hundred, while last night in
Sheffield it was about as many thousands. I have
rarely seen a better men's meeting, and to-night I
have another just the same. Moody has gone to
Manchester to-day to return to-morrow. I think
the work here is going to be splendid. All classes
are moved, from the Mayor to the beggar.'

'Reginald Radcliffe came last night to help me with
the men's meeting. His method was as peculiar
as it was successful. We went to the hall where
Moody was preaching, sang a hymn with the
crowd who could not get in, and then invited them to adjourn from the street to the
Young Men's Hall. By eight o'clock we had
five or six hundred of an audience, mostly men.
When Radcliffe began he asked the Christians to
stand up while he addressed them. About half
the audience rose, and he gave them a most
earnest charge on the subject of personal holiness for about ten minutes. He pleaded with
them to aim at more entire consecration and to
examine themselves to see what hindered them
from being filled with the Spirit. The effect
upon the unconverted who remained sitting was
wonderful. Then instead of asking the anxious
to retire to the hall below, as is usually done,
Radcliffe asked all the Christians to meet him
there for prayer for more holiness. I gave out
a hymn, while he and his party withdrew, and in
a few minutes was left alone with an audience of
two or three hundred unconverted people. Many
of them must have been under deep conviction.
I addressed them for fifteen minutes, and then
made a dedicatory prayer. A minister followed
in prayer, and then I asked all who had decided
for Christ to rise and leave. Somewhere about
fifty were left behind, and we then turned the
meeting into an inquiry meeting and spoke
personally to each of them. I had about a
dozen men in a corner and one after another
came to the light. All over the hall the same

thing was going on, and the result, so far as
the unconverted were concerned, was one of the
best inquiry meetings we have ever had, and so
far as the Christians were concerned, one of the
most delightful and memorable prayer meetings
of their lives.'

'QUEEN'S HOTEL, BIRMINGHAM, Friday, Jan. 29, 1875.

'A telegram this morning from Moody sent me off
here post-haste. I have just tea'd with him and
had a long talk over things. The work here has
been far greater than anywhere else — far, far
greater. Of course I do not know very much
about it yet. I was quite prepared to leave this
morning, as I knew Moody's ways and I knew I
must be in Birmingham before he left it, and that
is to-morrow morning. As usual I was sorry to
leave the last place, as the work had got into
splendid trim. The young men put out the bill
which I enclose, without my knowledge, and our
meeting was crowded till there was not standing
room and about fifty inquirers at the close. . . .
Moody is not at all the worse for this great work
here, speaking to fifteen thousand people every
night. These figures are not exaggerated. He
is very careful, and he says so himself.
Tell J. I was all over Rogers the cutler's ware-
house to-day in Sheffield. It is a magnificent
business. I saw one knife with one thousand
eight hundred and seventy-five *blades* — quite
true. It is a great curiosity. They add a blade
every year. Yesterday I saw electroplating, so
you see I am picking up information!'

'Birmingham, February, 1875.

'Once more I am on the eve of a flitting. When you get this I shall either be in Liverpool or on the road to it. A telegram in the usual style from Moody settled the arrangement last night. My work here has not been so great as I should have liked, but still I think a little real honest work has been done. And I have great hopes of a meeting last night with some of the leading young men of the town resulting in permanent work among young men. . . . I am almost sorry to leave this, as I have fallen into the houses of such very nice people; but of course that is not my business, so I must be off. I have lived so much at hotels lately that it is quite a pleasure to catch a glimpse of home life again.'

'Compton Hotel, Liverpool, Monday, Feb. 15, 1875.

'"Liverpool." Well, the programme is running out, you see, town by town. This is the last of the *provinces* now; and in another month we shall be on the big campaign. I came here on Saturday afternoon, and after dinner at the hotel was carried off by one of the Committee on an exploration expedition thro' the theatres, music halls, concert rooms, and public buildings generally to pick one out for our meeting. I think the prospects are very good. Yesterday was a great day here. Moody's four services were splendid — hundreds of inquirers. In the evening I had a theatre full of " overflows " to look after. This morning there was a monster breakfast of gentlemen interested in the movement, which went off very well. I have fallen quite among friends here — Stewart, who worked with me in Sunder-

land, and two college classmates, Fraser from
Alloa and M'Leod have churches near here. I
quite enjoyed meeting them, as they are about the
only "kent faces" I have seen for some time. . . .
I got a treat last night. Moody sat up alone with
me till near 1 o'clock telling me the story of his
life. He told me the whole thing. A reporter
might have made his fortune out of it!'

The mission of Messrs. Moody and Sankey to Liverpool produced greater results than they had achieved
in any other town. On the last day of their visit a
meeting was held for anxious inquirers who were
admitted by ticket.

'Not less than five thousand presented tickets. Mr.
Moody's address was directed to the clearing away of
doubts and difficulties, and at its close he called upon all
who were willing to trust themselves to Christ there and
then to rise to their feet. With much manifest emotion a
vast multitude of persons, quite two-thirds of all who were
present, stood up. This was followed by an after meeting,
when some four hundred or five hundred awakened souls
were conversed with personally.' Another witness says of
this meeting: 'It was a time of solemn surrender: no
startling appeals had been listened to; the noonday sun, and
not the glare of gaslight, shone into the building; there was
nothing to excite any one; yet the close-pressed phalanx of
city merchants and ministers on the platform had a struggle
to repress emotion.' 'An equal number remained after the
women's meeting in the afternoon, but perhaps the most
remarkable meeting was that of the men in the evening.
The great hall was crammed with some twelve hundred.
Mr. Moody delivered the same sermon as to the women in
the afternoon. It is a fact worthy of notice that a very much
larger number of men seemed to be impressed than of women
in the afternoon. In the afternoon three hymns had to be
sung after the address, and repeated invitations given, before

the inquiry room was filled with women, whereas in the evening no sooner was the address finished than the same room
was crowded with men before the first hymn was ended,
while hundreds more remained to seek and to find in the
large hall.'

Drummond's meetings with young men in the Circus are said to have been 'as much owned as Mr.
Moody's were.' For weeks he had ten or twelve
hundred every night. I can find only two of his own
letters about them, written after Moody left for London.

'COMPTON HOTEL, LIVERPOOL, March 19, 1875.

'. . . Must still hold the fort here for a little. We
are getting up deputations all over the country.
Last night I was at a place fifteen miles off by sea
starting a young men's meeting, and I go back
there to-night and to-morrow. To-night I shall
hurry the meeting and take cab and ferry back to
Liverpool to my own meeting in the Circus at
nine, and the same to-morrow. . . . The people
here are very kind: I have got to know nearly
the whole religious public, and could be out to
breakfast, dinner, or tea every day, but I decline
all invitations. . . . This is the great race week
in Liverpool, and the town is swarming with all
manner of blackguards. [He had his pockets
picked by one.] . . . Moody is much encouraged
by London. To tell the truth, I am in no hurry
to get there. I daresay I shall have had enough
of it before the four months are out.'

'LIVERPOOL [undated, about the 8th April].

'My last week in Liverpool. Moody was here
again and almost insisted upon my going with
him on Monday last, but the committee here

begged for another week, and I do not regret having stayed on. We have had some real good work. 'We have still wonderful work here. I have a theatre full of young men to "farewell address" at three, a circus full of working-men at four, another theatre full of men and women at seven in Birkenhead, and the usual circus full of young men again at nine. I shall never forget these young men's meetings here. You have no idea of them. We have never less than one thousand each night, and that is full six weeks without a break. There is not a man in the world that would not envy such a congregation. One can do a year's work in a month in times like these. I have no doubt but that we shall turn out a number of missionaries from among the young men here.'

'The aspect of the Circus,' says a newspaper correspondent, 'after the meeting was ended and many gone home, was inexpressibly touching. There two men in fustian jackets kneeling in prayer together. In one corner a dozen men standing round an energetic speaker. In another two men are anxiously debating what seems a question of life and death. There are many groups throughout the hall intent on matters of serious moment. There are tears flowing, but hastily wiped away. There are rough lads in dress and manner, whose looks make you regard them with a brother's love ; and ever and anon the speakers and the spoken kneel down in the sawdust or on the boards in prayer, and then, with a wring of the hand and gratified look, they go home.'

The London Mission was begun on March 14th in the Agricultural Hall, Islington, which was seated for thirteen thousand persons, with standing room for a thousand or two more.[1] The evening meeting for men

[1] There were at first grave exaggerations of the number : it was said that there were twenty-four thousand seats and twenty-five thousand persons present.

filled it to its utmost capacity, and during the following week the gatherings varied from four to fourteen thousand. One of them was addressed by Dr. R. W. Dale, who afterwards published the very impressive account which he gave of the work in Birmingham. On Sunday, the 21st, the meetings were nearly as large as on the preceding Sunday. The noon prayer-meeting was held in Exeter Hall. The Opera House, Haymarket, was taken for West End meetings, the Victoria Theatre in the Waterloo Road for the south side, and a large wooden hall was built in the far east. With scarcely an exception the daily press 'spoke of the work in terms of respect, even of hopefulness'; and the interest in it spread to all classes of society. There is no doubt that an immense proportion of those who attended the monster meetings were already church members, and in so vast a population as London, even so strong a movement could touch only the fringes of the careless and the vicious masses. Yet even these fringes amounted to much. There were as many as two hundred anxious inquirers every night at the Agricultural Hall; many more whose hearts had been touched went away without confessing it; while nearly every one of the tens of thousands of Christians who heard the evangelists was quickened and stimulated. The work spread rapidly. In a leading article, the *Times* of Good Friday declared that it was falling off. On that evening, on Easter Sunday, and all the following week the meetings were larger than ever.

Drummond came up to London about the close of the first week in April.

To John F. Ewing

'FRIDAY, April 23, 1875.

' If you knew how I am torn to pieces with work, you would not abuse me. You are a good fellow to write, and you deserve to be encouraged. I like to hear from young ministers! The last I heard of you was that you were doing " a most plucky thing." I am thoroughly glad of the line you have gone into.[1] When I become a young minister it is exactly what I shall do.

' I wish I had time to tell you of myself. The Liverpool work was very grand. London has been a fair success only, I mean after Liverpool. Many things were against work among the young men, but still we have had a very real work. I leave the N. meeting to take care of itself after this week, and go "away down east," as Moody would say. There we have pitched a tent to hold a thousand young men, which we expect to have crammed every night. After setting that a-going, I think the next move will be to the Haymarket Opera House, where I expect Stalker and you will make your first appearance in a London theatre, and I shall announce you beforehand as two swells from the provinces! Pardon me for being in such a serious vein. I have been writing Moody's sermons all day; you know they are being published under my most distinguished editorship.'

'LONDON, Saturday, April 24th.

' A sudden turn in the state of affairs yesterday has banished me to the South of London, and I fear

[1] Ewing had undertaken the formation of a new congregation in a working-class district of Dundee.

it will be impossible for me to come to the station on Tuesday, but I shall meet you at the Noon meeting at the Opera House.   The reason of my going to the S. is because Stalker and you are coming.   Moody, the moment he heard of it, put you both down for work there, and " the young men from Edinburgh " are to have full swing of the Victoria Theatre for the whole week.   [He reports on the arrival of others.]   I am divided equally between revival and arrival work.'

To His Father

'CANNON STREET HOTEL, LONDON, May 11, 1875.

'Everything is bright outside and inside, and I only wish you were here to share in the enjoyment. How would you like to see *an acre of people?* That is exactly the size of the audience to which Mr. Moody preaches every night in the East of London.   Here is Moody's programme: Drive three miles to Noon meeting; lunch; Bible reading at 3.30 followed by inquiry meeting till at least 5 ; then preaching in the Opera House at 6.30; then very short inquiry meeting; then drive five miles to East End to preach to twelve thousand at 8.30; then inquiry meeting; then drive five or six miles home.   This is *every day* this week and next—a terrible strain, which, however, he never seems to feel for a moment. The work is coming out grandly now, and I think the next two months will witness wonderful results.   It is deepening on every side, and even " London " is beginning to be moved.   Moody says Sunday was the best day of his life.'

'CANNON STREET HOTEL, May 14, 1875.

'Your *huge* remittance came to me all right this
morning *via* James.   I shall ride once more upon
a 'bus, and pay my way like a man and a Drummond.[1]

'I expect to leave this on Wednesday night after
the meetings are over by the night mail, and as I
am so *flush* I should not wonder if Mr. Pullman
Sleeping Car should have the honour of conveying
me and my co-worker, Captain Moreton, R.N.'

He goes to a great convention in Liverpool, and
looks forward to another at Brighton, though he does
'not at all approve of views held by some of the leading supporters.'   'We had a splendid young men's
meeting last night in London, the best we have had
there.   It is growing every night.   Moody takes it
to-morrow, and I shall be back for Saturday.'

To His Mother

'LONDON, May 27, 1875.

'Your flowers made me just a little homesick, they
had such a country air about them.   I declare I
had almost forgotten there were such things as
daisies.   However, at latest next week, I shall
renew my acquaintance with fresh air.   The
greatest event in my programme this week was
a large children's meeting in the Opera House.
I am to have another on Saturday along with Mr.
Sankey, and expect a great hubbub!'

---

[1] Drummond appears to have refused during this mission all remuneration and
only sometimes to have taken all his expenses.

'HAYMARKET OPERA HOUSE, May (?).

'A large number of inquirers are just waiting from
the afternoon Bible reading, and I must give my
afternoon to them.'

To His Father

'CANNON STREET HOTEL, June 23, 1875.

'The 12th of July is Moody's last day, I think.
He goes for a short tour after that, and his berth
is taken for the 4th of August by the National
liner *Spain*. The Eton affair makes much noise,
but will do great good, Moody thinks, in making
the higher circles show their colours on the general question. He expects his friends, who are
very influential, will come out and show who they
are. The actual meeting at Eton was a great
success. Never believe a word the papers say
about the work. They are, almost without exception, always wrong. . . . I am to have the
privilege of joining Moody (and three others) in
a series of Bible studies every morning for full
two hours. You must know how much I stand
in need of teaching, with so much preoccupation
and so much attempt to teach others. You will
approve this, for I think you must have been
frightened for me sometimes.'

In July he went to start a mission at Epsom.

'CANNON STREET HOTEL, July 9.

'I had a grand meeting on Monday night at 9 P.M.
The district is terribly dead, so we had at first a
general meeting at 7.30, and then the men's meeting [for which he had specially gone] at 9. The

latter was crammed away out into the street with
men, many of them jockeys and racing men, just
the kind to reach.   It was a most interesting meeting, and some thirty or forty remained anxious.
Next night there were one hundred in the inquiry
room, and the following night two hundred.   I
have agreed to go down again on Saturday night.
It is a magnificent chance for work, and I look
forward to a hundred or two in the after meeting.
I believe I am to have the honour of being sent
home on a special engine after the meeting, some
of the gentlemen who are getting up the work
having an interest in the railway.   A young man
who has been recently converted stood up in our
meeting the night before last, and told us he had
gambled away half a fortune before his conversion, and kept five race horses.   He is a splendid
young fellow, and a most genuine case.   He has
been having meetings himself near his own house,
and has done a great deal of good.

'The crowds now to hear Moody are terrific; the
panic of the papers was of course exaggerated.'

Twenty-five years have passed since the American
evangelists began their mission to Great Britain.   We
have seen how profoundly the churches were stirred,
and the crowds outside the churches; the tens of thousands who thronged the meetings; the hundreds upon
hundreds who filled each inquiry room, professing
penitence, and, in the great majority of cases, new
faith in Jesus Christ and experience of His power to
make them better men.   No one can doubt the enormous power of the movement so long as it lasted.
What has it left behind?

Probably, as we have seen, there never was a move-

H

ment of the kind in which religious extravagance and
dissipation were more honestly discouraged. In the
leaders there was no want of the healthy discrimination and genial charity without which our religious
zeal so fatally develops into Pharisaism. The preaching was Biblical and ethical. The doctrines were those
of Catholic Christianity. The salvation proclaimed
was, with some exceptions, salvation not from hell
but from sin. And the new faith and energy of the
converts was nearly everywhere guided into profitable
forms of activity, with effects upon character and service that, as we shall presently see, have endured until
to-day.

To form, however, a just appreciation of the movement, we must recall some things upon the other side.
We must remember the perils to which, in our civilisation, such enormous crowds of converts were immediately exposed. While revivals rise and fall, the
influences of worldliness and of vice abide among us
with fresh and awful persistency. Many of the converts, some even of the prominent workers, of the
great Mission, fell to that hereditary taint of drunk-
enness which infects our nation's blood; others not
so cursed fell as low before our careless and cruel
drinking customs, although not all of these were
slain, but in the end many won the victory to which
the Mission first inspired them. We must remember,
too, that so vast and rapid a movement was bound to
suffer the defects of its qualities. Among the large
numbers who were certified as adhering to the Mission,
there was a proportion of the comfortable middle class,
who spent their leisure in running from meeting to
meeting, and who, from that day to this, act as if they
believed that such conventions were at once the highest duty and happiest privilege of religion. Their

excitement and the habits which it has formed have not been beneficial to Christianity. Further, we cannot help observing that the idealism of the movement, the emphasis which it laid on general principles, and the speed with which multitudes were roused to the conviction of these, conspired with the general excitement to destroy, in a certain class of minds, all sense for facts, and to corrupt their conscience for accuracy. This is, perhaps, natural to every idealist movement, — one marks it in certain philosophies of the century, — but it appears to be the besetting temptation of a zealous and sanguine evangelicalism. It was curiously realised in the frequent exaggeration of the numbers reported to have attended the various meetings. But some of the forms which it assumed were more serious. One was a temptation to ignore all religious experience which lay outside the definite theology of the movement, and a stubborn refusal to recognise the manifest fruits of God's Spirit apart from the formulas and processes by which its converts had arrived at the truth. And another form of this vice was the unwillingness to see in Scripture any facts save such as might be used to confirm a very narrow theory of inspiration, nor any teaching save the few lines of evangelical doctrine and special providence upon which the preaching of the movement mainly ran. Mr. Moody himself was free from all these defects — except that of a narrow and unscriptural theory of inspiration. But during the last twenty-five years they have all developed in the circles whose religious life God used him to quicken so powerfully; and much of evangelicalism, both in its preaching and in its journalism, has been beset by narrowness, inaccuracy, and the fear to acknowledge some of the healthiest and divinest movements of our time.

But while all these defects have to be noted, how much falls to the bright side of the reckoning! Every one who shared in the movement or who has read its history will admit without question those beneficial effects which we have already noted, upon the membership and the ministry of all the Churches. This Mission lifted thousands and tens of thousands of persons already trained in religion to a more clear and decided consciousness of their Christianity. It baptized crowds in the Spirit of Jesus, and opened the eyes of innumerable men and women to the reality of the great facts of repentance and conversion, to the possibility of self-control and of peace by God's Spirit. We have admired the organisation of its converts. The young men who came under its influence are now in middle life, and to-day one can point to ministers in many churches, and to laymen in charge of the municipal and social interests of almost every town, who were first roused to faith and first enlisted in the cause of God and of their fellow-men by the evangelists of 1873–75. The Spirit of our God works among us in many other ways than by 'revivals' and church services, and the evangelical movement which Messrs. Moody and Sankey did so much to reinforce has required every iota of the influence of science to teach it tolerance, accuracy, and fearlessness of facts, and all the strength of the Socialist movement to rewaken within it that sense of civic and economic duty by which the older evangelicalism of Wilberforce, Chalmers, and Shaftesbury was so nobly distinguished. Among the men who have seen this, and who have not only preserved their faith amid the new distractions of our time, but to their faith have added knowledge and patience, and the brotherly love that means service of the commonweal, have been many—very many—converts of the two American evangelists, whom God in His grace sent to our shores twenty-five years ago.

We shall see in the rest of this biography how Henry Drummond contributed to this wider evangelicalism of our day; meantime let us understand how he helped the movement which did so much to inspire it, and how the movement helped him.

From April, 1874, to July, 1875, he followed up the work of the evangelists in the cities of Ireland and England, and he laboured by their side in London. His letters have made us familiar with the general character of his work. The bulk of it was the preparation and delivery of addresses, and as he sometimes spoke every night for weeks in the same hall his material began to grow in quantity. During this period he probably composed the first drafts of most of the discourses for which in later years he became famous. The discourses published after his death in the volume entitled *The Ideal Life* were produced either now or in the immediately subsequent years; so also his great address on 'Seek ye first the Kingdom of God.' But he had also spoken on 'The Greatest Thing in the World,' and 'The Changed Life.' His preaching, therefore, ranged over all the great doctrines and facts of Christianity: Sin and Salvation, Penitence, The Atonement, Regeneration, Conversion, Sanctification, The Power of the Spirit, Christ's Teaching about Himself and about a Future Life—on all these, in contrast to the smaller list of topics to which he limited himself in later years, he preached again and again and with great detail. He stuck close to the Bible. He used the incidents of the Old Testament to enforce the teaching of the New, just as older evangelists did. His theology was

practically that of the leaders of the movement, and
among crowds who were always more or less ready to
mark the slightest deflection from orthodoxy there
appears never to have arisen any suspicion of a difference between his teaching and the teaching of the
authorities. But his manner of presentation was
entirely his own, and in speaking to young men he
never forgot that he must put things differently from
the way in which things were put to their elders.
He acted on the principle, which he so often enforced, that 'a young man's religion could not be
the same as his grandmother's.' His style of speaking was simple and clear; he kept to the concrete, and
already revealed his famous powers of illustration and
analogy. His manner was quiet and self-possessed.
He had the opportunity, so invaluable to the young
preacher, of giving the same addresses again and
again, so that he could sift and balance them; nor did
he ever yield to the temptation, which such an opportunity often brings with it, of relaxing his preparation,
but this was always hard and thorough. 'One thing
has impressed me more than anything I heard at the
[Agricultural] Hall, and that is the quiet yet deep
and sincere manner in which he always prays and
speaks at the Young Men's Meeting.' 'I thank God
for His goodness in sending you to tell the Gospel of
Christ in a manner so simple and loving that many
together with myself were brought to a saving knowledge of the truth.'[1] He had not a strong, nor in any
way a remarkable, voice, but he used it easily in the
largest meetings. There was no attempt at oratory,
nor any sign of strain; and, besides the absence of all
ambition after personal effect, this was due to careful
preparation for each occasion and to that exquisite

[1] From a man, a member of the Church of England.

taste which the last few years of discipline in reading
and in writing had perfected.   He grew, too, to be
very expert in managing meetings.   What chances he
had! Who could ever again fear or fail, that at twenty-
three had organised the meetings he had to organise
or had faced the crowds he had to face night after
night!   But his opportunities would have been nothing without himself.   Not experience only nor coolness, but quick sympathy which does not always go
with coolness, rapid appreciation of other men's gifts
and the power of enlisting them, perfect courtesy, good
humour, and a strong dramatic interest, made him an
ideal chairman.   There was the tall lithe figure, the
keen eyes, the unstrained voice, the imperturbable
spirit, the purity and earnestness which were behind
all, the nameless radiance that surrounded him as of a
fresh spring morning — but indeed it is his biographer's despair to explain to those who never felt it the
equal charm and force which came out from him.

   In higher things, too, the movement must have re-
fined the character we found so perfect in after years.
Dr. Stalker, who shared so much of the work among
the young men, has written the following notes, which
illustrate both this and the other features of which we
have been speaking : —

   'Your letter has made me recall that glorious time ;
but I find that while I remember the general impressions most distinctly, I have not a very precise recollection of details.

   'Perhaps the impression which oftenest recurs to
me is the absolute purity of motive which at that time
possessed us.   Though suddenly thrust into unusual
prominence, we thought of nothing whatever but the
work itself.   This produced a curious confidence, in
which there was not the least touch of self-conscious-

ness. The very largest meetings were in no wise
formidable, and if the highest in the land had been
present, we should only have been glad to have additional hearers for the message of salvation. If we had
little of the humility which thinks disparagingly of
self, we had what has always since then seemed to me
the better humility which forgets self altogether. Indeed, at that time, we had many experiences which
have ever since made Christ intelligible; and the
Book of the Acts of the Apostles especially has a
meaning to those who have passed through such a
movement which it could scarcely, I should think,
have for any one else.

'Henry retained this humility of self-forgetfulness
throughout life; but at that time, when he was only
about three-and-twenty and very youthful looking, it
must have been curious to see him handling meetings
of thousands with the most perfect ease, though this
did not occur to any of us then. I was with him con-
ducting meetings scores of times, and from the first
he had the most perfect, effortless command of every
audience which I have ever seen in any speaker. It
was like mesmerism; and I have often wondered
whether it actually had any connection with the mes-
meric powers which he occasionally exhibited for the
amusement of his friends. His speaking was never
loud nor excited; there was never any straining
after profundity or picturesqueness or effect of any
kind; but every person in the audience followed
the speaker from the first word to the last without wandering for a moment. He never spoke of
his preparation, as other speakers do; and to this
hour I am not quite certain whether or not he prepared elaborately, but I should think he did. At all
events I know that his books were written with the

thoroughness of a French stylist. I have heard his
young disciples trying, in evangelistic addresses, to repeat his stories; and then one realised by contrast the
perfection of his way of telling them. He was not at
his best in addressing very large meetings, but in an
audience not exceeding five hundred his quiet voice
and simple manner found their natural range.'

But to associate Henry Drummond only with meetings and addresses would be to misrepresent him.
Had he ever been carried away with the size and
success of these, had he ever been tempted to swerve
from his own principle that the individual was the
aim and object of religion, he must have been brought
back by one element of the meetings themselves. At
each of these there were handed up to the chairman a
large number of requests for prayer, which in nine
cases out of ten had to do with the darkness or the
tragedy of some individual life. Carefully preserved
among his documents are some scores of these anonymous scraps of paper, shabby, soiled, and often mis-
spelt, each of them the confession of a fallen soul, or
the sob of a broken heart, or the cry for warmth of a
cold and a starving one. From vice or servitude to
some besetting sin, from long doubt and vain struggle
to the light, from wrecked and dreary homes, or
wasted by love and fear that had battled for years
over the characters of those who were dearest to
them, they had crept to the meetings, and felt the
strength of the faith that was present, and cried to be
lifted upon it as their last chance. Drummond sought
out many of these, and was sought by many more.
He worked hard in the inquiry rooms, but shy men,
who would not stand up in a meeting, nor enter an
inquiry room, waited for him by the doors as he came
out, or waylaid him in the street, or wrote, asking him

for an interview. He took great trouble with every one of them, as much trouble and interest as if each was a large meeting. His sympathy, his leisure from himself, his strength, won their confidence, as his personal charm on the platform had first stirred their hope, and he thus became acquainted with the secrets of hundreds of lives. Men felt he was not a voice merely, but a friend, and on his arm they were lifted up.[1] He was always hopeful about the most hopeless, picked out some good points in the worst, and sent a man away feeling that he was trusted once more, not only by this friend, but by Christ, by God. The affection which such treatment aroused was extraordinary. I have seen numbers of letters, commonplace enough but for the intense love and gratitude which they breathe, and which sometimes approaches worship. It was such power as was possessed by some of the greatest of the mediæval saints — and he was not twenty-four. One man said to me only the other day, 'Since Drummond died I have not been able to help praying to him.'

He had a great love, too, for all odd and grotesque characters. His patience with bores was his friends' wonder to the end; but he dearly liked to come across the unconventional, the Bohemian, and the vagrant. Showmen of all sorts were such a joy to him, and he got on so well with them, that we used to nickname him Barnum. A Spanish guitar-player, a laddie who performed on the penny whistle, music-hall singers, a cornet-player, a concertina-player — he had a knack of picking them out and giving them work to do in the

---

[1] Mr. R. R. Simpson sends the following: 'At an inquiry meeting in the Assembly Hall I spoke to a bright-looking young man and found that he had decided for Christ. On my asking him what led him to decision, the striking answer was, "It was the way Mr. Drummond laid his hand on my shoulder and looked me in the face that led me to Christ."'

meetings.   Nor was he often taken in.   So great a
movement had, of course, among its adherents many of
sordid and worldly motives : some contemptible, some
very amusing.   One good lady, who had never spoken
to him, wrote that she is 'sure he is her friend, wants
to introduce him to her eleven children and nineteen
grandchildren, and has asked them all to a one o'clock
dinner to-morrow to meet him : ' she is sure he will
not disappoint her.   People who had lost heavily by
American railways passionately urge him to get Moody
and Sankey to undertake among their countrymen a
crusade for the recovery of their lost investments.   Men
and women of the idle middle class and busy stock exchange brokers send him verses and tracts to publish.
There were countless appeals for employment; offers of
'Christian lodgings' for young men ; requests for sermons for collections from clergymen whose churches
were in debt; plaintive notes from flute-players to know
why their offers to give solos at the meetings have not
been attended to; claims to be reimbursed for losses
caused by faithful adherence to the movement; re-
proaches from speakers and other workers that they
have never had one word of praise — and so forth.
One of the kinds of appeal that gave him most trouble
was that from well-intentioned people who wanted him
to speak to their young relatives about their souls, when
these young relatives had no wish to be spoken to.   On
the occasions when he could not escape such conversations, he would begin thus : 'I suppose you know this
is a put-up job,' or thus, 'What you are suffering from
is too much religion, isn't it ? '   His insight was marvellous.   In one of the London after meetings, he said
to a girl, 'You must give up reading James's *Anxious
Inquirer*,' and she wondered how he guessed she was
reading it.   A fortnight of the Testament set her

right. When he helped another, she said, ' It's not so simple as that in James's *Anxious Inquirer.*'[1]

A great deal of the work was very painful. He once said, ' Such tales of woe I've heard in Moody's inquiry room that I've felt I must go and change my very clothes after the contact.' Thus at twenty-three he saw life on all its sides, learned the secrets of countless characters, and was trusted and hung upon by thousands of his fellow-men.

Yet he stepped from it all unspoiled, and the next session went quietly back to college.

[1] From notes by Professor Simpson.

CHAPTER V

HENRY DRUMMOND did not go back to college without a struggle. Invitations to conduct missions poured in upon him from all quarters. The leaders of the work pleaded that the last two years had surely proved his calling as an evangelist; and on his part he shrank from settling down as the minister of a congregation, with two sermons to prepare every week. But his parents had renewed their pressure upon him, and in letters, which he has kept, his wisest friends warned him of the perils of the wandering evangelist's life, the faults which it breeds in the best of characters, and the hindrances which it sets to conscientious preparation and general intellectual growth. Between these opposite influences he was still hesitating, when he went, in August, 1875, to spend a holiday with his friend Robert W. Barbour, at Bonskeid, in Perthshire. Barbour had just finished a brilliant course at Edinburgh University,—nine class medals, the prize poem, and a double first degree in Classics and Philosophy,—but had found time with it all for work among young men in Moody and Sankey's mission. After his success at Edinburgh—we who followed him there believed that there was no distinction beyond his reach—and with his political opportunities as the son of a large landowner, Barbour had been urged to go to Oxford, with a view to entering Parliament. But he resolved to give himself to the

109

ministry of the Free Church, and was now intending
to enter New College in the following October.
Drummond and he discussed their future at some
length, and his mother, Mrs. George Freeland Barbour, although fully aware of Drummond's powers as
an evangelist, lent her influence to persuade him to
complete his studies for the regular ministry. Drummond described the result in a statement made to
Professor Simpson shortly before his death : —

> 'For a year and a half after Moody's visit (he said)
> he was sure that he had found his vocation, till
> one Sunday forenoon on the steps of Bonskeid he
> had a long talk with Mrs. George Barbour, who
> showed him how the evangelist's career was apt
> to be a failure — perhaps a few years of enthusi-
> asm and blessing, then carelessness, no study, no
> spiritual fruits; too often a sad collapse. That
> sent him back to his last year at college.'

This is confirmed by the following letter to Robert
Barbour. The 'sore leg,' on which so much depended,
was a sprained ankle from a stumble over a stone on
the slopes between Fincastle and Bonskeid.

'GLEN ELM LODGE, STIRLING, Oct. 23, 1875.

> 'MY DEAR BARBOUR, — . . . Very sorry to hear you
> have been ill. You are much more to be pitied
> than I, for I count my sore leg one of the best
> things that ever happened to me. It was the
> very thing I needed. I have got time to look at
> all sorts of things, and have even made an attempt
> to write a first sermon. Altho' the first sermon,
> it was not the first, or the fiftieth, attempt, but
> only differed from the others by being, if any-

thing, a greater failure. I suppose I shall have
to do penance for this some day, but I don't
understand how men can knock together two
sermons a week — as if they were rabbit hutches.
'My main object in writing is to tell you that I have
decided to go to Edinburgh this winter. For the
last fortnight things have been growing clearer,
and my mind is now quite made up to go. I
hope I am doing the right thing. My horizon
was very dark when I was at Bonskeid, but I
know being there did me good. Besides, it is the
pleasantest recollection I have of this autumn; so
I emphatically demur to your statement that it
was " unfortunate." '

A year later, looking back to the same accident, he
writes again to Barbour:—

'I should rather like to make a pilgrimage to that
stone at Bonskeid. Sometimes I think I owe
more to it than I know. Perhaps if it had not
been for that stone I should not have been at
college this winter. " That stone!" I wish it
had been anything else but a stone. A wheel-
barrow would almost have been as poetical.'

How strong the temptations were to continue as an
evangelist may be felt from the following letter which
Drummond received after he had begun the winter
session, but which was only one of many similar
appeals that reached him while his mind was still uncertain. Mr. Moody had begun his American campaign at Philadelphia in November.

From Mr. Moody

'PHILADELPHIA, Dec. 4, 1875.

'MY DEAR DRUMMOND, — The work among young men in this country is growing splendidly. I am glad I went to England to learn how to reach young men. Could you come over and help us? We want you much and will see that all expenses are paid. I think you would get a few thousand souls on these shores, if you should come. I miss you more than I can tell. You do not know how much I want you with me. Come if you possibly can. . . . Since I got your letters I think of you and the College. May God bless you, and make you thrive in His Kingdom, is my prayer. Yours with a heart full of love,

'D. L. MOODY.'

When Drummond came back to college, he found his contemporaries gone from it, his juniors already in the Fourth Year, which he entered, and a fresh set of men in the years behind them. Some of the latter, like Richard Cameron, Frank Gordon, and Robert Barbour he knew: they had taken part in the great Mission; but the men who had shared with him the first and most profound experiences of it were already in the ministry; and, while the College as a whole was still under its glamour, and the students regarded himself with respect and admiration, their religious interests were far from being identified with its methods. Among them were an unusual number of able men. The ablest of all was Peter Thomson, the son of an Aberdeenshire farm-grieve, who had graduated with first-class honours at Aberdeen, and carried all before him at New College. He was now President of the Theological Society, and assistant to Professor Davidson. We who were entering the First Year had learned from him any Hebrew we knew, and looked up to him with great respect. His ability, kindliness, and weight

of character formed the chief influence of that session.
Round him, in his own year, were a group of solid and
thoughtful men, — among them George Steven, now
of Free St. Bernard's Church in Edinburgh, — who
set the life of the College upon scholarly but strenuously religious lines. The First Year contained the
phenomenal number of five men with first-class honours — three of them with double firsts. There was a
strong intellectual rivalry. The debates in the Theological Society were vigorous and extremely interesting. Thomson, who had already studied at Leipzig,
followed up Dr. Davidson's lectures, and brought before the meetings the facts which recent criticism had
laid bare in the Old Testament. But the chief interest of the society was in Dogmatic Theology. A number of the members were strong in philosophy ; D. M.
Ross was assisting Professor Campbell Fraser at the
University, and Barbour and Sorley had just come
from it with first-class philosophical honours. Others
had been at German universities, and those who had
not were reading Dr. George Matheson's *Introduction
to the Study of German Theology*, which had just been
published. Thomson, who had left Aberdeen with
the very singular conviction that in Mill's philosophy,
as interpreted by Bain, he was furnished with a defence for the Christian faith, had found this fail him,
and a great deal of his faith fail with it.[1] After
seeking in vain for another philosophy reconcil-
able with Christian doctrine, he was finding, and
leading others towards, a dogmatic based upon the
facts of religious experience. In this pursuit, the students were helped by the lectures of Dr. Davidson,
who taught them Old Testament Theology, not as the

---

[1] See his very interesting Memoirs, entitled *A Scotch Student*, by the Rev.
George Steven, M.A. Edinburgh, Macniven and Wallace, 2d ed., 1881.

I

dogmas of a church, but as the living experience of a great people and its greatest individuals; by the lectures of Dr. Rainy upon Church History, with their fascinating presentation of the personal religion of the chief doctors of the Church; and by the study of Schleiermacher, for the reading of whose *Der Christliche Glaube* a small club was formed. In the same direction we found of value Müller's *Doctrine of Sin*, Rothe's *Dogmatik*, with its priceless paragraphs upon the religious roots of each dogma, and his essays, *Zur Dogmatik*. The effect upon the debates in the Theological Society was that all the best men argued for truths which they had lived upon, or had seen working in the lives of others; it can be imagined how much they were helped in this by their experience of the Great Revival in which so many of them had taken part. The practical and the theoretical thus developed in close coöperation, with inestimable benefit to both. The strong intellectual activities of the College were in the healthiest possible touch with real life. At the same time the College was full of happy play, and there was a good deal of joking. Two comic papers were started by the Fourth Year and by the First: *The Patagonian Candle, a Missionary Record*, and *The Soap and Towel*, a parody upon Spurgeon's famous title. The fun of these was more furious than witty.

Into this life Drummond slipped from his great experiences very quietly. We younger men, who had not been in the Moody movement, were a little afraid of him and of the chance of his tackling us upon our own religious life. But we found him unaggressive, treating us as equals, willing to be our friend, entering into our fun, and even contributing to our comic papers. After dinner some of the students used to gather in a coffee-house to drink coffee, and one of

my earliest visions of Drummond was as he stood up
with the rest in due solemnity to chant a nonsense
verse, which invariably accompanied this function.
Soon our feeling of his friendliness deepened to gratitude for his power of doing us good.   It was a power
somewhat difficult to define, for it was exercised
almost imperceptibly.   We felt that he was interested
in us, and his interest being without officiousness
won our confidence and made us frank with him.
We could tell him, as we could not tell others, the
worst about ourselves, — the worst, and just as easily
also, the best, our ideals and ambitions, of which
men are often as ashamed to speak as they are about
their sins.   To the latter he was never indulgent, or
aught but faithful with those who confessed to him.
But in every man he saw good, which the man himself
had either forgotten or was ignorant of.   'He and
Robert Barbour,' said a fellow-student, 'were the only
two men I ever knew who helped you to feel that you
were stronger and your work better than you had
dared to believe.'   His sunniness brought hope with
it to everybody about him; and the air of distinction
which he carried was so manifestly an air of purity,
and not of pride, that it helped you to keep yourself
separate from what was base or trivial.

On his part Drummond laid himself out to learn
from the new men among whom he was thrown; and
in his constant humility he made no difference between those who were older and those who were
younger than himself.   For philosophy he had never
any gift, and he often chaffed those who had.   But
the effort of the leaders of the College to find a dogmatic based on experience enlisted his sympathy, and
I think it was this year that he mastered Müller's
great work on Sin, which had ever afterwards some

influence on his thinking. He had a keen sense for facts; and the facts of Old Testament criticism, of which he heard from Thomson and others, made a deep impression on his mind. He did not yet throw off the narrow theory of inspiration upon which he had worked with the Bible, but all he learned prepared him for further influence in the same direction, and engaged his sympathies for the great movement which was now rising in Scotland under the hands of Professor Robertson Smith.

Drummond did not forget the duties of an evangelist, nor fail to infect some of his fellow-students with an enthusiasm for them. During the winter he engaged the 'Gaiety' Music Hall in Chambers Street for a number of Sunday evenings, for meetings of men. When he spoke the hall was full, and at the after-meetings there were groups of inquirers. But he took few of the addresses himself, and the speaking was mostly by other students. The audience, chiefly of students in arts and medicine, clerks and working-men, must often have been puzzled, for one address was entirely on the Kenotic Theory of the Humiliation of our Lord, and in another, Spinoza was quoted three times. One would like to know how Drummond dealt with the criminals. Possibly he intended the mission more for the speakers than their audience, for his criticism of them was unsparing.

From these meetings came the name of the Gaiety Club. It was founded at a small gathering invited by Provost Swan of Kirkcaldy to his country-house near Cupar, and was at first called, after this house, the 'Springfield Club.' Besides Provost Swan, the original members were James Stalker, then minister at Kirkcaldy, James Brown of Tillicoultry, John F. Ewing, of Dundee, John Watson of Logiealmond;

and from New College, Drummond, D. M. Ross, Frank Gordon, and Robert Barbour. Alexander Skene, now of St. Kilda's, Melbourne, joined them a little later, the present writer in 1883, and Dr. Hugh Barbour upon his brother's death in 1891. An arrangement was made to meet every spring from a Monday to Saturday at some country inn; and for twenty-two years these annual gatherings have been sustained without a break. Drummond attended every one of them save three. At first some of the evenings were set apart for criticism of each other's growth upwards or downwards during the year. But as time went on this grew less formal, and the gathering became simply one of close friends, members of the same church, with very sacred memories of work and study together in the service of Christ, and with common interests in literature and religion. Every man discusses with the rest his own work planned or achieved, and I do not think that there can be anywhere a group of friends who have more constantly shared each other's aspirations, or who have more benefited by each other's criticism. If one could be more loyal than another it was Drummond. This was the innermost circle among his countless friends; and for our part, while we look back with thankfulness to the three lives of our fellowship that are now completed and have passed to God, Ewing's, Barbour's, and Drummond's, it is our chief pride that Drummond was one of us.

In April, 1876, Drummond finished his four years' course of Divinity, and passed the second part of the exit examination.[1] The ensuing summer he spent

---

[1] In Church History (Puritanism), Systematic Theology (The Person of Christ and Doctrine of the Church), and Biblical Theology. He made 636 marks out of 800.

partly on holiday and partly in short courses of evangelistic work. He received several invitations from
ministers to become their assistant, and several others
to preach as a candidate for vacant charges, but he
declined them all, and though in the ordinary course
he should have taken license to preach, he was still so
uncertain of his future that he postponed this first
step towards the full orders of the Presbyterian
ministry.

The following letters were written by him during
the summer to Mr. and Mrs. James C. Stuart,[1] with
whom he had stayed in Manchester for six weeks in
1874. They are interesting for two features, which
he subsequently dropped, the use of conventional
religious phrases, and the underlining of portions of
the sentences. In the first, he tells how he walked from
Grasmere to Keswick and chose the hotel from which
he writes in order to meet a party of Oxford students.
He is sorry to have missed a good Sabbath at Manchester, but has 'found a mission here.'

'ATKINSON'S LAKE HOTEL, KESWICK,
Monday, Aug. 7, 1876.

'I had some wonderful "leading" on Saturday —
all the more that it was unexpected. It would
take too long to tell, but I had two distinct and
valuable opportunities of talking *personally* and
in *detail* about the "unsearchable riches." The
outline of the first case is something like this.
I started in the morning for Ullswater, missed a
seat on the two coaches, walked half-way, was
picked up by a private party, who offered me a
seat beside the driver. At first he was very quiet,
and after some time I noticed tears in his eyes.

[1] Now of Grove House, Altrincham.

I found *he had just buried his wife.* He was in very deep distress. He was a good respectable man, a teetotaler, but plainly did not know the truth. I did not tell him much then, but I got his address and mean to write him to-night. I hope something will come of it; the poor fellow seemed very anxious. Another of the cases was in coming down Helvellyn. I went to Ullswater, dined, and started for Helvellyn alone about two. It was a lovely afternoon and the view from the top was marvellous. In coming down I met a young fellow who was in great anxiety about a companion whom he had *lost* on the mountain. He had searched everywhere, night was coming on, and he feared his friend had been seized with a fit. He didn't know what to do, but the question, " What do you think of praying?" led to a long and earnest talk. He was a Swedenborgian, but had practically no religion. . . . I do not know that any positive good was done; I mean I saw no immediate effect; but we talked the whole matter round very freely and plainly. I am afraid these details will be uninteresting on paper, and I will not trouble you with a third. For my own part, I felt very grateful for them.

'To-day to Grasmere Chapel. *I got nothing.* It poured all afternoon. I read *Tersteegen.*

'I have met one Moody party at each hotel. I am glad to see the Christian world goes round too. Religion is in a deplorable state in —— ; I quite felt for it. I should have given something for your "little river." The big sea is wonderfully shallow sometimes. I suppose that is when we are big ourselves.

'I go to Newcastle on Wednesday. Thanks for

that brave text. It made me feel quite strong to-day. I do not forget C.'

'STIRLING, Aug. 15, 1876.

'. . . I enjoyed my last day at the Lakes exceedingly, and was perfectly enchanted with Derwentwater. I got a beautiful little canoe and spent the evening on the Lake, and did not paddle home till it was about dark. The tints on the hills and the lights on the water and the quietness — well, everything was perfect.

'The transition to Newcastle was abrupt. There was a marriage and the inevitable meeting! Young folk alone. I ran away to hear Henry Moorhouse [the American evangelist]. He wants me to go to America with him.

'He said to me, "You must not let any person gather manna for you — you must go every day and gather it for yourself."

'I give you the beautiful text I got this morning: "Now the Lord my God hath given me rest on every side" (1 Kings v. 4).'

'GLEN ELM, STIRLING, Sept. 21, 1876.

'. . . Thank you very much for *Pulsford;* I like it extremely. It has almost become part of myself already, as I have it always by me. What I like about it is its great reverence, not only for religion, but for everything and everybody. It seems to be full of " points " besides. Excuse me also remarking on the binding; one likes to see one's friends decently dressed. I used to wish your *Tersteegen* was not quite so dilapidated! I am very glad you are at Brighton. . . . B. is a place of few, but very happy, memories to me. Firstly, it is associated with Frederick William Robertson, from whom I got a great deal of good; and secondly, with the Brighton convention, from which I got no harm. The first thing I should do if I were there again would be to visit Robertson's grave. He used to be one of my few heroes.

'My life is still the same knotless thread that it used to be. I have been trying to do a little here and there, but personally I see no further than before. And, do you know, a strange thought comes to me sometimes that "waiting" has the same kind of effect upon one that affliction has? I do not know truly if this be so, for I do not know what affliction is; but I sometimes wonder whether or not the effects may not to some small extent run in the same lines. My freshest truth is still "the will of God." May it always be so. It has been a great help to many of my friends here.'

In September he was preaching and evangelising in various parts of Scotland. He took a few Sundays in the church in Ayr, and in answer to an invitation from Bonskeid writes from Ayr as follows:—

'I have had no opportunity of deserving a holiday. My programme is full. . . . I like Kenman exceedingly; he came with me to G—— on Sunday, and we tackled the beadle at the close of the service. I really believe the man was converted. At all events, he prayed. Did you ever hear of a beadle praying? I am to be in Ayrshire till Wednesday, and then I hope to be at the Glasgow convention. The programme is rather clumsy, I think. I am hacking my way through two old sermons for Sabbath.'

In the end of the year he accepted an invitation from Mr. Wilson of the Barclay Church to assist him for some months.

'6, LONSDALE TERRACE, EDINBURGH,
Feb. 1, 1877.

' . . . Was I "forlorn" when I wrote last? I daresay I might have been, feeling the loneliness of a new position. But that is past now, and I am in full swing of work and very happy. Rather I should say I am very interested. I do not feel that I am in my life-work, however, but am certain it is a splendid and unique training for it, and I am sure I shall thank God for it long afterwards if I am spared. The work is very heavy, but all very interesting and enjoyable. It includes a sermon on Sabbath, a prayer-meeting address on Wednesday, a children's meeting on Friday, and an evangelistic meeting on Sabbath night. This is the regular weekly programme, but the unengaged nights are generally occupied with meetings of some sort or private work with inquirers, of whom there are always one or two *somewhere*. Indeed, this last is the best part of it all, and there have been some deeply interesting cases behind the scenes to keep the old fire from quite burning out.

'I have to make new sermons every Sabbath, which take much time and study. . . . I have preached a regular series on the "Will of God," and am going to write two or three more still. It is a profound and marvellous subject. But I do not think I am getting the people to take it up.[1] . . . I have had dreams of coming to Lon-

---

[1] He rather bored his friends these months with his continual insistence on this subject.

don, as I have a very urgent and warm correspondence from Dr. Dykes just now to come and
be his assistant, but I cannot see anything more
than dreams in them in the meantime. . . .

'I am trying to live on the text I sent you at
Christmas, which seems to me to be one of the
most beautiful pieces of teaching in the whole
Testament.[1] I think I have got a little way *in*
to its meaning, and find it very wonderful . . .'

I think that it was at this time of his life that he
used to go down every night of the week to the Grass-
market and convoy a man home past the public-houses.
In March he again wrote that he could not come to
Bonskeid.

'6, LONSDALE TERRACE, Saturday.

'I must deny myself this and all other forms of
worldliness for at least six weeks, unless the Barclay steeple comes down in the interim, which is a
consummation devoutly to be wished.   I feel like
a squirrel in a cage just now — *hinc illæ lach-
rymæ!*'

He had thrown himself into the Barclay work with
great diligence, not a little inspired by the feelings of
affection and admiration which he always felt towards
Mr. Wilson. The latter had gathered round him a
strong band of young men, and they and the inquirers
whom he constantly drew to him were Drummond's
chief joy in the work.   But the congregational routine
was not, as the last letter shows, to his taste, and he
felt cramped.   Most, if not all, of the discourses published in the *The Ideal Life* were delivered from the
Barclay pulpit.   His work there came to a close with
the end of April.

[1] 1 Tim. i. 12 (?).

To Mrs. Stuart

'GLEN ELM, STIRLING, June 28, 1877.

'My story is soon told. I stayed with Mr. Wilson
till 1st May. Then he got so thoroughly well
that I saw I was no longer a necessity, and
struck my tent accordingly. I was a little tired,
as the work was not light, and I was glad to get a
chance and go knapsacking with Professor Geikie
for a little. A fortnight's mission in Kirkcaldy
followed, and then a week at the General Assembly. Since then I have been studying at home
with an occasional flight into evangelism.

'My future as usual is all in the clouds. Everything
is as dark as ever — or shall I say as bright as
ever? *Faith-colour* would be the best word, only
I am not quite assured enough to use it.'

In June he went north to address a meeting of the
Pitlochrie Young Men's Association. There was a
cricket-match in one of the Bonskeid parks, in which
he took part, and when it was over and the visitors
gone, four of us were left together to spend the evening, which closed in dark and rainy. With his usual
resource Drummond invented a game for us. 'They
play it in America,' he said, 'with bowie-knives. Four
men are locked into a dark room, each in a corner,
and the survivor wins. We'll do without the knives;
the door and the shutters shall be shut, each of us will
stand in a corner, and the first who gets on another
man's back will be the winner.' It was, I think, the
most exciting game I ever played. Nobody stirred
from his corner for twenty minutes. Then I heard a
scuffle between two of the others, felt my way to fling
myself on both of them, when Drummond pounced on

me, and we all rolled in a heap, he of course on the top — as he always was.

In July he went for a tour in Norway with Robert Barbour, to whom he afterwards sent this letter, notable at least for its charming definition of a holiday: —

'GLEN ELM LODGE, STIRLING, Aug. 21, 1877.

'My programme since coming from Norway has been very simple and very happy. I have scarcely stirred from my den. I have studied some, and read crowds of, books. *The Ring and the Book* I have gone through with increasing interest, and Hutton's *Essays* have filled me with admiration for everybody except myself. I have just got Shairp's new book, which I think will delight you, if you have not seen it, *The Poetic Interpretation of Nature*, my only other novelties being Pulsford's new volume of sermons and a book by *Enigmas of Life's* brother, *A Layman's Legacy*, which is only mediocre. Norway did me a world of good; it was a clear month out of reading, out of thinking, out of planning for the future, out of responsibility for others. Not a shred of those things followed me; I forgot them all and I think this is the true holiday — to be one's simplest self, forget the past, and ignore the future. This is fearfully heathenish, and I sometimes had my misgivings, but I think now it is right. I never came back to work, to books, to Christianity, I might almost say, with such a spring; the world seemed new born. The first sermon I heard was heaven opened; preaching myself was inspiration. I should like to have your version when you write; or you can write a treatise if you like "On the Philosophy of Holidays," which is a subject quite worth thinking about, seeing that most men in our line give at least one-twelfth of their year to it.

'I went in to the Commission ten days ago, mainly to recover my ecclesiastical vocabulary. I had really forgotten all the more important words, also in theology, from pure disuse. . . .

'I am a missionary again — sad relapse from an assistant's airy height. A handful of colliers, in a place near Polmont, were needing shepherding, and I go down every Sabbath to preach twice to them. It is most delightful work, and I would not exchange it for anywhere.'

In spite of these bright intervals of holiday and work, Drummond, still uncertain of his future, was not happy. He afterwards called [1] this year 'the most miserable time of his life, not seeing what definite work he could do to earn his bread, and yet get time to preach. When he came from Norway he went to New College to see in the Calendar what subjects were required for examination for license, though he did not want to be licensed. He had been blamed (he says), as if he had given up the ministry, but he has never been a minister, nor wanted to be. At college he found some numbers of *Nature* that had been accumulating for him, and then all his scientific studies came back upon him. But he saw no use for his *Natures* now that his college career was at an end; and as he went down the Mound he gave them to an engine-driver, saying they were some journals he might find interesting. In a day or two he noticed the death of Mr. Keddie (lecturer on Natural Science in the

[1] To Professor Simpson, with whom he had a long talk about his career a few months before his death.

Free Church College, Glasgow), and wrote to Principal
Douglas to ask if it was any use his applying for the
lectureship. Dr. Douglas encouraged him. He got
a very commendatory testimonial from Professor Archibald Geikie, as well as some others, but he thinks
Geikie's got him the place.' On September 17th the
General Assembly's College Committee appointed him
to the lectureship for one session, and so he found
the work that ultimately formed the profession and
settled post after which he had been groping for two
years.

During these years of uncertainty and painful waiting for the issue of his life, Drummond had been much
sustained by studying the teaching of the Bible upon
the Will of God. He had put the result in three sermons which he preached from the Barclay pulpit, and
which now form the last of his volume, *The Ideal Life*,
'What is God's Will?' 'The Relation of the Will of
God to Sanctification,' and 'How to know the Will of
God.' But he has summarised the knowledge which
the study and experience of three years of waiting
brought him, in eight maxims, which he inscribed
upon the fly-leaf of his Bible.

To find out God's Will

1. Pray.
2. Think.
3. Talk to wise people, but do not regard their
decision as final.
4. Beware of the bias of your own will, but do not
be *too much* afraid of it (God never unnecessarily
thwarts a man's nature and likings, and it is a mistake
to think that His will is in the line of the disa-
greeable).
5. Meantime do the next thing (for doing God's

will in small things is the best preparation for knowing it in great things).

6. When decision and action are necessary, go
ahead.

7. Never reconsider the decision when it is finally
acted upon; and

8. You will probably not find out till afterwards,
perhaps long afterwards, that you have been led at all.

CHAPTER VI

SCIENCE AND RELIGION. 1877–1883

THE presence in a divinity hall of a lectureship on Natural Science is a phenomenon which requires some explanation. In the case of the Free Church of Scotland it was not due, as has sometimes been supposed, to the Roman policy of qualifying so inevitable an influence as modern science by straining it through a theological filter; but it arose very reasonably out of the condition of the Scottish universities in 1843, when the Free Church separated from the State.

At that time the Arts chairs in the universities were still under tests, and the Free Church felt herself obliged to supply for her students not only a theological curriculum, but a full Arts one as well. New College, Edinburgh, at first included professorships or lectureships in Classics, Mathematics, and Philosophy, and these continued till the university tests were abolished.[1] But in addition a chair of Natural Science was founded, at the instigation of Sir David Brewster, Hugh Miller, and others, who had strong feelings of the need of it in training young men for the ministry.[2] These feelings were due to the healthy opinion that Natural Science should be a factor in the Arts curriculum, in which nevertheless no Scottish university save that of Aberdeen had yet placed it. Other mem-

[1] Two of the New College Professors, Macdougall and Campbell Fraser, afterwards became the University Professors of Moral Philosophy and Logic.
[2] See a speech by Principal Rainy in the General Assembly of 1884.

bers of the Church, too, felt that science would so largely enter into Christian apologetics, and into the materials for preaching, as to justify a separate class for its treatment.   Consequently, when the other Arts chairs in New College came to an end, that of Natural Science was continued, first under Dr. Fleming, then under Dr. Duns; and a lectureship was established in the second Free Church College at Glasgow.   The latter was held till 1877 by Mr. Keddie, F.R.S.E., and on his death, as we have seen, Henry Drummond secured the temporary appointment for session 1877–78.

The students in Glasgow College varied from seventy to one hundred.   Drummond lectured to the First Year, from twelve to twenty-four in number.   He had no lines prescribed to him and chose to instruct the students in the rudiments of geology and botany and in the general methods of modern science.[1]   The salary was £150 a year, the lectures four a week from the beginning of November to the end of March.   Their preparation occupied the whole of his time, and I find in existence no letters from him during this session and no record of other work.   The following was written when the session closed : —

'GLEN ELM LODGE, STIRLING, April 20, 1878.

' . . . I am in the *statu quo*.   Session ended well. We wound up with four days' geologising in Arran, and had a glorious time.   Eleven men mustered, the cream of the class, and we hammered the Island almost to bits — nothing left but the hotel and a ledge of rock to smoke on !'

In May he had ten days more geologising, this time among the Cairngorms and with Professor Geikie.

[1] See further, p. 268.

In the end of the month he returned to Glasgow, to attend the meetings of the General Assembly, the first for many years held outside Edinburgh. The most important business before this Assembly was the consideration of the 'relevancy' of the charge made against Professor Robertson Smith before the Presbytery of Aberdeen, of contravening by his articles in the *Encyclopædia Britannica* the doctrine of inspiration in the Westminster Confession of Faith. The question was narrowed to the Professor's statement of the non-Mosaic authorship of Deuteronomy. A motion by Sir Henry Moncrieff that such a statement would, if proved, contravene the Confession, was carried by a small majority over one by Principal Rainy, that the charge was not relevant; and the case was sent back for proof to the Presbytery of Aberdeen. But the moral victory was felt to lie with the Professor's opinions, and as it turned out he was acquitted by the Presbytery and, on a narrow majority of three, by a subsequent Assembly.[1] At this stage of the famous trial Drummond's own mind was not very clear, but he was evidently impressed by the speeches for the defence.

'ASSEMBLY HALL, Saturday [first Saturday of June], 1878.

'MY DEAR MOTHER, — . . . The Smith and Dods cases are very well over, and every one is thankful for the peace of the end. [Alas, it was not the end!] The speaking of Smith, Rainy, and others has been extraordinary, and has made the Assembly very profitable. Last night I spent at an evangelistic meeting in Grove Street with Willie Ferguson and MacGill. I was with the same party on Wednesday morning, having an open-

[1] 1880. See p. 141.

air meeting in a foundry during the breakfast hour; so I have not been altogether useless.'

By this Assembly Drummond was appointed to another session of the lectureship; but the summer was free, and, eager for some religious work, he accepted an invitation to take charge of the Free Church of Scotland's station at Malta, in the absence of the chaplain, the Rev. Mr. Wisely. The following letters are to his friends Ross and Barbour: —

'VALLETTA, MALTA, July 4, 1878.

'My DEAR ROSS, — This is the day of your ordination, and I am not unmindful of you. My thoughts are Dundeewards, and if good wishes can do you any good in your new work you have them in abundance from this far-off land. . . . I am not going to bother you with much of this tissue-paper caligraphy, as I have little to say yet about Malta that would interest you. Besides, with the thermometer at 90° in the shade letter-writing is far from being a luxury, especially as I have to sally forth on a mosquito hunt between every second sentence. I had a splendid tour here. It began with a peep at the Paris Exhibition, then with a run through Italy and Sardinia, and wound up with a voyage to Africa, where I stayed a week.

'I have only been three days here. It is a splendid place. If the heat allow it, I am sure I shall enjoy the work greatly. The chief items are three services on Sundays, one or two in the camps through the week, and hospital visitation. It will be pretty hard, but I am only to have two months of it. . . .

'Now do write me a line and tell me "wie es sieht in der Welt aus," to quote your famous Tübingen phrase. I hope you have had a good start.'

'REV. MR. WISELY'S, VALLETTA, MALTA,
July 4, 1878.

' LIEBER ROBERT,—This time last year we were sing-ing chorales on the North Sea. You no doubt are singing them still in the North of Scotland. I am killing mosquitoes in Malta.

'. . . Malta seems a most interesting place, thoroughly civilised, and inhabited by every nation on earth. There is a magnificently equipped English library, where I spend the morning before work begins, and there are museums when one is tired of the endless museum of the streets. I came here *via* Paris, Marseilles, Italy, Sardinia, and Africa. In Africa I spent a week. My headquarters were Tunis, the second largest city in Africa. The change to Oriental life was most interesting, in fact, Tunis is the most interesting place I have ever seen. Arabs, deserts, palms, and camels are strange sights to a European, and I would recommend every one who comes near the Medi-terranean to give a few days to North Africa. I was all alone, and it is out of the tourists' track, so sometimes I felt rather eerie. One day I spent among the ruins of ancient Carthage — profoundly interesting. . . . Yours most sin-cerely,   HENRY DRUMMOND.

'P.S. *Paul* was three months here!'

'GLEN ELM LODGE, STIRLING, Sept. 17, 1878.

' LIEBER ROBERT,—. . . I came home on Friday. The chief event on the way was a sunrise from

Etna. Etna is only three thousand feet lower than
Mt. Blanc, so the climb was glorious and the view
from the crater a miracle of grandeur. After
Sicily, I did Naples, Pompeii, Herculaneum,
Vesuvius, the Island of Capri, Pozzuoli; then
Rome, Florence, Milan, the Italian Lakes, and
home over the St. Gotthard Pass with Switzer-
land; thence by Basle, Paris, and Calais.'

In September Drummond settled down again in
Glasgow. He was happy in his lectureship, and very
happy in his colleagues, with whom he was to work
for nineteen years on terms of the closest affection
and confidence. Principal Douglas, who was Professor of Hebrew, Professor T. M. Lindsay, who had
the Church History Chair, Professor James Candlish,
who taught Systematic and Pastoral Theology, and
Professor A. B. Bruce, who had the Chairs of Apologetics and the New Testament. Drummond's few
lectures gave him leisure for other work, and he had
not forgotten his calling as an evangelist. ' I want,'
he had written in April of this year, ' a quiet mission
somewhere, entry immediate and self-contained.' He
had attached himself to Renfield Free Church, under
the ministry of Dr. Marcus Dods, and was ordained
as an elder. The congregation had recently adopted
a mission station in Possilpark, and in April Dr. Dods
had offered the charge of it to Drummond, who entered upon his duties when he returned from Malta.
Possilpark is a northern suburb of Glasgow. In 1878
its population was said to be about six thousand, mostly
working-class families settled in recently built houses.
They were nearly all well-to-do people, but in the
autumn of 1878 the City of Glasgow Bank failed and
cast hundreds of them out of work. It was a terrible

winter; the social distress was aggravated by very severe cold, and city missionaries, not in Glasgow only but all over Scotland, passed through experiences which they can never forget. The ordinary labours of charity were increased tenfold; investigations had to be made into hundreds of new cases, and, owing to the number of honest families thrown into a distress to which they were absolutely new, the work required extraordinary patience and tact. But the rewards were great. The missionaries came into personal relation with a large number of lives they would probably never have touched, and obtained abundant proofs of the courage and honesty of the mass of Scottish working-men. One missionary, who was given £40 for distribution in his district, found that the most of it would be accepted only in the form of loans, and had not less than £23 repaid to him when work grew better in the course of the following year.

To Robert W. Barbour

'September 17, 1878.

'On Sunday I was "introduced" to my new flock in Glasgow by Dods, and I begin work there at once. I have a splendid prospect for the winter — a district of six thousand people, none of them lapsed as yet, no opposition, and many willing, helping hands.'

To Mr. and Mrs. Stuart

'POSSILPARK, GLASGOW, Nov. 22, 1878.

'. . . In the first place I have my college lectures, which is enough for any man. Secondly, I have now a church. On Sabbath I preach twice,

attend schools and classes. On Mondays I look
after a bank; on Tuesdays I give a popular lecture. On Wednesdays a mothers' meeting in the
afternoon, a lecture to children at seven, the congregational prayer-meeting at eight. The other
two nights I visit the poor and the sick, or hold
meetings elsewhere. I am just starting now,
ten miles, for a meeting to-night. This is my
programme every week. In addition to all this,
I have had the horror of my examination for
license hanging over me from the hour I landed
from Malta.'

'POSSILPARK, March 21, 1879.

'. . . So you have been to America and seen Moody.
For myself I have had a long, quiet, busy winter.
My little church gets on bravely, though it has
been a dreadful winter in Glasgow. Thousands
have been really starving all winter, and out here
I have had to feed scores of families with the
meat that perisheth, and a scant seasoning only
of the other. We are past the worst now, I hope,
though the snow is still thick on the ground.

' Although I have a church, I am not a minister *yet*.
Mrs. Grundy, I am glad to say, has not prevailed.
I am not ordained, nor have I any desire to be,
or prospect of being. My old desires and aims
are there still, unchanged. I have taken what we
call *license*, and which is often mistaken for ordination, but it is little more than a college certifi-
cate of a theological education. And my church
is a mere appendage to my college work to fill up
spare interest and time. By and by I give it up,
and plunge into evangelism. I shall retain my
college work — it will be corrective without being
absorbing. I have had several calls this winter

to be *ordained* to churches in different places, but have refused them all on this secret ground. No one, however, can understand me. I am looked upon as "queer." *You* will understand, however, that I have not bowed down and worshipped Mrs. G. If you ever write Mr. Moody, I wish you would tell him that. He, too, thinks I have fallen.

'I am going to take my class down to the Island of Arran for some days' geologising. . . .'

'POSSILPARK, GLASGOW, July 25, 1879.

'. . . You wrote me on the eve of your departure to America. It is now my turn. I start next Thursday. I am to be away three months — all the time in the Far West. I am going with Professor Geikie, whom you know. We are to geologise in the Rocky Mountains. I suppose we shall be camped out all the time, shooting, fishing, and hammering, so we shall see nothing of the States. I mean, of course, to make a great effort to run off for a day or two with D. L. M.,[1] but I shall have to reserve civilised America for a future occasion.

'Now that I have introduced myself, I must recall events since I wrote last. My life has been very humdrum, toiling away in a mission district since college closed last March. My college appointment was made permanent by my election to the Chair[2] last Assembly, so that there is no fear of my being a settled minister. I shall lecture five months and be a vagrant, or a city, missionary during the other seven. It is an odd life, but it suits me.'

[1] Mr. Moody.   [2] Lectureship.

On the 31st of July he sailed for America. The account of his geological expedition to the Rocky Mountains with Professor Geikie may be postponed to a separate chapter.

On his return from the Rockies, Drummond found himself at Boston, and in a curious dilemma. He had five days before he sailed for home. He was in the city of Lowell and Longfellow, Bryant, Emerson, Channing, Agassiz, and Holmes; and he had an invitation to meet Longfellow and Holmes at dinner.

'Longfellow I had learned to love from my youth up; Holmes, ever since the mystery of the three Johns and the three Toms caught my school-boy fancy years ago, has been to me a mouth and wisdom. And naturally the attraction of these names was a powerful inducement to me to spend my last days in quiet worship at shrines so revered and beloved. But some eight hundred miles off, away by Lake Erie, were two men who were more to me than philosopher or poet, and it only required a moment's thought to convince me that for me, at least, a visit to America would be much more than incomplete without a visit to Mr. Moody and Mr. Sankey. It was hard, I must say, to give up Longfellow, but I am one of those who think that the world is not dying for poets so much as for preachers. I set off at once. . . . Neither of the men seemed the least changed. There they were before me, the same men: Mr. Sankey down to the faultless set of his black necktie, Mr. Moody to the chronic crush of his collar. . . . I can scarcely say I have much to record that would be in itself news. For my own part I am glad of this. We do not want anything

new in revivals. We want always the old factors —
the living Spirit of God, the living Word of God,
the old Gospel. We want crowds coming to
hear — crowds made up of the old elements; per-
ishing men and women finding their way to
prayer-meeting, Bible reading, and inquiry room.
These were all to be seen in Cleveland. It was
the same as in England and Scotland. I was
especially pleased to find that it was the same as
regards quietness. I had expected to find revival
work in America more exciting; but, although a
deep work was beginning, everything was calm.
There was movement, but no agitation; there was
power in the meetings, but no frenzy. And the
secret of that probably lay here, that in the speaker
himself there was earnestness, but no bigotry, and
enthusiasm, but no superstition.'[1]

No more signal proof could we have both of Drummond's enthusiasm for the Gospel and of his loyalty to
old friends. Probably never in all his life did he feel
a greater wrench than this from Boston and the
chance of meeting the two poets; probably never
greater happiness than when he burst in — uninvited,
unannounced — upon the astonished evangelists at
Cleveland. And yet, — and yet, — O Henry, why
didn't you dine with Longfellow and Holmes?

From America Drummond returned to his third
winter as lecturer on Natural Science, and as missionary in Possilpark. The years '80 and '81 passed away
in this double work, without incident and almost without the break of a single holiday.

The case of Professor Robertson Smith was proceeding from one church court to another, with vary-

[1] From a letter to *The Christian*, November, 1879.

ing and ambiguous fortunes. No one knew how it would end; and indeed comparatively few were certain on which side, at the end, they themselves would be found. The truth is, it was not so much the trial of one man which was proceeding, nor even the trial of one set of opinions, as the education of the whole Church in face of the facts which Biblical criticism had recently presented to her. The Great Mission of 1873–75 had quickened, as we have seen, the practical use of the Bible, and the Church was studying her sacred books in the congregation and in the Bible class, with a freshness and a thoroughness hardly seen before. But now came the necessary complement to all that, in the critical study of the Scriptures; and by those who believe in God's providence of His Church, it has always been a matter of praise that the revival of the experimental study of the Scriptures in Scotland preceded that of the critical. Those who, with Professor Robertson Smith, instigated the latter, were some of the devoutest men in the Church, of whom it is right to instance especially one of Drummond's own colleagues: the late Professor James Candlish, a teacher of undoubted orthodoxy, a most spiritual preacher, a finished scholar, and, in spite of his weak health and a rare modesty, which made him the least aggressive spirit in the movement, a man of courage and the most perfect justice. These men believed that Christ's promise of the Holy Spirit for the education of His Church was being fulfilled, not less in the critical than in the experimental use of the Bible; they defended criticism on the highest grounds of faith in God and loyalty to Christ. But as in every other discipline of the Church in new truth, so in this, pain and restlessness prevailed. Within, as without, the church courts discussion ran high and hot for three years. The old parties were broken up, and even groups of friends and fellow-workers divided sharply under the new tests. At first Drummond could not but share the general uncertainty. Many of his dearest friends and leaders were opposed to Professor Smith's views; he himself was not equipped with the knowledge of the original languages of the Bible which could have enabled him to form conclusions of his own. And in the letter he wrote from the Glasgow Assembly, we have seen that he looked for peace arising out of some compromise.

But Drummond's scientific training had given him a sense for facts, an appreciation of evidence; while his strong and cheerful faith in God saved him from the confusion into which so complete a revolution in his views of the methods of inspiration must otherwise have cast him. The Assembly of 1880 decided by a narrow majority in Professor Smith's favour, and Drummond rejoiced at the decision. When new articles by the professor appeared in the *Encyclopædia Britannica*, and led the Assembly's Commission of the following October to suspend him once more from his chair, Drummond refused to be satisfied with a verdict which, while it saved the Church from a pronouncement against the new views, prepared to sacrifice, for the peace of the Church, their foremost representative; and when it became apparent, next spring, that the General Assembly would complete the work of the Commission, and remove Professor Smith from his chair, Drummond wrote in great sorrow:[1]—

'We are all much dejected here by the suicidal policy of the majority in their recent determination to lynch Smith. It will be a very serious blow to the Church, and I fear nothing can avert it now.'

[1] Glasgow, May 21, 1881.

He was right.   Professor Robertson Smith was sacrificed; but whatever may have been the motives of the
leaders of the majority,—whether the general peace of
the Church, or the more subtle desire to save the
Church, by his suspension, from a condemnation of
the critical views,—the latter result was secured, and
the Church was allowed to find room for methods of
research and for views of inspiration more free from
the errors of tradition, and more true to the facts of
Scripture itself.   With these new views, Drummond,
though he took no share in developing them, was
henceforth in hearty sympathy.   His religious teaching was as much based upon the Bible as it had ever
been; but in his own practical use of the Bible he
exercised a new discrimination, and he often said
that the critical movement had removed very many
difficulties in the Old Testament which once puzzled
him, and had set him free for the fuller appreciation of its divine contents.

Several years afterwards, speaking of the contest of
Science and Religion, he is reported to have said:—

'The contest is dying out.   The new view of the
    Bible has rendered further apologetics almost
    superfluous.   I have endeavoured to show that
    in my articles on Creation.[1]   No one now expects
    science from the Bible.   The literary form of
    Genesis precludes the idea that it is science.
    You might as well contrast *Paradise Lost* with
    geology as the Book of Genesis.   Mr. Huxley
    might have been better employed than in laying
    that poor old ghost.   The more modern views
    of the inspiration of the Bible have destroyed
    the stock-in-trade of the platform infidel.   Such

[1] See below, chap. x.

men are constructing difficulties which do not exist, and they fight as those that beat the air.'[1]

Drummond once asked me to help in the preparation of a popular tract on the Higher Criticism. A rhetorical Bishop, a defender of the Mosaic origin of the Pentateuch, had asked what the critics would answer when in the next world Moses met them with the challenge, ' How dared you say that I did *not* write the Pentateuch?' I pointed out that, considering the absence of all claims of Mosaic authorship in the Pentateuch itself, it was equally reasonable to put the question in the very opposite form; and Drummond's proposal was to write the tract in the form of a dream by the same Bishop, as though, being conveyed to heaven and meeting Moses, Moses should ask him, ' How dared you say that I *did* write the Pentateuch?'

But among all the influences which were bearing on Drummond during these years, the strongest came through his intercourse with Dr. Marcus Dods. In the Possilpark Mission Dr. Dods was his ecclesiastical superior, and they shared work in those practical movements for which the religious life of Glasgow is famous; while, in Dr. Dods' knowledge of literature and of the philosophical tendencies of our time, the younger man found numerous opportunities of repairing the defects in his own education. Years afterwards Drummond said: ' I can claim Dr. Dods, not only as a friend and elder brother, but as the greatest influence in many directions that has ever come across my life; and that if I have done anything in my poor way to help anybody else, it has been

[1] From ' A Talk with Professor Drummond,' by Raymond Blathwayt, in *Great Thoughts*, I think, about 1890.

largely owing to what he has done, and mainly by his own grand character, to help me.' Among the 'many directions' in which this influence told were those of Biblical criticism and the application of the hypothesis of evolution to the interpretation of religion.

Most of the members of Drummond's Club had married by 1881, and the experiment was tried of asking the wives to the annual reunion. This is the letter that one of them got from Drummond shortly afterwards.

To Mrs. Robert W. Barbour

'POSSILPARK, GLASGOW, May 21st, 1881.

'. . . I am so glad you enjoyed Moffat. I must confess I was afraid the ladies would find us a very queer set of beings. We are so accustomed to one another, that when we get together we drop all the graver responsibilities, and become schoolboys once more. This, of course, is a great and a natural joy to us, but I fancy you must often have been bewildered at us. Moffat reminded me even of an earlier stage than the school-boy this year. You know the curious old memory of "going thro' a wood when we were children," that was what Moffat was to me: young, fresh, and buoyant, "children going thro' a wood "; yet I trust we will never forget this memory, nor lose this spirit. . . .'

Early in 1882 Messrs. Moody and Sankey began a new mission in Scotland, passed in the late summer into Wales and the southwest of England, preached in Paris for the most of October, and returned for the winter to the cities they had already visited in England and Ireland, and to a number of others in addition. The mission was not so powerful as that of eight years before, but a good deal of real work was done.

To Robert W. Barbour [1]

'POSSILPARK, GLASGOW, March 13, 1882.

'DEAR ROBERT, — I wish you could spend a few days in the Moody work. Stalker is coming on Wednesday. The movement amongst men in the East End has been the main feature, and I have had some very wonderful cases. Brown and Ewing are both over head and ears in it; and for the workers at least, it is quite as good as the last revival. At the same time, the movement has not seized the city as it did before, and the scarcity of ministers at the meetings is marked. I have got a few students to come to the inquiry room, but the attitude of the college as a whole is largely one of simple toleration.

'I am afraid it will be impossible for me to come up in April. I expect Moody in my own parish, where I have long been expecting to see some work. I must say I believe in personal dealing more and more every day, and in the inadequacy of mere preaching. The inquiry room this time, as before, brings its terrible revelation of the vast multitude of unregenerate church members. I have dealt with several men of position who knew the letter of Scripture as they knew their own names, but who had no more idea of Free Grace and a Personal Christ than a Hottentot.'

'POSSILPARK, GLASGOW, June 8th, 1882.

'DEAR ROBERT, — ... I now see things a little clearer, but unfortunately I do not see Cults. Moody, too,

[1] Then Free Church minister at Cults.

L

has made me promise to "hitch on to him," as
he calls it, for the summer, so that my arrangements are very much taken out of my own hands.
My only reserve is a few weeks in July, which I
spend with Dods somewhere on the Continent.

'I had Moody in my church last Sabbath — one of
the most wonderful meetings I ever saw. A crowd
of my own members stood up at the close and
asked to be prayed for, and a number of other
inquirers waited to the second meeting. I have
been following up all week with nightly meetings.

'On Tuesday night there was a special meeting for
reformed drunkards in the City Hall. They
were admitted by special ticket, received on
formal application and after cross-examination.
Over 800 sat down to tea, of all ages and ranks.
Mr. Moody presided, and a number afterwards
gave their testimony: all was most thrilling and
pathetic.

'Altogether the work has taken a powerful hold, and
immense numbers have been reached. I have
given up my church.'

The Possilpark Mission, in which Drummond had
been working hard for four years, had prospered.
There were nearly three hundred communicants, a
large Sabbath-school, a Young Men's Christian Association, and various other agencies. A church had been
built, costing nearly £4000, and it was free of debt.
The General Assembly of 1882 raised the mission
to the status of a full charge, and Drummond resigned
the missionaryship in order that an ordained minister
might be appointed. This set him free to work with
Mr. Moody through the rest of the summer, and in
October he came back to his college lectures.

To Mrs. Stuart

'POSSILPARK, GLASGOW, December 20th, 1882.

'Of myself I have little to report. I am growing older and, as you know, wickeder. I was with Moody all summer in Scotland, Wales, and England. I have been very busy, and have not had a holiday for a year and a half. I have also been writing a book, now in the press. When I add that I am not married yet, and as far away from it as ever, my year's autobiography is ended.

'I hope you will see something of Moody when he is in your neighbourhood in the early year. My admiration of him has increased a hundredfold. I had no idea before of the moral size of the man, and I think very few know what he really is.'

A month before his death Drummond said to one of his doctors, ' Moody was the biggest human I ever met.'

During the winter he worked hard at the book, rewriting most of it, and joined Moody again for a little when the session was over.

To Mrs. Stuart

'POSSILPARK, GLASGOW, March 31st, 1883.

'. . . The book will not be ready for two or three weeks yet. I am going to Liverpool next week to work for a short time with Moody. . . . Moody has asked me to go to America with him, but I do not think I shall be tempted. From your letter I see you are afraid my book will not be orthodox, but I hope you will not find this to be the case. I am getting sounder and sounder !'

The book was the one which made him famous, *Natural Law in the Spiritual World.* It was not his greatest work. Its main argument rests upon a couple of unproved, and, in the opinion of many, impossible assumptions. And Drummond himself became discontented with it. But because it made him famous, and is still, with many, the chief cause of his reputation; because of the enormous circulation it achieved, the multitudes it helped, the wild hopes it raised, and the bitter controversy, — it is right that we should form some clear idea of how this book began, and what it aimed at effecting. Drummond has himself described its origin.

'For four years,' as he says in his Preface, he had 'to address regularly two very different audiences on two very different themes. On week days I have lectured to a class of students on the Natural Sciences, and on Sundays to an audience consisting for the most part of working-men, on subjects of a moral and religious character. I cannot say that this collocation ever appeared as a difficulty to myself, but to certain of my friends it was more than a problem. It was solved to me, however, at first by what then seemed the necessities of the case — I must keep the two departments entirely by themselves. They lay at opposite poles of thought; and for a time I succeeded in keeping the Science and the Religion shut off from one another in two separate compartments of my mind. But gradually the wall of partition showed symptoms of giving way. The two fountains of knowledge also slowly began to overflow, and finally their waters met and mingled. The great change was in the compartment which held the Religion. It was not that the well there was. dried; still less that the fermenting waters were washed away by the flood of science. The actual contents remained the same. But the crystals of former doctrine were dissolved; and as they precipitated themselves once more in definite forms, I observed that the Crystalline System was also changed. New channels also for outward expression opened, and some of the old closed up; and I found the truth running out to my audience on the Sundays by the week-day outlets. In other words, the subject-matter of Religion had taken on the method of expression of Science, and I discovered myself enunciating Spiritual Law in the exact terms of Biology and Physics.'

The simple style of this paragraph masks a considerable vagueness of meaning, and one desires some more explicit description of the state of his Science and his Religion when he 'kept them shut off from one another in two separate compartments of his mind.' He cannot have intended this to be taken literally. For, since coming to Glasgow, Drummond's eyes had been opened to the great signs of evolution within Scripture[1] itself. And, on the other side, he was equally aware how Natural Science corroborates the Scriptural assumption that behind the visible universe there is a creative mind. Although he had judged Darwin's own teaching to be defective on this point,[2] he thankfully acknowledged that Science in general bore to it unmistakable and even lavish witness. To his students he emphasised these mutual contribu-

---

[1] We shall get his opinion on this later on.
[2] See above, p. 47.

tions of Religion and Science, and on the last day of
1878 he wrote to one who inquired of him what
Science had done to corroborate the teaching of Scripture upon the origin of life, as follows : —

To Hugh Barbour

'I think it is quite clear that Science has gone as
far as she ever will on her side of the border.
And she has gone a wonderful length — *towards
us*, as I am convinced. The old cry, " How far
Science has wandered away from God (Creator),"
will soon be entirely obsolete; and " How near
Science has come to God" will be the watchword
of the most thoughtful and far-seeing. Instance
the argument of the " Unseen Universe" *in
toto;* instance Tyndall's article in the November
number of the *Nineteenth Century;* instance a
hundred passages in Huxley's *Lay Sermons* and
many other places.

'My Huxley is in Glasgow, or I would send you
reference to a quotation which would surprise
you if you have never seen it.'[1] He is describing
the development of an ovum. He watches the
process through a powerful microscope. "Strange
possibilities lie dormant in that semi-fluid globe.
Let a moderate supply of warmth reach its watery
cradle, and the plastic matter undergoes changes
so rapid, and yet so steady and purposelike in
their succession, that we can only compare them
to those operated by a skilled operator on a form-
less lump of clay." He sees, as it were, "a skilled
modeller" shaping the plastic mass with a trowel.
He sees "as if a delicate finger traced out the line

---

[1] The reference is to *Lay Sermons.*

to be occupied by the spinal column, and moulded the contour of the body, pinching up the head at one end, the tail at the other, and fashioning flank and limb into due salamandrine proportions in so artistic a way that, after watching the process hour by hour, one is almost involuntarily possessed by the notion that some more subtle aid to vision than an achromatic would show the hidden artist with his plan before him, striving with skilful manipulation to perfect his work."[1]   The above are Huxley's own words.   That is to say that the first biologist in Europe (according to Virchow) when he comes to describe the development of life can only do so in *Terms of Creation.* This, of course, was just what *we* might have expected, but I find it very remarkable that our anticipation should have been so literally fulfilled and by such authority.   The materialists have never got credit for this most advanced standpoint, and I think it cannot be too widely explained.   Your desire evidently is to state all that Science can with reference to the evolution of living things.   I do not see that they could go one step further than Huxley in the passage referred to; for the next step would be God.'

Drummond, therefore, was never troubled by any fears that Science would contradict the fundamental postulates of the Bible on the field of the natural universe on which Science worked; and he already recognised, within the historical origins of the Christian religion, the same method of evolution at work as Science had recently revealed in the growth of physical

---

[1] In Drummond's letter the quotation, written from memory, is not given, of course, so fully or accurately.

life. What, then, did he mean by saying that he 'kept Religion and Science shut off from one another in two different compartments of his mind'? In these words he was speaking of religion as the experience of the individual — conversion, regeneration, the growth of character, the assurance of immortality — the phenomena, in short, with which he himself had been practically busied in hundreds of lives during the last ten years. This set of facts, comprising the religious life of the individual, was what he had kept in one compartment of his mind, while the other was filled with the facts of physical life. By 'keeping them apart,' he did not, of course, mean that the religious facts had not their laws, as the physical had theirs, for Drummond had never treated religion in the manner of certain preachers, as if it were utterly without the great laws of life, a moral-less magic of arbitrary formulas, expedients, and even dodges. But he meant that the laws which are visible in the phenomena of the individual's experience of religion were at first felt by him to be different from, and without the slightest resemblance or relevance to, the laws which are visible in the phenomena of physical life. But a teacher who teaches in parallel lines two different subjects of human knowledge cannot help, sooner or later, stating the one in terms of the other; and this, of course, happened in Drummond's case the more easily that teachers of religion had from the very first perceived analogies or resemblances between spiritual and physical phenomena, and that some of the greatest of them had even conceived of Nature as therefore sacramental — the designed mirror or symbol of religious truth. No one, however, had proposed as yet to define these comparisons between the two sets of laws in more stringent terms than those of analogy and sacrament. Drummond went farther, and with great boldness—whether rightly or wrongly we shall inquire afterwards — asserted the two sets of laws to be identical.

Perhaps this is the best place at which to introduce a very curious story concerning a similar suggestion made by Drummond's grandfather, William Drummond, who died in 1824. It is told by Henry's brother-in-law, the Rev. Thomas Crerar: 'I was with Henry after his father's death [1] in Glenelm, when we found among his father's papers a note-book of *his* father, the old William Drummond, in which he had some reflections on religious matters. I think the old man wrote, after noting some facts in the Spiritual and the Natural Life: "Would it not be strange if it turned out that the laws of Nature and of the Spiritual World were the same?" and Henry remarked to me: "How strange! That is just my idea as expressed in *Natural Law*. Can there be an inherited idea as well as an inherited tendency?"—or words to that effect.'

Drummond, then, asserted that the laws governing both spheres were identical. But he insisted that he arrived at this position by the inductive method; that first of all he awoke to the actual presence of certain natural laws in one department after another of the spiritual life — regeneration, growth, degeneration, and so forth. This he emphasised again and again. He had not first supposed his theory, and then tried if the facts would fit it; but he had first encountered the facts, gradually recognised their significance, and then deduced his general principle from them. His method, in short, had been the *a posteriori*. But having thus reached his conclusions, he had found for them the corroboration of an *a priori* argument in the

[1] January 1, 1888.

scientific principle of Continuity.   Scientific writers
had recently emphasised the Continuity of Law in the
Physical Universe.   Was it not probable, Drummond
asked, that this continuity should extend still farther,
and cover the spiritual world as well?   Drummond
thought that the affirmative reply to such a question
was obvious.

It is not within the province of a biographer to expound in detail, still less to criticise, the writings
of the man whose life he is portraying; yet, if for
nothing else than to point out the direction in which
Drummond — who was far bigger than all his books
— grew away from the positions which he so con-
fidently occupied in the first of them, it is necessary
that we should here indicate the two unproved — and
most people will think impossible — assumptions by
which he reached his famous conclusion of the operation of natural law in the spiritual life.   In the first
place, Drummond's *a priori* argument from the principle of Continuity was a huge *petitio principii*.   It
does not necessarily, nor even probably, follow that
because laws have a certain continuity throughout
the physical universe they must also prevail in the
spiritual experience of man.   Drummond maintains,
indeed, that the principle of Continuity is so well established that the burden of the disproof of its extension to spiritual life remains with those who deny this.
Emphatically this is not true.   The gulf is so great
between matter and mind, the respective contents of
the two spheres are so very different, that the burden
of proof in the question of a continuity of Law between
the two rather lies with him who maintains the affirmative.   Drummond has simply begged the question;
and since, as he himself points out, laws are not independent substances, but forms or conditions by which

the actions of forces are invariably governed, the fact
that the forces of the spirit life are different from
those of the physical life makes the presupposition
very strong that, though the Lawgiver be the same,
the laws in the two spheres are equally different.

And this leads us to his other unproved assumption; that, namely, in the inductive portion of his
reasoning.   In his belief that he had discovered some
laws of biology in the religious experience of the individual, Drummond was apparently fascinated by the
use of the term *life*, to describe the phenomena in
both departments, without pausing to inquire whether
the two kinds of life had anything more than the
name in common with each other.   Had he entered
upon this inquiry, he must have made it obvious (as
indeed it afterwards became to his own mind) that
spiritual life contained elements, and was realised in
conditions, so foreign to physical life, that the identity
of the laws governing the phenomena of both might
be reasonably regarded as an impossibility.   This fundamental objection to his argument has been stated by
many of his critics, but by none better than by the
author of *On 'Natural Law in the Spiritual World,'*
by 'a Brother of the Natural Man,' who, it is no harm
now to state, is the Rev. Professor Denney.   He says,[1]
'We find that natural life comes from preëxisting
natural life — according, we must add, to a certain
law, a law of necessary physical determination; and
we find that spiritual life comes from preëxisting spiritual life — according, we must add again, to another
law, a law of free moral determination in correspondence with the idea of that life; and these two laws
are quite different.   What is more, till we appreciate
the difference, we are not within sight of the spiritual

[1] P. 15.

world.   From this point of view, which also takes in
the whole complexity of the spiritual facts, we can see
the error and irrelevancy of much of Mr. Drummond's
preface and introduction.'   And, it may be added, it is
from this point of view also that we can appreciate
the defects of the body of the book: the illustrations
of the working of natural laws in several departments
of the spiritual life.   The want of the volume is the
want of regard for the moral character of religious
experience.   The spiritual life which the various chapters describe is one perilously near sheer passivity: in
its beginnings as independent of responsibility on the
part of those who receive it as their physical life is,
and in its continuance as destitute of the elements
of effort and struggle.   Take the beautiful chapter on
Growth, one of the most justly admired in the book.
It inculcates the advice not to try to grow spiritually,
but to leave one's growth, *first*, to the power of the
Spirit, and, *second*, to the effect of a good environment.
And, in support of this advice, it quotes our Lord's call
to *consider the lilies of the field how they grow: they
toil not neither do they spin.*   But Drummond forgot
that in this part of His discourse our Lord was speaking, not of our spiritual struggles after character, and
perfect obedience to the Will of God, but of our
physical anxieties and labours for our daily bread.
Christ's own spiritual life was full of moral effort, yea,
to the pitch of agony; and so it has been with the
lives of all the greatest saints.   This defect of the book
has another as its consequence.   Drummond denies
that the man who 'by hard work and self-restraint
attains to a very high character' is really growing.[1]
According to him, the unregenerate man is in the same
relation to the regenerate as the inorganic in the

[1] Twenty-fourth edition, p. 131.

physical world is to the organic, as a stone is to a plant.
And this leads him to a further assertion, which completely ignores the moral identity of the individual before and after conversion. ' The plant stretches down
to the dead world beneath it, touches its minerals and
gases with its mystery of life, and brings them up ennobled to the living sphere. The breath of God, blowing where it listeth, touches with its mystery of life the
dead souls of men, bears them across the bridgeless
gulf between the natural and the spiritual, between
the spiritually inorganic and the spiritually organic,
endows them with its own high qualities, and develops within them those new and secret faculties by
which those who are born again are said to see the
Kingdom of God.' But the man before and after his
conversion is the same man, with a continuance of
consciousness and will which are certainly absent in
the other case. The identity or analogy breaks down
at the vital point.[1] In short, this omission of all regard
for the moral distinctions of the spiritual life is so fundamental, that its effects are seen almost everywhere
throughout the book. Drummond himself came to
recognise this. Some years afterwards, I think about
1890, he said: ' I would write the book differently if I
were to do it again. I should make less rigid application of physical laws, and I should endeavour to be
more ethical; and this I have stated in a new translation of the book in Germany.' Yes; but he did
not even then see that to introduce those ethical
elements which had been so conspicuously absent
from his volume would be to destroy its primary
argument that natural law still prevailed where those
elements predominate, for he immediately added:

[1] This is finely put in On ' *Natural Law in the Spiritual World*,' by ' a Brother
of the Natural Man,' p. 35.

'But it is still clear to me that the same laws govern all worlds.'

The introduction, into which these fallacies mainly enter, was not given by Drummond to his Possilpark audiences of working-men, nor indeed was its thesis formulated till after his work in Possilpark was closed. It is a far more welcome task to turn to the great virtues of the addresses themselves. Their analysis and orderly arrangement of the facts of Christian experience; their emphasis upon the government of the religious life by law; their exposure of formalism and insincerity, conscious and unconscious, in the fashionable religion of the day; their revelation of life in Christ; their enthusiasm; their powers of practical counsel and of comfort; and their atmosphere of beauty and of peace, — must have made these addresses to the hundreds who heard them, as afterwards to the hundreds of thousands whom they reached in the volume, an inspiration and a discipline of inestimable value. But these aspects of the book we may postpone till we come to treat of its wonderful reception by the public; and here need only state that they have an enduring value which not even the fallacies of the introduction to them can wholly destroy. What Drummond would have done with the volume had he lived is quite uncertain. But a month or two before his death, when he said that he wished it withdrawn from circulation, a friend answered, 'Remember the religious good which it has done, and is still doing, to multitudes who either never read the introduction, or do not concern themselves with the philosophic questions it raises.' This friend might have added that the effort of the book to reduce the phenomena of the Christian life to reasonable processes under laws — whether or not these laws were what the volume alleges them to be — constitutes of itself a valuable contribution to religion.

At the time he gave his 'talks to working-men,' as he called them, Drummond had 'not intended to make a book out of them.' But the editor of the *Clerical World*, a London periodical no longer in existence, asked him for a contribution.

> 'I had never published anything before, and it was only after a second appeal that I resuscitated some faded lectures, which once had voices for a local public, but which with other "dried tongues" had been long since packed away in a forgotten drawer. These papers, which are now reprinted almost as they stood in *Natural Law*, passed through many vicissitudes, as I shall relate, before they became a book, but in connection with this reference to their origin I may answer a question. I am asked: Were these papers, or are such papers, even with the addition of *viva voce* explanations, not above the people? I can only say I did not find it so. My conviction, indeed, grows stronger every day that the masses require and deserve the very best work we have. The crime of evangelism is laziness; and the failure of the average mission church to reach intelligent working-men rises from the indolent reiteration of threadbare formulæ by teachers, often competent enough, who have not first learned to respect their hearers.'

The papers were five in number: 'Degeneration,' which was published on September 28, 1881; 'Biogenesis,' on November 30; 'Nature abhors a Vacuum,' founded largely on Paul's words, *Be not drunk with wine, but be filled with the Spirit* (these did not appear in the volume); and two on 'Semi-Parasitism,' which appeared in 1882.

'Though printed almost *verbatim* as they now stand, no one, I then thought, seems to have read the papers in their fugitive form. Presently the journal which published them died, leaving in my mind a lingering remorse at what share I might have had in its untimely end. To give continuity to the series, and as a title under which to publish them, I had given the editor the phrase "Natural Law in the Spiritual World." At that time I had not thought much as to what this title actually meant. The few laws which formed the theme of the papers certainly seemed common to both the natural and the spiritual spheres; but it did not occur to me to regard this as a general principle. I mention this to show that the principle came to me through its applications, not *vice versa*. . . . I am well aware that many see no such thread binding Nature and Grace. Others not only see no thread, but see no use in one. I can only say that for me there is no alternative but to see it; that I saw it before I knew what it was, and that if this were taken away much of the solidity of religion would go with it.

'Now, a thing that we cannot help seeing must either be really there, or one's vision must have some constitutional defect. To test this I wrote out the rough sketch of the principle which now forms the introduction to *Natural Law* and submitted it to a small club, which met for the dis-

cussion especially of theological subjects.[1]   With
one dissenting voice, it was unanimously condemned.   Some of the criticisms were just and
helpful, and others mercilessly severe.   One
pleasantry I remember as especially discouraging,
for its source compelled me to treat it with respect.
The essay, said this candid friend, reminded him
of a pamphlet he had once picked up, entitled,
" Forty Reasons for the Identification of the
English People with the Lost Ten Tribes."

' But for two things I should have received this
verdict as final, and abandoned my heresies forever.   The first was the one dissenting voice.
But for its encouragement at the outset, my book
had never been begun, and without its ceaseless
assistance afterwards, it would never have been
carried through. . . .   The second was that I
remembered that the membership of the aforesaid club consisted almost exclusively of men
who worked from the philosophical, rather than
from the scientific, standpoint.   My own point
of view being exclusively the latter, I imagined
that, in many particulars, we might have been
working at cross purposes. . . .

' After this misadventure there remained in my
mind the desire to submit the essay, if only for
my own satisfaction, to a more public criticism.
About this time, also, I received a letter from an
orphanage[2] in England, asking permission to

---

[1] Glasgow Theological Club, ' January 9, 1882, at 5 Ashton Terrace.   Paper by
Mr. Drummond on " Natural Law in the Spiritual Sphere." '

[2] The request came from Mr. Newman, a member of the Society of Friends, in
the interest of a Home for Orphans at Leominster.   The tract was entitled
' *Natural Law in the Spiritual World.   Degeneration —" If We Neglect*," by
Henry Drummond, F.R.S.E., F.G.S., Leominster: printed at the Orphans' Printing Press.   Price, 1*d*. ; 6 s. per 100.'   Drummond used to call Mr. Newman his
' guiding star.'

M

republish as a booklet one of the papers which
had already appeared. The printing, I gathered,
was to be done by the orphans themselves, and
the proceeds were to go to the institution. What
the orphans could want with this paper, except
to practise printing long words on, I could not
imagine; but, as they had no parents, I overlooked the eccentricity and consented. Whether
the orphans had ever made anything by it, I
never knew; but presently letters dropped in
from unknown correspondents, telling me that in
another sense the paper had done some good.
This decided me at once. The world did not
need being made wiser, but if there was the chance
of helping any one a little practically, that was a
thing to be done. In a rash hour, therefore, I
addressed the introduction, along with some of
the " Natural Law " papers, to a leading London
publisher. In three weeks the manuscript, as I
wholly expected, came back "declined with
thanks." A slight change was made, and a
second application to another well-known London
house; and again the document was returned with
the same mystic legend — the gentlest yet most
inexorable of sentences — inscribed upon its back.
To be served a second time with the Black Seal
of Literature was too much for me, and the
doomed sheets were returned to their pigeon-
holes and once more forgotten. I suppose most
men have a condemned cell in their escritoire.
For their consolation, let me tell them further
how at least one convicted felon escaped.
' Time had gone, when one day, passing through
London on returning from a Continental tour, I
happened along Paternoster Row. I encountered

Mr. M. H. Hodder of Messrs. Hodder and
Stoughton. In the course of conversation he
made a sudden reference to my ill-starred papers.
My guilty secret, alas, was known! By the treach-
ery of the other publishers, I was already the
laughing-stock of the Row — the whole trade had
been warned against me. But I was wrong.
This most guileless and indulgent of publishers
knew nothing! He had seen the papers in their
earlier form, and was merely sounding their
abashed author with a view to a possible reprint.
I was honest enough, in the light of previous
tragedies, to commit neither him nor myself, but
promised to exhume the manuscript for his further
consideration. From this interview I learned
one lesson — that the search for a publisher is a
mistake. The right way is to let the publisher
search for the author.

' The next step was to hold a *post mortem* examination on my Rejected Addresses. I found mortal
wounds in one or two of the papers, but the few
which seemed most fit for resuscitation were forwarded as a first instalment to the publisher. . . .
I would have given anything just then to have
gained time, for nearly half my remaining material
was useless. . . . I set to work replacing the most
decayed of the papers with new ones, and these
were literally written, I believe, like most literary
work — with the printer's demon waiting at my
elbow. The subjects were chosen as I went
along, and, as the printer was exasperatingly
punctual, they received the barest possible justice.
. . . Owing to the lengthened interval between
the writing of one paper and another, consistency
was almost impossible. I was careful in the

Preface to point out the unsystematic nature of the book and the almost haphazard arrangement of the papers; in point of fact, it was little more than the printer's necessity of paging; but, in spite of all protest, some of my critics have wandered through these *disjecta membra* in search of a philosophic or theological system, and have come back laden with spoil of every description to confound and discomfit the illogical author.'

But for a long time Drummond was out of reach of his critics.

'A few days after the publication of *Natural Law* and before it had reached the booksellers' shelves, I was steaming down the Red Sea *en route* for the heart of Africa.'

CHAPTER VII

The Yellowstone: Canyons, Geysers, Antelopes, and Beavers

HENRY DRUMMOND made three expeditions to distant and at the time little known parts of the earth, — the first, in 1879, to the Rocky Mountains; the second, in 1883–84, to Central Africa; and the third, in the summer of 1891, to the New Hebrides. We may take the first of these in this chapter.

The expedition to the Rocky Mountains was a geological one, and Drummond joined it on the invitation of Sir Archibald (then Professor) Geikie, who sends the following reminiscences leading up to it: —

'My first acquaintance with Henry Drummond began in the University of Edinburgh at the commencement of the winter session of 1871–72. The Chair of Geology and Mineralogy had then recently been founded there by Sir Roderick Murchison, in conjunction with the Crown, and at his request I had been appointed Professor. At the end of my opening lecture, the first student who came to my retiring room to be enrolled as a member of the class was Drummond. I well remember his frank, open face and the gentle timidity of his manner as he gave in his name. The instinctive impression of that first interview was deepened by further intercourse with him. During the session frequent excursions were

made to places of geological interest around Edinburgh, and these rambles afforded excellent opportunities for the teacher and the students to become
personally acquainted with each other.   I soon recognised the earnest enthusiasm and remarkable capacity
of the young man who had been the first to join me.
He was conspicuous by his zeal in the field, and he
took a good place in the periodical examinations,
finally coming out in the first class.   At the end of
each session I used to take my students for a longer
excursion to some more distant part of Scotland,
where we spent ten days or so in constant field work.
The first of these most enjoyable trips was devoted to
the isle of Arran.   Drummond was one of the party,
and I remember being struck with his feeling for the
beauty of natural scenery and the meditative look that
often marked his features when we sat down on some
rock or hillside to rest and enjoy the landscape.

'In later years, though no longer in my class, he
used to come occasionally to the field excursions, and
I was delighted to have these opportunities of enjoy-
ing a closer acquaintance with him.   He had entirely
won my affectionate regard, and I think he felt this
himself, for he often came to consult me as to his
career at college.   In the year 1879 I planned an
expedition into Western North America for the purpose more particularly of studying the volcanic phenomena displayed on so wonderful a scale in that
region.   Desiring a companion, I at once turned to
my favourite pupil, and found him willing to join me.'

The invitation was given in June, and Drummond
had a month for preparation.   Letters to Professor
Geikie discuss their equipment, and the risks the
expedition might run from the unsettled condition of
the Indians in the Rocky Mountains:—

To Professor Geikie

'POSSILPARK, GLASGOW, July 3d, 1879.

'. . . I see from Reuter's telegram of last night that
the Indians are at war among themselves on the
Canadian frontier. This will probably drain the
south of Montana, and leave the Yellowstone
clear. The reports in the *Field* lately have been
also more encouraging.'

Professor Geikie and Henry Drummond sailed for
America on the 31st of July, and after a few preliminary arrangements in the Eastern States, they
travelled straight to the Rocky Mountains. Drummond used to speak of the great generosity of the
United States Government, which on the request of
Professor Hayden, then at the head of the Geological
Survey, provided these British geologists with an
escort of soldiers, their needful equipage and supplies,
and introductions to the various military posts in
Indian territory.

To His Mother

'FORT BRIDGER, ROCKY MOUNTAINS, Thursday, Aug. 21, 1879.

' MY DEAR MOTHER, — At last we are in the heart of
the mountains, and very comfortably quartered,
with a famous man in these parts, Judge Carter,
to whom Geikie had introductions. We make
his house our home for a couple of nights, and
go cruising among the mountains during the
day. Then we go off for a few days' camping,
and return here for a night next week on our
way further west, and north to the Yellowstone.
Judge Carter lives in a desert in an old fort

which was occupied until May the year before
last by a post of soldiery for protection against
the Indians.   The Indians are quiet, and the fort
has been abandoned, but "the Judge" and his
cattlemen occupy it as a kind of farm and store.
The fort is simply a collection of huts of wood,
but everything is very comfortable.   We shall be
fitted out with waggon, and riding horses, and
baggage animals for our camp by the Judge,
which will be a great saving both of trouble and
money.   At present we are some seven thousand
feet above sea level, and the climate is simply
perfect. . . .

'On Monday rather a curious thing happened.   We
were at a place called Boulder, in Colorado, in a
new gold-mining district right up among the
mountains.   As I was standing at the hotel door
a man came up, and in an excited way asked the
landlord if he knew where any minister lived, as
a miner had died ten miles off in a lonely canyon
(deep valley), and his mates had subscribed to
bury him, and had sent him in to try and find a
minister.   He had already called on one, but he
was from home.   I told him if he could not find
one anywhere he might come back to the hotel
for me and I would go.   In an hour he returned
saying he had searched far and near, and could
find no one.   I had my tweeds on, but ran to a
store, and fortunately found a white tie, which
gave one quite a sufficiently professional look for
the mountains.   We drove ten miles in a two-
mule buggy through one of the most wonderful
glens I have ever seen.   On reaching the mining
settlement I found the whole camp turned out.
It was the first death in the camp, and evidently

it was no common occasion to the gold-diggers.
Not a stroke of work had been done all day. All
were dressed in their best, and the whole population of the district, men, women, and children,
were turned out to attend the funeral. We got
the coffin put in the buggy, and the whole party
proceeded up to a little chapel of wood, which
had been built for any occasional service. A harmonium was there, and a choir of the miners'
daughters all ready to sing our hymns. I found
I was expected to make an "oration," as they
called it, and as the chapel was crammed to the
door I had one of the best audiences I have ever
seen in my life. The diggers are a very rough
lot — kindly, brave, but wild and lawless — and I
suppose few of them had ever been in that chapel
before. All were emigrants who had come to
seek their fortunes — some from the far East,
some from Germany, some from England, and
two young fellows with whom I spoke were from
Glasgow. The man who had died was an Englishman. They listened with profound attention,
and when the service was over they slowly filed
past the open coffin, and took a last look at the
dead. At last all were gone but one, a genuine
rough specimen, who looked all round to see if we
were alone, then bowed his face in his hands, and
wept like a child. He was the dead man's mate.
'The grave was far up the valley, as there was nothing here but the solid granite. The procession
formed once more, and when we reached the spot
the miners begged for another service. This was
gladly granted, and I hope I did not lose so
golden an opportunity. It may be years before
there is another service in that camp, as it is one

of the loneliest inhabited spots on earth.   Before
I came home they gave me tea, and loaded me
with specimens of gold.'

On the 2d of September the friends left Fort Ellis
in Gallatin County, Montana, driving southwards, and
by the way shooting grouse and prairie-dogs and fishing for trout.   In the afternoon they entered the
Yellowstone Valley, 'an old lake basin with a canyon
at each end.'

DIARY

'Long, low undulating line.   "Moraines, if ever I
saw them!"   "Is that an erratic against the sky?"[1]
Porphyry boulders, granite, flint, fragments of chalcedony.   The Lake Terraces.   The Basalt Plateau, flat
tables.   Caught a dozen trout, average half a pound,
in half an hour.   Camped at Bottler's, just opposite
Emigrant Peak; a hundred prospectors gulching for
gold and silver.

'WEDNESDAY, Sept. 3d.— Trout breakfast.   Our
horses, old cavalry "condemned."   Open valley.   Passed
several "wailing" heaps of stones, made by Indian
squaws to the Great Spirit when any of their braves
died.   "Nooned" at Canyon Creek, eleven miles from
Bottler's:[2] cold trout, tongue, and crackers.   Fishing,
caught a two-and-a-half pounder, sluggish, not game.
Broke camp at two, entered second canyon.   At mouth
on right magnificent glaciated gneiss (no granite in
canyon).   Moraines of immense size.   Yankee Jim
gave me a fine specimen of gold quartz from Bear
Rock Canyon, Yellowstone.   Camp at 4.30.   Deer

---

[1] These words were the exclamation of his companion. The existence of
former glaciers in these valleys had not previously been observed. — *Note by Professor Geikie.*

[2] He spells it Boetler's.

hanging between willows. Meteor, camp talk, buffalo robes.

'THURSDAY, Sept. 4th. — Up at 5.30, washed, breakfast at 6. Broke camp at 7.15. Rode along flank of Cinnabar Mountain — limestone mostly. At the south end of the Devil's Slide upturned beds of limestones and bands of red and cream-coloured marls, almost vertical; the walls of the slide composed of straight planed walls of limestone, exactly parallel, soft layers worn away but still quite distinct in part along the west wall; firs scattered through the gap, morning sun shining straight in and bringing out the vivid colouring of the great bands of rock curving down the mountain slope. Came to log shanty, store for miners, got gold specimen from miner in next shanty; a ranch burned by Indians two years ago. Passed waggon with magnificent head of elk, passed dead rattlesnake. For two or three miles on this side of junction of Yellowstone with Gardiner rivers magnificent moraine mounds and lovely little lake basin. Struck across Gardiner River, long wearisome ride over high mounds and ridge of landslides and moraines, passed two or three moraine lakes. Suddenly, without a minute's warning, half a mile off, [what looked like] a gigantic glacier, glittering through the pines. Camp on a rill, lunch.

'EXAMINATION OF SPRINGS. — First approach, exceeding beauty and delicacy of fretwork, cascades above cascades. The hot springs, basins all temperature; the orifice, 140°. Edge colours of leaf fronds and seaweeds, white with orange veining; sacrilege to tread upon it. You look for notice-board in vain. Pools of every conceivable shape and size, rim usually two to four inches cut out like coral. Each basin a slight slope upwards, successive deposits marked upon sides as if they were made of piles of coins, framework of hills all around, dark pine forests and grass.   Rise on to a plateau, you are in an arctic scene, everything is white like snow, the trees are growing up through it here and there.   Water where it reaches the downmost lips is tasteless; where it bubbles up it strongly tastes of sulphuretted hydrogen.

'THE PULPITS.— One place has fifty; in shade cream-coloured, in sunshine spotless white.   Stalactites here and there.   Bottom of each pulpit covered with soft tufts of most delicate moss.   Whole ground sounds hollow.

'THE FOREST.— A little farther on, the remains of a burned forest.   The springs have come down through a wood and destroyed the trees.   Now they stand up, some erect, some half-prostrate, just as in the living forest, but blanched, grey, dead, holding out thin, gaunt, bare arms as if in protest.   Here and there an *arbor vitæ* has survived and put on greenness once more.

'THE CASCADES.— Water falling over a hundred little balconies.   On either side these balconies are as white as stucco.   Where the cascades come down the walls are dyed near the top a deep orange, almost red, farther down a deep yellow, then saffron and exquisite shades of pink, then cream, then white. The water itself is milk-white, steaming at the top, and pattering and splashing like the fountains in gardens.   This is at the top of the forest; the most wonderful colouring is at the southwest corner, above the petrified wood, and running through it.   The fountain basins here are as regular as if chiselled by hand; the colours are pink, salmon, dark and light purple, white, cinnamon.

'THE UPPER BASIN.— The blue colour of the water

— the photograph — looking for a place to bathe —
the cascades — the variegated tables — marble, ala-
baster, etc.

'Friday, Sept. 5th. — Seymour, the artist — Yellowstone Kelly, Miles's scout, — where the Indians killed.
Crossed Gardiner River — rode up valley of east fork
of Gardiner River, like Black Forest scenery. After
an hour's ride we surmounted the plateau of basalt
(waterfall) at the head of the valley. Then for hours
wound over an undulating country, ridges and mounds,
covered with erratic blocks of granite. The ice action
quite remarkable, showing that the country has been
covered with ice and not simply a local glacier;
grand stream, with chalcedony, many agates; elk-
heads and horns of deer and buffalo scattered everywhere. Then began descent through valleys of pine
and poplar; camp waiting in a meadow, open pastures,
animals turned loose. Only 2.30; ramble after lunch;
rocks, roses, squirrels. Jack went to look for an
antelope, failed. O that bacon! Dark at 7.30; bed
by 8.30.

'Saturday, 6th. — Awoke at five, thermometer in
tent 36°; outside the ground was covered with frost,
ice in dishes and on creek, wash cold.[1] Bacon again!
Tomatoes. The ceremony of packing. Three miles
to Lower Creek — not time to visit the Fall. Struck
up the long ridge of Mount Washburne, over hillside
and forest; long ride, seven hours in saddle. Andy's
shooting — a prairie chicken. When riding three
paces behind him suddenly fired, . . . [?] our horses
into the air, a diabolical smell — the skunk! Our
camp at end of long meadow in full view of Washburne, the usual streamlet.

'Visit to the Falls and Canyon; the evening light

----

[1] They were about six thousand feet above sea level.

the most favourable; two things — the colouring from
an æsthetic standpoint, the erosion from a geological.
The section at camp in stream: a devitrified obsidian
(pumiceous base, abundantly filled with currant-like
fragments of the original obsidian), resting on perlite
and covered by an obsidian tuff.   The great interest of the march lay in tracing the granite boulders right up the flanks of Washburne.   The ice
sheet must have been of enormous thickness, and not
merely local.   The tracks of the glacier flow and wind
round the mountain, and are caught up again in the
long plateau traversed the day before along the east
fork of Gardiner River.

'SABBATH, 7th. — Remained encamped all day, spent
the day wandering around the Canyon, the magnificent
timber like a gentleman's park for thousands of acres,
soft yellow glades, withered flowers, one herb like the
maidenhair, only with a thicker stem.   The N. T.

'The Squirrel; Jack off hunting, Andy ditto; the
cranes.   Return to camp.   "There's Jack," a minut-
est figure in the distance — "Has he got anything?"
Nothing — another week on bacon!   "Something
white?   A crane?   What — a sack.   What have you
got?"   "Elk!"   The unpacking — the choice bits,
the supper!

'THE CANYON.[1] — The most grand and memorable
spectacle of my life, the inconceivable beauty and
glory of the colouring; a colossal gorge zigzagging;
green, foaming, spraying, roaring river.   The sides of
the gorge — not clean-cut, but carved into alcoves, pin-
nacles, spires, of the most picturesque and fantastic
forms.   The original colour of the rock is pure, dazzling white from river to crest, but little of the white

[1] That is, the Grand Canyon of the Yellowstone River at the south foot of
Mount Washburne.

is left save here and there a brilliant scar. The first weathering is a pale lemon yellow, deepening into saffron, sulphur, and through all the shades of yellow into the deepest orange. Then another gradation is the most tender rose-pink into vermilion and dark blood-red. The tone of the whole is a rich cream colour, deepening into russets and yellows and oranges — a kind of artificial sunlight. The distance tones were first in the yellows, a faint spring green; and the usual purple, shading into the deepest blue of distance as the canyon lost itself in the distant gloom, at the foot of Mount Washburne. The Fall — the lush green at the cauldron, the purple mists, the roar, the emerald green at the crests succeeded by dazzling spray — for three hundred and fifty feet. The lichen colours, brown here and there. The dark green pines mantling the whole, and straggling here and there in single file right down to the water's edge.

'GEOLOGICAL. — The rock is rhyolite — a solid mass of volcanic formation. Then the interest of the vast erosion, first, of the stream; second, of the weather, frost, and jointing along the sides. All through the forest and on all the plateau around the great blocks of granite and gneiss are records of the glacier age. The three elements combine: fire, water, and ice.

'MONDAY, the 8th of September. — Followed trail through magnificently timbered country with parks, glades, and streamlets, then across prairie country to head of Alum Creek — deposits, effluvium [from] steaming springs, sulphur mountain, Solfataras. Trail through timber again. Over the Divide. Down steep forest-clad hill to the east fork of Madison River. Fire Hole River. Through long swamp — timber again. Camp in glade by river-side. Seven hours in saddle. Lunch, bathe, bear, theological discussion

with Jack.   Geology, volcanic all day.   Obsidian
blocks everywhere; schistose obsidian.

'Tuesday, Sept. 9th.— Broke camp about 8.30, magnificent ride through glade and forest, crossed Fire
Hole River several times: clean turf banks, meadow,
green and golden grass.   Puff of steam here and there
through the forest, white patches of geyser deposit.
Lovely little basin by side of trail, green emerald
water.   Then struck through fallen timber — suddenly
the forest opened — an immense glade encircled by
pine mountains, the further end covered with snow.

'Old Faithful.— Notice his spurt at lunch, 1.21
P.M.   Went up at the hour of next performance.
Precisely at the hour almost, 2.20, he gave a grunt
and then threw up a little water.   Visitors rushed
back in alarm.   Then at intervals, say at $1\frac{1}{2}$ minutes,
he made another feint; then the feints became more
frequent, each succeeding better than the last.   Finally
he ran up twenty or thirty feet and then, as if climbing
on the shoulders of this he ran up his column to the
full height.   This began about 2.30, and the maximum
was reached about 2.31; it remained at this height,
say one minute, and then gradually lessened.   The
eruption lasted till $2.36\frac{1}{2}$ — about $4\frac{1}{4}$ minutes.   *Appearance* — in the distance a low flat mound appears
rugged as you approach it, then as you get near you
imagine it to be made of coral-madrepore.   A little coral
island, — on narrower inspection urns, pools, basins,
fantastic shapes, every conceivable design and colour,
— pink, yellow, orange, umber.   Many of the pools
contain water — very pure — a faint but perceptible
taste of sulphuretted hydrogen.   One or two orifices
in the mound were steaming — small caverns as large
as a coal-scuttle, some of them too hot to hold the
hand in.   The "valleys" along the flank of the little

island were made of tesselated pavement of imma-
ture [?] workmanship, like sections cut smooth from
brain coral. Some, nearly all, held little lakes from
the size of a walnut shell upwards, with pink bottoms.
Others had a little rivulet trickling down. At one
side quite a little stream wound down to the river a
hundred and fifty yards off. The bed of this rill was
covered with fragments of silicified wood. The ridges
were made of masses of pearls without the tesselated
look; ruggedly smoothed lumps, bosses like botryoidal.
After the eruption the whole sides were running with
rills which sparkled in the sun gloriously, as they
trickled from basin to basin.

'Sitting on the mound after making notes, a rhythmic
thud at one minute interval. Hot to the seat. The
orifice of the geyser—a roughly oval hole, large enough
to let two tolerably stout men slip through. Noise
like a barn threshing-mill, giving occasional explosions,
water coming up but not over edge, cloud of steam,
sides lined with dark orange, slimy coating, with a pale
sulphurous colour round the margin. The moment
the lip was reached the beautiful madrepore formation
began. Two handkerchiefs and a hat recovered, my
handkerchief forfeited.

3.15   boil in tube.
3.20   spurted thick about 5 ft. in air, boiling and increasing.
3.21½   spurted thick about 5 ft. in air.
3.22½   spurted twice, once about 5 ft., once 3.
3.23   spurted once about 5 ft.
3.25   spurted once about 2 ft.
3.26   thick stream, 5 ft.
3.27   thick stream, 5 ft.
3.28   very thin shower, 4 ft.
3.29   shower, 12 ft.
3.29½   shower rising.
3.29¾   shower rose to full height and continued at this maximum, till

N

3.30¾   then dwindled but action brisk, till
3.35   the last half minute steam alone but in a thick mass.   The
    geyser steams always.

'Old Faithful occupies a very prominent position on a white sinter plateau raised above the valley and looking down on all the other geysers.   Three extinct geysers surround it at fifty paces, and another lies to the west the same distance, which was slowly steaming. These four attendants are all perfectly symmetrical, of the same size, and equidistant.[1]   Vast pine-woods encircle the whole geyser basin, and straggling islands of timber are scattered through the whole undulating valley.   Here and there white colour of steam, now one in full blast.

4.30   "there it goes"—signs.
4.32   low spurt.
4.34   low spurt.
4.37   high.
4.37¾   higher.
4.38   up to max., lasts 4 minutes, very high.

5.39, date of next eruption, seen from Beehive — 3½ minutes.   First water falls back into funnel — after that the temperature is so high that when pressure is relieved it turns into steam [?].   Geysers damming up river with sinter.   Springs on both sides meeting. The river banks simply show sections of geyserite. Overlapping curves.   Mounds raised by overflow from the basin.   Hyalite (or millerite?) the usual (?) structure in Old Faithful.   Took temperature of two springs, 1st, 185° F., 2d, 200° F.   Boiling briskly.   Appearance an irregular tube, tawny, ugly throats.   A third with a thin crust of ice floating on the top, such was the appearance.   The water was very deep and of the most perfect crystal, blue in shade — green in sun.[2]

1 Here follows a rough sketch.   2 With this a rough sketch.

'Explored the Giantess, the Beehive, the Jokers [?]. Played at stopping up a would-be geyser. Different forms: mermaid grottos, ulcers, gashes, gaping mouths with horrid yellow umber lips; grunting, snorting, hissing, bubbling, gurgling, spluttering. A pink tube, six feet — pink coral. Rugged coral sides, like a cancer.

'WEDNESDAY, Sept. 10. — Up at 6, wash in creek. Elk and tomatoes. Old Faithful played at 6.26, a very fine display, and again at 7.24; just saw him finish, at 7.25 to .27; saw two minutes' play, not at maximum. Examined the Castle, Vesuvius, the Grotto, the Punch-bowl, the Cancer. Adjoining this, a deep grotto, with dentate or serrate margin — orange fringe all around. At the side of this a blistered crust — about ten feet diameter, with five ragged holes, lined with sulphur and black mineral [?], three steaming, one little pond still, and fringed with delicate lace [?] work. The fourth boiling, and spluttering boiling water, and gurgling. One of these mouths has raised, pouting lips.[1]

'Old Faithful played at 8.30 and 9.30 precisely. The Castle in full blast, 9.15.

'Collecting diatoms, heard shouting, two men hollering; great spluttering and tremendous clouds of steam. Suddenly they ran down bank and struck across river — up to knees at least. "The Castle!" Reached it breathless, thinking it was as short in its period as Old Faithful — played on and on and on. Booming. Party came here on Monday evening; Castle has not spurted since then. Hats in, thrown high in the air, handkerchiefs, stones; showered out.[2]

[1] Rough sketch given of 'a very perfect form of geyser, perfectly round, shallow saucer, with an irregular funnel mouth — boiling.' Three other larger sketches.

[2] Sketch of 'outline of Castle against blue sky, the rainbow, the whole sides running with steam.'

' After lunch walked on to examine the remaining
geysers: Fan, Grave, Sawmill, etc. Saw Sawmill in
action. Snow came on as we were emerging from the
basin. Walked to the half-way group. There over-
taken by pack train. Struck [1] camp in a bay of the
wood overlooking geyser basin (lower). Went off to
examine many lively geysers.

' THE MUD GEYSER. — The most comical thing in
nature! On a summit of a pine grove — grass and
wild flowers. You come to a low oval basin, marked
out by an undulating rim of some dazzling white material. The one-half of the basin consists of a pink,
sun-cracked mud of the consistency of the finest
stucco — not a flat surface, but a score of large mole-
hills, each made of concentric cones, the rings quite
well marked, and each terminating in a perfectly round
mouth, like a miniature crater. Here and there the
cone is inverted, leaving a round hole. One or two of
them are steaming faintly, and a dusting of sulphur is
sprinkled over one or two of them. One or two of the
craters are also smoking, hissing briskly. The majority are stiff and cold. The pink colour is exceedingly
beautiful and delicate, very pale — a mere tinge — yet
quite decided in its tone. The other half of the pond
is altogether deposit. It consists of the purest white
mud, boiling as briskly as the viscous nature of the
material will permit. The spurts come up in little
domes, some only the size of a thimble-top, some a
walnut, a teacup, a sugar-bowl. They blow up like a
soap-bubble, quite suddenly, and burst in a tiny fountain. The rings which they make in falling remain
fixed round each, so that each bubble has a number of
concentric circles surmounting it, giving a very peculiar symmetrical pattern, which adorns the entire sur-

[1] Pitched?

face of the geyser.[1] Sometimes, instead of one bubble coming up like a cup, half a dozen little thimbles dance up, each with its little rings around it. A small island of solid mud stands to one side. This is shaped like a small model of a mountain in stucco, and the dancing bells all around it give a very curious effect.

'But the most peculiar thing is at the junction of the solid pink with the white. The greatest heat is apparently at the white end, and the pond is slowly becoming solid. The mud near the junction is much thicker, and the spurts in the thicker crust much more constrained; the noise here is loudest, the motion slowest, but the patterns infinitely more amusing. Here is one circle of mud as big as a large dinner-plate; a ring or two, like a thick rope, surrounds it. These ropy rims are so thick that the power below can scarcely destroy them, and they remain constant for several minutes at a time. The centre of the plate is the great scene of action. At first there lies upon it a little shape of jelly, like a custard just turned out of its cup. Suddenly it is heaved up in the air. A ragged mass of mud hangs in the air for a moment, and then as suddenly another custard is lying on the plate, just like the last. Another moment of pause, the bottom of the plate is slowly knocked out once more, the custard disappears, and this time a *pear* lies on the plate. Then another custard, then two. Once three came all at once. There was a whole basin of these plates, all going through the same legerdemain at once. This was going on in a small bay formed by the hardened crust, standing two feet above the surface. I was standing on this crust (I am now), within an inch of the edge of the boiling custards, right in

[1] Rough sketch.

the centre of the pond.   One spurt of mud lit on my hand from the next bay, where the most interesting operation of all was going on.   This bay was six feet long by two and a half, yet it only contained four spouters.   The rest were all closed up.   One of them deceived me for a long time.   I thought he was stopped up, too, but he suddenly began to grunt and throw up pellets of mud five feet in the air.   One fellow was shut up, all but a hole the size of your finger. He was a little dome of plastic mud, and every bubble of steam made him heave an inch or two, so that he was riding up and down like a ship at anchor, or a buoy in a ground swell, all the time.   The little orifice was alternately being stopped up and blown out, and the grunting he kept up was tragic to behold.   The colour of these last was the delicate pink which made the sight a most beautiful one, and quite destroyed one's notion of a mud geyser.   A faint steam was rising all the time.   The sky was the most exquisite blue, the snow-shower of the past hour having cleared off the smoke from the burning forests, which filled the air all the past week.

'The *symmetry* of the bubbles is the next most noteworthy thing.   The rings are perfectly formed and rise like mounds.[1]   The thickened spurts obviously mark the declining energy of the spring.   The mud is thicker, the ebullition less brisk, and here and there in the "bays" has already become quite stiff and impervious to the passage of steam.   One plate or cone became silent and quite stopped up apparently while I was standing by; it was the one closest to the solid mud behind, and was the next in natural course to shut up.

'The white colour resembles molten porcelain or

[1] A sketch.

china. The present circuit of the pond is about 150
(paces) yards, but it is evident that at the solid end
has once been much larger. The grassless part equals
150 yards. The *independence* of all the geysers —
each on its own hook — sometimes one boiling, three
feet off another perfectly quiet, next one another
roarer.[1] Jack assures me that in [?]'s time the whole
pond was like meerschaum. The last escort made
pipes, bowls, ornaments. Next morning they were
all cracked.

'On the way back to camp shot a skunk; immense
brushlike tail, slow motion; only measure of defence
the smell. Small black head, glossy black fur; skin, 20
cents. Supper, mock-turtle soup, brandered elk steak,
bread, and tea. Andy cut down two trees for fire-
wood. Put one bodily on fire. Intense cold. The
wolf barking, the red squirrel cracking in the wood
below.

'THURSDAY, Sept. 11th. — Thermometer at 5.30,
outside tent, 19°. Everything froze stiff. Breakfast
of elk, green corn, jam, coffee, hard tack, bread, and
more of Andy's stories. " It does a fellow good to get
out a string of oaths — four or five miles long — to be
continued on the next page." The plain before the
camp bounded by fine forest, volumes of steam coming
up everywhere around. The white puffs in the distant wood, the great clouds over the main geyser
group, the cold condensing the steam rapidly. Counted
fifty from the trail a few yards from camp. Soon
struck Madison River — peculiarity of flow, no flood
mark, uniform banks of turf, like travelling through
Hyde Park heavily timbered. The Madison Canyon
— very fine scenery, wide-timbered glen, splendid
crags here and there. Trail crosses river four or

---

[1] Here a sketch-map of all these mud geysers.

five times. After passing through canyon crossed and camped on meadowy bank by a small clump of firs. Lunch.

'At 3 or 3.30 went hunting antelope with Jack; struck through timber for a mile and a half, crossing little prairie. Abundant sign everywhere. Sign of antelope in timber is unique: " been down there?" Struck high prairie; soon sighted game; made fine stalk behind clump of trees; Jack to fire, for camp wanted meat: threw down hat, crawled on belly thirty yards under bush and fallen timber; fired at doe on the watch. Herd (unseen till now) all started and ran. In one hundred and fifty yards the doe fell dead, after running full speed all that distance. I got a long shot with Andy's cavalry carbine at the retreating herd, six, with one fine buck, but they were just disappearing over the brow of a hill. Sighted game next by a watercourse in glade one mile off. On nearing the place crept up a slope and saw game two hundred yards away. Hat off, down on belly; wormed through the grass till within a hundred and fifty yards; wind blowing right from me to them. Fired. As usual, all started. Jack ran to the right to catch them as they ran back, I to where they would round the hill. Presently the magnificent buck dashed past at full speed — flying shot, must have missed. Fired at a doe coming behind — must have struck her originally, as, although Jack fired at her, three bullets were in her when she dropped. Jack had shot another through the fore legs, which I killed with my revolver. During the retreat Jack surprised a second herd and killed one more. Total, four antelopes — all does.

'Note. — The antelope is a prairie animal. Witness in the first place its splendid speed. It is the fleetest of all animals, and to see a herd of six or eight dash-

ing along the prairie is a sight to keep the keenest
sportsman from touching his trigger.   Powers of
speed like the antelope's would be useless in Switzerland.   Nevertheless, they do inhabit some districts
which are essentially timber lands, but they make
their home in the long grassy glades with which nearly
every forest in the West is studded, or in the small rich
prairies of rising ground, interspersed among the
woods.   For another thing, their fur is altogether
inappropriate to forest life.   If you put your fingers
into it and pull gently you can pull the whole hair out
by handfuls.   A forest animal requires a fur which is
well rooted in the skin to resist the rough friction of
the trees, brush, and especially the sharp prongs and
spines of fallen timber.

'TENACITY OF LIFE. — Jack's first shot entered at the
breast, and ploughed clean through the body, coming
out within an inch of the tail.   The animal, however,
bounded off as if nothing unusual had happened; ran
down hill at full speed along with its companions for
one hundred and fifty yards, and then dropped stone
dead.   Another, which was shot through both legs,
hobbled along a considerable distance like a kangaroo,
using the hind legs and the breast, until I shot her
dead through the neck with my revolver.   The effect
of the cry, " Hoo, hoo," in making them turn round
even when scared.   On the plains they feed with
buffalo in countless herds.   Their fur is almost useless, for the reason mentioned, but their skin is valuable for gloves, gauntlets, etc.   The bucks are the
most difficult to stalk.   They always manage to get
into a place in the herd where no stalk is possible.

'FRIDAY, Sept. 12th. — Broke camp precisely at
eight.   Ice outside tent, sponge inside frozen into a
boulder, but the night much warmer than the preced-

ing. Crossed the Madison, and followed through woods and glades for several miles the general course of the river, though often out of sight of its banks. The trail lay over an ancient river-terrace (perfectly well marked — compare terraces on Madison between Virginia City and Bozeman), which made the riding easy. After leaving the river struck through timber with prairies and abundant game, antelope, everywhere for twelve miles, when we crossed a fork of the Madison. The trail next led up the low Divide, across the main chain of the Rocky Mountains through the Tangee [?] Pass. The ascent is very gentle, and it is almost inconceivable that this should represent the Divide between the Atlantic [?] and Pacific waters. On the Madison side of the water-shed we passed a splendid beaver-dam, where the beavers are still working. Jack gave us the natural history of the beaver as we crossed the pass. After a gentle descent of a mile or two we left the so-called waggon-road and followed the brook — the source of Snake River — down to Henry's Lake. Camped about a couple of miles from the lake by the creek's side, and just below a very fine beaver-dam, which we had the opportunity to examine. It is either now in use, or has been very recently abandoned. Home by three o'clock, seven hours in saddle. Lounging [?] Creek here is full of trout at grasshopper season, but now apparently is empty. On Henry's Lake a company of soldiers are encamped, for protection from the Indians. A short stone's throw from our camp I stumbled on a rough trench or breastwork. Jack says it was thrown up in 1877 by General Howard, who was encamped here several days when chasing the Nez Percé Indians. They were only one day ahead, and sent back a band who captured his baggage-train. General Howard followed the Indians

right over our route, but they were not captured till
General Miles headed them in Clark's Fork (of Yellowstone?).[1]   Twenty-seven white soldiers were killed
during the short resistance, and some threescore Indian
braves — the number captured was three hundred and
fifty.

'We saw lodge poles frequently along the route, but
these probably belonged to a tribe of Bannock Indians
who were camped a few hundred yards from this spot
only this week.   They had been up the Madison from
their reservation below Camas Prairie after antelope.
They are supposed to be friendly.   We shall likely
overtake them to-morrow or next day.

'Before dinner strolled up the creek to examine the
beaver-dam more thoroughly.   The creek is of the
usual character, soft turf banks of uniform depth, a
few inches, and pebbly bottom.   An even flow wets
even banks, like a shallow mill-lade.   Breadth quite
within a very good running jump.   We traced it up
from camp to the first dam.   Poplar trees and willow
brush fringed the ground, and these had been cut
through and dammed across the stream.   Pebbles and
mud had been baked down upon the whole.   The
dam, therefore, was a sort of wicker work, with rough,
big base, and more compact top of interlacing willow,
mud, and stones, formed into a stiff, impervious em-
bankment.   Along the sides of the streamlet the log
stumps were left standing about two to two and a half
feet from the ground, just gnawed off where the animal
could best reach with his teeth.   This dam extended
far across the little valley beyond the bounds of the
stream a hundred [?], and the result was the formation of a swamp of quite considerable size.   Here
peat formed.   The beaver, as a geological agent.

[1] Or Clark's Fork, south of Flathead Lake.

The situation of the dam was admirably chosen. The opening valley, opening out from the hills, a thin patch of timber on either side to furnish the material for building.'

Here the diary abruptly closes, though the expedition lasted for another fortnight. Sir Archibald Geikie writes of it: —

'In this journey, thrown into closest contact with him under the most varied conditions of travel, including even sometimes hardship and risk, I learned to appreciate more than ever the beauty of his character. His singularly placid and equable temperament was like a kind of perpetual sunshine. Nothing seemed ever to discompose him or overshadow that winning smile that used to fascinate the wild men among whom we were thrown. And yet he was singularly impressionable. The grandeur of the scenery through which we passed appealed powerfully to his imagination, and his eyes would flash with delight as each new landscape unfolded itself before us.

'He looked on everything with the eye of a poet first, and of a man of science afterwards. The human interests appealed to him before he began to dissect and compare and classify. But the marvellous interest of the geological phenomena which unfolded themselves as we rode on through those primeval solitudes roused his enthusiasm sometimes to the highest pitch.

'Drummond's keen sense of humour was another feature in his nature that came out vividly during that memorable journey. How he would draw out our attendants over the camp-fire at night, getting each to cap the other's thrilling and incredible tales of adventure! I would sometimes watch him playing them as if they were the trout or salmon he was so fond of alluring in the streams of his own country. And how he would laugh over their exaggerations, and suggest possible omissions and lapses of memory!'

After their return to Scotland Drummond wrote a very warm letter of thanks to his chief:—

To Professor Archibald Geikie

'POSSILPARK, GLASGOW, Nov. 22, 1879.

'. . . For my part, I feel the Western expedition has been a very solid gain, and I know it will be helpful to me in very many ways all my life. The short interval since coming home has been sufficient to strike out of the picture all that was merely incidental; and now the perspective of the whole begins to shape itself. The whole of America impresses me now as a *revelation* — a revelation in civilisation, in politics, in human nature; and if not a revelation in geology, a confirmation, elevation, and consolidation, which is more than equivalent. I feel the gain in every department of my work. . . .

'For all your other kindnesses to me I cannot attempt to thank you. I am sure I would find it not only difficult, but impossible, to express how much of all that I have enjoyed and learned during these past months I have owed to you. You will allow me at least this reference to it.'

CHAPTER VIII

In the year 1859 David Livingstone, invested with the powers of a British consul, led a government expedition to the Zambezi. His instructions were 'to extend our knowledge of the geography and of the mineral and agricultural resources of Eastern and Central Africa; to improve our acquaintance with the inhabitants, and to endeavour to engage them to apply themselves to industrial pursuits and to the cultivation of their lands, with a view to the production of raw material to be exported to England in return for British manufactures.' It was hoped that 'by encouraging the natives to occupy themselves in the development of the resources of the country, a considerable advance might be made towards the extinction of the slave-trade.' Upon this expedition Livingstone discovered Nyasa, an enormous fresh-water lake some three hundred and fifty miles long by fifteen to forty-four broad. It is surrounded by high tablelands, fertile, and bearing a considerable population, whose material and moral interests Livingstone left as his last bequest to his countrymen. 'I have opened the door,' he said; 'I leave it to you to see that no one closes it after me.' The task was taken up by three British Churches. The Free Church of Scotland, under the leadership of Dr. Stewart, founded a station, which they named Livingstonia,[1] at the south

---

[1] The United Presbyterian Church joins with the Free Church of Scotland in the Livingstonia Mission, paying the salary of Dr. Laws, the head of the Mission.

end of the Lake; but they afterwards transferred it to Bandawé, about two hundred miles farther north. The Established Church of Scotland founded a station at Blantyre, in the Shiré Highlands between the Lake and the Zambezi. The Universities Mission of the Church of England began work on the east of the Lake. These missions did not confine themselves to preaching, but among their agents are doctors and nurses, male and female teachers, masons, carpenters, and gardeners. About the same time a few British traders began the cultivation of coffee and certain cereals in the neighbourhood of Blantyre. But all these settlements were hundreds of miles from the coast; and, in order to convey their supplies, as well as to develop a commerce strong enough to supplant the slave-trade which devastated the region, a carrying agency was needed, with stations on the Zambezi, the Shiré, and the Lake. In 1878, therefore, the African Lakes Company, or Corporation as it now is, was formed by Glasgow gentlemen who were in sympathy with the missions and with Livingstone's policy of developing industries for the natives and keeping from them spirits, gunpowder, and arms. The Company was not started for gain; or for gain only in the sense that commercial soundness is the one solid basis on which to build up an institution that is to permanently benefit others. A large amount of private capital has been expended by this Company; yet, during the years of its noble enterprise, it has reinvested in Africa all that it has earned there. In a short time it founded twelve trading stations, manned by twenty-five Europeans and many native agents. It ran a

---

Old Livingstonia, at the south end of the Lake, was by Cape Maclear. The name has been transferred to the Livingstonia Training Institution at the head of the Lake, near Mount Waller (p. 205), three thousand feet above the Lake.

steamer up the Shiré, and another upon Lake Nyasa. It started a coffee plantation and other agricultural works. 'For the first time on the large scale it taught the natives the meaning and blessings of work. It acted as a check upon the slave-trade, prevented inter-tribal strife, helped to protect the missionaries in time of war, and in short, modest as the scale was on which it worked, and necessarily limited as were its opportunities, it was for years the sole administering hand in this part of Africa.'[1]

In 1883 Mr. James Stevenson, F.R.G.S., was chairman of the Company. It occurred to him that it would be important to have a scientific examination of the countries extending to Lake Tanganyika, and this he thought Henry Drummond could carry out. In June, Drummond went to Crieff to meet Mr. Stevenson, and, leave of absence having been granted to him by the College Committee, the plan of the expedition was arranged.

To Mr. and Mrs. Stuart

'GLEN ELM LODGE, June 16, 1883.

'. . . I am going off to Africa next Wednesday. I am going right into the heart of the country to make a scientific exploration of the Lake Nyasa and Tanganyika region. I shall be away a long time, probably a year or more. The whole scheme has come upon me like an avalanche, and I am in a whirl of preparation.'

He crossed the continent to Brindisi, and took steamer to Alexandria, his travelling companion being the Rev. James Bain, of the Free Church Livingstonia

[1] *Tropical Africa*, p. 82.

Mission. They found traces of the bombardment on every hand, and saw the battle-field of Tel-el-Kebir, 'still thick with cartridges; the desert all round is streaked with the marks of gun-carriages as if our cannon had rolled over them yesterday.'

To His Brother

'S.S. RAVENNA, RED SEA, July 2d, 1883.

'I take a full course of sea-bathing, and hope to land in Africa as strong as a lion. My beard grows mightily, although I am a terrible object to be in the cabin of a P. and O. mail. A lot of Indian Government agriculturists are on board, and I am getting terribly wise in tea, coffee, cinchona, and spices. If my wisdom can be transferred to practice, I really think the Lakes Company may yet get back my expenses. We reach Aden to-morrow. The Pole Star is sinking fast, and in a day or two I shall sight the Southern Cross.'

At Aden, Bain and Drummond were joined by Dr. and Mrs. Scott, of the Livingstonia Mission, and Messrs. Hedderwick and Henderson, of Blantyre. They had a bad voyage to Zanzibar through the monsoon. Drummond crossed the equator in an ulster. At Zanzibar he had his first sight of tropical vegetation, and was fascinated with the spectacle of the bazaars. On July 26, after a couple of days at Moçambique, they reached Quilimane, in Portuguese East Africa. Hospitably entertained there by Mr. and Mrs. Shearer, of the Lakes Company, they started up the Qua-qua in shallow boats — 'a splendid week, like a continual picnic, with gipsy breakfasts and teas by the river

bank'—to where a portage of five miles brought them
to the Zambezi and the Company's steamer.

From Quilimane Drummond kept a full journal and
also wrote regularly to his home. In *Tropical Africa*
he has given a charming sketch of his travels, of
the general nature of the region he crossed, and of
the geological discoveries which he made upon it.
Many of even the most finished sentences and paragraphs of his volume have been printed just as they
stand in his daily notes. But his diary contains a
great deal of interesting matter which he did not
publish; and besides giving this and a general outline of his journeys, I have felt it due to his memory
to state, a little more fully than he has allowed himself to do, the interesting and original observations he
made upon the structure of the African continent.[1]

On the voyage up the Qua-qua, Drummond noticed
the ibises perching upon the trees—'which struck me
as a peculiarity in waders.'   'The only annoyance was
the mosquitoes, which were very numerous, but their
bark, I honestly confess for my part, I find worse than
their bite.'

'A geological feature of considerable interest was
observed about half a mile from Mogurrumba [about
fifty miles from the sea]. Since leaving Quilimane
we had seen nothing but mud,—mud black, mud
grey, mud dry, mud wet, mud eroded, mud in slopes,
mud banks, mud channels—everywhere mud, mud,
mud. But, in a high, clean-cut bank, where the river
curved and deepened, this monotony was broken by
a dark-coloured boss of what appeared to be rock. It

---

[1] *Tropical Africa* was published in 1884. Since then many editions have been
sold of it; besides 5000 of a small volume of extracts, entitled *Nyasaland*. A
German translation, *Inner-Afrika*, appeared at Gotha in 1890; second edition,
1891. Translations into some other European languages have also been made,
but I have not seen them.

was but a few yards in breadth, rising out of the water to a height of some six or eight feet, where it was again lost in the universal enswathement of clay. Had the clay been anything else, and had the place been almost anywhere else but Africa, I should have pronounced it a basalt dyke. But here this was out of the question, and with some expectancy I watched the natives pole towards the spot. A blow with the hammer revealed, beneath the blackened crust, a dull reddish rock, porous in texture, and considerably decomposed. There was no doubt whatever as to its nature. It was coral. Sponges were scattered through it in considerable quantity, as well as other organisms of smaller size. Possibly this may be the old fringing reef of the continent. Nowhere else in the Qua-qua have I seen or heard of any similar exposure. Señor Nunes, the English consul at Quilimane, told me that coral reefs appeared in the Zambezi delta at two places. Is there any relation between these three, and any coincidence of general outline between this ancient reef and the first inland belt of raised country—the first plateau?

'Aug. 7th, 1883.—Two or three miles above Shupanga[1] I noticed from the steamer two or three thin strata of what appeared to be sandstone rising above the water-line. We had followed the exposure only for a few hundred yards when a fine flock of guineafowl appeared at the water's edge, at which we fired, and stopped the steamer to pick up the slain. I had thus time to bring on board three specimens — the first a very fine grained sandstone; the second a reddish marly sandstone also very fine; and the third a somewhat more highly siliceous sandstone of a brick red colour through which were scattered small peb-

[1] On the Zambezi.

blets of quartz. These deposits were buried under ten or fifteen feet of sandy alluvium. They are only visible for a short distance, and if the river had been two feet higher, would have been entirely concealed. I kept a close look-out upon the banks all day, but saw no trace of rock until the custom-house near the mouth of the Shiré was reached. Near there two or three low conical hills make their appearance, a fine artificial section being obtained immediately behind the custom-house. It is a pure white quartz; not quartzite, but vein-quartz apparently. Distinct traces of a matrix are visible in the section — in the shape of small granitic or mica-schistose masses.

'A low bar of rock seems to stretch across the Shiré at the very mouth, but only a few boulders near the side were above water. It had the same appearance as the last.

'At the custom-house I had an opportunity of seeing the geological structure of the low conical hills which anticipate the rising ground of the continent. Behind the rough shanty which serves as the custom-house a fine section is cut in one of those hills. It seems to consist almost entirely of a pure white ungranulated quartz. Traces of a granitic or mica-schistose matrix appear here and there, but the great mass is essentially pure quartz. The next specimens were obtained at Chinga-Chinga, where we anchored for the night. I sent a couple of men to the hill on shore to bring me specimens, which I found to be quartz of the same kind as at the custom-house. The views all the way up the river are very fine, the valley being richly wooded, the trees rising up all the hills, and crossing even the loftiest parts of Morambala.

'Aug. 8th, 1883. — Our first stop was at the south end of Morambala,[1] at the Company's "station" (a grass

1 On the Shiré.

shanty) presided over by a native named "Sam." . . .
Great piles of wood for the steamer are arranged on
the bank opposite Sam's house, and an hour was spent
in loading. I spent the time with my gun and hammer in a morning stroll, with a native as guide, through
a mile or two of the adjacent country. On every side
I found a rather poor granitic soil, with boulders of
granite scattered everywhere. It is a coarse grey
variety.

'It was about two hours' steam from Sam's when the
natives signalled to stop for the projected visit to
the hot springs. We started in single file, headed by
two natives, one of whom carried a short sword with
which he assisted in clearing a path through the long
reeds lining the bank. We waded straight inland for
a few hundred yards through grass and reeds which
were often far over our heads, when we struck a small
footpath running parallel with the flank of Morambala. This we followed through a country rich with
shrubs, trees, and wild flowers, for about a couple of
miles, when we reached the springs or spring, for there
is only one. (Our exact time was twenty-five minutes'
hard walking.) There is nothing of the geyser-like
character about this spring. It is a little spring of the
usual kind, bursting up among the granite pebbles,
and, but for its temperature and chemical composition,
might be the head-waters of a highland burn, or one
of those exquisite fountains which bubble up among
the granite hills of Arran. Steam was being given
off in small quantities, and a strong smell of sulphuretted hydrogen announced the presence of the mineral water at some little distance. Unfortunately,
neither of my thermometers registered over 150°, so
that I dared not risk them in the water, which was
plainly considerably above that temperature. Proba-

bly Livingstone's figure, 170° Fah., expresses the exact
truth. We found it impossible to hold a finger in
the water for a single moment; but in a pool some
twenty yards beneath the opening of the spring we
enjoyed a very agreeable bath. . . . The taste reminds
one of some of the home mineral waters, such as
Bridge of Allan, the sulphurous taste not being dis-
agreeably strong. The position of the spring in
Ravenstein's map is decidedly too far north. It is
quite a mile or two from the end of Morambala.
Morambala is also incorrectly placed, its direction
being not due north and south, but to the west of
north. In the Portuguese map the position is exactly
right.'

The only other facts not mentioned in the volume,
which are recounted in the diary, are the tobacco
manufactured by Chipitula, the Shiré chief [1]—'capital
stuff, a fine, mild tobacco, if anything wanting in
strength, but extremely pleasant to those who prefer
the gentler varieties of the weed;' the female ornament known as the pelele ring, 'a most hideous
fashion, especially in the older women, who wear it
of the largest possible size.

'Conceive of a thick upper lip standing out from
the face like a shelf. Let into this is a metal or ivory
bone cup, its rim flush with the surface of the skin.
The cup lies with its open mouth turned upwards just
underneath the nose, and suggests a device for receiving the drip from that organ during a cold in the head.
In the case of one old hag the pelele was quite as
large as, and exactly resembled in appearance, the
brim of the lowest segment of a pocket telescope-
drinking-cup.'

On August 11 the party halted at the river-side,

---

[1] *Tropical Africa*, p. 21.

where for two seasons Chipitula's people have come to manufacture salt. The natives tried to hide from the white men the locality of the soil from which they extracted the brine; but a troop of women coming in laden with the soil, and 'the natives, seeing the clue to the mystery was in our hands, accepted the situation with great merriment, and a boy was despatched to conduct us to the spot.

'There are two characteristics of the natives. They are full of secrets. Of the white man they stand in constant awe, which in practical matters becomes suspicion, and makes them continually on their guard in case he should take some advantage of them. Accordingly they always refuse to give him information when the object for which the inquiries are asked is not perfectly patent to them. In this case no amount of explanation could have given them any satisfaction, and it would have been impossible to drive the idea out of their heads that we either wanted to make salt ourselves or would work some charm upon it which would spoil the supply for them for all time to come. The second peculiarity is their fondness for everything in the shape of a joke. The unexpected procession of salt-bearers, whose whole appearance showed that they had only travelled a short distance at the very moment they were protesting the salt came from far on the other side of the river, was plainly a case of " caught," and like children they simply laughed heartily all round.

'SUNDAY, Aug. 12th. — On the Shiré above Katunga's, the terminus of the steamer's voyage, and beginning of the road of sixty-five miles up the Shiré cataracts.

'The valley here is fine and rich, and heavy crops might be expected. On reaching the edge of the val-

ley the hills begin to rise at once, and one has a good
climb for the next three-quarters of an hour(?).   The
rock is granite (grey) and gneiss, and a few yards from
the plain the geological eye is refreshed by the sight
of a good, honest whin dyke.   It ran right up the hill,
about a yard wide, with the prismatic structure well
developed.   I find this only the precursor of many
other dykes, some of considerable size, and the amount
of basalt strewn over the hills almost surprised me.   It
seemed to have left its influence on the soil even more
than the granite in many places where the underlying
rock was undoubtedly granite.   The stain of iron quite
colours the soil over all these hills.   I should describe
these lower hills as consisting of granite and gneiss,
riddled with basalt dykes of the ordinary type.   (This
applies to the entire section as far as Blantyre and
onward.)'

On the 13th, in good health, none of them having
had the least touch of fever, the travellers reached
Mandala, a station of the Lakes Company, and were
welcomed by Mr. and Mrs. John Moir to their house,
'the largest for some hundreds of miles on the one
side and some thousands of miles on the other.   The
Blantyre mission is a mile off.'   At Mandala, Drummond had to wait a month, as the Lake Nyasa steamer
had just started for the north and could not return
within that time.   He spent part of the interval in the
excursion to Lake Shirwa, or Chilwa, described in
the second chapter of his volume.

His companions were Messrs. Hedderwick and
Henderson of the Blantyre mission; they had a small
caravan of ten porters, an interpreter, a boy cook,
and a youth whom Drummond constituted his body-
servant.

To His Mother

'Sept. 5th, 1883.

'. . . At Zomba on the Sabbath we had a service
for the natives — the real *Missionary Record*
kind of thing; white men with Bibles under a
spreading tree, surrounded by a thick crowd of
naked natives. We sang hymns from a hymn-book
in the native tongue to Scotch psalm tunes, and
then spoke through an interpreter. Unfortunately
the service was brought to rather an abrupt conclusion. I had just finished speaking when a
tremendous shriek rose from the crowd, and the
congregation dispersed in a panic in every direction. A huge snake had fallen from the tree
right into the thick of them. A bombshell could
not have done its work faster, but no one was
hurt, and the beast disappeared like magic beneath some logs. The snakes rarely do harm,
and I have never heard of a serious case.'

From Mandala, on September 10th, he wrote his
father in strong praise of the Blantyre Mission,[1] and
of the Company's treatment of the natives, and the
letter concludes thus: —

'Summer has well begun here, but I have never
felt the heat. I am thankful to say also that my
health is better than it has been for a long time,
and I have no doubt I shall be better every way
for this long and strange break. If all goes well
this expedition will be of life-long service to me
in my college work, and I hope also I may have
a voice some day in our Foreign Missionary Committee.'

[1] *Tropical Africa*, p. 124.

After some delay two hundred carriers were engaged
for the portage to the steamer, and on September 11
Drummond started with Dr. and Mrs. Scott and Mr.
Bain. The Lake and the voyage upon it are described
in the second chapter of *Tropical Africa*. But the
following are some extracts from his journal not included there: —

' 12th Sept. — Matopé being honoured with a place
in the map, we expected to find a centre of some
importance. The reality is a few grass huts on the
river-flat. Its interest for us was centred in two slender white poles rising above the largest of the huts —
the Company's store — which we rightly conjectured
to be the masts of the *Ilala*. We were welcomed
on board by Mr. Harkiss, and found lunch spread for
us inside the hut. The river looked tempting for a
bathe, but in the Shiré generally the attentions of the
crocodiles are too assiduous to risk, and this place is
particularly infamous. The natives are afraid even to
stand near the water's edge, and the villagers have to
get all their supplies of water by scooping it up in
pumpkin ladles with a handle of bamboo cane some
eight feet long. I saw the tsetse fly here for the first
time. It is found on the Mandala road as far as the
Luangwa [?]. But for this we should have been helped
on our way by the Mandala donkeys, which dare not
venture in this direction more than a few miles from
Blantyre, though they go to Katunga's with impunity.
We went to sleep to-night amidst a perfect chorus of
hippopotami. Their heads were rising like buoys all
up and down the river — the female a red buoy, the
male black. Shooting at these ironclads with any
ordinary rifle is simply a waste of ammunition. On
her last voyage some got between the *Ilala* and the

bank while moored close in shore, and at a few paces'
distance two bullets from an " Express " were sent into
parts that ought to have been vital, but the animal
waded coolly ashore and disappeared as if nothing had
happened.   Their vocal performances are somewhat
stale by this time, and are by no means musical.   First
the creature slowly heaves his square skull above
water and gives vent to a tremendous sniff, as if he
had just caught a severe cold in the head.   This
seems to relieve his vocal organs of a considerable
quantity of water, and he straightway proceeds to fill
the vacancy with air.   This he draws in with a series
of terrific grunts suggestive of a huge trombone
worked by a blast furnace, and sufficiently startling
when heard at close quarters.   The performance concludes by the creature raising himself bodily in the
water almost up to the middle, and this achieved he
sinks out of sight with a sudden plunge.

' My beard is now of age, and I look very old and
important.

' THURSDAY, 13th Sept. — The *Ilala* was off by
ten, with thirty on board, all told.   This included
our own party — Dr. and Mrs. Scott, and Mr. Bain;
seven boys from Bandawé who had been sent by Dr.
Laws to be vaccinated at Blantyre (the lymph at Bandawé being exhausted and smallpox raging); seven
men who are to accompany me to Tanganyika; Jingo,
Chessiemaleera, Mrs. Scott's native maid, Mr. Harkiss, Mr. Wells, " Bandawé," the " steward," native
deck hands, stokers, etc.

' Two or three hours' steaming brought us to Pimbé,
where limestone is said to be found.   It is being
tried just now at Mandala; and as I was anxious to
see it *in situ*, I got a native to take me to the place.
We struck across a flat at the back of the small

village for half a mile, and then reached a low range
of hills running almost parallel to the river, and a
few miles in length. We skirted the base of these
for another half-mile and then crossed a small wood
ridge into a dry watercourse occupying a valley of
some little depth. Among the boulders of this dried
" burn " blocks of limestone were scattered in considerable quantity. The surrounding rock was gneiss,
but the bed of limestone could not have been far off,
as the hills were of small size. I did not wish to
detain the steamer, or would certainly have followed
it up to the limestone. It is a dazzling white marble
with black mica in small spangles scattered through
it. In the bed of the stream I also found blocks of
fine basalt, and a good deal of quartz was lying all
over the hills.

' 14th Sept. — Towards the head of Lake Pomalombé
the hills approach on the east side. Large trees clothe
the flats along their bases, among them a number of
fan-palms, but few of any size. The few miles of
winding river between Lake Pomalombé and Nyasa
traverse a country of great beauty. The baobab,
tamarind, and fan-palm grow in profusion, and shelter
one or two of the largest villages I have yet seen in
Africa. One of the largest of these is M'Ponda's,
exquisitely situated among trees on the slope of the
west bank. A bold spur of red granite on the opposite side runs to within half a mile of the water's edge.
Behind this are ranges of low hills, succeeding one
another in an unbroken line as far as the eye can
reach. A similar range rises in the distance behind
M'Ponda. As it stretches away northward the hills
increase into the mountains which mark the southwest end of Lake Nyasa, and under a spur of which
nestles Livingstonia. We passed through this on a

fine afternoon, the cool breeze from the distant lake
tempering the heat and giving to the whole journey
the aspect of a tour among the English lakes. But
for the difference in the vegetation, palpable only at
close quarters, the sudden apparition of a hippopota-
mus crossing the steamer's bows, or the spectacle of
a naked savage fishing in his canoe, there is nothing
in the general surroundings of the upper Shiré to
remind one that he is out of Europe. The villages,
however, are certainly unlike anything one has ever
seen before. There is one above M'Ponda's, occupying nearly half a mile of the river-bank. The huts
are huddled together for the most part without any
attempt at order, a few being reduced to something
like neatness by a high stockade, which gives in the
distance to the whole the appearance of an English
cottage with its garden. At close quarters, however,
the huts are more like the moss summer-houses one
finds in country seats than human habitations. They
are all of the same toadstool pattern, and miniature
toadstools are often built at the side to form barns.
Smaller toadstools still are built on high piles and
connected with the ground by rude ladders. These
are the fowl-houses, which have to be garrisoned in
this fashion for fear of leopards, wild-cats, hyenas,
and other beasts of prey.

'16th Sept. — At ten native service in the school;
large turnout of natives and my men from *Ilala*.
Mr. Harkiss conducted, and gave an address. After
dinner we went to a native funeral.[1] The cortège had
come a couple of miles, and were waiting for the
white men under some trees. They consider it a
great honour to have white men present on such an
occasion, and have been used to it in the mission

[1] Cf. *Tropical Africa*, p. 155.

days.   The body—a native in his prime—was merely
wrapped in calico (his own suit), and placed in two
palm-mats, formed into a litter with two rough
branches, and carried by four men.   The burial-place
was the wood behind the station at the rise of the
hill.   The funeral itself was interesting as a mixture
of the heathen and Christian mode of sepulture.   Had
it been in the old days it would have been very different, but the whole of the tribes are gradually
"reverting to type."   The grave was at least ten feet
deep by eight in length.   Some sixty natives stood
round about, an equal number of women remaining in
the background about fifty yards off.   Two long strips
of bark were laid across the grave—a copy and
reminiscence of the ropes used by the English.   These
ropes were held by four natives while the body was
slowly lowered.   This was done with great decorum,
and up to this point the funeral might have been that
of an Englishman conducted by his countrymen.
But now commenced the heathen or native ceremonies.
First, the dead man's two knives were handed down
to the two men who stood beside the corpse in the
unfilled grave.   These were placed beside the body.
His bow and arrows followed—the bow *with the bow-
string cut across with a knife*, a most touching symbol.
Then, with some ceremony, his pipe, the long stem
covered with blue and white beads, was laid beside
his head.   Next followed a large calabash cooking-
vessel, a smaller one with a handle used as a drinking-
cup, two baskets—one large and one small.   These
were arrayed about the body.   About a foot above
the body a groove was cut in the earth all round,
and into this were then fitted a number of strong
sticks.   These were then covered with leaves and
twigs, and all was ready for the soil to be thrown in.

The mounds of earth were slowly scraped in with the small native hoes, assisted by a shovel borrowed from the Mission. When all was finished two field baskets were broken up with an axe and thrown upon the grave. By this time I began to realise what all this meant. It was the burial with the dead of all his earthly possessions. This man probably owned not another article in the world. I never realised so much as here the absolute simplicity of the native life. Even the unsmoked tobacco was to be laid over his ashes. It was strewn near a small fire kindled under a tree, but when we tried to find out the exact mode in which it was to be disposed of the information was refused. Chimlolo told us they would come back and finish that part of the ceremony when we had gone. No word was spoken by the natives of the nature of a service. They were mostly grave, sober-looking men in middle life, and the faces of some were fine and intelligent. A white man's funeral in Scotland could scarcely have been attended by more intelligent-looking men, and one could not help feeling keenly for them in what they lacked. All the native graves around had their pots and baskets over them — some had empty cases from the English — all *holed*.

'Chimlolo, on this occasion, was dressed in his best Sunday clothes, and nothing could illustrate better the folly of encouraging the natives to don European garments. He had on an ancient and discoloured tweed coat over his naked body, a pair of rough pilot-cloth trousers over his naked feet, and on his head a faded green helmet, which bore the legend "31st Lanarkshire Rifle Volunteers." Yesterday, with his fine frame wrapped in his robes, he looked every inch a chief. To-day he was a perfect object. He resembled nothing so much as the negro loafers who lounge about the quays in the Southern States.'

On the 19th September the *Ilala* reached Bandawé, the central mission station of the Free Church of Scotland. Drummond's visit and the communion service in which he participated are described in *Tropical Africa.*[1]

To his Father

'KARONGA'S, N. END OF LAKE NYASA,
Sept. 28, 1883.

'. . . We stayed at Bandawé from Thursday at midnight till Monday at midday. . . . Dr. Laws goes home in a month. He has been seven years here without a break, and much needs a holiday. . . . The native service on Sunday was a grand sight. Five or six hundred were present, all squatting on the ground and listening with all their might. I had the pleasure of talking to them a lot, Dr. Laws translating. There was also a good Sunday-school and an English service in the evening, which I took. These were sad days for the Mission, however. The steamer had gone round to a bay twenty miles up the coast for repairs, and came back on Saturday with the flag floating at the half-mast. All knew that this meant death, and a crowd gathered on the beach. It was too stormy for a landing, and no boat or canoe could venture out, so we waited in suspense. At length a board was hoisted, on which the telescope was at once focussed. In chalk we read the words, " Mr. Stewart." The steamer had met some natives coming down the Lake shore from here, and they brought the news. Mr. Stewart's name

[1] Page 148.

you must have heard. He is a civil engineer,
and was at the head of the operatives on Mr.
James Stevenson's road from here to Tanganyika. He laid out Livingstonia, Blantyre, and
Bandawé, and has been a foremost figure in
mission work in Africa for several years. He is
a cousin of Dr. Stewart of Lovedale. On reaching this place, we found the flag on the store also
half-mast, so we knew it was too true. He died
of a complaint contracted by a residence in India
— jaundice. He lies near where I write, under
a huge baobab tree. He chose the spot himself
only six weeks before for the captain of the *Ilala*,
over whom he read the burial service, one other
white man only being present. One of the Company's men had to do the same service for him.
I was looking forward with great pleasure to
meeting him here. He has few relations living,
only a sister, Mrs. Vartan of Nazareth.

'We were from Monday to Thursday in getting
here. This included a whole day on shore cutting wood. The men are now busy unloading
our things, and I think I shall get under way
to-morrow. Bain may possibly wait here for a
fortnight yet, as things are not quite ready for
him at Mweni-wanda. But if he came, he would
only accompany me some fifty miles farther. He
is very well and in capital spirits. His manse
will be something to look forward to on his home-
ward march. My caravan is almost ready for
the start. I brought twenty men with me in the
steamer, and will not need many more. Some
were brought from Mandala, the rest from Bandawé. Dr. Laws has given me one of his best
natives to act as captain over the men. "James"

P

is a really trustworthy man, and I am very fortunate in having got him, though he knows no
English. He was one of three natives who sat
down to the Lord's Table with us on Sabbath
last at Bandawé. I have got a thoroughly good
tent and any quantity of provisions and calico
(money), and I think the journey will be most
enjoyable. After this is over, I shall track home-
wards as rapidly as possible.'

Drummond started from Karonga's on September 29, and began his tramp northwards across the
plateau towards Lake Tanganyika. He left white
men behind him. He had a caravan of twenty-eight
blacks, including his three faithfuls — Jingo, Moolu,
and Seyid. Not one could speak a word of English.
'They belonged to three different tribes, and spoke as
many languages; the majority, however, know something of Chinyanja, the Lake language, of which I also
had learned a little, so we soon understood each other.'
Drummond has given, in Chapter V. of *Tropical Africa*,
some extracts from his diary on this journey, illustra-
tive of his general experiences. The following additions are taken, some from the same source, others
from his letters home.

After entering the fringe of hills, bordering the
higher lands as described on page 92 of *Tropical
Africa*, he took some geological notes.

'Sept. 29th. — A herd of cows browsing along the
banks and the newly cut road give to this part quite a
homelike character. For about two miles the road
winds along with the stream through a richly wooded
valley. The mark of the pick is still fresh upon the
great rocks which flank the narrow glen, and here are

not only the best, but the only artificial, geological sections in Central Africa.   The hills rise high above the
river on either side, and their structure is evident from
a hundred well engineered bits of the road as it cuts
room for itself alongside the river channel.   A fine
study in metamorphic rocks.   (Bits of mica-schist of
many varieties alternate with bands of quartzite?)
These beds are all thin, seldom more than a few yards,
and are pitched at a very high angle, in several places
being all but vertical.   Gneiss also gradually appears,
and the different rocks alternating repeatedly add considerable variety to the section.   Scarcely two of the
beds are alike.   Here is a coarse schist (granite?)
with plates of black mica three inches in length.   Next
it a band of the most pellucid quartzite.   A variegated
bed of waving gneiss follows, to be succeeded by a
schist (granite), in which the flakes of mica are so
small as only to be distinguishable by their mass.
(Others of the schists are strongly talcose?)   The
quartzites run through every shade from white to iron
brown, one very beautiful variety being a delicate
salmon pink.   I describe these thus minutely, for in
another year or two the geologist may look for them
in vain, or only expose a fresh section with much labour.
All these varieties may be found within half a mile,
and probably a hundred yards might be found in which
the whole series was represented.

'Sept. 30th. — Rested all day, being Sabbath.   Held
service in the morning with the men.   They gathered
in front of my tent after breakfast, I sitting on a box
at the door.   Gave out a hymn verse by verse, from
Dr. Laws's book, three or four joining in the singing
to the tune of " Scots wha hae " (!).   I then read the
Lord's Prayer in Chinyanja, the natives repeating as
they have been taught at the Mission service.   Then

James gave a short address which I should have given a great deal to have fully understood. We then sang another hymn, "Come to the Saviour"; I offered prayer in English, and James closed with prayer in Chinyanja, or rather Atonga.

'This day month, August 30th, Mr. James Stewart died in this place — a hundred yards, I believe, from where I write.

'WEDNESDAY, Oct. 3rd. — After crossing the valley, the path — the road is not cut here yet — struck over a steep ridge of sedimentary rocks, coarse sandstones, or fine conglomerates, with one or two beds of limestone. We then descended into another long and narrow valley in which lay the dry bed of a considerable stream. The path follows this for a mile, but leaves it shortly after a stagnant pool is passed, the road recommencing at this point. It is freshly made, and winds up the hill in long sweeping curves. Fresh exposures of purple, chocolate, and dark red sandstone occur on the roadside. These evidently belong to the same series as those in the opposite valley. They are all inclined toward the earth at an angle of about 35°. They soon give place to the old series of gneisses and granites which occupy the country now as far as Mweni-wanda, possibly as far as Tanganyika. These granitised beds are exposed in all the burns (all dry), which are numerous along the line of march. They are all pitched at a very high angle — all but vertical. Quartz predominates apparently in the composition of the granite, and the path is littered with quartz pebbles. In this respect the rocks probably differ from the Blantyre beds, where there is an unusually large proportion of black mica, which accounts for the greater fertility of the latter district. From Maramoura to Kamera the country cannot be described as

poor; the soil is thin and strong, covered with trees of
a uniform height of about twenty feet, thinly planted,
with grass and underwood not luxuriant.   Large trees
are absent.   The general features of the country are
the same as far as the eye can reach on either side,
undulating hills of thin forest unvaried by any exceptionally distinctive features.   The "billows" are all well
rounded, and present their long axis towards the lake
which receives their drainage.'

Under the same date occurs the following interesting note upon African habits:—

'After leaving the sandstones (a short distance) the
new road is left to the right, the men insisting on
striking across country, but in reality the road is only
made for a few hundred yards farther.   I do not suppose the roadway is constructed much farther, but at
any rate it proved a superfluity in this case.   Mr.
Ross, one of the engineers at work on the road, told
me that his own men who had helped to make it, in
taking him to Karonga's (where I met him, the incident happened that very morning), left the road at
one point to cross a hill by the native path instead of
rounding it by the road.   He recalled them at once, a
fine sense of loyalty to the undertaking, but on sight-
ing the point of re-convergence he was disgusted to
see the tail of his caravan defiling into the main road,
and now considerably in advance of him, although
they were formerly too far behind to hear the order.
These natives were all carrying heavy loads.   Even
where they use the road they never vary their custom of walking in Indian file, so that a beaten path
exists in the centre of the road itself.   The difference
between the English road and the native's path is
simply this—the former, made with line and level, is
straight in detail but winding as a whole; the latter,

made by naked feet and instinct, is winding in detail but straight as a whole. The native strikes a bee-line to his destination, but the exigencies of the case, the avoidance of trees, logs, and large stones, cause it to be irregular throughout.'[1]

On the 3d and 4th of October Drummond noted the almost entire absence of water from the country through which he was passing, till he struck the main stream, an enticing little river, and fine volume of water. 'The path crosses it at some gneiss blocks. I spent the rest of the day plashing and wading about the river-bed.

'Towards nightfall a small native caravan arrived at the crossing and camped on the opposite bank. I found it was a sub-chief under Mweni-wanda, whose name is Wanimaver, travelling to the coast. The old fellow came across to pay his respects to the white man, accompanied by two or three of his counsellors. A native carried a small stool, which he placed for him in front of my tent. I did not know the natives enjoyed this luxury, but probably the age of the chief demanded it. He told me he was ill, and was on his way to a medicine man at Karonga's village. I shared my cocoa with him, and presented him with a little salt and a needle. He seemed much awed all through the interview. Next morning he was over by daylight to wish me good-by. He seemed a simple, kindly, childlike old man, quite the chief in appearance. His sole garment was a maize-coloured and faded drab loin cloth. His men, meantime, were up the trees adjoining the river throwing down great branches, with which they soon made him a very pretty bower by the river's brink. The camp-fire twinkling through this; the native music played before the tent—a sere-

[1] Cf. *Tropical Africa*, pp. 34–36.

nade to the chief by three voices and some stringed
instrument; the brawling river; the young moon and
the bright starlight, — made up a very pretty tableau
for my after-supper smoke on the grass by my own
camp-fire.'

On Friday, 5th, he arrived at Kamera, and on the
6th at Mweni-wanda's village, and Chirenjé, 'a future
Free Church station.' There he paid his men, and
checked Mr. Bain's goods which arrived by another,
caravan. He stayed in the rough mission-house for a
week, shooting, collecting, talking with Mweni-wanda,
and entertaining Mr. Griffiths, of the London Missionary Society, on his way home from his station on
Lake Tanganyika. On Friday, the 12th, he started
again and travelled that and the next day by the
Stevenson road till it stopped at 18½ miles — 'a fine
avenue through a level or gently undulating country.'
His camp was at Zockye's village. 'After a twenty-
mile tramp in the sun, this village, with its dirty water,
its shocking sanitary conditions, almost shadeless
stream, and staring crowds, was simple torture, and I
confess the reasons against enduring other forty days
of it by going on to Tanganyika seemed at that
moment most convincing.' Next day he moved on to
the camp beyond Chewakunda, where he spent the
week so beautifully described on pages 109 ff. of *Tropical Africa*. In addition to the observations recorded
there he read a number of books, 'Howells's *Undis-
covered Country*, *Old Mortality*, Miss Edwards's
Modern Poets, and much of the Revised Version.'
'On Monday, 1st, service as usual, James (Moolu)
very eloquent on "Lazarus."' They started (as *Tropical Africa* says, page 112) on the 22d and marched
northwest. 'This day the tropics have dried up my
stylograph.' The next part of the diary is in pencil.

He stalked, shot at, and missed some fine hartbeest.
He was going to sit down, when, in the very place he
had chosen, he

'Observed a curious patter among the leaves. It
was a puff adder. I drew my revolver and shot it,
but the brute slowly sank down the bank and lay
down, as I thought, to die, by the water. Some
hours after, when I sent for it, it was gone. A
day or two later my men were frightened to death
by finding it at the pool where they drew water for
the camp. It was still alive, but I finished it with
another shot. It was not very lengthy, but very
fat in the girth. The men said it was a python,
but I have my doubts, especially as they also said
its bite was certain death — a fact which was quite
evident from the shape of the jaws. It had two
bags on the side of its head with poison enough
to kill a village.'

The journal for October 24 and 25 is fully given in
Tropical Africa. Till the 30th they stayed (because
of the bearer wounded by the buffalo) in the same
'enchanting camp,' and then 'steered west and southwest up a valley running into the Lejangé, with steep
sides. The main rock is gneiss, but here and at the
former camp there are beds of mica schist, very hard
and compact for schists, however.' They crossed the
watershed of the range, descended a little, and camped
eight miles from their previous camp at about 4900
feet above the sea. On October 31 he sent back to
Mweni-wanda for a medicine chest and 'some books,
as my small box was read to death. Spent Monday
studying White Ants. There was much thunder, and
rain fell uninterruptedly from three to six, but as it
was not heavy my tent held out.'

But the rainy season had commenced and it was time to turn. On the 24th of October he had written home: —

'I started from the Lake with thirty-two men, most of them from a distance, but I had to engage some local men to take extra loads. I had the universal fate of African travellers, for a number deserted at the first hill. I got their places filled, but gradually the local men dropped off, and now I have only seventeen left. These are all good men and true, but I have had to leave many stores at a log cabin at Mweni-wanda. The crippling of my caravan made me consider seriously whether I ought to go the whole way to Tanganyika, and you will perhaps be glad to hear that I have decided to turn now. I am within 130 or 140 miles of it, but the rainy season is due immediately and I should catch it coming back in all its fury. I have enjoyed such perfect health that I do not think it is right to run unnecessary risk. I could probably weather anything in my tent, but my men would suffer severely. They are not accustomed to this high country, and already many of them have had fever. Scarcely a day passes but I have to doctor some of them. Besides this, the rest of the way is just the same thing over again, and it would be dreary work toiling all the way back over exactly the same ground. All things considered, therefore, I have resolved to wander slowly back to Nyasa and make my way to Quilimane as the rain permits. I may weather out the first plumps in the aforesaid log cabin, which is to be Bain's manse and where he will now be. Word will be sent there when the *Ilala* arrives at Karonga's to take me down the Lake again.'

Besides, as he confessed afterwards, he was beginning to feel lassitude and depression, the precursors of fever, though he did not yet know them as such.

On October 31 they moved to a deserted village and felt safe from wild beasts behind its stockade. The wounded man was still in evil plight. They remained there till November 3, when a letter came from Mr. Bain, with a postscript from Mr. Fred Moir (returning from Tanganyika), that they would wait for Drummond at Mweni-wanda. Carrying the wounded man in a litter he reached Mweni-wanda on November 5 and stayed till the 14th. 'Moir and Lieutenant Pully went off to shoot elephants at Kimbashi. Much tempted to go with them. The steamer went for their mails after they had been five or six days in the field. They sent *eighteen tusks back*, capital sport.'

On November 15 he started for the Lake and on the 18th camped fifteen miles from it beside Mr. Munro, the engineer who was at work on the road, and Mr. Bain, who like himself was waiting for the steamer. It was here that he made his discovery of fossils — he believes 'the only fossils that had ever been found in Central Africa.' They lay in 'thin beds of very fine light grey sandstone and blue and grey shales, with an occasional band of grey limestone — but especially in the shale, one layer being one mass of small *Lamellibranchiata*. Though so numerous, these fossils are confined to a single species of the *Tellinidæ*, a family abundantly represented in tropical seas at the present time and dating back as far as the Oolite. Vegetable remains are feebly represented by a few reeds and grasses.' [1]

[1] *Tropical Africa*, 'A Geological Sketch,' p. 192.

But here is his journal: —

'MONDAY, Nov. 19th. — Terrific thunderstorm with heavy rain broke out late last night. I awoke, lit a candle, and sat watching for the first sign of leakage in my tent. A trench had been dug all round, but the slope of the road made a perfect torrent sweep past, and I had to keep building up the banks. One trench ran parallel with my bed, as the side of the tent was tilted aside to meet the hill, so that I could see from where I lay the brown torrent sweeping sticks, leaves, and insects before it. The wind rose to a hurricane, and I was afraid every moment I would be unroofed and left to weather the storm in the open. But my tent behaved bravely and the combined elements failed to dislodge me. A few drops only got through. Bain, who shared Munro's tent, was less fortunate, in spite of his tent having a good fly. The rain soon penetrated both fly and canvas and flooded him out of bed at midnight. They were in a terrible plight all night, and Bain was down with fever in consequence a couple of days after.

'On the Sunday morning, when sitting at breakfast on the newly made road, I saw at my feet a small slab of slate with markings which struck me at once as familiar. I eagerly seized it, and saw before me a fossil fish. I had marked this very spot on my way up country as a place for a possible " find " in this direction, and I had planned to spend two or three days here fossil-hunting on my way back. I had little idea that so fine a section would be waiting me; and the road-cutting here was a most singular coincidence, as this was the only mile of rock between Tanganyika and the mouth of the Zambezi where I should have wished such a thing, or where I would have expected to find fossils. Monday, therefore, I devoted to a regular fossil-hunt, but I am sorry to say with no very satisfactory result as far as fish were concerned. I got several teeth, however, innumerable fish-scales, and a great number of shells, these last all belonging to a single species. I set all the boys to work, and offered a knife to whomsoever would bring me a fish, but although several of them worked hard they all failed.'

The fossil fish remains were submitted to Dr. Traquair of Edinburgh, whose identification of them is given in full in *Tropical Africa*, pages 193–195. He says of the largest: —

'. . . Belonging to the order *Ganoidei*, this fish is with equal certainty referable to the family *Palæoniscidæ*, but its *genus* is more a matter of doubt, owing to the fragmentary nature of the specimen. Judging from the form and thickness of the scales I should be inclined to refer it to *Acrolepis*, were it not that the dorsal and anal fins seem so close to the tail, and so nearly opposite each other; here, however, it may be remarked that the disturbed state of the scales affords room for the possibility that the original relations of the parts may not be perfectly preserved. I have, however, no doubt that, as a *species*, it is new; and as you have been the first to bring fossil fishes from those regions of Central Africa, you will perhaps allow me to name it *Acrolepis (?) Drummondi.*

'No. 2 is a piece of cream-coloured limestone with numerous minute, scattered rhombic, striated, ganoid scales, which I cannot venture to name, though I believe them to be palæoniscid. . . . Among these minuter relics is a scale of much larger size, and clearly belonging to another fish. A little way off is the impression of the attached surface of a similar scale, and there are also two interspinous bones probably belonging to the same fish. This is probably also a palæoniscid scale, which we may provisionally recognise as *Acrolepis (?) Africanus.* . . . No. 5 is a piece of grey, micaceous shale, with scales of yet a fourth species of palæoniscid fish; . . . the outer surface not being properly displayed, renders it impossible to give a sufficient diagnosis. No. 6 is a piece of the same shale having the clavicle of a small palæoniscid fish, which it is, however, impossible to name.'

'These fossiliferous beds,' adds Drummond, 'seem to occupy a comparatively limited area, and to have a very high dip in a southeasterly direction.   At the spot where my observations were taken they did not extend over more than half a mile of country, but it is possible that the formation may persist for a long distance in other directions.   Indeed, I traced it for some miles in the direction in which, some fifty or sixty miles off, lay the coal already described,[1] and to which it may possibly be related.'

It was in the same camp, twelve miles north of Karonga's, that Drummond made a discovery of a very different kind, and one of greater personal interest to himself, — the phenomenal success among his countrymen of his book on *Natural Law*, while he had been wandering in these savage regions.

'THURSDAY, Nov. 22d. — After I had gone to roost, sometime about midnight I was aroused by talking in Munro's tent.   Could it be the arrival of natives with the mails from the coast?   " Mails," came in response to my shout; and in a few moments a boy came in with a huge packet of letters and papers.   My lamp was lit in a twinkling and I was for the next three hours devouring the first news I had had from home for five months.   Letters from all the family twice over, as the bag contained two months' despatches.   *Spectator* with critique enclosed — which much surprised me.   I had almost forgotten about the book!   Sleep was hard after so much interesting news, and it was early morning before I dropped over.'

On the 26th they marched for Karonga's, ' Bain very weak with fever, so our progress was very slow.'   After three days at Karonga's they embarked on the *Ilala* on the 29th, and coasted along till opposite the re-

[1] *Tropical Africa*, pp. 187, 188.

ported coal-bed south of Mount Waller. 'Landed and
spent the afternoon among the coal. Stewart's description is accurate as regards the topography, but he is
wrong geologically.' The matter is fully discussed in
Tropical Africa, pages 188, 189, with the conclusion
that 'the Lake Nyasa coal, so far as opened up at
present, can scarcely be regarded as having any great
economical importance, although the geological interest of such a mineral in this region is considerable.'
'Probably,' he says in his journal, 'the coal is a mere
fragmentary portion thrown down by a "fault."'

On November 30 he was at Deep Bay, where they
slept on shore through heavy rain that nearly put out
their carriers' fires. 'This was about midnight. It is
wonderful how they manage to keep hold on "motu"
(fire) under the most trying circumstances. The rain
was enough to quench anything, but they must have
kept some embers screened in their hands, which they
had carried to the hut and back.'

On December 1 (with a ton of ivory aboard) they
anchored at Bandawé, partook of the Lord's Supper at
the service next day (Sunday), and witnessed the bap-
tism of five native converts. Sailing down the Lake
with Dr. and Mrs. Laws on board, they reached Matopé on December 8, and stayed there, waiting for carriers, till the 13th, 'killing time and catching fever.'
On the 14th they camped in rain at the first stream
to the south of Matopé.

'Dec. 15th. — Off with the sun, walked hard till 10
o'clock, when we reached stream and took breakfast.
Then all started for Blantyre, still 10 or 12 miles off.
I was last to leave, as I felt lazy — the same inertia
that I had so often felt up country, and which I now
knew to be incipient fever. Lay down, with Jingo and
another of my men with the N'tonga, a few hundred

yards from the start, and rested quite two hours.
Meantime a thunderstorm was raging ahead, and the
rain threatened to reach us every moment.　However,
we had not a drop; but I had not gone 500 yards
before the ground became quite wet, and we were soon
almost wading in the stream of muddy water which
rushed down the path.　Rain itself we had none.
There might have been five or six miles of this, and
then, at the stream at Mulunga's village, the wet
ground as suddenly ceased.　I learned afterwards that
Dr. Laws and the others had got over this rain-zone
before it came on, and escaped quite dry.　We both
must have made a narrow escape.

　'Stopped at the burn to make a hasty cup of tea,
and had just finished when I saw Mr. MacIlwain
coming to meet me on one of the donkeys.　I thanked
him with all my heart, and after he had a cup of tea
he walked by my side into Blantyre (four or five miles).
At B. I was welcomed by Messrs. Scott, Henderson,
Hedderwick, and all the staff, and, after a plate of soup
at the Manse, went on to Mandala.

　'SUNDAY, Dec. 16th. — Felt rather lazy about going
to church, but, as I wished to go, a donkey was placed
at my disposal, which I accepted.　I felt unaccounta-
bly tired, but had no other symptom.　In the evening
I did not go out, but, feeling rather knocked up, went
early to bed.　Dr. Laws insisted that I had fever; and
when I took my temperature and found it read a degree
or two above the normal, 98.6, I was as much astonished as disgusted.　I took no medicine, but heaped
on clothes to induce perspiration, which came in an
hour or two and necessitated two or three changes of
pyjamas.　I had no sickness, but slight oppression and
headache of a new variety, though not very severe.
Slept fairly.

'MONDAY, Dec. 17th. — My fever was short-lived,
though I kept my bed all day.   I fancy I might have
been up.   Was glad to get it over.   There seems now
no doubt that I had a good deal of fever up country
without my knowing it.   Certainly I can now account
better for the want of spirit, want of appetite, laziness,
weakness, and general limpness which I felt so often.
Indeed, for a month or six weeks, this was almost my
normal state.   Yet, at the time, I did not realise the
extent of it, but set it down to sheer laziness.   No
doubt my cinchonised condition helped me greatly.

'TUESDAY, Dec. 18th. — Up even to breakfast,
though feeling a little weak and top-heavy.   This
giddiness remained all day.'

There had been great illness at Blantyre while
Drummond was up country, and the only two white
children in the community had died.   Drummond
stayed a whole month at Mandala, hospitably entertained by Mr. and Mrs. John Moir, and without adventure or incident, save numerous cases of fever in the
little colony, and the arrival of the first consul appointed to the region, Captain Foote, R.N., and his
family.   On January 15 Drummond started down
stream for Katunga's, where his journal closes.   He
retraced his journey of some months before, descended
the Shiré and Zambezi, crossed the portage, and came
down the Qua-qua in a boat with eight rowers to
Quilimane — finding the country, because of the rains,
in a very different aspect from that he had seen on his
way up.

'My faithful Jingo was with me to the last.   I had
serious thoughts of taking him home, but at last reluctantly resolved to leave him in Africa, as I felt sure he
would weary away from his own tribe.   He was a most
useful servant, and every white person I met begged

me to hand him over to them when I left the country. Black servants very soon get spoiled, but my boy was awarded first prize by universal consent. He actually *belonged* to me as long as I was in the country; and if I had wished to *keep* him, I should simply have had to send a few yards of cloth to his chief. I was really very sorry to part with poor Jingo, and he looked very lugubrious over it likewise. He came on board with me, carrying my umbrella as his last service, and I took him round the great ship. He was utterly lost and bewildered, and I should give a good deal to hear his report to the natives up country of all the wonders he saw at Quilimane. It seems quite strange to be afloat once more, and I am almost as bewildered as poor Jingo!'

From Quilimane Drummond sailed in the Currie liner *Dunkeld* to East London, which he reached on the 21st of February. In South Africa he visited King Williamstown, Pirie, and Lovedale, the famous mission-station under Dr. Stewart of the Free Church of Scotland, where he stayed the first half of March, Fort Beaufort, Grahamstown, Port Elizabeth, and Uitenhage, the home of his old college friend Paterson, who died there in 1875. Cape Town was 'dirty, windy, and city-like,' so he went to Wynberg — ' out of sight the loveliest place I have seen in South Africa ' — and spent a fortnight wandering about the base of Table Mountain. There he heard of the death of the Shiré chief Chipitula, whom he had visited : shot in a quarrel by an English trader, who was also killed. ' This is a serious matter and may lead to further disturbances, as the whites are all looked upon as one tribe, and the next European who passes will have to look out. I do not think the affair will be carried farther owing to circumstances, but there is no saying.

Q

Anyway I am glad to be now on the safe side of it.
It is a rough country up there, say the best for it.' On
the 9th of April he sailed from Cape Town, and by
the end of the month was in England.

Central Africa left a deep mark upon Drummond.
He accomplished his mission and was able to give
to the African Lakes Company a valuable report on
the geology and resources of the great country which
they were administering. He added infinitely to his
knowledge of natural history, and did original work
by his discovery of fossils and by his observations
of the effect of white ants upon soil.[1]   But it was
not along any of these lines that the country left its
chief influence upon him. He had entered Africa
in perfect health and at the best season; with almost
boyish glee he had revelled in his journey of exciting
scenes and adventures as 'one continual picnic from
first to last.' Then he met the first European graves
— Mrs. Livingstone's, Bishop Mackenzie's, the pathetic
cemetery at Old Livingstonia.[2]   He saw the missionaries laid down with fever, some like his companion, the heroic Bain, suffering in solitude hundreds of
miles from another white man. The news of Stewart's
sudden death smote him at Bandawé. A white mother
died in childbirth—every white birth in Central Africa
up to that time had cost a life—and the only two British children in the land died while he was up country.
In short, Drummond saw all the cruel sacrifices, inseparable from the first heroic assaults of Christianity upon
the heathendom of the Dark Continent. He saw, too,
the slave-trade in its most ghastly features, the cruel
Arab dealer, the tracks dotted with human bones, the

[1] See *Tropical Africa*, Chapter VI., 'The White Ant: a Theory.'
[2] *Tropical Africa*, pp. 15, 16, 22, 23, 41–45.

stockades with human heads impaled on them.   Then
came his own fits of lassitude and depression, attacks
of fever in his tent under the pitiless rain, and a
month of weakness and inertia.   All this marked him
for life.   When he returned to Scotland we noticed a
splash of grey hair upon his head.   And although beyond this he seems to have suffered from his African
travel no other physical injury, there is little doubt that
his spirit was affected by all he had seen and suffered.
This is visible between his letters on arriving and
his letters on leaving the Continent.   It coloured his
views on certain aspects of life and religion.   Up till
1883 Drummond had never suffered personally, except
from the long trial of uncertainty with regard to his
vocation.   He had never known loneliness.   Death
had not come into his family, and hardly within his
sight.   To a friend who had lost a little nephew in
1877 he had said, ' I cannot write on these things, for
I know little of their reality or awful mystery.'   But in
Africa he learned to know.   When on his work with
Moody he had almost fiercely resented the statement
of a speaker that suffering was inseparable from Christian service.   But now he knew that it was so ; and I
do not think it is a fault of memory to say that from
1884 onwards there came upon his always pure and
sympathetic temper a certain tinge of sadness with
which we had not been able to associate him in previous years.   Upon his return to Scotland he said to
a friend, ' I've been in an atmosphere of death all the
time.'

CHAPTER IX

THE FAME OF *NATURAL LAW*

WHILE Drummond was in Central Africa his book achieved a most amazing popularity. No one was more amazed at it than himself. He had left England within a week of its publication, in June, 1883, and was beyond all news till the following November. Then suddenly, one midnight, between Nyasa and Tanganyika, a bundle of letters was thrust into his tent. He jumped from bed, and, hastily lighting a candle, fed his long famine of tidings from home. Nothing had changed there except his own reputation. He read that his volume had passed immediately through a first and a second edition, that the reviewers were carried away by it, and that in especial the *Spectator* could recall ' no book of our time (with the exception of Dr. Mozley's *University Sermons*) which showed such a power of relating the moral and practical truths of religion, so as to make them take fresh hold of the mind and vividly impress the imagination.' This review enforced the already great popularity of the volume; and, by the time Drummond reached England in the following May, the popularity had risen to fame. At the end of the eighth month seven thousand copies had been sold, and the circulation still went up by leaps and bounds. The more important Reviews printed long articles upon *Natural Law*. While some of them disputed both its theories and conclusions, others considered it ' the most impor-

tant contribution to the relations of science and religion
which the century had produced;' and all attributed
its extraordinary success 'to its undoubted merits, —
the originality of its ideas and its style.' 'A pioneer
book'; 'full of the germs and seeds of things'; 'a
remarkable and important book, the theory which is
enounced may without exaggeration be termed a
discovery'; 'the reader is stirred to the depths of his
spiritual nature'; 'an unspeakably fascinating volume,'
— these are but a few drops of the almost weekly
showers of praise which were poured upon *Natural
Law* during the first year of its life. But not even such
praise can measure the extent of its vogue among the
people. The book was read almost everywhere. At
the end of the second year thirty thousand copies had
been sold; at the end of the third, forty thousand; at
the end of the fifth, sixty-nine thousand, and still the
numbers grew. To-day the sales have reached one
hundred and twenty-three thousand in Great Britain
alone.

About this rush of public favour one fact is conspicuous — it was proportionally much greater in England and in America than it was in Scotland. The
principle that a prophet has less honour in his own
country does not explain this, for no part of the Eng-
lish-speaking race exceeded in admiration for Drummond his own countrymen, and especially his private
friends. But the hostile criticism, which the main
idea of the book had received from the Glasgow Club
to which it was first communicated, was repeated
nowhere more persistently than in Scotland, and by
none with greater conviction than by a few of the
author's closest companions.

The causes of the immediate popularity of *Natural
Law* are obvious. With the exception of a few pas-

sages the book is beautifully written. But the clear and simple style is charged with an enthusiasm and carries a wealth of religious experience which capture the heart, and tempt the thoughtful reader to become indifferent to almost every prejudice which the introduction has excited in his mind. A teacher who, with such gifts, founds his teaching upon the facts of Christian experience, is always sure of a welcome; and the welcome will be the more cordial if he expounds these facts, as not arbitrary, but subject to reason and law — and this apart altogether from the question whether the laws he alleges be the true ones. When, besides, he deals with the relations of science and religion, he presents a subject that is not only of great intellectual interest to most persons of education, but to many thousands also is a topic of the most acute personal significance. Among the letters which Drummond received between 1883 and 1892 are a large number from men and women of all degrees of culture, whose faith, once strong, had been shattered by the new convictions of science, and who looked for the reconciliation of the claims of science with religion as they that look for the morning. Science had proved the universe to be subject to exceptionless laws; and the form under which those persons had received religion — as if it were outside of reason and independent, if not defiant, of law — had collapsed beneath their impressions of science. They were now not concerned whether Drummond made out a case for the special laws which he illustrated, nor whether his main thesis, that physical law continues within the spiritual sphere, had been proven. It was enough for them that they encountered a teacher who expounded, defended, and enforced their deepest religious experiences upon what appeared to be the dominant intellectual methods of their generation. There were also a number of scientific men who had not passed through a definitely Christian discipline, and who called themselves agnostic, but who yearned to receive from the methods they avowed gifts to the religious side of their nature, and a number of these also felt that what they needed they got from Drummond. Then, too, devout and poetic souls who rejoice in Nature as the sacrament and divine expression of spiritual truth, welcomed the book as though it were a consummate interpretation of this. And finally, there were crowds of commonplace men and women who were touched by neither the poetic nor the scientific spirit, but who were in need of the pure comfort, the shrewd counsel, and the lofty ideals in which the volume is rich, or who in their weariness of the world rested simply in its pure light and peace.

Of all these classes, illustrations may be given from the heap of letters which the author of *Natural Law* received from every part of the world. To his biographer, who has gone through them, these letters have brought an almost overwhelming impression of the hunger of this generation for religion and the spiritual life. Next to Drummond's experiences during the Great Mission of 1873–75, this correspondence must have helped to develop his wonderful expertness in dealing with the men and women of his time in their religious needs and aspirations.

The first letter we may take is one of scores of its kind. The writer gives her name and address in a town of New York State. The date is late, December 9, 1893, but Drummond had received many similar tokens within a year of the publication of the book.

'I know you are a grand good man, while I am only a poor working-woman; but if you would really care to know, your book has comforted many a weary hour of my life. I have read it over and over again, thoughtfully, and sometimes prayerfully, until I know many of its pages by heart, and so can always have them with me to make me better, more thoughtful of my fellow-men, and more faithful to God. I thank you for giving it to the world, for I may have it to purify my heart and life. Your book is one of my treasures, and has made me realise and believe the most momentous truth that Christ must be in the Christian, and created a longing in my own heart to love Him more and serve Him better.'

Another wrote, echoing beautifully the expressions of many: 'Your book has been a benediction to me;' and numbers traced to it their conversion from wild and profligate lives, or from a careless and formal Christianity. The late Mr. Campbell Finlayson, in sending to Drummond his very able criticism of the volume, added that it 'has interested and stimulated the minds of many who, like myself, are unable to accept some of its conclusions.'

But welcomes more specific than these were given by authorities in the departments both of science and religion. It was one Anglican divine who wrote the article in the *Spectator*. Another said enthusiastically, 'it was the best book he had ever read upon Christian experience.' Several men, well known for their contributions to theology, congratulated Drummond on having placed the argument for the spiritual life upon a sound basis. One wrote thus in June, 1884: —

'I daresay from the seven thousand purchasers of your book on *Natural Law* you have had more letters than you care for, but I trust you will not allow this to deprive me of the pleasure of saying how delighted I have been with it. I feel that you have added

enormously to the avenues of my own spiritual existence, and therefore I warmly thank you for it. I regard the application of your method as most meanful
(*sic*), and think your conclusions impregnable. You
have provided a splendid apparatus of additional
inductive probability to show the existence of a
spiritual world, which to those who are prepared to
accept it must be final. I am not sure, however, of
its effect upon those who start with the denial of its
existence.'

On the part of many men of science the book received an immediate and a cordial welcome. A great
London physician said of it in March, 1884: 'One of
the best books I have ever read — I have given away
six copies of it.' From this side take the following,
written in July, 1883, — about a month after the book
was published, — by one of the foremost authorities in
his own branch of science : —

'MY DEAR SIR, — I have just been reading with
extreme interest your very able and suggestive book,
Natural Law in the Spiritual World, and cannot
refrain from writing you these few words of thanks
for the strengthening of my own convictions, which
you have given me. It is now many years since I felt
that Christianity is not in harmony with the Science
of Nature, and that to commend it to students of
Nature some other mode of presentment was required. Long pondering over the question in my
own case has led me through much difficulty and
doubt and pain to see the matter just as you see it,
and I can hardly say how glad I am to find these
notions, or rather convictions, so clearly and convin-
cingly set forth as they are in your work. I believe
your book will be of inestimable value to many a
troubled and distracted soul. Living as I did for

many years a somewhat lonely life in the country, practically cut off from personal converse with fellow-workers, I yet was well aware that materialistic views of life were rampant amongst biologists, but until I came to —— to reside I was hardly prepared to find materialism so victorious. And yet among the many positivists with whom I have recently come in contact, there is much doubt and restlessness. Their religion of death and annihilation is not a religion of peace. And I have been quite touched by the avidity with which they will listen to any argument that seems to open for them a possible means of escape from their melancholy conclusion. One of my students, who called for me last Sunday evening, told me, with the tears in his eyes, that he would fain believe as his mother taught him, but that his scientific training would not let him. It is very sad to think how many hearts are breaking — how many souls are being eclipsed all around one. But the dawn, I feel assured, is breaking. I do not know any thoughtful Agnostic who does not doubt his own conclusions, and who would not readily escape them if he could. Such a book as yours will appeal with great force to all such, and it will give me the greatest pleasure to recommend it to every thoughtful biologist I encounter.'

These typical letters, which represent the kind of effect the book so suddenly produced, I give without the names of the authors, for some of them are dead, and some who live may no longer adhere to the opinions they then expressed. It is remarkable, indeed, how many, both on the evangelical and the scientific sides of life, at first welcomed the book as a proof of religion and a reconciliation of her claims with those of science, but afterwards fell away from this opinion.

Besides the gratitude which a book wins from those

whom it has helped in the hard struggle of head or
heart, there are two other standards by which its
power may be measured — the serious criticism which
it calls forth from philosophic minds, and the fascination it creates upon all the restless race of faddists,
quacks, 'cranks,' and monomaniacs in general. *Natural Law in the Spiritual World* triumphantly passed
both of these tests.

To take the latter first — I suppose Drummond had
more correspondence with theorists and with dreamers
than any other author of our generation. Their name
was legion. A number hailed him with eerie joy as a
fellow-spirit. They have been working, they write, for
years in the same direction; they have reached the
same conclusions by 'electro-biology,' 'medical psychology,' 'mind-healing,' 'Christian science,' 'interpretation of prophecy,' and I know not what else, and
they are eager to point out defects and omissions in
Drummond's arguments which can be repaired only
by their peculiar methods. They are generally retired
army officers, doctors without practice, dreamy school-
mistresses, lonely squatters. Some are retired profli-
gates, into whose minds, swept empty of vice but also
destitute of principle, the devils of vanity, curiosity,
audacity, paradox, and unreason appear to have rushed
with riotous vigour. One extraordinary letter comes
from a man who describes himself as 'fifty-nine years
of age, converted at fifty-six from a life of sensuality,'
and now recovering health and social usefulness
through 'Christian Science,' to which he welcomes
Drummond as a powerful adherent. Some offer the
author an additional chapter in which his principle is
applied to the phenomena of reproduction. Others
tell him that he has sinned by forgetting the tri-
partite constitution of man, and disclose to him three

analogies of life where he has discovered only two.
And, of course, there are more than one — fortunately
far away in Australia and the Western States of
America — who propose marriage to him.   It is all a
curious chapter in the history of human delusions.

Of a different class are those who claim Drummond's adhesion to their own denomination or particular heresy.   It was very natural that Swedenborgians
should assert that many of his positions have been anticipated in 'the divine correspondences' of their master; and no doubt they were right in pointing out
that the Swedenborg's method of working down from
the spiritual to the physical was preferable to Drummond's of working up from the physical to the spiritual.   A similar claim with even more justice was
made by the disciples of James Hinton.   It was
equally natural for those Christians who believe in
the theory of conditional immortality — that short
cut through many mazes — to read *Natural Law* as a
corroboration of their creed.   Perhaps the greatest
number of letters which Drummond received upon
his volume came from such promoters of the application to the future life of the doctrine of 'the survival
of the fittest.'   Then the foes of ' Bibliolatry,' as they
call it, congratulate him on having removed religion
from a Scriptural basis, though they 'look with suspicion upon his employment of so many texts' to illustrate his arguments.

The letters which criticise omissions in *Natural
Law* are not only proofs of the unreasonableness
of the writers, but form an impressive tribute to the
power of a volume which could evoke such colossal
expectations of what its author might have done, had
he willed, in meeting the intellectual demands of his
age.   Many blame him for not settling all the great

problems of religion and life. Upon a number of these problems some letters dwell with an ignorance and a hunger which pathetically reveal how much intellectual starvation may linger in our midst within sight and touch of the rich supplies that it desperately supposes do not exist. A squatter, writing from 'the lonely wilds of the Australian bush,' thanks Drummond for 'a great intellectual treat,' but angrily asks him, — with pretty much the same petulance as a savage beats his fetich or a mediæval churchman used to sulk at his saint, — why he has not settled other difficulties. Why has he not dealt with 'the atrocities of the Old Testament,'[1] 'with the miracles of the New,' 'with the virgin birth of Christ,' 'with the ultimate fate of the heathen,'— and so forth. The same questions followed Drummond wherever he lectured during the next ten years and were sent up on scraps of paper to every platform on which he appeared. 'What is your theory of the Atonement?' 'Can you explain it on the principles of your volume?' 'What place do you leave for free will?' 'Does man's immortality depend on the gift of free grace?' 'Why were the Jews, on your theory, specially selected by God?' 'Why was Jesus Christ born a Jew?' Every kind of question, soluble and insoluble, relevant and irrelevant to the volume, was thrown at the head of the author. But with some pertinence the questions on free will and 'conditional immortality' far outnumber all the rest.

The many gleams of reasonable objections to *Natural Law* which these letters and questions reveal were formulated with great ability, in a number of serious articles and pamphlets, the long list of which, though they are in the main hostile, bear unmistakable tribute to the impression made by the book on

[1] See below, p. 400.

the mind of our generation. Appended is a catalogue of the greater number.[1] The most able and effective are the treatises by Mr. Campbell Finlayson and 'a Brother of the Natural Man.' I do not know who wrote the article in the *British Quarterly;* that in the *Church Quarterly* was, though generally hostile to Drummond's logic, by Mr. Lyttleton, the author of the previous article in the *Spectator* which had so largely helped to lift the book into fame.

But, from the first, *Natural Law* encountered more than criticism of this honest and able kind. No volume of our time has provoked more bitter and passionate blame. It roused both the *odium theologicum* and that which is scarcely less savage, the *odium scien-*

---

[1] 1. *Biological Religion;* an essay in criticism of 'Natural Law in the Spiritual World.' By T. Campbell Finlayson. London: Simpkin, Marshall, & Co. Bd. 2*s.*

2. *On 'Natural Law in the Spiritual World';* by a Brother of the Natural Man. Paisley: Gardner. Paper, 1*s.*

3. *Drifting Away.* Remarks on Professor Drummond's 'Natural Law in the Spiritual World.' By the Hon. Philip Carteret Hill, D.C.L. London: Bemrose & Sons, 6*d.*

4. *'Natural Law in the Spiritual World' Examined.* By W. Woods Smyth. London: Elliott Stock. Bd. 1*s.* 6*d.*

5. *Remarks* on a book entitled 'Natural Law in the Spiritual World.' Being the Substance of Four Lectures given in London by Benjamin Wills Newton. London: Houlston & Sons. Paper 1*s.* 9*d.*

6. *A Critical Analysis of Drummond's 'Natural Law in the Spiritual World.'* With a Reply to some of its conclusions. By E. C. Larned. Chicago: Janson, M'Clurg & Co.

7. *Review of 'Natural Law in the Spiritual World.'* By J. B. Fry.

8. *Drummond and Miracles.* A Critique on 'Natural Law in the Spiritual World.' Paisley: Gardner. 1*s.*

9. *The Laws of Nature and the Laws of God.* A Reply to Professor Drummond by Samuel Cockburn, M.D., L.R.C.S.E. London: Swan Sonnenschein. Bd. 3*s.* 6*d.*

10. *Mr. Drummond's Book.* With special references to Biogenesis. Shrewsbury: Adnitt & Naunton. 6*d.*

11. *Are Laws the Same in the Natural and Spiritual Worlds?* By A. C. Denholm. Kilmarnock: Herald Office. 2*d.*

12. *Are the Natural and Spiritual Worlds One in Law?* By George F. Magoun, D.D., Iowa College. Reprinted from the *Bibliotheca Sacra.*

Besides articles in the *Church Quarterly* for January, 1884, and in the *British Quarterly.*

tificum. An 'Old Man,' signing himself 'Agnostic' and writing from the Athenæum, flings in Drummond's face the differences of doctrine among Christians, assails him with quotations from Schopenhauer, and rails at him for daring to believe either in a revelation, or a spiritual world, or a God. 'The whole thing is an enigma beyond the grasp of the human intellect!' On the religious side there arose a most extraordinary irritation. Certain evangelicals caught at the statement on page 30 of *Natural Law*, that it (religion) has not yet been placed on that basis which would make them (many of its positions) impregnable. They took this as meaning that Drummond did not recognise the authority of the Bible as the witness of God's most gracious dealings with the race, whereas what he meant by 'religion' in the sentence they quoted was not the teaching of the Bible, but the experiences of the Christian believer. These, he felt, had been treated in too loose a way; he examined them as facts, and attempted to explain the laws by which they are governed. Sheer misunderstanding of this provoked many to virulent attacks upon him. They withdrew from religious associations of which he was a member; they would not speak from the same platform; they published pamphlets against him, and wrote him bitter and contemptuous letters. They said, 'He founds religion upon science, and to do so is to be an infidel.' It was extraordinary how they succeeded in poisoning against him the minds of a number of people with whom he had shared the work of the Great Mission of 1873–75. There were hot controversies in many evangelistic committees as to whether he should be asked to conferences and conventions; and some societies cancelled their invitations to him to lecture. One religious paper, which had reported his work with

Moody, and to which he had often contributed, not only styled *Natural Law* a dangerous book, but gave orders to its reporters at a large convention in America not to take down anything that Henry Drummond might say.   His services as an evangelist, his character and influence, the great amount of positive Christian doctrine that he taught, were all ignored by these hot hunters of a fancied heresy.   They would have been (from their own point of view) more profitably occupied in proving it a fallacy.   But this none of them seemed to see.   Drummond met all attacks upon him with great good temper; and where the assailants were old comrades in religious work, or had any other right to be answered — and even in many cases where they had no right to be answered at all — he replied with gentleness and courtesy.   One never heard him say a word against the most violent of his opponents.   But of his temper towards his critics there will be more to say in connection with his later works.

A few lines may be added upon the vogue which *Natural Law in the Spiritual World* enjoyed upon the Continent of Europe.

Within a very short time after its publication in England reviews of it appeared in religious and literary journals in France, Germany, and Scandinavia. But the news of its religious value was more widely scattered over these countries, as well as in Holland, Italy, and Russia, by private correspondence.   In a year or two requests for permission to translate it were received by Drummond from every land in Europe except Turkey and Greece.   There are two translations into German,[1] the earlier of which appeared in 1886.   In 1885 the French edition was ready, and by

---

[1] The first was published through the Hinrichs'sche Buchhandlung of Leipzig, *Das Naturgesetz in der Geisteswelt,* and had a large circulation; the other, by

1887 Danish, Dutch, and Swedish translations were published.

The book appears to have excited the greatest attention in Germany, Scandinavia, and Russia, if we may judge both from the letters Drummond received, and the number of pamphlets published, in the language of these countries, both in defence of the book, and in controversy with its main positions. It is almost superfluous to give a *résumé* of these letters and pamphlets; in substance they reflect the British and American letters summarised above. They contain the same fervent testimonies from individuals who have been lifted to faith and a better life; the same inquiries from evangelical Christians as to Drummond's attitude to the doctrines of Christianity; the same bitter attacks upon his belief in evolution; the same solid discussions of his argument; and the same eerie ejaculations of sympathy and welcome from persons who believe they have found in him a prophet for their particular 'revelations,' and 'systems of thought.' One Swede begs Drummond to tell him how exactly the manifestations of new truth which *Natural Law* contains were let down from heaven.[1] There are letters of gratitude and inquiry from several of the Russian sects. Some sign themselves 'disciples' and 'devoted adherents.' In Germany, as in England, though of course in less proportion, a

Velhagen Klasing of Berlin, reached by 1897 a circulation of 4000. It was done by Miss Julie Sutter, to whom also was intrusted the German translation of Drummond's Christmas addresses.

[1] 'Do tell me if you have holy treasures lying by, containing sacred *revelations* from the realms above? You *must* have them, or you could not have written as you have written. . . . You must, like Daniel and other great seers, have seen visions; you must have been introduced, "whether in the body or in the spirit," into the far regions of spiritual spheres. If I dare ask you these questions, it is because I do not hesitate to tell you it has only been through such means that I have formed my opinions, and only through some *special grace* that I believe you could have come to such clearness.' There are nine pages of this.

R

small literature appeared both of articles and pamphlets, and — one symptom among many others — a new magazine, to which many good names were attached, promised in its prospectus to give an ' exakt-naturwissenschaftliche Seelenanalyse (nach Art Drummond's).' The book does not appear to have impressed any German authorities in Natural Science in Germany as upon its first appearance it did impress some such in England. But it received attention from theologians; and many capable writers discussed it seriously and with respect. Their hostile criticism was largely on the lines on which criticism had been directed in Great Britain. It is summed up by Dr. Otto Zöckler — a scholar and a thinker of repute as well in this country as in his own — in the following words : —

'One may grant that the criticism of Drummond, which has appeared in quite a considerable number of pamphlets and articles, has given expression to much that is correct. Such an acknowledgement, however, must not be allowed to mislead us into ignoring the high value of the healthy stimulus which has proceeded from Drummond's writings. If several English critics have complained of Drummond's "evolutionist gospel" as scarcely different from ordinary Darwinism, and as issuing in "Entwickelungsunglauben" (development-infidelity) [sic], there is not only strong exaggeration in such a complaint, but also disregard of the fact that the Glasgow scholar has several times expressed himself — especially in *The Ascent of Man* — against the unlimited validity of the Darwinian principle of the "Struggle for Existence." And if one of the German critics — Oberpastor Dr. Joh. Lütkens, of Riga, in the brochure *Henry Drummond's Traktate gewürdigt in drei Briefen an eine Freundin*[1] (which, we may remark in passing, is one of the most solid we know) — has found fault with the Pelagian tendency of Drummond's

[1] Riga, Hoerschelmann, 1891.

ethic (das Pelagianisierende der Drummondschen Ethik), its mitigation (Verflachung) of the conception of sin, and its disregard of God's free pardoning grace in Christ, he does so only by ignoring the profound manner in which the greater [1] work of the noble Scotsman speaks of the necessity of the new birth. He forgets that the individual's utter inability to deliver himself from the yoke of sin and of death is for Drummond a fact of fundamental importance, and that, when Drummond takes the field against the superficial and shallow (am Peripherischen haftende) modes of thought of one-sided modern moralists, he at the same time declares war against Pelagianism.'

[1] *I.e.* than his booklets.

CHAPTER X

EVOLUTION AND REVELATION

MUCH of the hostile criticism of *Natural Law* which has been described in the last chapter turned upon the question of Drummond's attitude to the relations of science and religion, and upon the view which he took of the authority of the Bible. Upon those topics, he published, soon after his return from Africa, three articles, two in the *Expositor* for 1885,[1] on the 'Contribution of Science to Christianity,' and one in the *Nineteenth Century* for February, 1886, on 'Mr. Gladstone and Genesis.' The growth of his opinions cannot be sufficiently traced without some quotations from these : —

The former articles open with a beautiful introduction, which describes the expansion, by modern science, of 'the intellectual area of Christianity,' and the power of Christianity to assimilate new facts without either false hopes or false fears.

'It knows it can approve itself to science, but it has been taken by surprise, and therefore begs time. It will honestly look up its credentials and adjust itself, if necessary, to the new relation. Now this is the position of theology at the present moment. And theology proceeds by asking science what it demands, and then borrows its instruments to carry out the improvements. The loan of the instruments constitutes the first great contribution of science to religion. What are these instruments? We shall name two — the Scientific Method and the Doctrine of Evolution. The first is the

[1] Third Series, Vol. I.

instrument for the interpretation of nature; the second is given us as the method of nature itself. With the first of these we shall deal formally; the second will present itself in various shapes as we proceed.'

After stating that science has had no exclusive right to the use of the scientific method, but that theologians have employed it again and again, Drummond says that the things on which the method insists are chiefly two — the value of facts and the value of laws. 'On bare facts science from first to last is based. Now if Christianity possesses anything, it possesses facts. So long as the facts were presented to the world Christianity spread with marvellous rapidity. But there came a time when the facts were less exhibited to men than the evidence for the facts. Theology, that is to say, began to rest upon authority. . . . Then there came another time when this authority appealed to the secular arm. It is these intermediaries between the facts and the modern observer that stumble science. It will look at facts, and facts alone. The dangers, the weakness, the unpracticableness in some cases of this method are well known. Nevertheless, it is a right method. It is the method of all Reformation; it was the method of the Reformation. . . .

'Now Christianity is learning from science to go back to its facts, and it is going back to facts. Critics in every tongue are engaged upon the facts; travellers in every land are unveiling facts; exegetes are at work upon the words, scholars upon the manuscripts; sceptics, believing and unbelieving, are eliminating the not-facts; and the whole field is alive with workers. And the point to mark is that these men are not manipulating, but verifying, facts.

'There is one portion of this field of facts, however, which is still strangely neglected, and to which a scientific theology may turn its next attention. The evidence for Christianity is not the Evidences. The evidence for Christianity is *a Christian*. The unity of physics is the atom, of biology the cell, of philosophy the man, of theology the Christian. The natural man, his regeneration by the Holy Spirit, the spiritual man and his relations to the world and to God, these are the modern facts for a scientific theology. We may indeed talk

with science on its own terms about the creation of the world,
and the spirituality of nature, and the force behind nature,
and the unseen universe; but our language is not less scientific, not less justified by fact, when we speak of the work of
the risen Christ, and the contemporary activities of the Holy
Ghost, and the facts of regeneration, and the powers which
are freeing men from sin. There is a great experiment
which is repeated every day, the evidence for which is as
accessible as for any fact of science; its phenomena are
as palpable as any in nature; its processes are as explicable,
or as inexplicable; its purpose is as clear; and yet science
has never been seriously asked to reckon with it, nor has
theology ever granted it the place its impressive reality demands. One aim of a scientific theology will be to study
conversion and restore to Christianity the most powerful
witness. . . .

'But not less essential, in the scientific method, than the
examination of facts, is the arrangement of them under laws.
And the work of modern science in this direction has resulted
in its grandest achievement — the demonstration of the uniformity of nature. This doctrine must have an immediate
effect upon the entire system of theology. For one thing,
the contribution of the spiritual world to the uniformity of
nature has yet to be made. Not that the natural world is to
include the spiritual, but that a higher natural will be seen
to include both. . . .

'There may be laws, or actings, in the spiritual world, which
it may seem to some impossible to include in such a scheme.
God is not, in theology, a Creator merely, but a father; and
according to the counsel of His own will He may act in
different cases in different ways. To which the reply is that
this also is law. It is the law of the Father, the law of the
paternal relation, the law of the free-will; yet not an exceptional law, it is the law of all fathers, of all free-wills.
Besides, if in the private Christian life the child of God
finds dealings which are not reducible to law, grant even their
lawlessness if that be possible, that is a family matter, a relation of parent and child, similar to the earthly relation, and
scarcely the kind of case to be referred to science. Into

ordinary family relations science rarely feels called to intrude ; and it is obvious that in dealing with this class of cases in the spiritual world, science is attempting a thing which in the natural world it leaves alone.   If ethics chooses to take up these questions, it has more right to do so; but that there should be a reserve in the spiritual world for God acting towards His children in a way past finding out is what would be expected from the mere analogies of the family. . . .

'The relations of the spiritual man, however, are not all, or nearly all, in this department.   There are whole classes of facts in the outer provinces which have yet to be examined and arranged under appropriate laws.   The intellectual gain to Christianity of such a process will be obvious.   But there is also a practical gain to the religious experience of not less moment.   Science is nothing if not practical, and the scientific method has little for Christianity after all if it is not to exalt and enrich the lives of its followers.   It is worth while, therefore, taking a single example of its practical value.

'The sense of lawlessness which pervades the spiritual world at present reacts in many subtle and injurious ways upon the personal experience of Christians.   They gather the idea that things are managed differently there from anywhere else — less strictly, less consistently; that blessings or punishments are dispensed arbitrarily ; and that everything is ordered rather by a Divine discretion than by a system of fixed principle.   In this higher atmosphere ordinary sequences are not to be looked for — cause and effect are suspended or superseded.   Accordingly, to descend to the particular, men pray for things which they are quite unable to receive, or altogether unwilling to pay the price for.   They expect effects without touching the preliminary causes, and causes without calculating the tremendous nature of the effects.   There is nothing more appalling than the wholesale way in which unthinking people plead to the Almighty for the richest and most spiritual of His promises, and claim their immediate fulfilment, without themselves fulfilling one of the conditions either on which they are promised or can possibly be given.   If the Bible is closely looked into, it will probably be found that very many of the promises have attached to them a condition—itself not infrequently the best part of the promise. True prayer for any promise is to plead for power to fulfil the condition on which it is offered, and which, being fulfilled, is in that act given. We have need, certainly in this sense, to know more of prayer and natural law. And science could make no truer contribution to modern Christianity than to enforce upon us all, as unweariedly as in nature, the law of causation in the spiritual life. The reason why so many people get nothing from prayer is that they expect effects without causes; and this also is the reason why they give it up. It is not irreligion that makes men give up prayer, but the uselessness of their prayers.

'One other gain,' he continues, 'may be expected to Christianity from the wider use of the scientific method. It must attract an ever-increasing band of workers to theology. . . . We are warned sometimes that this method has dangers, and told not to carry it too far. . . . The danger arises, not from the use of the scientific method, but from its use apart from the scientific spirit. For these two are not quite the same. Some use the scientific method, but not in the scientific spirit. And as science can help Christianity with the former, Christianity may perhaps do something for science as regards the latter. And so just is the remark of "Natural Religion" that the true scientific spirit and the Christian spirit are one, that the Christian world is probably prepared to accept almost anything the most advanced theology brings, provided it be a joint product of the scientific method with the scientific spirit—the fearlessness and originality of the one tempered by the modesty, caution, and reverence of the other.

'To preserve this confidence and to keep this spirit pure is a sacred duty. There is an intellectual covetousness abroad just now which is neither the fruit nor the friend of a scientific age—a haste to be wise, which, like the haste to be rich, leads men into speculation upon indifferent securities, and can only end in fallen fortunes. Theology must not be bound up with such speculation. . . .[1] The one safeguard is to use the intellectual method in sympathetic association with the moral

[1] Here comes a fine quotation from Bacon's *Works*, v. 132, 133.

spirit. The scientific method may bring to light many fresh and revolutionary ideas; the scientific spirit will see that they are not given a place as dogmas in their first exuberance; that they are held with caution and abandoned with generosity on sufficient evidence. . . .

'So much for the scientific method. Let us now consider for a moment one or two of its achievements. . . .

'Itself at an elementary stage, we should be wrong to look [to it] for any very pronounced contribution as yet to the higher truths of religion. We should expect the first effect among the elements of religion. We should expect science to be fairly decided in its utterances about them, to become more and more hesitating as it runs up the range of Christian doctrine, and gradually to lapse into silence. Proceeding upon this principle, we should go back at once to Genesis. We should begin with the beginnings, and expect the first serious contribution to theology on the doctrine of creation.

'And what do we find? We find that upon this subject of all others science has most to offer us. It comes to us, not only freighted with vast treasures of newly noticed facts, but with a theory which by many thoughtful minds has been accepted as the method of creation. And, more than this, it tells us candidly it has failed — and the failures of science are among its richest contributions to Christianity — it has failed to discover any clue to the ultimate mystery of origins, any clue which can compete for a moment with the view of theology.

'Consider first this impressive silence of science on the question of origins. Who creates or evolves; whither do the atoms come or go? These questions remain as before. Science has not found a substitute for God. And yet, in another sense, these questions are very different from before. Science has put them through its crucible. It took them from theology, and deliberately proclaimed that it would try to answer them. They are now handed back, tried, unanswered, but with a new place in theology and a new power with science. . . . If there are answers to these questions, and there ought to be, theology holds them. . . . In its investigations of these questions science has made a discovery. It has seen plainly that atheism is unscientific. It is a remarkable thing that, after trailing its black length for centuries across European thought, atheism should have had its doom pronounced by science. With its most penetrating gaze science has now looked at the back of phenomena. It says: "The atheist tells us there is nothing there. We cannot believe him. We cannot tell what it is, but there is certainly something. Agnostics we may be, we can no longer be atheists." '

He illustrates this by the passages from Huxley's *Lay Sermons*, quoted above in Chapter VI.[1]

'When we turn now to the larger question of the creation of the world itself, we find much more than silence, or a permission to go on. We find science has a definite theory on that subject. It offers, in short, to theology a doctrine of the method of creation in its hypothesis of evolution. That this doctrine is proved yet, no one will assert. That in some of its forms it is never likely to be proved, many are convinced. It will be time for theology to be unanimous about it when science is unanimous about it. Yet it would be idle to deny that in a general form it has received the widest assent from theology. But if science is satisfied, even in a general way, with its theory of the method of creation, "assent" is a cold word for theology to welcome it with. It is needless at this time of day to point out the surpassing grandeur of the new conception. How it has filled the Christian imagination and kindled to enthusiasm the soberest scientific minds is known to all. For that splendid hypothesis we cannot be too grateful to science, and that theology can only enrich itself which gives it even temporary place. There is a sublimity about the old doctrine of creation — we are speaking of its scientific aspects — which, if one could compare sublimities, is not surpassed by the new ; but there is also a baldness. . . . The doctrine of evolution fills a gap at the very beginning of our religion ; and no one who looks now at the transcendant spectacle of the world's past, as disclosed by science, will deny that it has filled it worthily. Yet, after all, its beauty is not the only part of its contribution to Christianity. Scientific

[1] P. 150.

theology *required* a new view, though it did not require it to come in so magnificent a form. What it wanted was a credible presentation, in view especially of astronomy, geology, and biology. These had made the former theory simply untenable. And science has supplied theology with a theory which the intellect can accept, and which for the devout mind leaves everything more worthy of worship than before.'

'We might pass on,' the second lecture begins, 'to mark the effects [of science] upon many other theological truths [than that of creation]. One shall be the doctrine of revelation itself. According to science, as we have already seen, evolution is the method of creation. Now, creation is a form of revelation; it is the oldest form, the most accessible, the most universal, and still an ever-increasing source of theological truth.

'If, then, science, familiar with this revelation, and knowing it to be an evolution, were to be told of the existence of another revelation — an inspired word — it would expect that this other revelation would also be an evolution. Such an anticipation might or might not be justified; but from the law of the uniformity of nature there would be, to the man of science, a very strong presumption in favour of any revelation which bore this scientific hallmark, which indicated, that is to say, that God's Word had unfolded itself to men, like His works.

'Now if science searches the field of theology for an additional revelation, it will find a Bible awaiting it — a Bible in two forms. The one is the Bible as it was presented to our forefathers; the other is the Bible of modern theology. The books, the chapters, the verses, and the words are the same in each; yet in form they are two entirely different Bibles. To science the difference is immediately palpable. Judging of each of them from its own standpoint, science perceives, after a brief examination, that the distinction between them is one with which it has been long familiar. In point of fact, the one is constructed, like the world, according to the old cosmogonies, while the other is an evolution. The one represents revelation as having been produced on the creative hypothesis, the Divine-fiat hypothesis, the ready-made hypoth-

esis; the other on the slow-growth or evolution theory. It
is at once obvious which of them science would prefer — it
could no more accept the first than it could accept the ready-
made theory of the universe.

'Nothing could be more important than to assure science
that the same difficulty has for some time been felt, and with
quite equal keenness, by theology. The scientific method in
its hard, scientific theology has been laboriously working at
a reconstruction of biblical truth from this very view-point of
development. And it no more pledges itself to-day to the interpretations of the Bible of a thousand years ago than does
science to the interpretations of nature in the time of Pythagoras. Nature is the same to-day as in the time of Pythagoras, and the Bible is the same to-day as a thousand years ago.
But the Pythagorean interpretation of nature is not less objectionable to the modern mind than are many ancient interpretations of the Scriptures to the scientific theologian.

'The supreme contribution of Evolution to Religion is that
it has given it a clearer Bible. Science is the great explainer,
the great expositor, not only of nature, but of everything it
touches. Its function is to arrange things and make them
reasonable. And it has arranged the Bible in a new way,
and made it as different as science has made the world. It
is not going too far to say that there are many things in the
Bible which are hard to reconcile with our ideas of a just and
good God. This is only expressing what even the most devout and simple minds constantly feel, and feel to be sorely
perplexing, in reading especially the Old Testament. But
these difficulties arise simply from an old-fashioned or unscientific view of what the Bible is, and are similar to the
difficulties found in nature when interpreted either without
the aid of science, or with the science of many centuries ago.
We see now that the mind of man has been slowly developing, that the race has been gradually educated, and that
revelation has been adapted from the first to the various and
successive stages through which that development passed.

'The moral difficulties of the Old Testament are admittedly
great. But when approached from the new standpoint, when
they are seen to be rudiments of truth spoken and acted in

strange ways to attract and teach children, they vanish one by one. For instance, we are told that the iniquities of the fathers are to be visited upon the children unto the third and fourth generation. The impression upon the early mind undoubtedly must have been that this was a solemn threat which God would carry out in anger in individual cases. We now know, however, that this is simply the doctrine of heredity. A child inherits its parents' nature, not as a special punishment, but by natural law. In those days that could not be explained. Natural law was a word unknown, and the truth has to be put provisionally in a form that all could understand. And even many of the miracles may have explanations in fact or in principle, which, without destroying the idea of the miraculous, may show the naturalness of the supernatural.

'The theory of the Bible, which makes belief in a revelation possible to the man of science, Christianity owes to the scientific method. It is not suggested that the evolution theory in theology was introduced to satisfy the mind of the scientific thinker, any more than that his appreciation of it is the test of its truth. As regards the latter, it is to be weighed on its own evidence and judged by its fruits; and as regards the question of origin, its ancestry is much more reputable, for it was not a concession to any theory, but rose out of the facts themselves. Indeed, long before evolution was formulated in science, discerning minds had seen, with an enthusiasm which few could at that time share, the slow, steady, upward growth of theological truth to ever higher and nobler forms. . . . [He here quotes John Henry Newman on the development of theology.] However physical science may have contributed to this result, it is certain that the method is not the creation of science. . . .

'Evolution is the ever-recurring theme in theology as in nature. We might indeed almost have grouped the entire contribution of science to Christianity around this point. No truth now can remain unaffected by evolution. Evolution has given to theology some wholly new departments. It has given to it a vastly more reasonable body of truth about God and man, about sin and salvation. It has lent it a firmer base, an enlarged horizon, and a wider faith.   But its great contribution, on which all these depend, is to the doctrine of revelation.

' What, then, does this mean for revelation?   It means, in plain language, that Evolution has given Christianity a new Bible.   Its peculiarity is that in its form it is like the world in which it is found.   It is a word, but its root is now known, and we have other words from the same root.   Its substance is still the unchanged language of heaven, yet it is written in a familiar tongue.   The new Bible is a book whose parts, though not of unequal value, are seen to be of different kinds of value, where the casual is distinguished from the essential, the local from the universal, the subordinate from the primal end.   This Bible is not a book which has been made; it has grown.   Hence it is no longer a mere word-book, nor a compendium of doctrines, but a nursery of growing truths.   It is not an even plane of proof texts without proportion, or emphasis, or light and shade; but a revelation varied as nature, with the divine in its hidden parts, in its spirit, its tendencies, its obscurities, and its omissions.   Like nature, it has successive strata, and valley and hilltop, and mist and atmosphere, and rivers which are flowing still, and here and there a place which is desert, and fossils too, whose crude forms are the stepping-stones to higher things.   It is a record of inspired deeds as well as of inspired words, an ascending series of inspired facts in a matrix of human history.

' Now it is to be marked that this is not the product of any destructive movement, nor is this transformed book in any sense a mutilated Bible.   All this has taken place, it may be, without the elimination of a book or the loss of an important word.   It is simply the transformation by a method whose main warrant is that the book lends itself to it.

' It may be said, and for a time it will continue to be said, that the Christian does not need a transformed Bible; and fortunately, or in some cases unfortunately, this is the case. For years yet the old Bible will continue to nourish the soul of the Church, as it has nourished it in the past; and the needy heart will in all time manage to feed itself apart from any forms.   But there is a class, and an ever-increasing class,

to whom the form is much.   Theology is only beginning to
realise how radical is the change in mental attitude of those
who have learned to think from science.   Intercourse with
the ways of nature breeds a mental attitude of its own.   It is
an attitude worthy of its master.   In this presence the student
is face to face with what is real.   He is looking with his own
eyes at facts, at what God did.   He finds things in nature
just as its Maker left them; and from ceaseless contact with
phenomena which will not change for man, and with laws
which he has never known to swerve, he fears to trust his mind
to anything less.   Now this Bible which has been described
is the presentation to this age of men who have learned this
habit.   They have studied the facts; they have looked with
their own eyes at what God did; and they are giving us a
book which is more than the devout man's Bible, though it is
as much as ever the devout man's Bible.   It is the apologist's
Bible.   It is long since the apologist has had a Bible.   The
Bible of our infancy was not an apologist's Bible.   There are
things in the Old Testament cast in his teeth by sceptics to
which he has simply no answer.   These are the things, the
miserable things, the masses have laid hold of.   They are the
stock-in-trade to-day of the free-thought platform and the
secularist pamphleteer.   And, surprising as it is, there are not
a few honest seekers who are made timid and suspicious, not a
few on the outskirts of Christianity who are kept from coming
farther in, by the half-truths which a new exegesis, a reconsideration of the historic setting, and a clearer view of the
moral purposes of God would change from barriers into bul-
warks of the faith.   Such a Bible scientific theology is giving
us, and it cannot be proclaimed to the mass of the people too
soon.   It is no more fair to raise and brandish objections to
the Bible without first studying carefully what scientific theologians have to say on the subject, than it would be fair for
one who derived his views of the natural world from
Pythagoras to condemn all science.   It is expected in criticisms of science that the critic's knowledge should at least be
up to date, that he is attacking what science really holds, and
the same justice is to be awarded to the science of theology.
When science makes its next attack upon theology, if indeed

that shall ever be again, it will find an armament, largely
furnished by itself, which has made the Bible as impregnable
as nature.

'One question, finally, will determine the ultimate worth of
this contribution to Christianity. Does it help it practically?
Does it impoverish or enrich the soul? Does it lower or exalt
God? These questions, with regard to one or two of the
elementary truths of religion, have been partially answered
already. But a closing illustration from the highest of all
will show that here also science is not silent.

'Science has nothing finer to offer Christianity than the
exaltation of its supreme conception — God. Is it too much
to say that in a practical age like the present, when the idea
and practice of worship tend to be forgotten, God should wish
to reveal Himself afresh in ever more striking ways? Is it
too much to say that at this distance from creation, with the
eye of theology resting largely upon the incarnation and work
of the Man Christ Jesus, the Almighty should design with
more and more impressiveness to utter Himself as the Wonderful, the Counsellor, the Great and Mighty God? Whether
this be so or not, it is certain that every step of science
discloses the attributes of the Almighty with a growing
magnificence. . . .'

So much for the *Expositor* articles. About a year
after they were published, Drummond wrote for the
Nineteenth Century a short article entitled ' Mr. Gladstone and Genesis.' It appeared [1] under one on the
same subject by Mr. Huxley. Mr. Gladstone and Mr.
Huxley had been waging a controversy upon the relations between the teaching of Genesis and that of
modern science upon the creation or evolution of life.

In an article on the ' Dawn of Creation and Worship,' Mr. Gladstone committed himself to three propo-
sitions: The first, that, according to the writer of the
Pentateuch, the ' water population,' the ' air population,'
and the ' land population,' of the globe were created

[1] February, 1886.

successively in the order named; the second, that this
has been 'so affirmed in our time by natural science
that it may be taken as a demonstrated conclusion and
established fact;' and the third, that the fact of this
coincidence of the Pentateuchal story with the results
of modern investigation makes it 'impossible to avoid
the conclusion, first, that either this writer was gifted
with faculties passing all human experience, or else his
knowledge was divine.' And accepting, of course, the
second of these alternatives, Mr. Gladstone declared:
'So stands the plea for a revelation of truth from God,
a plea only to be met by questioning its possibility.'

In answer to this, Mr. Huxley had little difficulty in
showing that Mr. Gladstone's second proposition was
'not merely inaccurate, but directly contradictory
of facts known to every one who is acquainted with
the elements of natural science,' and arguing that
therefore the 'third proposition collapses of itself.' In
other words, Mr. Gladstone based his 'plea for a revelation of truth from God' upon the agreement, which
he asserted, of the first chapter of Genesis with the
discoveries of modern science. Mr. Huxley denied
that agreement, and concluded that with it there disappeared all argument for a divine revelation. It was
at this point that Drummond intervened, with the
assertion that the question which the two antagonists
debated, that, namely, of the harmony between Genesis
and modern science, was absolutely irrelevant to the
problem of revelation. On the one side he accepted
Mr. Huxley's statement that it is impossible to harmo-
nise Genesis and science; on the other side, he denied that the contradiction between them was fatal to
the belief that Genesis contains 'a revelation of truth
from God.'

He showed how from the standpoint of the new

s

science of Biblical criticism 'the problem of the reconciliation of Genesis with geology simply disappears.
The question, in fact, is as irrelevant as that of the
Senior Wrangler who asked what Milton's *Paradise
Lost* was meant to prove.' Biblical criticism, he says,[1]
has pronounced the Bible 'to be absolutely free of natural science'—he means, of course, in its modern shape.

'The critics,' he continues in the rest of his article, 'find
there history, poetry, moral philosophy, theology, lives and
letters, mystical, devotional, and didactic pieces; but science
there is none. Natural objects are, of course, repeatedly
referred to, and with unsurpassed sympathy and accuracy of
observation; but neither in the intention of any of the innumerable authors nor in the execution of their work is there
any direct trace of scientific teaching. Could any one with
any historic imagination for a moment expect that there
would have been? There was no science then. Scientific
questions were not even asked then. To have given men
science would not only have been an anachronism, but a
source of mystification and confusion all along the line. The
almost painful silence—indeed, the absolute sterility—of
the Bible with regard to science is so marked as to have led
men to question the very beneficence of God. Why was not
the use of the stars explained to navigators, or chloroform to
surgeons? Why is a man left to die on the hillside when the
medicinal plant which could save him, did he but know it,
lies at his feet? What is it to early man to know how the
moon was made? What he wants to know is how bread is
made. How fish are to be caught, fowls snared, beasts
trapped and their skins tanned—these are his problems.
Doubtless there are valid reasons why the Bible does not
contain a technological dictionary and a pharmacopœia, or
anticipate the *Encyclopædia Britannica.* But that it does not
inform us on these practical matters is surely a valid argument why we should not expect it to instruct the world in
geology. Mr. Huxley is particular to point out to us that the

---

[1] After repeating the paragraphs of his *Expositor* article given above on pp.
251 ff.

bat and the pterodactyle must be classified under the "winged fowl" of Genesis, while at a stretch he believes the cockroach might also be included. But we should not wonder if the narrator did not think of this.

'Scientific men, apparently, need this warning, not less than those whom they punish for neglecting it. How ignorantly, often, the genius of the Bible is comprehended by those who are loudest in their denunciations of its positions otherwise, is typically illustrated in the following passage from Haeckel. Having in an earlier paragraph shown a general harmony between the Mosaic cosmogony and his own theory of creation, he proceeds to extract out of Genesis nothing less than the evolution theory, and that in its last and highest developments : —

'"Two great and fundamental ideas, common also to the non-miraculous theory of development, meet us in this Mosaic hypothesis of creation with surprising clearness and simplicity — the idea of separation or differentiation, and the idea of progressive development or perfecting. Although Moses looks upon the results of the great laws of organic development . . . as the direct actions of a constructing Creator, yet in his theory there lies hidden the ruling idea of a progressive development and a differentiation of the originally simple matter." [1]

'With the next breath this interpreter of Genesis exposes "two great fundamental errors" in the same chapter of the book in which he has just discovered the most scientific phases of the evolution hypothesis, and which lead him to express for Moses "just wonder and admiration." What can be the matter with this singular book ? Why is it science to Haeckel one minute and error the next ? Why are Haeckel and Mr. Huxley not agreed if it is science ? Why are Haeckel and Mr. Gladstone agreed if it is religion ? If Mr. Huxley does not agree with Haeckel, why does he not agree with Mr. Gladstone ?

'George Macdonald has an exquisite little poem called "Baby's Catechism." It occurs among his children's pieces:

[1] Haeckel, *History of Creation*, vol. i. p. 38.

' " Where did you come from, baby dear?
Out of the everywhere into here.

Where did you get your eyes so blue?
Out of the sky as I came through.

Where did you get that little tear?
I found it waiting when I got here.

Where did you get that pearly ear?
God spoke, and it came out to hear.

How did they all just come to be you?
God thought about me and so I grew."

' For its purpose what could be a finer, or even a more true, account of the matter than this? Without a word of literal truth in it, it would convey to the child's mind exactly the right impression. Now conceive of the head nurse banishing it from the nursery as calculated to mislead the children as to the origin of blue eyes. Or imagine the nursery governess, who has passed the South Kensington examination in Mr. Huxley's " Physiology," informing her pupils that ears never "came out" at all, and that hearing was really done inside, by the fibres of Corti and the epithelial arrangements of the maculæ acusticæ. Is it conceivable, on the other hand, that the parish clergyman could defend the record on the ground that "the everywhere" was a philosophical presentation of the Almighty, or that "God thought about me" contained the Hegelian Idea? And yet this is precisely what interpreters of Genesis and interpreters of science do with the Bible. Genesis is a presentation of one or two great elementary truths to the childhood of the world. It can only be read aright in the spirit in which it was written, with its original purpose in view, and its original audience. What did it mean to them? What would they understand by it? What did they need to know and not to know?

' To expand the constructive answers to these questions in detail does not fall within our province here. What we have to note is that a scientific theory of the universe formed no part of the original writer's intention. Dating from the childhood of the world, written for children, and for that child-spirit in man which remains unchanged by time, it takes colour and shape accordingly. Its object is purely religious, the point being, not how certain things were made, but that God made them. It is not dedicated to science, but to the soul. It is a sublime theology, given in view of ignorance or idolatry or polytheism, telling the worshipful youth of the world that the heavens and the earth and every creeping and flying thing were made by God. What world-spirit teaches men to finger its fluid members like a science catalogue, and discuss its days in terms of geological formations? What blindness pursues them, that they mark the things He made only with their museum-labels, and think they have exhausted its contribution when they have never even been within sight of it? This is not even atheism. It is simple illiterateness.

'The first principle which must rule our reading of this book is the elementary canon of all literary criticism, which decides that any interpretation of a part of a book or of a literature must be controlled by the dominant purpose or *motif* of the whole. And when one investigates that dominant purpose in the case of the Bible, he finds it reducing itself to one thing — religion. No matter what view is taken of the composition or authorship of the several books, this feature secures immediate and universal recognition.

' " Mais s'il en est ainsi (says Lenormant), me demandera-t-on peut-être. Où donc voyez-vous l'inspiration divine des écrivains qui ont fait cette archéologie, le secours surnaturel dont, comme chrétien, vous devez les croire guidés? Où? Dans l'esprit absolument nouveau qui anime leur narration, bien que la forme en soit restée presque de tout point la même que chez les peuples voisins." [1]

' A second principle is expressed with such appositeness to the present purpose, by an English commentator, that his words may be given at length : —

' " There is a principle frequently insisted on, scarcely denied by any, yet recognised with sufficient clearness by few of the advocates of revelation, which, if fully and practically recognised, would have saved themselves much perplexity and

[1] *Les Origines de l'Histoire*, Préf., xviii.

vexation, and the cause they have at heart the disgrace with which it has been covered by the futile attempts that have been made, through provisional and shifting interpretations, to reconcile the Mosaic Genesis with the rapidly advancing strides of physical science. The principle referred to is this: matters which are discoverable by human reason, and the means of investigation which God has put within the reach of man's faculties, are not the proper subjects of Divine revelation; and matters which do not concern morals, or bear on man's spiritual relations towards God, are not within the province of revealed religion." [1]

'Here lies the whole matter. It is involved in the mere meaning of revelation, and proved by its whole expression, that its subject-matter is that which men could not find out for themselves. Men could find out the order in which the world was made. What they could not find out was, that God made it. To this day they have not found that out. Even some of the wisest of our contemporaries, after trying to find that out for half a lifetime, have been forced to give it up. Hence the true function of revelation. Nature in Genesis has no link with geology, seeks none and needs none: man has no link with biology, and misses none. What he really needs and really misses — for he can get it nowhere else — Genesis gives him; it links nature and man with their Maker. And this is the one high sense in which Genesis can be said to be scientific. The scientific man must go there to complete his science, or it remains forever incomplete. Let him no longer resort thither to attack what is not really there. What is really there he cannot attack, for he cannot do without it. Nor let religion plant positions there which can only keep science out. Then only can the interpreters of Nature and the interpreters of Genesis understand each other.'

From all this it is apparent how far Drummond had travelled from the positions of the older orthodoxy which he described in the college essay, quoted on pages 46, 47. These positions had been the intel-

1 Quarry, *Genesis*, pp. 12, 13.

lectual basis of the Christian faith for centuries. To question them seemed to many to be treason; to abandon them, madness. But Drummond was forced from them by his study of facts in the departments of natural science and of Biblical criticism and Biblical theology. And upon the new positions to which he was led he has evidently found a basis for his faith more stable than ever the older was imagined to be, richer mines of Christian experience and truth, better vantage grounds for preaching the gospel of Christ, and loftier summits, with infinitely wider prospects of the power of God and of the destiny of man.

Drummond's exposition of revelation, as also an evolution, needs to be supplemented by only one remark, which, when he wrote his articles it was not possible to make with confidence. Recent researches into the origins of the Old Testament have proved that the factor in the extraordinary development of moral and religious truth, which is so discernible in the history of Israel and in their gradual ascent to the loftiest heights of spiritual knowledge from the low levels of life which they had once occupied with their Semitic neighbours, was the impression upon the people as a whole through the wonderful deeds of their history and the experience of their greatest minds of the *character* of God. But to impress the character of God upon a people so sensitive and so responsive is revelation in its purest and most effective form.

CHAPTER XI

1884-1890

THE PROFESSORSHIP AT GLASGOW—THE GROSVENOR HOUSE ADDRESSES—ASSOCIATED WORKERS' LEAGUE—POLITICS AND HOME RULE FOR IRELAND—REFUSAL TO STAND FOR PARLIAMENT—SWITZERLAND—HIS FATHER'S DEATH—FIRST ATTEMPTS AT THE *ASCENT OF MAN*—SECOND SERIES OF GROSVENOR HOUSE ADDRESSES—THE '88 CLUB—SWITZERLAND AND VENICE—MEETING WITH BROWNING—COLLEGE SETTLEMENTS—PREPARATIONS FOR AUSTRALIA—OPINIONS ON MEN, BOOKS, AND MOVEMENTS

SOON after he returned from Africa Henry Drummond was promoted by the Church to the status of a Professor of Theology.

In April, 1883, Mr. James Stevenson, of Largs, had offered to the Free Church funds sufficient for a considerable increase of the salary of the Science Lecturer in Glasgow College, provided that the office was raised to an equal rank with that of the four Professors who formed the Senate. The General Assembly of 1883 accepted Mr. Stevenson's offer, and remitted the proposal of the Professorship to the Presbyteries. By a majority of four to one these decided in its favour, and by 260 votes to 167 the General Assembly of 1884 'enacted and ordained that the Theological Faculty of Glasgow shall consist of five professors instead of four, the additional professor being a professor of Natural Science.' The title was interpreted in the same sense as that of the corresponding chair in New College, Edinburgh, — so its occupant, Professor Duns, wrote to Drummond, —

which had been chosen 'as sufficient to secure the intimate theological relations of the chair, and to give free scope for the Professor to deal with all the questions of a physico-theological kind sure to turn up as science advances. The place of the chair in a *theological* college was from the first held to settle its character and scope.' The Assembly reserved the right to revise the constitution of the chair whenever Natural Science should be included in the Arts curriculum of the universities.[1]

On May 31 Drummond was unanimously elected to the new chair, and the Assembly instructed the Presbytery of Glasgow to arrange for his 'ordination and induction.' This took place on November 4 in College Free Church, according to the simple Scottish rite, and *by laying on of the hands of the Presbytery.*[2]

This rite is the same in the case whether of a minister or of a professor, for the Church of Scotland recognises no difference between her teachers and her

---

[1] The deliverance of the Assembly of 1884, constituting the chair, declared: 'In accordance with the wishes of James Stevenson, Esq., who has provided the endowment, that in the event of such arrangements being made for the teaching of Natural Science as part of the M.A. curriculum in the universities as may make it inexpedient or unnecessary to keep up this chair on its present footing, it shall be competent for the Church to revise the constitution of the chair, and to determine the subjects to be taught as may then be most suitable, retaining the basis of the relation of science and theology, and adding such subjects as are cognate.' — *Assembly Blue Book*, 1884, pp. 69, 70.

[2] There had been some uncertainty about this. Drummond was ordained an elder of the Church on his appointment to the lectureship, and Mr. Stevenson wrote Principal Rainy and Dr. Melville, the Principal Clerk of Assembly, that surely it was not necessary to ordain him as minister. Dr. Melville replied that the Assembly wished to place the Professor of Natural Science on the same footing as his colleagues, but that Drummond's ordination to the ministry need not prejudice any future appointment to the chair of a layman, who was an elder. This was what Mr. Stevenson had wished to secure. Probably also Drummond himself had been anxious not to be ordained as a full minister of the Church; for after the ordination, and to the end of his life, he persisted — to the amusement of his friends — that he had never been ordained as a minister. The fact, however, is beyond all doubt. On November 4, 1884, he received by the hands of the Glasgow Presbytery the full orders of the Presbyterian Church.

pastors, but lays them under the same vows and ordains them all as ministers of Christ's Gospel and of His Sacraments. The form is as follows: After public worship the candidate stands up before the congregation. In answer to the questions of the presiding minister he declares his 'belief in the Scriptures of the Old and New Testaments as the Word of God, and the only rule of faith and manners'; his acceptance of the doctrines of the Church as defined in the Westminster Confession of Faith;[1] his adherence to the Presbyterian form of church government; his loyalty to the 'spirituality and freedom of the Church under the sole headship of the Lord Jesus Christ,' for which the Free Church of Scotland testified and separated from the State in 1843; and that 'zeal for the honour of God, love to Jesus Christ, and the desire of saving souls are his great motives and inducements in entering into the function of the Holy Ministry.' Having signed the formula the candidate kneels before the Moderator (that is, the presiding minister), who offers the ordination prayer, the other ministers of the Presbytery standing round. When the prayer invokes the Holy Spirit upon 'this our brother whom we solemnly ordain and set apart to the office of the ministry,' the Presbytery lay their hands upon the head of the kneeling man. At the close of the prayer, he stands up and receives his induction from the Moderator 'in the name and by authority of the Lord Jesus Christ,' and the Presbytery give him the right hand of fellowship. He is then suitably charged by one of the ministers, and his congregation, or students, as the case may be, are also exhorted. When Drummond was ordained, the presiding minister was the Reverend

---

[1] Which confession is now interpreted according to a Declaratory Act passed by the General Assembly in 1893.

George Reith of College Free Church, who delivered
the following charge : —

'Your appearance this day reminds us of the faith our
Church wisely reposes in a trained and cultivated ministry.
No wise man will undervalue culture, especially in the line
of scientific investigations — the peculiar feature of our time.
The more of culture a man has the better for his hearers.
But, after all, we may mistake wherein lies power, and
besides it is not with a few cultured sceptics a Church has to
do.   It is with the great masses of men.   I very sincerely
rejoice that you have earned, I will not say a better title to
your chair, but I do say an equally valid title, by your sympathy with the evangelistic work of our Church, and your
very considerable practical acquaintance with it.   A professor
is all the better for having known the practical work of the
ministry ; and in your case, though the name has been wanting, the thing has been there.   We look to you as one especially qualified to show how culture and sympathy with evangelistic work are to go hand in hand.   We look to you to
impress your students with the love of men.   You can teach
them what culture can, and what it cannot do.   You can
teach them — and from your lips it will come with additional
emphasis — that to gain men we must lay down our lives for
them, and that our true power is the power of the Master we
serve, the love that moves to daily self-sacrifice.'

Professor Drummond then delivered his inaugural
address on the ' Contribution of Science to Christianity ' — virtually the same as the articles in the *Expositor*, summarised in the previous chapter.

To James Stevenson, Esq.

'3 CARLTON GARDENS, KELVINSIDE, GLASGOW,
November 13, 1884.

' Thank you for your very kind note on the morning
of my induction.   There was more interest in the
starting of this chair than in anything that has

happened publicly in the history of this Glasgow
College. The inauguration was advertised for
the College Hall, but the audience would have
filled it three or four times, and we had to have
it in Mr. Reith's church. I am quite sure there
is a great and increasing interest in the subject.
The *Philosophy* men find it hard to believe that
the day of science has come, but I am sure four-
fifths of our Church are not only favourable, but
enthusiastically favourable, to our science chairs.[1]
' I believe in the work of this chair more and more
every day. Indeed, perhaps it is due to you that
I should tell you what I have not told any one
here, that I lately refused a very lucrative government appointment lest it should hinder me in
my new work.'[2]

'Our session,' wrote Principal Douglas to Mr. Stevenson on December 8, 'has begun this winter, I think,
well. Drummond is very popular with the young
men, and I hope you will have evidence that he is
exercising a healthy and powerful influence.' There
were ninety-five regular students (twenty-five of them
in their first year), and twenty non-regular. The
course through which Drummond took his class continued to be the same as it had been.[3] He lectured
four hours a week, and, besides expounding the principles of modern science and their relation to religion,
taught the elements of botany and geology, and, I
believe, a little zoölogy. It is clear that in the short
session — the lectures numbered about eighty — a
thorough treatment of these sciences was impossible,

[1] This was not the case. The chair would never have been created but for
Drummond's personality, and Mr. Stevenson's generous offer.
[2] The secretaryship of the Shipping Commission.
[3] See above, page 130.

and students who had already taken any of them at the University must have found Drummond's teach-ing rudimentary. But, as an 'old student' has said,[1] 'Drummond did his students a world of good by teaching them some of the general principles which underlie all science, and by making them feel that truth is indivisible, whether it be of science or religion. He taught his students at least not to fear science; and if they could not get a complete reconciliation, meanwhile they must work with broad, flexible hy-potheses which would keep their minds from harden-ing and narrowing. Once a week at College he used to give his class special lectures, beginning with the evolution of the world, and coming down to the evolu-tion of life. These were intensely interesting, and had a certain apologetic purpose, and were more use-ful than the mere teaching of the rudiments of science.'

Probably Drummond did even more good to his students in another way. The education of nearly all of them had been confined to languages, literature, and philosophy, with some mathematics. He drew their attention to the common facts of nature. About three weeks after the beginning of the session, he used to set what he called an 'ignorance examination.' The questions were such as: 'What are air, water, earth? What is the use of a leaf? What makes a leaf fall? What is the use of a flower? What do trees live on? What makes the sea salt? Why are mountainous districts rainy? What colour or colours are the stars? Define a volcano. What happens chemically, *first* in striking, *second* in burning, a wooden match? Name any two of Mr. Darwin's works, and their theses. Define Natural Selection.' No marks were given for the answers. Each paper

[1] Article in the *Woman at Home* for 1897, by H. B.

was treated as if anonymous, but it was carefully reviewed before the whole class, and thus students received a healthy knowledge of their ignorance, both of the common facts of nature and of the dominant methods of science.

Drummond remembered his ordination vows, and welcomed his work in the College for the time which it left him to minister to a far wider congregation in the matters of morality and religion. Of this ministry an enormous increase was brought to him by the fame of his book. Having read his African journal, one is tempted to regret that he did not spend a quiet year in elaborating the results of his travels into a careful treatise upon the geology and resources of the Zambezi and the Nyasa regions. He could have given us such a work, and it would have established his scientific reputation upon a height from which his subsequent ministry might have been directed with perhaps even greater force than it actually achieved. That he considered the question is clear from the following letter from R. W. Barbour:—

THE FREE MANSE, CULTS, ABERDEEN, 17th August, 1884.

'Henry is here and it is good to entertain angels awares or unawares. I expect the Lord often looked like he does, a mere man of the world, dining out and living in rich men's houses — to the Pharisees at least.

'Henry says it is his birthday — he is thirty-three to-day — but it has felt liker my own. He spoke to us to-night on Paul's Hymn of Heavenly Love in the thirteenth of First Corinthians, and it was like being in heaven or in sight of it, to hear him. One had the sweet pain of seeing something which he might strive after for many days.

' I have just been down seeing Mr. ——, who was announced at eight. I went in fear and trembling, lest he should be going to raise a cry about Drummond's doctrine, or ask me to hold a franchise meeting, but — it was ordinary business. I expect Henry will leave to-day to see after his MSS. for winter. He is hesitating whether to give some time to vigorous scientific work, as a monograph on some of his African spoils, or whether to go in entirely for evangelism. I think the latter will have it.'

The latter did have it, and could not but have it. Since his return from Africa Drummond was met by numerous appeals for counsel in religious difficulties and for assistance in moral and social work. He found door after door opened to him among classes of men to which the ordinary ministers of religion had no access, or having access, upon which they had no real influence. Into two spheres, especially, there seemed to be a strong call for him to enter. His work in one of these, the life of our universities, was large enough to need here a chapter to itself. At present we may take the other.

So distinguished a writer as the author of *Natural Law in the Spiritual World* was bound to be sought after by the more religious portions of what is termed 'Society.' By 1884 the evangelical movement in Great Britain had lost much of the doctrinal influence which it previously exercised upon the higher ranks of the community. The more serious among the younger generation of these were loyal to Christ, anxious for His sake to do good works, but, like many men and women of their time, in considerable intellectual uncertainty. In the author of *Natural Law* they discovered a teacher, with a strong fresh mind of his own; not only a subtle expert in religious experience, but one who enforced the principles of Christianity apart from ecclesiastical formulas. From such persons of position there came in April and May, 1884, a number of letters, either addressed to Drummond himself asking an interview, or addressed to those who knew him asking an introduction. When the writers met him they found a man of simplicity and winsomeness, courteous, unassuming, and generous in the communication of his apparently exhaustless stores of experience in dealing with men and women with religious difficulties. Our national life is probably nowhere so sensitive to influence as throughout its upper ranks, and the individuals who had been benefited by Drummond busied themselves to extend the boon throughout their class. The correspondence which ensued is one of very great interest, but it involves the views and personal experiences of so many who are still alive, that it is impossible to quote largely from it. Among the new friends found by Drummond were Lord and Lady Aberdeen, with whom his relations for the rest of his life were most close and affectionate. The following correspondence with Lord Aberdeen relates to a movement for which Drummond's help was asked, and which took shape not only in the remarkable addresses delivered in Grosvenor House, but in the still more profitable enlistment of a number of the families of London society in various forms of philanthropy. The nine months which intervened between his return from Africa and the date at which this new crusade opened, Drummond spent in a visit to the Perth Conference; in an autumn visit to Haddo House,[1] with addresses and lectures in the neighbourhood; in a

[1] Lord Aberdeen's.

visit to the Y.M.C.A. Convention in Dublin; in his winter work at college; in lecturing on Africa in Liverpool, before the Edinburgh Philosophical Institution, and elsewhere; and in organising the religious movement among the students of the Scottish universities.

To the Earl of Aberdeen

'3 CARLTON GARDENS, GLASGOW, March 5, 1885.

'I quite thought I should have been able to have answered your letter and Lady Aberdeen's to-day. But light comes very slowly; and though I have been thinking over the request very seriously, I am still in the twilight. I fear I must therefore beg you to allow me a few more hours before writing in detail. My difficulties are: —

'1. To lecture in the circumstances named would be a matter of very great delicacy and difficulty, and to prepare a set of lectures worthy of the object would require months of careful preparation.

'2. I am seriously involved just now in the work among students. This is spreading daily, and is now extending to the other universities. Whither it may develop one cannot foresee; but, as nothing like this has ever happened in my lifetime, I am not sure but that my immediate duty lies here. We have many plans for April, and there are very few men among the professors who give any help. What makes me shrink from the idea of running away from it prematurely is the profound conviction that this university movement is a distinct work of God — such a work as I, after considerable experience of evangelistic work, have never seen before.

T

'I must not disguise from you, also, that I would have little faith in my lecturing producing any permanent result. The lecture, as a weapon, always has seemed to me a poor influence in religion; and although, as Lady Aberdeen very kindly says, my book has won for me some friends, I cannot shut my eyes to the fact that it has also won me many enemies — witness the critic who dances upon me so mercilessly in this month's *Contemporary*.

'I should really have some faith in addresses of a simple kind — not written lectures, but clear statements of what Christianity really is, what personal religion really is, and evangelical matter generally. To attempt this would be very much more trying; but if the call came I would feel that I dared not shrink from it. . . .'

'March 7th, 1885.

'Your most considerate letter, this moment handed to me, relieves me much. It was the word *lecture* that frightened me. This simplifies matters greatly.'

Finally Drummond agreed to give three addresses in the ballroom of Grosvenor House, the Duke of Westminster's, on the afternoons of the last Sunday in April and of the first two in May. Between the second and third he joined us at our club, held this year at Grasmere, and told us of his new work. The only record I have been able to discover is one by Robert Barbour in a letter to his wife.

From Robert W. Barbour

'PRINCE OF WALES' HOTEL, GRASMERE, May 5, 1885.

' I slipped along the passage here, guided by the sound of friendly voices, and slapped Ewing on the shoulder as he was entering the room. Such a burst of greetings met me from half a dozen voices and faces: Frank's and Henry's and George's, Mr. Stalker's, Mr. Ross's, Mr. Brown's, and Mr. Skene's. Mr. Watson is going abroad, so cannot come. The change from the darkness and the raw night air with a chill north wind blowing in my face as we drove, my dogcart-man and I, the ten miles along the lakes from Windermere, to the light and warmth of our snug dining-room, was very pleasant. I think the faces all look older — perhaps having missed a year makes a difference — and I am older too. The time alone last year drew me apart from every one, I think, only to be nearer of course, but still not to depend on any one outside so much henceforward. Henry looks least changed. His Master makes him ever young.[1] He came up from London, where he has been giving addresses in Grosvenor House these two Sabbaths past. At supper Mr. Stalker was the chief talker, taking off (in a genial sympathetic way) several of Henry's "colts," and what things they had said and done in his pulpit.'[2]

'May 6th.

'We are just in from a *herrlicher Tag*. We started at 10.30 for Helvellyn. . . . The climb was beguiled by Henry telling me of the Grosvenor House meetings. They are held in the ballroom of the

---

[1] At another 'Gaiety' meeting Barbour had described Drummond 'princely and bewitching as ever.'

[2] These were the members of the Students' Holiday Mission. See below, pp. 327 ff.

duke's house, which may hold 650. The invitation
is made through the society column of the *Morning
Post*. Any one who wants to come may call for a
ticket at Lord Aberdeen's. The first day the place
was filled, and none were turned away. The second
another room was thrown open. There is no service
— just an address for an hour. The first day Forster,
Childers, etc., were sitting next to him on the platform
and the room was full of members of the Upper
House. They came expecting to hear a lecture on
science, but Henry took the simplest evangelical subject he could — about Conversion. He never felt so
horrid in his life, but I think he must have been
greatly helped. At the end he asked them to engage
with him in prayer. He said it seemed to take them
by surprise, but they all knelt down. It is a wonderful opportunity God is giving him, and he is wonderfully fitted for it. Looking at him moving among
us, I have the feeling I used to have about——:
it is a noble creature of God. We must remember
him there again next Sunday.'

How those meetings impressed a part of London
society may be seen in the following extracts from an
article in the *World*, May, 1885, entitled 'Wanted, a
Religion': —

'Mr. Drummond has struck out a completely new line of
his own, in which there is nothing that is not dignified, nothing that is not telling. To be able to collect, even under a
ducal roof, on four [1] successive Sunday afternoons, four or
five hundred people, many of them of the highest distinction,
social and intellectual, is a triumph of ingenious ingenuity
[*sic*]. Mr. Drummond has invented a gospel, which, if not
entirely new, has just enough novelty about it to pique and
interest the fashionable public, and which can be perfectly

[1] Three?

well reconciled with the somewhat effete, but always to be respected, evangel of the New Testament. He applies the principle of evolution, the law of the survival of the fittest, to spiritual existence. He does not consign to perdition all who fail to lead a highly spiritual life here. He only reminds them that they are not qualifying themselves for the life to come. For the effect he has produced, everything depends upon his management of his material. Sometimes his religion and his science have fused their currents and travelled in a common stream. Sometimes they have run in parallel channels. Sometimes their relations have been of a different kind, and the lecturer has employed religion as the gilding of the pill of science, or science as the rationalising witness to religion. But whatever the method adopted, the result produced has been the same; and the audience has departed profoundly impressed by the words of wisdom and solemnity issuing from the lips of a young man with a good manner, a not ill-favoured face, a broad Scotch accent, clad in a remarkably well-fitting frock coat, and reciting, after his prelection, the Lord's Prayer in a tone of devout humility remarkable for the professors of the period. Mr. Drummond has, in fact, produced upon his hearers the impression that the teachings of science are, upon the whole, in favour of revealed religion. . . .

'Nothing could be easier, and nothing could be more contemptible, than to disparage or satirise the serious struggle which society is now making to obtain from some one of its many spiritual teachers a new revelation, or, if not that, to have its feet directed into the ways of a new religion. Nothing, again, could be easier than to take a more or less humorous view of Mr. Drummond's dissertations at Grosvenor House. Naturally, the professional religionists are a little jealous of his success. The Church papers hint that he is an amateur and a quack. But then that is only professional jealousy. There seems to be no reason why evangelists like Mr. Drummond should not coöperate with the salaried interpreters of another evangel, now some nineteen centuries old. Or it may be said that Mr. Drummond would scarcely take a leading part in a performance which certainly seems to have a good deal that is artificial about it, if he had any store of the sincerity and earnestness which ought to be the attributes of the religious teacher.   Upon this it is enough to observe that audiences as fastidious and discriminating, and as highly educated, as any in the world, have been won over by his utterances.   That he will produce a moral or social revolution is no more to be anticipated than that he will change the future history of the human race.   But that he will be instrumental in effecting an appreciable degree of improvement in our social tone is far from impossible.   He may, indeed, almost claim to have done this already.   He has caused society to talk, not only about himself, but about the subjects which he expounds. Perhaps the interest he has created in the topics that throng the borderland between physics and faith may not be permanent.   But what is permanent in these times?   And it is quite enough to know that his words do, for the time, provide matter for reflection.   Granting even that religion, or the new blend between science and religion, is taken up by society as a species of diversion, and occupies the same moral level as philanthropy, charity organisation, domiciliary visits paid to the poor at the East End, music, old china, or lawn tennis, that is no reason why it should be discouraged.   It is better for society to be occupied in this manner than in many others which might be mentioned.   And, indeed, to those who look a little beneath the surface, there is something not only instructive, but pathetic, in the avidity with which English society, supposed to be irreligious, but really the most religious in the world, snatches at the spiritual mixture prepared for it by Mr. Drummond.   What — such is the question which presents itself to many minds — might not be hoped for, if some new and authentic revelation were to be delivered to society by a greater even than Mr. Drummond?'

No one, however, can estimate the force of the Grosvenor House addresses who has not seen some, at least, of the appeals which they called forth.   As always when he spoke, Drummond drew to himself the secrets of many lives, and became, to a large number of them, an influence of light and hope.   The fol-

lowing letter from himself reports the beginnings of
an effort to organise women of the West End of London
don into an Associated Workers' League, for social
and religious help among the poor: —

To Mrs. Simpson, Edinburgh

'37, GROSVENOR SQUARE, LONDON, July 10, 1885.

'. . . You ask me what I have been doing? Meeting, meetings, meetings. These have been mostly
in private houses, and we are now seeking a little
fruit. It ripens slowly in this climate, but there
are signs of life on every hand. The latest development is a "Workers' League" to set all the
unemployed in the West End to work.'

The League was started in July at a drawing-room
meeting, at which Drummond gave an address, describing the need for 'some kind of link among
workers with a view to assistance in their difficulties
and encouragement in their efforts. The objects of
the League were to introduce those desiring work to
fields of usefulness best suited to their special gifts; to
reinforce existing agencies with workers; to form a
workers' exchange; and to help workers in the country
during their temporary residence in London by bringing them into contact with actual work there.' The
proposal was eagerly welcomed, and many names
were given in at the first meeting. In the second year
ninety-eight were added, and by 1890 the total membership was 240. Reports were periodically asked
from workers, and the endeavour was made to inspire
in the members 'the true temper of work, as distinct
from mere busyness in good works.' An appeal, signed
by Lady Tavistock, says: —

'Thought must be below all, and deep purpose and

much dependence on God, or our efforts will degener-
ate into mere restlessness, and we shall exhaust ourselves and other people, while we effect nothing of any
permanence or value.'

In the end of May, 1885, Drummond was the guest
at Holyrood Palace of Lord and Lady Aberdeen,
while the former filled the office of the Queen's Lord
High Commissioner to the General Assembly of the
Church of Scotland. In July he was back in London, holding meetings and organising the Associated
Workers' League, as above described. August he
spent at home in Stirling, and fishing at Lairg in
Sutherland. In September and October he passed
some weeks at Haddo House, and went to the Aberdeen meeting of the British Association, at which he
read a paper before the Geological Section. On Sunday
evenings he gave addresses in the chapel of Haddo
House to congregations consisting of the household,
the guests, and residents in the neighbourhood.

'HADDO HOUSE, Sept. 17, 1885.

'All the wise men from the Association are here,
resting after their labours — among them Lord
Rayleigh, Sir John and Lady Lubbock, Lady
Boyle, Professor Masson, Mr. Du Maurier of
Punch, and other celebrities.'

'Friday, Sept. 25, 1885.

'Still in the North, though I am now wearying to
have done with it. But I have a service on Sabbath and one or two of an important nature next
week, which will keep me a few days longer.
Most probably I will wind up Haddo with a
meeting on Sabbath week.'

The following letter from Robert Barbour gives a portrait of Drummond, as he showed to his friends in those days. The rapid descent upon them and the swift flight were very characteristic:—

'STUDY ROOM, CULTS, Monday night,
'Oct. 10, 1885.

' I have had a great treat to-day.

' As I was seeing A. into the train, who should seize me by the arms but Henry! He was the old charac- ter — black and white check tweeds, brown hat, dark green plaid, and princely swing — stepping into the 12.20 for Aboyne. He was fresh from Haddo, where he has been spending the time since the British Association salmon-fishing and men-fishing together. Lubbock, Sedgwick, Trevelyan, etc., were among his companions. . . . Each Sabbath evening he has spoken there in the chapel, suiting his theme to the special guests. On Saturday they had a kind of Perth Conference, with two or three hundred of the farmers' wives and daughters around, to start the Haddo House Association's work for the year. The earl and Henry were the speakers.

' I left my errands and came back to Cults by the 12.30, deposited his wraps at the Manse, and then had a glorious two hours' walk in the face of the bracing west wind, gazing with delight at the autumn woods and the grand blue hills and moors behind, round by the back of Hillton on to the Skene Road and so home by Countesswells and Craigton. " Das war eine Freude, nicht wahr?" . . . M. gave us dinner, all her *pièces de persistance et résistance* with coffee.

' Then followed a chat, face to face and heart to heart, by the study fire, and a solemn moment of prayer. And so the Bird of Paradise spread his wings, and I saw him no more.'

In October Drummond spent a week geologising, in preparation for a case in the Court of Session, to which he was summoned as an expert witness; and in the end of the month he started his short mission in Oxford, which we may reserve for the general history of the Student Movement in next chapter, From Oxford he returned to the winter session in Glasgow. Here are a few extracts from his letters during 'a terribly busy' session — his classes at college, lectures in many places, social operations in Glasgow, and a series of addresses to the Edinburgh students : —

'I am glad you are taking to Emerson. I have been reading Herbert Spencer this week, and I must say with great admiration. I read through *Queen Mab*, which is cleverly done, but does not come to much except destruction. The best thing in it is where the author calls the Thirty-nine Articles "tinned theology."

'Here I was suddenly interrupted by the advent of the Edinburgh deputation — four students, whom it really does one good to see. Only they won't go away. They have been five hours in the house already. . . .

'I had a great day with the students. They sat eleven hours, and we went the whole round of the theologies. Their request was that I should go to Edinburgh every Sunday in February and if possible March. I hope at least to do something. . . . On Sunday there is to be a monster meeting here at which Dr. Barbour and I are to speak. It was begun by the Edinburgh students, and I took it last night and found over a thousand people present.

' I have just (Dec. 12, 1885) finished an article for
the January *Nineteenth Century*.[1] You will be
shocked to hear that it is not about beetles, but
about Mr. Gladstone and Mr. Huxley. I fear it
is really hard on Mr. Gladstone; it certainly is,
though I have been as gentle as I could. But I
could not help the thing: it is a real duty; Sir
———— ———— also works on Mr. Gladstone's lines,
and they do incalculable harm to men of science,
so I write to repudiate their whole position in the
name of scientific theology. . . . In the original
MS. I had in a page of admiration, but, on second
and third thoughts, I reluctantly compelled myself to exclude it. It was not germane to the
subject, and would not come in without a sense
of forcing, which would have spoiled everything. . . .'

' *New Year's Day*, 1886. — I look over the clean figures of our Almanac and the yet as blank pages
of its diary with strange wondering as to what
they hold in store. We ought all to be getting
into the heart of our life-work now, and, in feeling how much there is to do and how short the
time is, one cannot but pray that no day of it
may be misspent.'

To Drummond and his correspondents, the year
1886 was to bring many changes and many cares. In
February the political life of the nation was convulsed
by Mr. Gladstone's return to power and his declara-
tion of a policy of Home Rule for Ireland. The Earl
of Aberdeen was appointed Viceroy of Ireland, and
offered Henry Drummond a post on his staff. He
replied as follows : —

[1] See above, end of chap. x.

To Lord Aberdeen

'GLASGOW, Feb. 12, 1886.

'My immediate feeling (after the blush of thanks, which you will so fully understand that I need not open with any formal reference to it) — my immediate feeling is one of intense shrinking from a post of such honour and publicity. I feel it is not for me at all. As I have often told you, the Tub is the place for me and not the Castle; and, at the moment, I do not see how I am to displace this feeling. But, of course, one's mere feelings are neither here nor there, and the real consideration is what is *right*. Now, I am not sure that it would be right for me to do this — right in connection with one's real work and mission in life. I need not enlarge upon this; you will know what I mean. Try for a moment to look at it from my point of view — not that you have not done that, but I mean in this relation — in relation to my friends and my *audience*, past and future. For Mrs. Grundy I do not care, I hope; but for others, for the students and for those to whom one may yet speak of a Spiritual World, one would like to avoid even the appearance of ambition. Is it not so? On the other hand, what more could I do in an official relation than as a full private? The difference could only be in name; and, if that name involves a loss in the highest sense without there being any real gain, ought I to seek it? This is how the thing strikes me at the moment. I wish I could talk it over with you, for writing is so stupid; but I have told you frankly what is in my mind. If I could be of real use in the more official capacity, that of course would weigh; but I can be of none, and I am fearful lest I injure any evangelistic work that may be given me to do. The Edinburgh work has broken out in a marvellous manner last Sunday, and I shall be going there for some time, so that the summer may have calls upon me which I cannot now foresee. So please leave me to think over it for a few days, and judge this base ingratitude as gently as you can.'

The result was that he did not accept the post. In April, in the midst of work for the student movement at Edinburgh, Aberystwyth, and elsewhere, he paid a flying visit to Ireland to lecture before the Royal Dublin Society on Africa, and to prepare for a student deputation to Trinity College. He was the guest of the Viceroy, and re-crossed the Channel with Mr. John Morley.

' Mr. Morley told me *en route* that he had come away from Ireland with at least one very definite impression — the extraordinary and widespread influence for good throughout the country of the present vice-regal reign, or, as I ought to put it, reigns. I think I shall get to Killin on Monday.'

It was at Killin that year that our club met, the last time we were all together, for Ewing left soon afterwards for Melbourne. Naturally we discussed the Home Rule question, on which we were divided, and the impending General Election. Drummond quietly stated both sides of the case and gave his reasons for adhering to the portion of the Liberal party which followed Mr. Gladstone. He had not been converted by Mr. Gladstone's own judgment, nor had he the materials to form an independent opinion. Some of his nearest friends were hotly opposed to Home Rule; his youthful experiences in Dublin had given him distrust of the Irish party[1] and his natural caution in such matters was so great that none of us would have been surprised if he had not taken a side. But he had been impressed by the evidence of Lord Spencer, Sir Robert Hamilton, and other statesmen responsible for the government of Ireland, who had declared for Home Rule; he recognised that the policy was in agreement with the Liberal principles which he had always professed, and he was attracted by the moral possibilities which he felt it to contain. Probably, too, he judged, as many other Liberals did, that even if Home Rule were never carried in the form in which Mr. Gladstone projected it, — and in a few weeks this was to become very likely, — Mr. Gladstone's policy had already created at least the kind of atmosphere in politics in which alone the Irish problem could ripen to a solution. And this may be said to have come to pass, for on whatever side of the question men have taken their stand, they must allow that Mr. Gladstone's effort has succeeded in making our former policy towards Ireland impossible, and has been the real cause, for instance, of the possibility of the Local Government Act recently passed by Parliament. In such opinions and expectations Drummond had been fortified by his recent visit to Ireland,[2] his conversa-

---

[1] See above, p. 37.

[2] On this point Mr. Gladstone had requested his opinion and he sent it. He received the following reply: —

'10 DOWNING STREET, WHITEHALL, June 1, 1886.

'DEAR MR. DRUMMOND, — I have handed your letter to Mr. Gladstone, who desires me to ask you to excuse him if he does not write himself as he is so very busy, and to say that he is greatly obliged to you for what you have written. Your testimony as to the change wrought in Irish feeling is very remarkable and has afforded Mr. Gladstone the *highest* satisfaction. Yours very truly,

'H. W. PRIMROSE.'

tions with Mr. Morley and Sir Robert Hamilton, and his experience of the effect upon the people of the reign of a Viceroy who represented a Government pledged to Home Rule. So he was not only prepared to give his vote for this at the coming election, but to speak in public on its behalf with conviction and even with enthusiasm.

The diminished Liberal party endeavoured to induce Drummond to take a further step. They were in sore need of candidates at the election — candidates of his class and culture — and he was urgently requested to stand for several constituencies.[1] The Partick Division of Lanarkshire was especially importunate, and Mr. Gladstone himself wrote a strong letter of persuasion. But Drummond was wiser than his advisers, and, as at so many other periods of temptation, refused to launch upon a line of life which would have distracted him from the vocation that he felt and had now so amply proved to be his own.

'3, PARK CIRCUS, GLASGOW, June 17, 1886.

'I found in possession of my Tub a horrid monster — a deputation from the Partick Division of Lanarkshire. All past refusals were fruitless, although I had an hour with their chairman yesterday, and they came to renew the attack. I fought single-handed for three hours, with what result you know.'

---

[1] There are letters to him from Partick, West Edinburgh, and the Inverness Burghs.

To the Right Honourable W. E. Gladstone

Copy dated June 15, 1886.

'MY DEAR MR. GLADSTONE, —

'A letter from you on the subject of going into Parliament I feel to be a most sacred call. It has touched me unspeakably. I am entirely unworthy of a thing so high and generous, and it is with a deep sense of responsibility that I now try to trust myself to reply.

'After the most serious and anxious consideration I fear I must ask your forbearance for an answer in the negative. I shall not waste your time by entering on the many reasons which contribute to a decision which I offer you with the profoundest respect and regret, but as far as my present light goes I feel that I can serve you and the great cause better in other ways than by myself entering Parliament. What little I can do as regards the present crisis I think I can do to equal purpose apart from the House of Commons, and in the long run for the good ends of which this is but a part.

'I believe that by working in the fixed walk of life which seems to be assigned to me, and which refuses, in spite of private struggles and the persuasion of the wisest friends, to release me for this special service, I can do more for every cause of truth and righteousness.

'What personal regrets and regards mingle with this letter you can form little idea of; and I shall not attempt to express my sense of gratitude for the extraordinary honour and kindness of your letter. — With great respect, I remain,

'Sincerely yours,

'HENRY DRUMMOND.'

But while refusing to stand for any constituency, Drummond gave help to several Liberal candidates. He went the round of the Ayr Burghs with his friend, Captain Sinclair, and spoke also in Possilpark and at Kilmarnock.

He was warmly attacked both by friends and by strangers.

> ' A torrent of wrath from —— over the advertise-ment of the Home Rule meeting. —— is not satisfied yet, and the general public is treating me to anonymous letters. But really neither are at all severe, and I am very far from complaining.'

His critics could have no idea of how seriously and how religiously he took up the work of which they complained. His few speeches were very care-fully planned; they rang high and true, and, as I find from some notes to friends, he did not appear on those political platforms without the same kind of prepara-tion that he invariably made for his religious addresses. When defeat came he reverently considered the mean-ing of it, and his letters to those to whom it shut doors of usefulness, hardly opened, are among the finest he wrote.

Drummond spent July fishing in Sutherlandshire and came to Glasgow for August.

> ' I have been working like a tiger. No Scotch moor is quieter than Glasgow just now, and I have not seen one white man since I came back. Half the churches were closed on Sunday, and I worshipped in the slums. . . . Germany is tak-ing shape, and I must work, work, work.'

U

This was for a visit to the German universities. But first Drummond went to Switzerland with his sisters for part of September.

To Lady Aberdeen

'HOTEL AXENSTEIN, LAKE OF LUCERNE, Sept. 2, 1886.

'There is but one spot in the world, and its name is Axenstein. In all my wanderings I never saw anything to approach the place from which I now scribble. I know you are a heretic about Switzerland, but ten minutes of this would win you for evermore. The scenery is of the very noblest type — mountain, lake, and forest — and this hotel is surrounded with shady walks, with views breaking out everywhere of the most bewildering beauty and sublimity. And — but really you are laughing. Do excuse me, for I had to blow this off before writing one word. I have often marked this spot in my knapsacking days — a forest ledge two thousand feet high, on a precipice falling sheer into the lake, with a great eagle's nest of a hotel — and I always looked forward to the quiet visit which has now come. We had engaged rooms in Paris on Tuesday, but the heat and noise were intolerable, so we took the first express and came right on to Lucerne, and then here by steamer. My main mission to Paris was to see Pasteur and go over his laboratory, but I found he had just left for a holiday. We got here yesterday afternoon, and we feel we would just like to stay here all the time.

'No words can — but I must not begin again. . . .

'On the Calais ferry I crossed with Count ——, and had an interesting talk with him. He has given up the Consulate (from political motives) and has nothing to do but travel. I feel very sorry for him, for he is an exceptionally good Frenchman. You would have been intensely amused to see the letter of introduction he gave me to a friend of his in Paris. I was "*un savant très-religieux, et au même moment double*[*ment*] *un homme du monde !*" Part of the humour of the thing consisted, as I afterwards discovered, in his friend Count T. being the leading man at the Paris Jockey Club!'

'HOTEL RIFFEL-ALP, ZERMATT, Sept. 12, 1886.

'I am very glad you are president. This sentence is good and contains all you want for a text to speak on: "These girls must be met, not by authority, but with sympathy and respect." I am sure these people will trust you and allow you to say almost anything you like, and I should not be afraid to speak plainly. It is a fine opportunity, though a very delicate one, to help on the modern movement towards a more real and solid faith and a truer Christianity. And I am sure we can do much without breaking with the evangelicals. . . . Last Sunday I went to church twice [1] and got two very fine sermons from Dr. Laidlaw of Edinburgh.'

'VALLOURMANCHE, Sept. 15.

'I am at this moment in a rustic inn in the most glorious valley in Piedmont. This is the most delicious travelling in the world. One wanders where one likes, stops where one likes, the weather is perfect, the scenery glorious, the wine good, and

[1] At Interlaken.

the inns as sweet as the Alpine roses.　To-morrow we make for Milan, and on Saturday start for the Italian lakes.'

Drummond stayed on in Switzerland to prepare his German addresses.　He had many opportunities of helping those in religious doubt whom he met at table or by the wayside, and who like all their kind were drawn to open their hearts to him.　On October 16th he left for Tübingen.　I do not know whether he visited other universities, but by October 25th he was in Bonn, of which we will hear afterwards.

By November 2 he was in Glasgow, and 'in a whirl of work.'

To Lady Aberdeen

'Dec. 16, 1886.

'One sees one's life in perspective when one goes abroad, and to be spectators of ourselves is very solemn.　I have been reading a new book this week which brings out in a startling light the old distinction between "the ourselves" in us and our mere outward talents.　Those last are but the Weapons; the Warrior is within.　The Weapons, it says, are but the accidents of birth, and no more to be placed to our credit than gold or clothes or worldly possessions.　Yet how often we think the Warrior is well if but the Weapons do their work; and how much self-satisfaction is based upon what we, *i.e.* the Weapons, not *we* have done; how little upon what we, the real we *are*. But the measure of the success of our life can only lie in the gains of the last, in the stature of our manhood, in the growth in unworldliness and moral elevation of our inner Self.　But I wonder what makes me ramble on like this.

Alas — it is the memory of a remorse which always follows one in one's own holidays. The text I oftenest think on then is this: "What is the Man profited if he gain the whole world — morally or spiritually — and lose his own soul."'

To Lord Aberdeen [1]

'GLASGOW, Jan. 6, 1887.

'MY DEAR ABERDEEN, — First, please look at the queer stamp on the outside of this letter. As Viceroy (temporarily Ex.) I thought you would like to see the new symbols of the Crown, and ordered a complete set, — for everything is changed except the penny ones this Jubilee year; but the telegraph boy who was despatched to the General P.O. for them — the local offices have to use up the old ones — is probably playing snowballs somewhere in the city, so I fear this must go before I can send them. I do not know if you have a weakness for stamps, but I confess this relic of boyhood still survives in me. Perhaps, however, in present circumstances, you would prefer the boy to send you the snowballs.

'*Pour moi*, I have nothing to report. My life flows on in silence, almost in solitude. These winter months I am the pure Diogenes. I read a little science, write *ein wenig*, skate when the frost pleases, and walk three or four times a week with Dods. I like it all, nevertheless, very much. I think I was made to remain "*in der stille.*"

'I begin Edinburgh on Sunday. It haunts me like a nightmare. The responsibility of these coming Sundays I feel almost more than anything in my life.'

[1] In India.

To Lady Aberdeen

'GLASGOW, Jan. 20, 1887.

'We had a splendid meeting last Sunday; and on
Sunday week the students open a campaign
among the bigger Edinburgh schoolboys. We
have got the athletic men, whom the schoolboys
all know, to take this in hand, and I think it
ought to succeed.

'Mr. Barbour, Senior, died on Saturday night. I
was present at the time . . . a very quiet and
beautiful end. Robert is in Corsica for his health,
and will feel it much. I go to Bonskeid on Saturday for the funeral.

'Jan. 27, 1887.— Edinburgh was *splendid* on Sunday.

'Feb. 17.— Edinburgh is as good as ever, both the
boys and the students. Much happier. " The
Lord is good to all."

'March 3, 1887.— Symptoms you now openly avow
of having caught the Travel Fever in earnest. I
have seen premonitory symptoms of this for some
time, and in A.'s last letter it had gone the length
of " *spots*," but I held my counsel and kept silent,
knowing the hour was at hand. And now it has
come, and I make merry. But is it not good?
And really wholesome and tonic, and expansive
all round? And what a new proportion it gives
to things; for example, "God so loved the *World*,"
and " The City had *twelve* gates, and *every one a*
Pearl."

'But what it is exactly that travel gives, and is, one
can scarcely define, though not the least of it

must be the immensely bigger Environment to *think* in.

'I had forgotten that Emerson did not appreciate roving, but then he was an American, and their big country saves them from insularity, so they did not need it. Speaking of Emerson, I heard this of him lately: Himself tottering on the verge of the grave, he went to Longfellow's funeral. (L. was his oldest friend.) For some time he stood looking at the dead poet's face, and then said, "He was a beautiful soul . . . but . . . I forget his name!" (I do not know in the least what recalls this here, but, as you see, I am just chatting to-night.)

'In Edinburgh the current is flowing deep and strong. I do not think I would exchange that audience for anything else in the world.'

Through March the Edinburgh meetings continued large and enthusiastic. They closed with a Communion Service on the third Sunday. For the first few days of April Drummond took his own class as usual to Arran, and throughout the month was busy arranging the Students' Holiday Mission.

'GLASGOW, May 10, 1887.

'Moody writes urgently about going to America for a students' gathering, and I think I must go. I am also asked to give some lectures at Chautauqua (excuse the word), and thereafter may evangelise about among the American and Canadian colleges. If I go, it will be in the beginning or middle of June.'

In America he arrived on the 18th of June. But his work there was among the colleges, and falls to be described in another chapter.

From America Drummond returned to find his father dangerously ill. To a friend watching beside her mother's bed he wrote as follows: —

'GLENELM, STIRLING, Nov. 10.

'This is sad news your telegram brings me. I wonder much how it is at —— to-day. I suppose —— will have come, but nothing in the world can take off the awe and solemnity of a time like this. I did not tell you before — for you have enough to bear — that I am one with you in trouble. They wrote to Queenstown to prepare me for it, but the meeting has been a great shock. The doctors seem to fear the worst, and I am living here at present, and going in to Glasgow every day for a few hours. So you will know how I can partly understand what is going on with you.

'How suddenly the water deepens sometimes in one's life! How fast the bottom shelves, and yet how little one knows the depths that lie beyond — or whether the currents are to be swift or still!

'Well, I suppose it must be better, this deeper sea, than the shallows where the children play. But this is not my line to talk aloud like this: so basta! But I must add this. One thing I am learning, slowly, to believe in prayer. So I pray for you all.'

'14th Nov. — The thing that crushes is to look on silently at the unalleviable pain of those we love. But God knows the end; and it is His natural order that generation after generation should pass away.'

'16th Nov. — I have been reading an exquisite essay by Edwin Arnold on Death, which I shall send you some day. After all, what an entrancing thing Death is! I am glad I am an evolutionist, yet its surroundings are very terrible, in your case terrible unspeakably.'

'18th Nov. — I look eagerly for every report from ——. The last looks as if there might be a resurrection. But *living or dying we are the Lord's.* Trouble is not such a new thing to you. But it is to me, and I hear it saying many things. Some I never knew before; others one has heard, but never believed; others one has heard often, and as often forgotten. But the great benediction of it seems to lie less in the personal elements than in the larger views one gets of what is permanent, eternal, and most worth living for.

' My father lived for these things if ever man did.

' Pardon me writing more. He is sinking fast, and the end must be near.'

' 22d Nov. — I hope you have found all well on your return. It is a kind of shock always to come back from a place of great and solemn experiences and find things all going on as if nothing had happened. We tread the winepress alone. And yet it is sight and healing that the world should be so busy and unsympathetic.'

' 29th Nov. — My father lingers on. We can forecast nothing.'

' 10th Dec. — I begin to think my father is rallying in earnest.'

' 31st Dec. — This is the last time I shall write 1887. I have lots to say, but the post goes earlier tonight, and I must commit my wishes to the south wind. *Nun Gott sei mit, durch dieses Jahr!* And please see the blue in the sky, and there is always more than we can see.'

' 1st Jan. 1888.— The end has come now. My
father has begun the *New Year.* He passed
away this morning at five o'clock. You did not
know him, but he was a good soldier.'

The winter and spring of 1888 were spent by Drummond on his college class, and on what had now become his yearly meetings for the Edinburgh students.[1]
He also did some literary work.

' Jan. 28th.— I have become a veritable hermit-crab,
so far as that is consistent with about ten meetings per week. In the intervals of making new
addresses[2] I am doing a little (strictly private and
confidential) to the *Ascent of Man,* but the progress is miserable.'
' March 5th.— I am too exhausted after this to add
more. The Tub has been as still as the Pacific
since you left. Little has happened to the *Ascent.*
Edinburgh has been unusually absorbing. I have
stitched together a wee book on Africa; written a
college lecture or two; prepared an article for the
Britannica;[3] and consumed infinite smoke. *C'est
tout.*'

There was the usual visit to Arran with his students
in the end of March, and assistance, all that and the
next month, to a friend who was standing for a vacant
constituency. Concerning certain intrigues in regard
to which he is tempted to say, ' " The more one knows
of men," says my favourite Artemus Ward, " the more
one thinks of dogs." '
On the Higher Education of Women he writes:—

[1] See next chapter. [3] On the Zambezi.
[2] For Edinburgh students.

To Lady Aberdeen

'The main thing surely is that it be *real*, and not the mere accretion of further "accomplishments." I do not think it has touched this ideal yet, certainly not in the case of men. *Wise* women, balanced women, are what are needed, not accomplished ornaments — or bores. Specifically, then, they should be educated to be E. *women* and not second-rate E. *men*. Hence (don't laugh) the three things they should know from the foundation to the top before they put on any stucco are : (Mind) *Education* (What? Why? How?); (Body) *Physiology* and Ethics; Psychology and (Soul) *Theology*, or Theology alone. Apart from the obvious reason, and the importance of it, in these days when even our novels are theological, or sham-theological, women should know their way about here. Then your Political Economy would come in, etc., etc.'

In May Drummond received a remarkable requisition to deliver another series of religious addresses at Grosvenor House during the London season. It was signed with the following names: Aberdeen, Arthur James Balfour, W. St. John Brodrick, George N. Curzon, R. Munro Ferguson, Alfred Lyttelton, W. S. Murray (of the Grenadier Guards), George W. Russell, John Sinclair, and J. E. C. Welldon. To Captain Sinclair, who acted as secretary, Drummond replied : —

'GLASGOW, May 5, 1888.

'I feel very unequal to this piece of work, but after the most serious consideration I feel bound to face it. The kind interest of yourself and of your fellow-conspirators in the matter is of itself almost enough to determine my decision; and on all grounds I am persuaded I ought at least to make the attempt.

'With reference to the points you raise let me say: —

'1. That I am strongly of opinion that only *three* addresses, and on the Sundays you name, should be announced. When a long series is intimated, men imagine they can go at any time; and a main object should be to keep the first day's audience through the course rather than to have new men coming in at the end. An isolated address is almost useless. If it turned out to be advisable to have a fourth, it could be intimated at the third meeting without the necessity of issuing fresh tickets. But on all grounds, I think we should wait developments before announcing more than three.

'2. I am quite at a loss for the title of my subject. Robert Elsmere is a good suggestion, but would scarcely give scope for what one would really like to say, and would give rather a polemical or apologetic cast to the address. Would it not do to name no subject? None was announced last time. With this precedent, and the fact that the addresses are on Sunday, the suggestion of a religious subject might perhaps be strong enough without a direct statement. I fear no title would quite cover the ground one would like to go over.

'3. As the limitation to *Men* only might create an impression that the *subject* necessitated this, and was of a private character, would it not be well to put a footnote on the card in small type to some such effect as this: —

' " The limitation strictly to men is necessitated by
the accommodation."
' I hope these suggestions will not be out of keeping
with your own views.'

In accordance with this, a circular was drawn up
and signed by the requisitionists, intimating meetings
for men only, on Sundays, 3d, 10th, and 17th June, at
4 P.M. ' The great square room was densely crowded
by an interested and representative gathering — poli-
ticians, clergymen, authors, artists, critics, soldiers, and
barristers, with a large sprinkling of smart young men,
whose appearance would scarcely have suggested a
vivid interest in serious concerns.'[1] The addresses
(I do not know in what order) were on ' Evolution
and Christianity,' ' Natural Selection in Reference to
Christianity,' and the ' Programme of Christianity.'
After distinguishing between religion and theology
and emphasising Christianity as life, Professor Drummond said that the truth of Christianity is manifest in
the fact that there is no real civilisation without it,
and that the purer the form of Christianity, the greater
the development of civilisation. ' Show me,' he said
with Matthew Arnold, ' ten square miles outside of
Christianity where the life of man or the virtue of
woman is safe, and I'll throw over Christianity at
once.' He defined its place in the evolution of the
universe and of man as the crown and consummation
of the process. He showed its adaptability to the most
pressing requirements of the individual and of society,
accounted for its apparent failure to accomplish its
mission by the unfaithfulness of Christians to their
own ideal, and compared the efficacy of Christ's Gospel in ministering to such common ills as poverty,

[1] *Pall Mall Gazette*, June 11th.

distress, melancholy, and bad habits, with that of
Socialism, Political Economy, and Natural Morality.
The address upon 'Natural Selection in Reference to
Christianity' applied the latter to the individual. They
were often told, he said, that so far from religion being
a question of the survival of the fittest, it was the very
opposite; that nature and religion here parted company; that while in nature the race was to the swift
and the weak went to the wall, in religion the weak
and heavy-laden were helped and the bruised reed was
not broken. Yet, he thought, the same law held good
for both. Illustrating the meaning of the term 'survival of the fittest' by the case of the tadpole, which
when the pond dies and myriads of other organisms
die, yet survives and develops into another creature,
because it is surrounded with a mysterious apparatus
which enables it to effect that transformation under
different vital conditions, Professor Drummond said
that when they came to religion they found exactly
the same state of matters. . . . At the dissolution of
their bodies those who had here, in their being, somewhere, an apparatus for living in an unseen environment would survive, and they would survive because
they were fit, and not because they were worthy of
eternal life. . . . They were told by many that all men
at last would have eternal life, that God was good, and
that it was out of the question to conceive that any
should not survive. He knew nothing about the
survival or non-survival of those who had not the
special apparatus for developing; but they had little
reason to believe that if a man had not developed in
him the faculties for communicating with the spiritual
world, he would have that kind of life at least, whatever his immortality might be. *He that hath not the
Son hath not life.* God had invited every man and

woman to come to Him that they might have life; and if they resisted that invitation, they could not fall back upon generalities about God's goodness. And instead of it being more likely for a man to get these faculties after death, he was afraid it looked as if the chance diminished every year of his life. They were told by many that the future was so vague they should just take their chance. There was no such thing as chance. It was a question of the survival of the fittest, and unless a man was fit he had not the ghost of a chance. This was not an arbitrary enactment on God's part. It was natural law: a natural selection, a selection of those who had become fit, done by nature, not by God. As to what constituted fitness, they were told in the Bible that *without holiness no man shall see the Lord. . . .* They were also told in the Bible that *if a man loves the world, the love of the Father is not in him.* The man who loved the world was by that incapacitated from loving God. It was a question of taste, and religion was the education of the taste in that particular. The Christian was not to go out of the world, but he was not to love it. . . . Again they were told, *If any man have not the Spirit of Christ, he is none of His.* Only those who were unworldly could live in that society. A man to get into heaven, which was simply a select family, must have the family interest at heart. . . . These three things constituted fitness, and it was impossible to survive without them. Could *they* tell whether they were fit to survive or not? Must they wait until the judgment day, or was there to be a judgment day at all? He did not think there would be any bar, or any trumpet, or the machinery of a human event. These would be unnecessary, because a man would know whether he was fit to live in that world the moment he was brought into

contact with it. The moment a man submitted his
soul to God's friends, he would see at a glance instinctively whether he was fit to live in that company or
not. The moment he came into contact with Christ
— there was the judgment. Those he was addressing
could know at that moment whether they were fit to
survive. It was not religiousness nor good works
that constituted fitness. It was the possession of the
mind of Christ, unworldliness, holiness. They who
had these would survive. That was eternal life. It
was a beautiful life, it was the life they would like
to have eternal, the only life worth being eternal.
They could see at once that the law of natural selection was a law which would keep heaven pure. Its
object was to produce fitness — not to keep some out,
but to make clear that those who got in should be
worthy of it, pure, heavenly minded, unworldly. All
men could be eligible if they would get into the environment suitable to the development of this fitness.
To do that, they must, in the first place, turn their
backs upon the old environment, upon the world; and,
secondly, they must live in the new environment, or,
in Scriptural language, *Abide in Christ*, and that environment would in itself produce these changes. There
was an undeveloped bud in every one, and they had
only to abide in Christ, and it would grow into beauty
and send its fragrance upon all around. A brief
prayer followed the address.[1]

The usual letters, appeals, interviews, ensued upon
these addresses; and years after they were given,
thoughts, questions, resolutions, and decisions of character which they had stirred came back to Drummond
for sympathy and counsel — often from lonely men
and women working on the far fringes of that world-

[1] From a newspaper report.

wide Empire to the whole of which you speak if you speak in London.

Besides the meetings for men at Grosvenor House, Drummond addressed a large meeting of young women of the West End of London in the residence of the Speaker of the House of Commons. This meeting was held in pursuance of the aims of the Associated Workers' League started in 1885; and a separate club was formed from among those present for the purpose of informing and guiding them in all the usual work to which they had given themselves. The '88 Club' (as it was called) was to consist 'of working members who will each undertake some definite work, however small, undertaking to help each other when so called upon, to remember each other at some set time, and to send in to the Secretary quarterly reports of their work.' A letter from the President 'rejoices that every one who has joined the "88" has in some way or other definitely recognised the obligation under which we are placed as human beings to make life better worth living to others. The *raison d'être* of the Club is not to impose any fresh duty upon us, but the Club was intended to act as a constant help and reminder that we are already bound, in some way or other, to make service for others the aim of our lives. We recognise to the full the paramount claim of home-duties.' The motto of the Club was '*Præsto et Persto*': 'I undertake and persevere.' In 1889 the Club started a magazine to give descriptions of philanthropic activity, and especially of such as are suitable for young women of the wealthier classes who live in the country, reports of the members' work, and notices of books relevant to the aims of the Club. A volume, from December, 1889, to September, 1892, contains articles on 'Women's Work in Large Cities,' 'Friendly Societies for Women,'

x

'Women's Work and Wages,' 'Women's Settlements
in London,' 'Clubs for Girls,' 'The Higher Education
of Women,' 'Country Neighbours,' 'Village Choirs,'
'Needlework Guilds for the Country,' 'Suggestions
how to help Servants,' 'An Experimental Household
Club,' 'Workhouse Suggestions,' 'Bee-keeping,' 'Children's Country Holiday'—and so forth.

'LOCHMORE LODGE, LAIRG, July 3.

'Arrived here one hour ago after a charming drive.
The place is buried in mountains, and London
already seems a million miles away. There has
been no rain, and till it comes I must simply
smoke and dream, for there is not a solitary fin
in the loch.'

'July 9.

'The change from London has been delightful. I
have had four days' absolute peace and indolence.
Yesterday I had a service at twelve in the servants' hall, to which keepers, foresters, and their
wives trooped in for miles and miles, and I liked
the thing much better than Grosvenor House.
The —— has been spreading its poison in the
Highlands, and one or two would not contami-
nate themselves by coming out to hear so awful a
monster. (This is quite true.) London ended
better than it began. The ladies' meeting went
off, I think, fairly well, and Harrow was of some
use also, I hope.'

In the middle of August Drummond started for a
tour in Switzerland with his mother and sisters.

'SONNENBERG HOTEL, ENGELBERG, Aug. 19.

'I am lost in wonder all day long. Switzerland is
the one place in the world which is never false to

old impressions, which never betrays one by a shadow of disappointment, but grows in grandeur with all one's faculties. I find this truer than ever this year, and I suppose this is my eighth or ninth time in it.'

He took his mother and sisters by Engsteln Alp, the Grimsel, Fiesch, and over the Simplon to the Italian lakes, where he left them and returned to meet Lord Aberdeen at Lucerne.

To Lady Aberdeen

'LUCERNE, Sept. 16.

'A printed notice at our hotel told us of the usual Free Church service here in the Maria Hilf Kirche. Mr. —— of —— to preach during September. When we got there we found a congregation, mostly American, standing outside the *locked* door. The hour struck, but no minister appeared, and not even a beadle was about. By and by A. and I hunted up an old woman, got the keys, requisitioned two Swiss urchins to blow the organ, and an American Miss to play it, and got under way with an extemporised sermon. A. gave out the hymns and precented from an organ loft, about a hundred feet above the floor, and after a little singing I read a chapter and discoursed, and then we had prayer and more singing and — no collection. The hymn-books had to be sent for to " The Swan," and no one knows why the parson did not appear. One idea is that the thing closes in the middle of September; another, that the parson had fallen down a crevasse. Anyhow, I mean to report matters to headquarters, as there was some unparliamentary

language going, and the Down Grade in the F. C.
must not be allowed to descend to glaciers.   I
hope —— at next Assembly will introduce an
overture that henceforth " all continental chap-
lains shall be roped." '

' ANDERMATT, Sept. 23.

' This has been a happy Sabbath.   In the morning
I went up the mountain alone; then spent an
hour with two old bauers in a wee Roman Catholic Chapel.   Hymns with A. and Dr. and Mrs.
—— in the afternoon and evening.'

' VENICE, Sept. 27.

' I met Browning[1] to-day and had a chat, also the
Queen of Portugal — and had no chat.'

' MONTE GENEROSO, Oct. 4, 1888.

' I left A. at Zermatt and ran off to Venice to my
mother and sisters.   We wandered up and down
with Ruskin's *Stones of Venice* in our hands till
it was too dark to read.   I never felt more be-
holden to any author than to Ruskin during these
days.   It was to me a revelation.   I must go
back.

' I met Browning on the street one day and had a
memorable chat with him.   He said this was his
ninth visit to Venice, and he always found out
new things.

' The Italian Bible I sent you is selling in every
kiosk, and by the ten thousand.   Issued simply
as classical literature by an irreligious man, it is
being read on every hand.

' I am now back again with A., and will stay quietly
reading and dreaming till the 10th or 12th.'

---

[1] H. D. had met Browning at Dollis Hill in June, 1885.   ' I had a walk with
him.   He is quite unlike a poet, and talks plain prose.   To meet him you would
think he was an elderly but well-preserved and smart French banker.'

The winter of 1888–89 passed in the usual labours
— college lectures, new addresses for Edinburgh, and
endless meetings of philanthropic societies. He was
kept very busy, and claim after claim upon him had to
be refused in the interests of his work for the students.
In February he wrote : —

> 'I shall need my Saturday night to myself, that is,
> to the students. I have not had a moment this
> week. There are always heaps of people for ———,
> and I am sure they do not need me so much as I
> need myself on Saturday. Try to see it in this
> way.'

Part of his work this year was the founding of a
University Settlement in Glasgow. His intense interest at this time in such work is proof of how far
he had advanced in his conception of Christianity since
the early days, when the social side of religion had
few charms for him.

'March 27.

> 'I am busy with the University men here, planning
> a Settlement in a poor district. The leader is an
> Established Church student, the second a med-
> ical, the third an Arts man coming on for the
> Free Church College. Plans are out, and the
> thing will be built by the beginning of next ses-
> sion. Thirty men are already at work in the dis-
> trict, and there will be fifteen residents. Is not
> this good? It will be on earnest evangelical
> lines, and ought to be a great blessing to the
> University. The first formal meeting of workers
> takes place in my house next Tuesday night.'

In the beginning of April Dr. Smeaton, Professor
of New Testament Exegesis in New College, Edin-

burgh, died, and Drummond threw himself with ardour
into the work of securing the election of Dr. Dods to
the vacant chair.

To Lady Aberdeen

'April 25, 1889.

'I have great hope.   The younger men are rallying
finely, and the issue is now seen to be, not the
personal one, but the large question of Liberalism
versus Toryism.   I have long wanted a test vote
on that point, as Scotland has changed much even
since Robertson Smith was put out.   His critics
have been watching a chance to get at Dods for
his Pan-Council Speech, and this will be made
the occasion of it.   The row will be very serious,
and many good people must pass through tribu-
lation — the price of progress.'

June 10.

'I hope you recognise the handwriting.   I believe
the writer has been in his Tub for some weeks.
The scenery there is at times monotonous, so the
poor wretch has seldom anything to write about.
These are placid days, and no earthquakes.

'One —— came upon me like a meteor on Friday,
and on Saturday went off again into Space.   His
talk was of fish, flies, and lochs, and at times in-
coherent, so I know not whither he has gone.
He used much guile to allure me from these
shades, but wild-horses could not draw me at
this moment.   Towards the end of the month
this pelican of the wilderness and owl of the
desert plumeth his wings for Stack.'

To a Friend

'All good wishes go with this for the 20th. Surely
your cup can never be much fuller than it is this
July. The sentries cry "All Well" from every
outpost, and only the one ubiquitous and never-
sleeping enemy within lives to be reckoned with.
What can I wish for you better, and for all of us,
than that he shall have less and less dominion
over us? With your thorn in the flesh the fight
is hard, but when the smoke clears we shall
wonder at the legions that were slain, and when
we almost thought the battle had turned against
us. Every bullet has its billet. That is one
thing sure. The moral is "Charge!"'

'GLASGOW, July 24.

'I went up to Stack, looked at it, then at the rain-
less sky, and said to the coachman, "Drive on."
It was absolutely hopeless. At present I am a
close prisoner, trying to work, but making almost
nothing of it. I hope your busy life pays you
better.'

'CUILFAIL HOTEL, KILMELFORD, ARGYLLSHIRE, Aug. 1.

'Interruptions to my work have been incessant all
summer, and I have run off here to try to get
some necessary things done before the Bonskeid
gathering stops my work at the end of the month.
You have heard —— rave about Loch Melford?
That is where I am. This hotel is at the head
of the loch, twenty-five miles' drive from Ardris-
haig, fairly lovely, very healthy, and lonely enough.
There are several people at the hotel, but I have
scarcely spoken to a soul for some days, and am
deep in a hamper of books.'

'Aug. 14.

'I am inextricably fixed here with a heavy programme to get through and a warning sent to
all my friends that I am not going to be visible,
audible, or accessible for the whole of August.
'I go to the Tub to-morrow, as my books of reference are exhausted, also the weather, and the
hotel has become a shooting-lodge, and a bedlam
of dogs has broken loose.'

'BONSKEID, Sept. 3.

'A thousand thanks for your letter. How well do
I know the experience you describe — the evapo-
ration of a great and moving thought when one
tries to expose it to the public air! "Hast thou
Faith? Have it to *thyself*," the Bible somewhere
says.'

'BONSKEID (no date).

'I must still be vague and say, "About the last
week." There ought to be *margins* left round
all lines where it is possible. We sometimes tie
up Providence as well as ourselves.'

After Bonskeid he spent a fortnight deerstalking
and fishing at Guisachan and Haddo, then came back
to Glasgow for work, and before the session began
went to Haddo and Rossie Priory for certain meetings
and services.

'Oct. 5.

'D—— has been saying very straight things lately,
and this crooked and perverse generation is doing
its best to drive him from the synagogue. He
does not like it, and is in very low water, but one
dare not wish him rescued.'

'Nov. 12.

'*P.T.O.* and you will find something worth reading.
I shall not spoil it by adding more at present. I
pray all goes well.— Yours ever,   H. D.'

'"Holiness is an infinite compassion for others:
Greatness is to take the common things of life
and walk truly among them: Happiness is a
great love and much serving."'

'Nov. 16.

'I am glad you are getting among your books.
With shame I confess I have never read Stanley's
Jewish Church. Long it has been on my *List.*
I have just been glancing at George Eliot's *Jubal*
and *Stradivarius.* . . . I see no new books worth
sending. I wonder if you feel, as I do, an un-
healthy liking for *new* books. I have continually
to pull myself up and go back to old and dusty
friends — to find them after all the best.
'I hope you did *not* have it out with ——. How
well I know the torture of suppression! "Many
things" had He also which He could not tell His
disciples.'

'Nov. 20.

'Your letter this morning is delightful. I am so
glad you have taken the veil. There is no life
like the Tub life. How calmly one regards the
passing show, now laughing at it, now crying
over it, now rushing in for a day to help some
poor wretch falling under his flag, but always
coming back again to the true Ark! I suppose
one ought to join the procession oftener, *i.e. me :
pour vous,* you have trudged till you are tired,
and others must pull your caravan a bit. You

see poor Elmslie [1] has fallen at his post. You did not know him or *see* him, the real Elmslie. But this is a real shock to me. He was one of the brightest and most living spirits of this age, one of the best equipped men for the future struggle; a hundred of us ought to have gone before him.

'I see that your thoughts still go out to the "new theology," and I am going to send you a few books in that line to glance over. You will doubtless already have discovered the points in *Jubal* and *Stradivarius*.'

'Bellamy I never heard of. Mackintosh I know as an acquaintance of some years' standing. He studied for the Free Church, but stuck at the Confession, and will not be ordained. He lives to expound the new theology. He is one of the acutest minds in the country, a thorough scholar, and has already written one book (*Christ and the Jewish Law*) and two pamphlets (one on the Confession, the other an attack on Revivalism). These pamphlets are too fierce. But his book is admirable. The *new* book [2] I have only glanced at. It is sure to be good. I shall send you a new book of Dr. Bruce's, which you will get much from.'

'GLASGOW, Nov. 28.

'To-night I preside at the opening of our University Settlement here.'

'Jan. 2, 1890.

'This is a delightful sketch of yours, and really important. If you ask my honest opinion, I shall give it on all the points you ask, but please

[1] Professor W. G. Elmslie, died Nov. 16, 1889, *ætat* forty-two.
[2] *Essays towards a New Theology*.

notice the above first sentence, and take what
follows for what it is worth. . . . Last. The
style is not good! Indeed, it is bad; once or
twice very bad. Sentences are overloaded; and
though words are always well chosen, no *work*
has been spent in improving it. You never do
spend enough work on that department, and how
can you when you are so busy? But please,
Mr. Editor, you must try. Pass the roller slowly
over your work. Now I have said it, and of
course feel a fiend for doing it. Tell —— not to
bring a horse-whip next time we meet. You *can*
do it, *i.e.* write better, if you will only keep the
simple rule of the Umbrian and "fence in the
morning hours." A *Nineteenth Century* article
should be written at least three times — once in
simplicity, once in profundity, and once to make
the profundity appear simplicity.

'This letter, being official, shall contain no more.
Other matters will follow to-morrow. — Yours
mercilessly,

'EXCELSIOR.

'What a horrid letter!'

'GLASGOW, Jan. 11, 1890.

'Dresden? *Freut mich sehr* to hear you speak of
    it. I did not think you would bridge across the
    Channel for all the doctors in the kingdom. I
    wish I could make it more tempting, but, do you
    know, I have never even been in Dresden. I am
    waiting for that German governess, who will help
    me to understand the pictures. But all I have
    heard of it is good, and you will get what you
    need most just now — art, both music and paint-
    ing, to your heart's content. To make it an
    epoch you must read up the Masters a bit be-

tween this and then. How I wish I could do
that! I believe a fortnight's reading is enough
to make one a cracked enthusiast for life. But,
like Darwin, most of us (not you) live dead to
it all.'

'Jan. 17.

'At Christmas-time I tried everywhere, both in
Edinburgh and Glasgow, for a bound copy of
Greatest Thing, but it was nowhere to be found,
and no copies are yet forthcoming. On New
Year's Day I ordered the fifty thousand from the
printers, but the binders cannot get the bound one
touched until orders for the other one are executed.
However, I hope it will come in a day or two, and I
shall then obey your behest, though much against
the grain. Of course I did not send —— one,
and I absolutely refuse to send "tracts" to him.'

This letter touches on a curious habit of Drummond's. He did not do his publishing like other
authors. He chose paper, type, and binding, and dealt
with the printers himself. It was a needless trouble,
but he said he enjoyed 'the sport' of it.

'Jan. 21.

'I am all but talked to death these days. One
meeting, Sunday; two, Monday; two, Tuesday;
one to-day, and so on.'

During the previous autumn invitations had reached
Drummond from the Australian colleges to come and
tell them of the Edinburgh Student Movement and do
what he had done in America. He had refused to go
to Australia the year before, but now he agreed.

'Feb. 28.

'I wish I knew better what Australia would be, and
how the work will open and develop. I must do

that thoroughly, for it is once in a lifetime, and I
shall " not pass this way again " in all probability.
And since I saw you I have had an urgent appeal
from Japan to go to Tokio University for a little
on my way back. The University opens there
late in autumn.'

'March 6.

' I should much like to meet George Macdonald.
He has been a real teacher to many. I am taking
Robert Falconer to read on the voyage. My *pièce
de résistance*, however, will be Browning. I am
taking him complete, and mean to go through
with him thoroughly. None can approach him
for insight into life, or even into Christianity.

'Imperial Federation begins to dawn upon me.
Perhaps you shall hear of me lecturing upon it!
I have a lecture all ready on the " Evolution of
Natives," and two pages added would make it out
and out Imperial-Federationesque. The idea is
great and worth working at. But as I have to
introduce into Australia the Boys' Brigade, the
Home Reading Union, and other modern improvements, I fear I have too many strings to my
bow.'

1884–90. — These seven years of Drummond's life,
which have been summarised in this chapter, were
the years of his fame and greatest activity along many
lines. Even in them he did nothing greater than his
work among students. We have already marked the
signs of its progress, but it was so big and the issues
so far-reaching that it requires a chapter to itself. To
follow the movement we must return to 1884, in which
year it started in Edinburgh.

CHAPTER XII

BESIDES his mission to young men under Mr. Moody, the greatest work which Henry Drummond achieved was his work among students. Started at Edinburgh in 1884, it spread to many other colleges of Great Britain. It took him to Germany, to America, and to Australia. Up to the very end it remained his chief interest and burden. He reckoned as mere distractions from it not only the most honourable of calls to positions of eminence on other arenas of life, but even many of those forms of work in which he had hitherto achieved success. He shut himself off from the pulpits of his Church, denied his friends, turned from the public, banished reporters, and endured infinite misrepresentation, if only he might make sure of the students. Had one asked him towards the end what the work of his life had been, he would certainly have replied, ' My work among them.' And measured by results, almost everything he did seems less; for the field was one on which other ministers of religion had many failures, and he conspicuously succeeded. Hundreds of men who never went to church were won for Christ at his meetings. He invented methods that are now employed wherever students join for religious service. He preached the Gospel of Christ with a fulness and with a pertinacity of personal application which he never excelled on any other platform. And so he influenced thousands of lives, which are

now at work among many nations, in all those professions of governing and teaching and healing, to
which the University is the necessary introduction.

As for all great religious movements, so for this,
there had been preparation and signs beforehand.[1]
In April, 1884, the University of Edinburgh celebrated the tercentenary of its foundation. Among the
many meetings was one under the auspices of the
Students' Representative Council, for the students
themselves, of whom there were eleven or twelve
hundred present. The Lord Rector, Sir Stafford
Northcote, was in the chair, and brief addresses were
given by Mr. Russell Lowell, then American Ambassador, Count de Lesseps, Count Saffi, Professors Pasteur, Virchow, von Helmholtz, and de Laveleye.
Robert Browning, too, said a few words. ' If the
speakers had merely given utterance to complimentary
commonplaces, such an assembly could not have been
commonplace. But the unexpected thing was that
from the deeply spiritual prayer of Principal Rainy
till the closing benediction, there was a reverential
tone, and throughout the addresses there sounded
an earnest call to the acknowledgment of God, which
rang out most clearly in the closing word of the last
of the illustrious orators, Professor de Laveleye:
" Remember the profound and beautiful words of
Jesus, which would put an end to all our troubles and
all our discords if it were but listened to: *Seek first
the kingdom of God and His righteousness, and all
other things will be added unto you.*" '

Again, at the beginning of the following session in
October, Principal Sir Alexander Grant, in his open-

[1] The following paragraphs owe much to Professor A. R. Simpson's pamphlet
The Year of Grace 1885 in the University of Edinburgh, published by the Inter-
University Christian Union, 93, Aldersgate Street, London, E.C.

ing address — the last he was to deliver — 'claimed for his University, founded by the Reformers, that it always had a distinctively Christian character,' and he called upon the students to ' recognise and sustain this reputation.'

In November the Medical Students' Christian Association held their annual meeting, and listened to more than usually helpful addresses from Professor Douglas Maclagan, the retiring President, and his successor, Dr. Greenfield, the Professor of Pathology. ' The Arts Students' Prayer Meeting also set out with much vigour, aided by a stimulating address from Professor Calderwood.' Outside the University some students and resident surgeons at the infirmary had been roused to an earnest faith by the work of Dr. Moxey, the Lecturer on Elocution at New College.

So things had been shaping, when on the 10th December Messrs. Stanley Smith and C. T. Studd,[1] the two Cambridge graduates who had given themselves to the work of the China Inland Mission, held in Edinburgh a meeting for students. Professor Charteris was in the chair, and had around him several of his colleagues from the different faculties, extra-mural lecturers and hospital residents. There were seven hundred students present, and the addresses were so impressive that the greater proportion remained to a second meeting, after which a crowd of students singing hymns accompanied the two young evangelists to the railway station. In January Messrs. Smith and Studd held three more meetings in Edinburgh under the presidency of Professors Charteris, Butcher, and Grainger Stewart, and attended by increasing numbers of students. ' At times in those days scenes were

---

[1] Smith had been stroke-oar of the Cambridge eight, Studd captain of the Cambridge eleven.

enacted that recalled the First of John, and young men who were disposed to think that no good could come out of the meetings were induced by their fellows to come and see; and they came and found Jesus. Some were impressed by the stirring eloquence of Mr. Stanley Smith's appeals. Others were attracted by the straightforward narrative of Mr. Studd's experiences. All were fain to recognise that it was no unmanly thing to become a Christian, and that there was some magnetic, mighty influence in the power of a life wholly given to the service of the world's Redeemer.'

All these facts it is necessary to give, in order to show how disposed to religion the life of a university is, and lest any might think that to start a great movement on such a stage requires the advent of one commanding personality.

In December Drummond had made his first appearance before his own university as a teacher by giving the annual lecture of its Christian Medical Association. Professor Geikie was in the chair; there was a fair number of students present, and Drummond redelivered his inaugural discourse on ' The Contribution of Science to Christianity.'[1] Whatever his audience had previously known, or not known, about him, they now saw before them a religious teacher utterly free from conventionalism, ardent and enthusiastic as any of themselves, fearless of facts, loyal to the intellectual methods of the age, but still with an unshaken faith in God and in the reality of spiritual experience. He was immediately urged to return and lead the movement which had just started. His reply was, ' I cannot address students in cold blood;' and besides (as appears from his letters), he was sure that he could not work

[1] Summarised above in chap. ix.

Y

with freedom upon all the methods on which the movement was conducted.   The difficulties, however, were
removed, and he engaged to give one address on the
Sunday evening subsequent to Messrs. Smith and
Studd's last meeting.   He stipulated that it should be
for students only, and upon new ground.   The Oddfellows' Hall was chosen, the nearest that could be
found to the University Buildings.   It was simply
announced that 'Professor Drummond would give an
address,' and an audience gathered that nearly filled
the hall.[1]

'It is difficult,' says one who was present, 'to describe the
impression one got in such a meeting.   We have seen young
men's meetings gathered before a platform crowded with
ministers surrounding a world-renowned evangelist.   But this
was not a random gathering of the young men of Edinburgh.
There were youths from all parts of Scotland.   There were
many from England and Wales.   India had some of her dark
sons there.   Australia, Canada, the Cape and all our colonies
sent their contingents.   They had all come to our city to
study, and were in various stages of their curriculum.   Knowledge had been for them the principal thing; and they found
themselves, somewhat wonderingly, in a scene where they
might haply get something they had not got in any classroom.
They saw the platform filled with their teachers, their class-
tutors, and some of their own number whom they might recognise as officials of one or other of the Christian Associations.
When they had sung the Hundredth Psalm, and the Professor
occupying the chair had led in prayer, and read a portion of
Scripture, they sang another hymn.   Then the young gentleman at the chairman's side, who was a stranger still to many
of them, came forward to the table, and the confidence at
once awakened by his open, earnest look at them was confirmed when he began to talk to them in the well-known
classroom tone of a lecturer who has some knowledge which
it is his business to impart to his auditors, and which it is their

1 It holds about nine hundred.

supreme business at this hour to acquire. He began by telling, with graphic detail, how a geologist had opened a mine
in search of a silver lode, and when his fortune had nearly
melted away, said to his people that for a few weeks longer
they might dig, and if they found no silver they must cease ;
how it was sold to one more fortunate, whose men had only
dug through two yards of soil when they came on one of the
richest veins of silver in England. "Now, I believe," said
the lecturer, "that there are some men in this hall who are
not two yards off from a treasure greater than can be found
in all the mines of earth." And then he proceeded to enforce on them the command of Jesus, *Seek ye first the kingdom of God and His righteousness.* After the address he
prayed, and before giving out a closing hymn he intimated that
an after-meeting would be held for personal converse with
any who might feel that they could get further help from
himself or any other believers present. No urgent appeal
was made; rather they were told that probably the best thing
for some of them would be to go home and speak with none
but God. Yet the after-meeting was large, and some declared
their willingness to be the Lord's.'

Drummond would not commit himself to a series of
meetings. Till the end of each it was left open whether
there was to be another. With one break, he returned
every Sunday evening till the end of the session.

'The atmosphere of the classroom seemed always to pervade the meetings, and at a telling illustration, or apt appeal,
there was often a suppressed sound of the pleasure with which
it had been received. It must have been at one of the early
meetings, when he had for text the grand Gospel invitation
in the end of the eleventh of Matthew, that Mr. Drummond
used an illustration which caught their attention and guided
some to the discipleship of Christ. "You ask what it is, this
coming to Christ. Well, what does Jesus Himself tell you
here? He says 'Learn of Me.' Now, you are all learners.
You have come to Edinburgh, some of you from the ends of
the earth, to learn. And how did you put yourself in the
way of learning what is here taught? You went to the Uni-

versity office and wrote your name in a book. You matriculated; and becoming a University student, you went to get
from each individual professor what he had to teach. So,
with definite purpose to learn of Christ, must you come to
Him and surrender yourself to His teaching and guidance."
Sometimes thereafter, when a happy worker had to tell of a
new addition to the number of Christ's disciples, he would
pleasantly say that So-and-so had "matriculated." '

In February the Indian statesman, Sir William
Muir, was appointed Principal of Edinburgh University. On the day after his inauguration, he attended
one of the meetings in the Oddfellows' Hall, and closed
his brief address by pronouncing upon it the benediction of the closing verses in Numbers vi. ' You will
more easily imagine than I can describe the thrill of
emotion that ran through the hall. It would have
sought utterance in the usual applause, but for the
reverent " Hush-sh ! " of the majority, and was finally
expressed by the whole mass in the galleries and floor
rising up and sitting quietly down again when the
Principal had bowed his acknowledgment of their
loving reverence.'

How real and deep Drummond felt the work to be
may be seen from his letters, which we have already
quoted. Even with his experience of such movements
he was taken by surprise. ' It is a distinct work of
God,' he writes ; ' such a work as I, after considerable
experience of evangelistic work, have never seen before.' ' It haunts me like a nightmare. The responsibility I feel almost more than anything in my life.'
' I do not think I would exchange that audience for
anything else in the world.'

The work in Edinburgh required Drummond's presence every Sunday, and he refused invitations to visit
other universities ; but these of themselves seemed

ready for the movement, several of their own professors organised meetings, and from Edinburgh deputations were sent to address these under the leadership
of Professors Charteris, Grainger Stewart, and Greenfield, and Dr. Cathcart, while several of their own professors and graduates worked hard to make them a
success. In Aberdeen, Dr. Hay, the Professor of
Medical Jurisprudence, organised three meetings before the end of the session. From about eight hundred
students at King's and Marischal Colleges, three hundred and eighty attended the first meeting, addressed
by a deputation from Edinburgh, and over *seventy*
remained to the after-meeting, the majority of them
discussing questions with the leaders till a very late
hour. More than three hundred attended the second
and third. The result was not only the formation of a
University Christian Association, and the decision of
many for a more strenuous Christianity, but the moral
elevation of the whole life of the University, which, as
I remember well, was not transitory.

In Glasgow the movement was still stronger. The
first deputation from Edinburgh consisted of Professor Grainger Stewart, Dr. Cathcart, Mr. G. P.
Smith,[1] one of the chief Organisers of the Edinburgh
work, and seven other students.

From James M. Macphail to Professor Drummond

2, MAULL TERRACE, PARTICK, March 16, 1885.

' The hall was crowded to excess by the most orderly
students' meeting I[2] ever attended. Dr. M'Kendrick
presided, and Professors Gairdner, Ramsay, Veitch,

---

[1] Now a medical missionary in China.
[2] James M. Macphail then a medical student at Glasgow University, and now
medical missionary among the Santhals.

Robertson, and quite a crowd of assistants were present.
The Edinburgh men spoke with power, especially, I
think, the young fellows who were making a public
stand for Christ for the first time. Four hundred
remained to the after-meeting. We were kept busy
till about ten o'clock [when the hall had to be closed].
Many men waited who had been thinking about accepting Christ for a long time, and who talked to us about
their difficulties. As far as we could see, there were
many cases of true conversion, and also of spiritual
quickening. Dr. M'Kendrick told me the meeting was
the finest he had ever attended. We are continuing
our union of prayer in our rooms at ten o'clock every
evening this week.'

'March 10.

' The meeting on Sabbath evening was not quite so
large as on the previous Sabbath, but the hall was
filled. Dr. M'Kendrick took the chair, and Professors
Dickson and Gairdner were on the platform, and quite
a number of assistants were present. The meeting
was a very impressive one, and Dr. M'Kendrick spoke
more clearly and earnestly than I had ever heard him
speak before. The after-meeting was a very remarkable and, I believe, fruitful one. The inquirers were
of all sorts—some convinced of sin, some atheists,
some anxious to be Christians, and yet with doubts and
difficulties in the way. I felt very much the extreme
delicacy of the task of dealing with many of these
fellows. Really this is the part of the work, above
all others, which demands earnest prayer. Professors
Gairdner, Ramsay, and Jebb have been waited upon,
and have expressed a very deep interest in the whole
movement. Dr. M'Kendrick is quite convinced that
it is a work of God and not of man.'

'March 24.

'The meeting last Sabbath was a most successful
one. Dr. M'Gregor Robertson presided. Dr. Barbour
gave an exceedingly beautiful and striking address,
and Dr. Woodhead's was also very impressive. The
inquiry meeting was a large and, we have good reason
to believe, a fruitful one.'

'March 30.

'Last Sabbath's meeting was, I think, the most
impressive of all. The hall was crowded in every
part, thirty or forty having to stand. Professor Jebb
presided, but did very little beyond giving out hymns
and introducing the speakers, yet the mere fact that
he was there bore testimony to the widespread interest
in the movement. Dr. Williamson of China gave an
address. Dr. Yellowlees, Lecturer on Insanity, and
Dr. Hay [of Aberdeen] followed. Our after-meeting
was the largest we have had. Dr. Williamson spoke
a few words from the platform; and after that Professor Hay, Dr. Yellowlees, and Principal Douglas
went among the students. One feature of this meeting was the large number who waited to discuss doctrinal difficulties. Several cases of apparent decision
for Christ came under my own notice.'

Though Drummond could not attend any of those
Sunday meetings, he met with the Glasgow students
on week-days for prayer and conference.

When the session came to an end, sixty or seventy
of the Edinburgh students volunteered to carry the
influences which had blessed themselves to young men
in other towns. So the Holiday Mission arose. It
spread to many parts of Scotland, England, and Ireland. The volunteers were carefully organised, and
Drummond, Dr. Cathcart, and some of the professors
superintended many of the operations.

'3, CARLTON GARDENS, March 24, 1885.

'Everything goes well. And, I think, by the time
you come back you will find fires lit in many
places. I hear that the third year's men, at their
meeting on Sunday afternoon in Edinburgh,
arranged to start eight Bible-classes, and they
hope to raise the number to fourteen. They had
the best inquiry meeting they have yet had.
To-morrow I am coming to meet our sixty new
evangelists. They have all been summoned by
post-card to meet in Oddfellows' Hall at five. . . .
Many of the medicals now want to be missionaries.'

Which of us does not still remember the advent of
these first 'Holiday Missioners' among our manses!
They were scattered upon us with the spring, and
they came young, hearty, and laughing to be free of
the long winter's classes. They were sent, not as
advocates, but as witnesses, and they gave their testimonies with a freshness and simplicity that went to
the hearts of the older people who listened to them.
Of course, there were crudities and indiscretions; but
one would rather have had these than undue maturity
and bumptiousness, of which there was next to nothing. Every deputation of five or six had one or two
really able men among them, carrying a good conscience from their past work, and well trained in
philosophy or science. They had little or no theology,
but they told of Christ's power upon themselves, and
did so in a manly, moral spirit that brought new hope
to every tempted man who heard them. They talked,
too, of their doubts and intellectual difficulties in a
way that proved very profitable to us ministers in
dealing with young men, and appealed most powerfully to those of their own age. Naturally, they

impressed their educated contemporaries more than others. But they seldom left any town or village, whatever its intellectual condition might be, without having moved several young men to a clearer and more strenuous life in dependence upon Christ.[1] Next to this, they interested us most by their open reflection of Drummond. His way of putting things, his stories, his accent, his characteristic reserve, his pauses and hesitations, were reproduced almost to mimicry. It was a great tribute to the influence of his personality; but how we used to chaff him about it!

The organisation of the Holiday Mission cost Drummond and his assistants very much thought and hard work. He held the reins firmly, and had full reports sent to him through the secretaries. From all the towns, large and small, of the Scottish lowlands he has kept letters with accounts of meetings and individual cases; and he was applied to almost every day for counsel as to the latter, as well as to the general strategy of the mission. He knew the perils to which his young missioners were exposed, and both received reports on the conduct of each, and returned frank warnings. There are many grateful letters from ministers, to whose parishes deputations had been sent. Finally, he started off to examine some of the work for himself.

---

[1] In Greenock a large circus was filled with men to overflowing; 'several openly professed decision for Christ in the after-meeting.' In Crieff Mr. Henderson said there had been nothing like the results since 1874. In Stirling the meetings were 'crowded and enthusiastic.' At Killin 'a meeting well on for two hundred men for a beginning;' in Wick week-night audiences varied from two hundred to three hundred; 'it is no metaphor to say that the whole town of Wick is moved just now;' unanimity prevails among all the churches. And so forth. In Edinburgh one congregation added forty-five young communicants, 'most of them the result of deputation work.'

To Professor Greenfield

'EASTBOURNE, April 25, 1885.

'. . . I came here, or at least to Brighton, on Monday, to see how a troupe of students were getting on with their holiday mission. I found half a dozen of them hard at work. They had had meetings for eight days before I came, and with real result. They are splendid fellows, and talked with the utmost simplicity, earnestness, and power. I have spent the last month in visiting the deputies at various places, and am greatly impressed with the *men*. Nearly all are medicals, some mere boys, and a finer set I never knew. It has been a real privilege to be among them. I hear four hundred new men are coming up to Edinburgh this summer. What a work is before you! My heart is in Edinburgh, and I should greatly like to be back again. But that dreadful business at Grosvenor House, of which I told you, is in full swing, and I am a prisoner till then.'

'LONDON, July 10, 1885.

' I met a Bradford man yesterday, who had been to all the students' meetings in B. (we sent a deputation there), and he reports a deep and enduring impression.'

In October Drummond made his mission to the undergraduates of Oxford. The proposal for this had begun with some of his hearers at Grosvenor House, and with one or two Oxford heads who had read his book. There were some difficulties in making the arrangements, for Drummond and those who knew his work were anxious that he should not appear under the auspices of any religious school, nor in continuance of the conventional methods of evangelistic work. Finally, there was a wonderful consensus of invitations to him from all quarters. Sir William Anson, Warden of All Souls; Canon Girdlestone; Canon Scott Holland; Mr. Butler of Oriel; Canon Percival, President of Trinity; the Rev. Mr. Christopher; Mr. George N. Curzon and Mr. George W. Russell all wrote wishing success, and offering to facilitate arrangements for his visit. Drummond went as the guest of Sir William Anson, and his 'first lecture' was advertised for the 'Hall of Trinity College on Sunday, October 25th, at 9 P.M., open to undergraduate members of the University.'

To Lady Aberdeen

'ALL SOULS COLLEGE, OXFORD,
Monday, Oct. 26, 1885.

' The Club dinner I found to be practically, though not nominally, a Liberal gathering, and I met quite a number of dons — the Provost of Oriel (Munro), with whom I dine to-night, the Warden of Merton (with whom I had tea yesterday), one of the other Heads — Fowler of Corpus — and Professor Bryce and Mr. Pelham.

' On my arrival on Saturday I found Mr. Christopher waiting for me. He had some hundreds of circulars printed for his proposed meeting next Saturday, but my telegram had stopped their issue. What could I do? I had really no excuse for refusing, so the thing must go on, though I fear he will find he has caught a tartar. After all, if anything is to be done in Oxford, this party[1] must

---

[1] The Evangelical.

be carried along with it. They will supply great and essential elements. And I am given to understand that the various parties are not nearly so distinct and alien as they were some years ago, and that a combined evangelistic work is not impossible.

'On the whole, therefore, I provisionally agreed to take the private meetings, provided no more urgent work opened. I now find that these meetings in New College and Christchurch will serve a very important function, and are perhaps the best service I can do here. I have had a long talk with the man of New College in whose rooms the Thursday meeting was to be held. He is an old Etonian, and rows in his college eight and the fours, and seems a capital man.

'The authorities at New College (as the result of the *Science* in last night's address) have to-day given the Common Room, or Hall, if we like, for the Thursday meeting, so that it is now under no auspices at all, but a College thing. The Musical Society has not only undertaken to postpone their meeting, but is going to distribute circulars for ours personally. The man at Christchurch who is getting up the meeting there to-morrow is not identified with any party, and I think things will go.

'When I got to Trinity (I had called on the President in the afternoon along with Sir William Anson, when we arranged that the President should take the chair), I found the hall so crammed that we could scarcely get in. All the passages were crowded, all the tables, forms, cornices, window-sills, with a seething mass of undergraduates. The door being blocked, they were pouring in through the windows and filling every inch of space.   So much for Mr. ——, to whom I have just written thanks.

'I need not say how inspiring this sight was. It was a most unconventional and picturesque audience — the thing I liked best.   I longed to give them something more than science, and I did, a little, at the end; but I suppose the science was right.   There are some splendid men among the undergraduates, but they are in danger of many things, especially cant and precipitate and too aggressive evangelism.   I am going to deluge them with cold water this afternoon.'

'Oct. 28. — We had a very large gathering at Wycliffe [Hall] on Monday, all the Low Church workers and one or two dons being present.   I gave them a sketch of the Edinburgh Movement, and explained at length our theological views and methods of work.   They seemed much surprised at the former, *i.e.* our *views*, but did not instantly burn me at the stake, as I feared.   On the contrary, they asked many questions, and, on the whole, I think, this meeting was useful.   I had no idea it would be part of my work here to run a tilt at the evangelism current in the place, but nothing is really more needed.   On Tuesday afternoon I had a Conference with a number of men — mostly Low Church workers — in ——'s rooms at New College.   We discussed the "situation" for two hours, and I learned a good deal. These men are eager to do something for the University, and had half engaged the Corn Exchange for me for next Sunday afternoon.   After much consideration, I refused to attempt this.

The time is not ripe yet; there are not the men to do it; it could not be followed up; and it might compromise my present mission, which I find is a very peculiar and delicate one. In fact, I feel this week more like reconnoitring than doing the actual battle — that must be done by somebody later.

'The meeting at Christchurch last night, I think, went off well.[1] We had a large roomful of men — mostly, I believe, freshmen, for whom the meeting seems to have been specially got up. I think the gathering at New College to-morrow will be much larger and more representative.

'As to social arrangements. On Monday I dined with the Provost of Oriel (whose people I know), and met Freeman the historian, Professor Bryce, Mr. Butler, and others. On Tuesday I lunched at All Souls with some of the Fellows, Sir William Anson being from home for the day. This morning Canon Fremantle came here to breakfast, and to-night the President of Trinity comes to dinner. Mrs. Liddell was at tea yesterday, and I had a short talk with her. To-morrow I breakfast with Mr. Butler at Oriel to meet Canon Holland; luncheon at Trinity with one of the Fellows; tea with Rhoda Broughton at her house; and dine before my nine o'clock meeting with the Vice-Chancellor. Mr. Jowett wrote me a very kind note —

'"OXFORD, Oct. 22, 1885.

'" DEAR SIR, — Would you, if I may make the proposal, give me the pleasure of your company at dinner *tête-à-tête*, either on Thursday or Friday at 7.30? — Believe me, yours very sincerely, B. JOWETT."

[1] The meeting was larger than the previous one in Trinity.

'Oct. 30. — I thought my dinner with the Vice-
Chancellor very sad. We were entirely alone,
and had a good talk, also occasional silences.
He asked me if in Scotland we were now generally giving up belief in Miracles — he meant as a
sign of progress.

' I called for Dean Liddell yesterday on his granting
the hall at Christchurch. He gave me pretty
clearly to understand that it was solely on Aberdeen's account. He thawed a little after twenty
minutes over tea, but I thought him very appalling. I said they wanted leaders here, but really
they are almost hopeless. I thought I had got a
number of the best undergraduates to understand
our Edinburgh methods of work and to attempt
something on our lines — *i.e.* to work with absolutely neutral and colourless men, both ecclesias-
tically and theologically. And this is what they
have done: made out a list, including ——, ——,
——, ——, and his wife to sing! I have implored
them to tear up the list, and I think they see it.
The only immediate counter proposal I can make
is to get a deputation of Edinburgh students for
the 8th, and some notable man (a young M.P., I
hope) for the chair.

' I think we have at least four first-rate men at
Edinburgh who would come, and I shall put this
in train at once. The chair can be arranged later.
I have told the Low Church men to repress themselves entirely and keep out of sight, but to work
behind the scenes to any extent. To the latter
our ways of work, our leading ideas, the absence
of cant and of evangelical formulas, are a complete revelation, and I really think they will adopt
them. It is inconceivable how left to themselves

they have been. The proposal is to take the
Clarendon for a few Sunday nights; but the great
difficulty is to get speakers. The High Church
party have arranged a special series of University
sermons in St. Mary's on Sundays at eight, and
have engaged some splendid men. The other
meeting might be grafted on to this as a species
of Second or Inquiry Meeting, and would have
to be at nine. I know some of the Committee of
this series — Mr. Butler and Canon Holland —
and both are anxious to have an Inquiry Meeting
afterwards, but do not see how it can be managed.
Perhaps our meeting may be the solution, but we
shall see how things develop before doing anything definitely.

'It would be a real gain to unite the low and high
factions in a piece of neutral evangelistic work.

'The meeting at New College last night interested
me greatly. A great many men turned up, the
men were most attentive, and I hope the occasion
was not lost, though of course one had no indica-
tion of how they took it.'

The following letter from the present Bishop of
Rochester, then Warden of Keble, reached Drummond after he left Oxford: —

'KEBLE COLLEGE, OXFORD, Nov. 2, 1885.

'MY DEAR SIR, — May I send a line to thank you
for taking the trouble to come up to me so early before
your journey? It was a great disappointment not to
see you.

'We have much reason to be grateful to you, especially for what I have lately heard of the motives of
your visit to Oxford. You have seen, I know, some

of my great friends, Holland and Butler, and I hope that some good may have its source in your talks.

'It is perhaps a happy feature of the present time, which is certainly one of revived religious feeling in Oxford, that one of our greatest difficulties is to discern the right ways of doing good and teaching it, to choose those which follow best the lines of God's own working, to handle safely such powerful but difficult instruments as emotional appeal and temporary enthusiasms and the like.

'Since writing this my wife tells me that you have just been discussing with her part of this very subject — the difficulty of maintaining impressions and of chronic work.　May God guide us all in truth and love. — Yours very faithfully,　　H. TALBOT.'

To Professor Greenfield Drummond had written : —

'ALL SOULS COLLEGE, OXFORD, Oct. 27, 1885.

'We had a tremendous turnout here on Sunday night; in fact, as the Americans say, it was necessary to take the paper off the walls.　I am at it every night this week, though in different colleges, and finish next Sunday night.　I think the place is ripe.'

If Drummond was right, — and he was an expert in the work, — there was nobody and nothing at Oxford to reap the harvest.　The man for whom he looked,[1] able to lead a movement and unsworn to any religious party, failed to appear; but if he had appeared and had been gifted with Drummond's own powers, it is doubtful whether he could have done such work in Oxford as for years Drummond continued to do in Edinburgh. The conditions were very different.　Earnest attempts

[1] See p. 334 f.

z

were made at Oxford. Men of all religious schools had been impressed by Drummond's addresses and his explanation of the methods on which he worked. I have been much struck, in the letters I have read, with the sincere desire on the part of the leaders, both of the High Church and the Low Church, to see what one letter calls 'more direct and faithful mission work among the students than we have yet had.' At least one deputation came from Edinburgh after Drummond had left, and were favourably received by a large audience, among whom were many leading dons. More than one conference was held to consult as to the continuance of the work. But however sincere those were, they only served to reveal (as Drummond's correspondence proves) insuperable differences of opinion as to methods. These were not differences between Church and Dissent, but between High Church and Low Church. The work was abandoned.

On the 8th of November, Drummond held a very large meeting for students in Glasgow. A few more followed at intervals, and were addressed by himself and other University men. But in Glasgow no movement arose, growing and permanent, like the movement in Edinburgh, and in subsequent years Drummond does not appear to have tried to start one. Why there should have been this difference is not very clear. The facts are, that in Glasgow there is not the large body of English, colonial, and foreign students who frequented the meetings in Edinburgh; in Edinburgh the bulk of the students reside in a comparatively small area; in Glasgow they are not only scattered over an enormous city whose distances can only be covered by railways not open on Sundays, but a large proportion of them live in the smaller towns around; and, above all, those Glasgow students who are most interested in religion, and who could have best organised a movement, are (part of them even in their Arts course) occupied with city missions, in which they have an amount of work and responsibility that effectually disables them from other interests.

In Edinburgh the movement continued and increased throughout session 1885–86. In October there was a meeting of fifteen hundred without Drummond's presence to draw them. The students urgently pressed him to return, and he went back for another series of meetings in February and March. The following are extracts from his letters to various friends:—

'Oct. 25, 1885.—When I shall get to Edinburgh, I know not. I have to begin the Glasgow meetings on Nov. 8th, but my heart is in Edinburgh.'

'Dec. 16.—I fear it will be impossible for me to get to Dundee. The students' work takes up all my time, and I have to refuse all outside engagements—even yours, alas!'

'Feb. 26, 1886.—You ask about the Edinburgh students. I send you a letter from one of them, which will let you know what is going on all round. The work is still very wide and deep, and I am still going there every Sunday. Four of the students went as a deputation to Belfast on Sunday week, and between Sunday and Monday night addressed *twelve* meetings, the most important being at the College there. . . .

'Now I must rush for the Edinburgh train.'

'March 13.—The Edinburgh work goes on with unabated interest. For the last two Sundays I have been trying to tell them something about the Kingdom of God—after *Ecce Homo*. We had a very large after-meeting last Sunday, and I

think the impression deepens as the term draws
to its close.   A desire has sprung up to have the
Sacrament all together in our own hall, the Oddfellows' Hall, on the last Sunday night of the
session, and we are making arrangements to have
it done.   It will be to-morrow fortnight, and I
think Professor Charteris will take the leading
part.   To-night we have a meeting to organise
the Summer Holiday Mission.   Belfast and the
North of Ireland are to have strong deputations
in April — especially the colleges at Belfast,
Derry, and possibly Dublin.

' I am starting now to see the International Football
Match at Edinburgh.'

' March 27.— Dr. Whyte and Dr. Charteris take
our Communion Service to-morrow night.'

' April 12.— We had a very happy party at Arran.
Twenty-two came, and Dr. Greenfield joined us.
He and I meant staying over the Sunday, but
smelt battle across the sea, and could not help
flying off to Ayr, where six Edinburgh students
were making their *début*.   We concealed ourselves till Sunday afternoon, and then dropped
suddenly among them, when they were "gathered
in one place for prayer."   They were on their
knees praying for help when we entered.   Two,
however, were in the secret, as they had discovered us at church.   We had a good meeting at
night, and the deputies kept at it all week, not
without result.'

The secretary of the Holiday Mission reported this
month deputations to between fifteen and twenty
places in Scotland, England, and Ireland.   ' On the
whole, the news from all round is good.   The work is

very much worth helping by all accounts.' Most important was the work at Aberystwyth, and Drummond himself went to it.

To Lord Aberdeen

'ABERYSTWYTH, May 1, 1886.

'MY DEAR ABERDEEN,— I arrived here, after a very fine crossing, yesterday afternoon, and found the place ripe for action.

'The students from Edinburgh began last Monday by a novel manœuvre: For two days they held no meetings at all, but attended the Annual Athletic Sports of the University, and otherwise threw themselves into the students' interests. They also were present at a social gathering on the Tuesday night; and the only one of them who spoke, instead of giving the company a sermon, proposed in a humorous speech the toast of "The Ladies." The effect of this was to secure the whole " 'varsity " for the meeting on Wednesday, and a profound impression was made. Thursday night was equally good, and last night we had to move into a bigger hall. Great interest is created both among professors and students, and I am very glad I came. We have a meeting again to-night, and three or four to-morrow; in fact, we shall be at it all day long.'

The difficulties were great, chiefly the jealousies between Church and Chapel; but the work progressed and spread to other places, with the result of many conversions and the dedication of a large number of young men to a life of service.

During the summer Professor Christlieb wrote from

Bonn to Professor Charteris of Edinburgh, inviting a deputation of students to come over to the German University. It was ultimately arranged that Drummond should go, along with Mr. G. P. Smith, a medical student, who had taken from the first a leading part in the Edinburgh movement, and was now studying at Vienna. *Natural Law* had by this time been translated into German, and Drummond's name was well known.

'BONN, Oct. 26, 1886.

'. . . The University has allowed a notice of my meeting on the "privileged" blackboard, and Christlieb, who has the largest theology class, has intimated it from the chair and urged the men to come. A good turnout is not to be expected, although Christlieb is sanguine. The difficulties here are enormous. Evangelism is *hated, loathed.* Still, a feeble spark may smoulder on, and time create a more accessible field for our bigger deputation, which I hope will follow next year.'

'GLASGOW, Nov. 6, 1886.

' I am in a whirl of work, and have only time to say one word about Bonn. It was a strange experience. The chief feature of the mission was one big meeting, at which some of the professors (one or two science men amongst them) were present, when I gave a detailed narrative of the Edinburgh movement. Questions were invited at the end, and for half an hour I was under a keen fire. The depth of ignorance shown in these questions was appalling. I think the men were interested, on the whole, and one or two have promised to take the thing up. By and by we shall send them another deputation.'

Drummond must have made a deep impression at Bonn; for among his papers, I find a requisition from a large body of students of the University, inviting him to return and hold a second series of meetings.

When he returned to Scotland in the beginning of November, the Edinburgh work occupied his attention.

> 'Nov. 13, 1886.— I ran in to Edinburgh this week to see the students. They are to go on with their meeting. I absolutely refused to go there meantime, as they have scores of men among themselves perfectly able to run the thing. So they will start to-morrow, the Principal in the chair. They have founded an East End University Settlement (like Toynbee), and have five or six first-rate men already in residence.'
>
> Dec. 16.— For me it will be a quiet winter. I see it pretty well before me. I have begun *The Ascent of Man*, though it climbs slowly, slowly. Then after the Christmas holidays I begin Edinburgh. You know, I have purposely left it alone this month to let them try themselves. And they have succeeded perfectly. I got a description of their meeting of last Sunday night, which really filled me with awe.'

His Edinburgh meetings began in the end of January. In addition to the usual gathering of students on Sunday evenings, in the Oddfellows' Hall, an afternoon service was started for schoolboys.

> 'Jan. 27, 1887.— Edinburgh was splendid last Sunday.'
>
> 'Feb. 17.— Edinburgh is as good as ever, both the boys and the students.'

'March 3. — Professor —— was in the chair last Sunday night at the students' meeting, and led off with a really fine address. The meeting deepens in interest, and I have many bad hours preparing for it every week. That sort of thing keeps the rush off splendidly. The current is flowing very deep and strong. I do not think I would exchange that audience for anything else in the world. The Boys' Meeting also, which was meant only to last a Sunday or two, has grown into an institution, and *will* not stop. Last Sunday, after the hour's meeting, I sent all the small boys home, and kept two or three hundred of the big ones for a private talk about decision. We did not think it wise to cross-examine them individually, or put any undue pressure upon them, but I am sure many of them are thinking most seriously. One difficulty is to get into their heads that they are to be religious *as boys*, and that they need not be so "pious" as their maiden aunts. I heard this incidentally the other day: The boys from one of the Edinburgh schools were playing a football match against a team from another public school (not Edinburgh). During the game the strangers used some bad language. At "half-time" the Edinburgh boys got together and resolved that they would do collectively what they saw it would be priggish to do individually — namely, tell the other side that they must stop this, or the game could not go on. They followed this up by saying that unless this were done, their school would never play a match with them again. It came on the strangers like a thunderbolt, but they gave in at once.'

'March 10. — We had very fine meetings again last

Sunday, and a conversazione for the students on Saturday evening. Among other things, we then got from sixty to eighty *entirely new* men to start a " Holiday Mission " next month.'

' March 24. — Sunday was our last great meeting for the winter, and I can never forget it. Our hall was crammed to the door, and at the close we asked all the men who had become Christians to remain and join in the Sacrament. Over six hundred waited — men of every kindred and tongue. Sir William Muir was present, and many of the professors, and Dr. Charteris dispensed the Sacrament. Some of the students acted as elders, and the leading prizemen were all with us. The work has been outwardly very quiet this winter, and none of us had the least idea it was taking such marvellous hold until we gathered around the Communion table. Forty or fifty have volunteered to work in the " University Settlement " in the East End, and about a hundred have given in their names for a Holiday Mission in summer, and especially in April next. All this, and the Boys' Meeting, — which is bigger than ever, — has kept me very busy for the last month or two, and it has been a great strain.'

' STEAMER " BRODICK CASTLE," March 31, 1887.

' The above heading may suggest Timbuctoo, but it is only *Arran*. I take my students for a week's geology there every year, and I cannot tell you what a relief it is to get out of the smoke. Greenfield and some of the Edinburgh medicals are to join our party at Arran, and we are looking forward to some capital climbs.

' Edinburgh still glows. We have not been able to

stop the meetings. I had four last Sunday, and
have four more next.

'Now I must go to my brethren of the hammer,
who are having a lively time on deck.'

'April. — It would be splendid to get among the
heather and the fish for a little, for my spirit pines
in this tunnel.

'I am just rushing off to Uddingstone, where a band
of the Edinburgh students have been at work all
week.

'The Holiday Mission is in full swing, and quiet
good doing all round. All this keeps one's mind
away from the shame of politics. The sides get
more and more bitter.'

So from year to year the work went on. The
summer and autumn of 1887 saw it carried by Drummond himself to the American Universities, as will
be described in another chapter. When he returned
to Scotland he found the Edinburgh students as eager
as ever to continue the movement, and the arrival of
a deputation from America gave the movement a new
impulse.

'November 8, 1887. — The students at Edinburgh
are determined to start work at once; and I was
already advertised for next Sunday, although I
had written protesting that I would have nothing
more to do with them, as they could now get
along themselves. But a deputation came to
Glasgow, and my heart melted. In any case,
however, I could not get away from my Glasgow
work; and, although it is hard often to be tied,
so incorrigible a free-lance as myself needs it.'

'November 14. — My father is also a case of
hoping almost against hope. But at the moment

there is a hairbreadth of improvement, and ——
said I might go in to Edinburgh for the students
yesterday. We had the hall crammed, and the
American deputation gave an account of their
work. It was wonderfully interesting, and told
palpably on the hundreds of new men who were
there.'

'November 24.—I am advertised for the Edinburgh students next Sunday. It was the same
last Sunday, and I disappointed them, and if at
all possible I ought to keep the engagement this
time. But, to tell the truth, I had all but given
up hope of getting there, as my father's condition
has been most critical for the last day or two.
He could not well be much worse than he is,
but if he were, I fear I could not go to Edinburgh. . . .

'If, however, my father's condition remains satisfactory, I feel I ought to go to Edinburgh. I
would very much rather not, but I see no way of
escape from so plainly the line of "ought."'

'December 10.—You do not know what an unver-
satile being I am, and how I recoil from all but
one or two special lines of work.

'We had a big meeting of the students on Saturday
night, and the biggest of the term on Sunday.
We also started the schoolboy meeting yesterday
afternoon.'

'January 1, 1888.—These terrible medicals are at
it again,—a conversazione,—this time in George
Street Hall next Saturday evening. They will
not let one eat one's dinner in peace. I do
hope you have made no plans, for they have
upset your arrangements every time.—Growl-
ingly yours,   H. D.'

'January 28, 1888. — Edinburgh takes a lot of time,
for we are in full sail there again, and I had three
students' meetings last Saturday and Sunday.   I
am also in the middle of a persecution.

'Did you see a letter in the *Christian* about my
heresies, signed by a medical student?   A small
clique has addressed a printed circular to the
Edinburgh ministers, begging them to suppress
me and my views.   Of course, I have taken no
notice, and I think it has not hindered the work
at all, which is the main thing.   Now I have
brought myself up to date.   You see I am not
doing much.

'My one engagement is Edinburgh, which I fear I
dare not abandon, even for a Sunday, in the
present persecution, though I would fain let it
go, for none knows what a nightmare that work
is.   I have an important commission for —— as
soon as he gets into Parliament, to rush a Bill
through securing a Copyright in Public Speech;
i.e. to prevent these irresponsible miscreants, the
reporters, from doing their work except when
permission and revision are granted by their
miserable victim.

'This scream is not *àpropos* the Pope, but many
other enormities.'

'March 26, 1888. — It is very hard to be called
names, but very right, and in the nature of things
altogether inevitable.   "It is enough for the servant that he be as his Master."'

In session 1888–89 it was still the same.

'November 12, 1888. — Really fine students' meeting yesterday, hall filled to standing, and much

interest. I fear I am in for it again this winter,
but I really wanted a few months' peace.'

'November 26, 1888.— I dinna think I can come.
Edinburgh is at it again, and I must stick there.
You know, I have no faith in a stray shot, and
mean to bombard the students steadily both here
and at Edinburgh. It is too dreadful to have to
refuse you so often, but you know your man.'

'February 26, 1889.— May I spread my mat at
No. ——? I fancy we shall have only two more
meetings after next Sunday, so one may not have
the chance of a cigarette again for a little, so I
hope you can give me a corner.'

So week after week during January, February, and
March he held the Edinburgh meetings. In August
there was a Students' Conference at Bonskeid, very
active and very successful. And session 1889–90 saw
the work as engrossing as in previous years, the
freshmen who had come up as interested and responsive as their predecessors had been.

'January 6, 1890.— *All* the Sundays now for two
months or so must be in Edinburgh — at least I
think so.

'We begin next Saturday night with a conversazione in the new Students' Union Building,
which is just opened. Twelve hundred invitations
are out. A deputation of Cambridge men are
coming. On Sunday the old meeting in the
Oddfellows' Hall begins, but though I preside,
the Cambridge men will do the bulk of the
talking.

'I have been flying everywhere during these last
days — first accompanying my mother to a place

near Edinburgh for a little, and then going a round of meetings both in Edinburgh and Glasgow. It is the busiest time amongst the poor, and especially among the tempted, and it has fallen to my lot this year to devote my holiday mainly to them, turning up at my mother's from time to time as I could.'

'January 11, 1890.—I have been in Edinburgh— meetings, meetings, meetings—and am just start- ing back again for more.'

Such was the outer history of the Student Move- ment so far as Drummond himself has told it, and his notes for the years 1884-90 hold good also for 1891-94.

In these ten years the work covered about three generations of students, and Drummond was able to give many of his better-known addresses more than once, but always with varieties and additions suitable to the occasion. At first he confined himself to very simple themes: '*Seek ye first the Kingdom of God*,' Christ's call to the weary and heavy laden to *learn* of Him, and similar texts. Sometimes he had these printed upon cards and distributed to his audience as they entered, as thus:—

> Let the wicked **forsake** his way
> And the unrighteous man his **thoughts** :
> And let him return unto the Lord,
> 　　And He will have **Mercy** upon him,
> And to our God
> 　　For He will **abundantly Pardon.**

> STUDENTS' MEETING,　　'HIM THAT COMETH UNTO ME
> 　MARCH 8, 1885.　　　I WILL IN NO WISE CAST OUT.'

Those addresses were all upon the relation of the individual to Christ. In 1886 he began to emphasise the social aspects of religion, and gave some addresses on the Kingdom of God, based on *Ecce Homo;* his *Programme of Christianity* from Isaiah lxi.; and his address, or parts of it, on 1 Cor. xiii. Then while preparing his lectures on *The Ascent of Man*, he took up the relations of science and religion, and illustrated the naturalness of Christianity as the crown of all human evolution; but always drove home to the individual his place and duty in the process. Take the very remarkable series of addresses delivered in the winter of 1890, a summary of which will be found in the Appendix to this volume. They start with science; but as they go on, one is impressed no less by the fulness of the Gospel which is in them than by their persistent pressure upon the individual to accept Christ and consecrate life to Him. It is a seer who speaks, stimulated like the prophets of old by the intellectual conditions of his own time to a new view of the things that are eternal. Modern science has enabled him to view life as a whole, and to perceive, with an eye which, as he tells you, he also owes, partly to science, that in the universe Christianity is at once the most natural and the most sublime of facts. He sweeps before us, in a magnificent panorama, the forces which have built the world, developed the individual, and fashioned human society, and he relates Christianity to them as their continuance and consummation. But the individual is made to feel his place in this and his duty towards it. And for all those purposes the speaker excites not the imagination only, but reason and common sense. There is no sensation in the addresses, nor any imposition of authority; no artificiality nor false mysticism; but the style is as simple as the thinking; it is one sensible man talking to others of his own generation.

In the Christianity which he presents as the crown of the life of the universe, the spring and cause is Jesus Christ. He is the Source of all life and light; the assurance of the forgiveness of sins; the daily nourishment of the soul; the one power sufficient for a noble life; the solution of all problems; the motive and example of all service. Night after night this teacher shut up the reason of his young hearers to the acceptance and obedience of Christ. Night after night he pleaded before their hearts God's love in Christ and God's need for them in the life of the world. This is the most striking feature of the addresses, and next to it is their adherence to the Bible and Christ's own words, which are expounded with a simplicity and homeliness that remind one sometimes of Luther, and sometimes of Robertson of Brighton. And next is another feature which will surprise many who did not hear the addresses — their loyalty to the Church and to the doctrines of the Church. Church-going, they say, is not Christianity, and belief in doctrines is not Christianity, but no sane man will refuse the regular nourishment and strength of fellowship which church-going supplies; and, as in every department of science, so here also a reasonable mind will recognise that there must be doctrines, and will go for their explanation only to their highest authorities. But description of these addresses is useless save to tempt the reader of these lines to study them himself. He will find them among the best which Drummond ever achieved.

Nor will he who reads these addresses need to be told how ignorant and irrelevant was the criticism from which their author suffered. It arose, in the first instance, because he excluded all reporters from the meetings. He adopted this policy, not from any wish to hide his teaching, but — apart from the obvious fact that the daily press can give only fragmentary, and therefore to some extent misleading, reports of long religious addresses — because his mission was to students only, and he was persuaded that the very personal and sacred work which it involved would thrive better if kept to himself and his audience. Every one who is familiar with such work can perceive the many reasons for this. But at the same time it was bound to provoke criticism and misunderstanding. Some of the misrepresentations from which the addresses suffered were wilful; bits torn from their context by a young prig or two in his audience, and flung to the rapacity of certain of the lower-class religious papers, who followed the author of *Natural Law* with an insatiable suspicion. Others were the effect upon good but unduly sensitive minds of the inevitable distortion of the half-reported teaching of an evangelist with unconventional ways of stating the truth. Such charges are mentioned here only to emphasise how unfounded they now appear to be in face of the addresses themselves. And, in fact, when any of Drummond's harder critics went to hear him, they generally came away disarmed. The newspaper which attacked him most persistently for his exclusion of reporters acknowledged that he had intelligible reasons for this, and published at least one candid appreciation of his power by an outsider to the work.

The following account of the addresses has been sent me by one who was a medical student at Edinburgh from 1888 to 1892, Mr. George Newman, now Lecturer on Bacteriology at King's College, London, and lately Warden of Chalfont House Settlement : —

' The first time I saw Professor Drummond was in the winter time in 1888. I was a freshman ; and though I had, of course, heard of him by name, I had no idea at all as to

2 A

any connection he had with the University of Edinburgh. Some fellow-undergraduate gave me a card to attend "a meeting for students in the Oddfellows' Hall, to be addressed by Professor Drummond." It seemed only by chance that I went to the meeting. I believe Sir William Muir, the Principal of the University, was in the chair. There were several of the leading men in the University upon the platform, and the room, which seats, I think, about a thousand, was full. I suppose I shall never forget — I certainly do not wish to forget — the impression I gained of Professor Drummond that night. He spoke with evident earnestness, but with marked control, if not reserve. His whole bearing was calm and collected. There were no gestures. Nor was there a suggestion of the " preacher " — natural voice, natural demeanour, natural and dignified from beginning to the end. At the close of his remarks he uttered a few words of prayer. A hymn was sung, and the great gathering dispersed with preternatural quietness and decorum. The impression left on my mind was such as to cause me to reflect upon what I had seen and heard. Taken at the very lowest estimate, here was a disciplinarian of no ordinary skill. To those who have not heard Drummond, or have wondered at his influence, I suggest a consideration, viz., that his *methods* were of a rare kind, and obtained for him a hearing which many religious teachers never seem able to secure. The matter of a sermon is clearly of first importance, but is it not possible that great matter is frequently spoiled by not being greatly uttered?

' Now, whilst in my judgment Drummond was not an orator, he had a most exceptional faculty of simple, beautiful, and dignified expression. His style and mode of procedure appealed, I think, to his hearers in Edinburgh. He was admittedly a tall, well-built, handsome man — almost a king among men — and no one who has looked into those eyes can ever hold any other opinion than that they were attractive. He was rather particularly well and neatly dressed. These things, combined with his skill of style, all had their influence upon his hearers. But there was another characteristic which struck me that night. I had heard a real *Teacher*. Such are rare. Many professors in our universities can no

more teach than fly! At best, possibly they are crammers
in. But Drummond *e*-ducated men. He drew them out —
and drew them onwards and upwards. His ideas may have
been, or may not have been, orthodox, scholastic, theological,
scientific — but they resulted in *leading out* a young fellow's
mind. His teaching opened men's eyes — not to wondrous
doctrines, but to *see*. After a course of Drummond, men
began to look about for themselves.

'A considerable experience of those meetings of Professor
Drummond's only convinced me the more that he was a
Teacher possessing an admirable style. But it was not long
before I learned of at least two other features which made
this visitor to Edinburgh such a power in the University.
He held no position whatever in the University. He came
as "unofficial preacher"; but in that capacity he had, in my
judgment, a greater and a more lasting effect upon the
University at that time than any of the University teachers
themselves. And for a very simple reason. He dealt not
with technical subjects, but with ethics and life. The Professors of Divinity might be said to be his only competitors.
But while they spoke to small compulsory classes reading
for a degree, Drummond spoke to the largest class in the
University, and it was a voluntary one, composed of students
in all the Faculties. Moreover, he possessed his influence
very largely because he went beneath the surface of things
— beyond formularies, creeds, definitions — to the elementary
questions of life and conduct. It is true, such a course led
him inevitably into controversy and misapprehensions, but it
accomplished that which he desired. I should sum up his
entire teaching in those meetings in one sentence from the
pen of George Macdonald: "*Life and religion are one thing,
or neither is anything.*" Here was a minimum of theology
and a maximum of simple common sense. How well it acted
was proved by experience.

'For three winters, to my personal knowledge, these large
gatherings of students took place. Nor was the effect immediately transient. It acted in a perceptible measure as the
salt of the University. The foremost men in the University
gave these meetings their support, and were often present

themselves. Lord Aberdeen presided on several occasions, and frequently distinguished visitors to Edinburgh were present. Otherwise the meetings were absolutely limited to matriculated students. The elementary basis of doctrine — if such it is to be called — was of a nature to bring men of all shades of religious feeling, and of "no religion at all," together in one hall. Professor Drummond has frequently been criticised respecting the matter of his addresses to the students of Edinburgh. Of that I am not qualified to speak. Many of those who might be considered as representatives of the children of Israel were sore afraid that the religious spirit of Evangelism was absent. The world of exact science declared that Drummond was "unscientific." In a measure he was guilty of both accusations. He was not, I should say, an evangelical teacher in the general acceptation of the term. Professor Masson, in an essay written, I think, about 1852, on "Scottish Characteristics," selects finally as those most often found: (1) An intense spirit of nationality; (2) the habit, in thinking, speaking, and writing, of laying emphasis upon certain points rather than in co-ordinating them into one entirety. Drummond erred — if it be erring — in the latter of these two characteristics. He was a philosopher, yet he has left us no philosophy. Like Jowett at Oxford, though in a less degree, he *individualised* his creed and his teaching. Though his entire contribution to religious thought has done much to co-ordinate, still it must be recognised that he had, or thought he had, a very definite part or side of Truth to enforce. This he did with as great pertinacity as he declined to speak to audiences outside those he deemed desirable. He emphasised, not to misplace or isolate Truth, but to bring out the finer points, which he felt were so often neglected, because they lay below the surface. The final result was a revealing of unity, co-ordination, and adaptation in the Truth of the Christian Religion and Nature. Nature was to Drummond a sympathetic background to human life and the kindred revelation of a divine intelligence. Most of the many misconceptions of spirituality may be traced, as T. H. Green of Balliol pointed out, to the notion that it is attained by eliminating, leaving behind, and transcending

what is natural. Drummond believed and taught that, on
the contrary, the spirituality which was real, and which would
stand the test of time, was attained by absorbing, assimilat-
ing, and developing what was Natural. "Nothing," said
Drummond, "can ever be gained by setting one-half of Nature against the other, or the rational against the ultra-
rational." That is a fine quotation — the whole of it, in my
judgment, absolutely representative of Drummond's best
thought and contribution. Seeley declared for Natural Religion : Drummond demanded that religion should be natural.

'As I have said, his whole tenor of thought inevitably led
him into differences with the exact sciences. He was above
everything else the Poet of Science. And the general run of
exact scientific men have little or nothing to do with poetry.
I imagine Drummond has left comparatively little original
work behind him. He *interpreted* the Ethics of Nature rather
than investigated new matter.

'From what I have said, you will gather that I think
Drummond's immense influence was due to solid reasons, and
neither ephemeral nor superficial. The reasons were three :
(1) His style and methods; (2) his power of teaching; (3) his
creed. But more, I think, than all these, and inspiring them
all, was his own personality and pure spirit. He practised,
so far as we could judge, what he preached. His life was
the home of fair visions and noble thoughts and courteous,
kindly deeds. He seemed to many of us to be removed from
the sordidness of life.

'After my first experience I saw a great deal of him, and
had the delight of being of some little use in the furtherance
of his work at Edinburgh. Of this he often spoke, and any
little service done for him was amply repaid by his gratitude
and appreciation. He was not a frequent correspondent, but
his letters were admirable, and contained much helpful and
wise advice. My time in Edinburgh was certainly a very
happy one. But I learned to measure many things as but
poor and common compared with our friendship. It was the
most precious thing I found during my course. Nor was I
alone in this experience. I remember not a few who shared
it. Drummond was prepared to take almost endless trouble

with men who desired his help. " After-meetings," I think, he disliked as strongly as some of us did. But if a man wished to see Drummond privately and have a talk with him, he was always ready. Indeed, he would come through from Glasgow on a week-day simply to see a man who desired his help. Few teachers have ever had such confidences bestowed in them as Drummond, and yet he was strangely reserved as regards his own heart. He would not be drawn just by anybody at any time. He was fastidious to a degree in all spiritual matters. His taste was the essence of refinement.

' The last walk we had together was along Princes Street and towards the Dean Bridge. It was a Sunday night at the end of term in 1892, and we discussed amongst other things his meetings during the four years. He spoke very modestly of his share in them, though, of course, his share was everything.

' I loved him with all my heart and soul and mind — I think I have never loved any man so much, so strongly, so continuously. I have never seen in any man so much that was admirable — for he seemed to possess all the graces and virtues of which as *perfect man* I dreamed.'

As in his mission in 1873-75, so in this work among the students it was not so much the addresses themselves which told, as the personal intercourse with hundreds of young men to which they formed the introduction. One who heard Drummond through several years of the students' movements said there was one power which distinguished him beyond every other preacher to men, and that was the power of so speaking as invariably to move from one to two hundred of his audience of seven or eight hundred — not merely to stay to an after-meeting, but to talk with him one by one and face to face. This power never failed him with the students, and it was by it he left an abiding mark on many hundreds of lives.

What it cost him he alone could tell, and even his closest friends during those years had only glimpses of

the labour, the thought, and the anxiety which it en-
tailed.   In mere talk or writing, that take up time, it
occupied him for a part of every day during the winter
session.   To deal with a single case he would come
through from Glasgow to Edinburgh for an afternoon.
On Saturdays, when he was free, he arrived in the
morning and spent several hours fulfilling appoint-
ments with men.   And on Sunday, after the meeting
was over, he would talk with one and another far on
into the night, in the Hall, on the winter streets, or in
his lodgings.   One of his hosts tells me that after
having worked all night with men in trouble, he came
in to breakfast on Monday morning, fresh and happy
as any round the table, and was off to Glasgow before
they knew what he had been doing.   That must have
been a night when men were given to him for his hire,
and God's grace was so evident as to be meat and
drink to him.   But there were other times at which
the confessions of some of the men and his disappointments with them strained and wore him out.   One,
with whom he stayed over a Sunday, writes as follows:—

' One Sunday evening we were having prayers when
he returned.   I did not know that he was in, and went
down to the dining-room to see if the soup was ready
and hot for him.   (He laughingly called our house the
" Sign of the Ox-tail.")   I found him there leaning
with his head bowed on the mantelpiece, looking into
the fire.   He raised a haggard, worn face when I spoke
to him, and I made him take a glass of wine, and asked
him if he were very tired.   " No," he said, " not very.
But oh, I am sick with the sins of these men!   How
can God bear it?"'

If his experiences that night were the same as were sent to him in a large number of letters, anonymous and signed, then one cannot wonder that coming forth from the living face and eyes they stunned and sickened him. He has kept letters with strange and awful stories of sin, told for the most part in utter despair. Some are from men who have fallen once, and cry for his quick hand to lift them. Some are from those whom he has befriended before, and perhaps shepherded for a time, but away from him they have yielded.

'I suppose you will be coming to Edinburgh for Sunday. If you are not specially engaged and would come through early, I should be very glad. . . . The winter before last I was always at your meetings, and a year last Easter was on deputation. Now I am off the mark and fully aware that things cannot go on this way much longer. A talk quietly with you might do good and help me.'

There are many letters like that.

'DEAR SIR, — Can you tell me what will help me in the first second succeeding moral defeat and the consciousness of it? What, when we have but a moment to think before plunging into the next bit of work that lies to our hand, will save us from losing heart at the consciousness of our weakness and giving way to a feeling that it is useless to prolong a struggle which can only end in our total defeat? I have found that the first moment of defeat is the crucial instant determining whether it is to be a stumble from which we shall recover, or whether it is to usher in a period longer or shorter of listlessness and wasted opportunities. I feel certain there must be some way of doing right at every instant independent of the rightness or wrongness of previous acts. Can you help me and possibly others? — I am yours expectantly,

'VICTOR SÆPE VICTUS.'

'DEAR PROFESSOR DRUMMOND, — I was at your meeting to-night, and was also present at your after-meeting. I may say that I am a member of ——'s church. . . . When a fellow leaves home he finds it pretty hard work to keep straight sometimes, and I frankly say I have come to grief since I came to Edinburgh. I have been trying for some time back to live a better life and be more like Christ. I am taking advantage of your offer to give us advice.'

'DEAR SIR, — How past sins are to be blotted out is a matter of special difficulty to those who enter upon the Christian life, leaving a dissolute career behind them. The usual method of meeting this difficulty is that of the Atonement. Some perplexity has been caused through your making no reference to this, and it is felt that you would render a great service by elucidating the matter. If convenient, would you kindly refer to the subject this evening?— Yours respectfully,
'A STUDENT.'

'DEAR SIR, — I have been attending your Students' meetings for some time, and am now resolved to follow Jesus Christ. But my past life has been a very wild and sinful one, and I want to know how I am to regard the past. What assurance may I have that the past is forgiven? Do you believe in the Atonement of Christ?'

This last letter Drummond 'read to the meeting, and, laying it down, declared his unequivocal faith in the efficacy of Christ's Atonement. That Atonement (he said) furnished the ground and assurance of the forgiveness of sins. There were many theories of the rationale of that doctrine; and he would not venture there to offer any theory of his own, but he took the opportunity of magnifying the Atonement as one of the central facts of Christianity.'[1]
Another sends the following: —

'I recollect particularly well an answer he gave once in private conversation to the question, "Do you believe that the sacrifice of Christ is the essential and basal thing in the Christian religion?" The interrogator desired an answer, Yes or

[1] From a student who was present at the meeting.

No.   It was at a time when Drummond's position was being
assailed from almost every quarter.   I shall not soon forget
the slow, deliberate reply : "Then my answer must be No."
The questioner remarked that it was satisfactory to have such
a plain answer.   But there was in store for him something
which probably made matters plainer still : "If I may venture
a supplementary remark," said Drummond, "I would say that
in my opinion the sacrifice of Christ is a part of the very
essence of Christianity, but the basis of Christianity is the
eternal love of God." '

I have been told by those who assisted Drummond
at the after-meetings, that you could not know him till
you saw how he pleaded there with groups of men, and
still more with individuals.   He was very straight;
and God's forgiveness made sure in Jesus Christ was
what he pressed home, with all the simplicity of Scripture itself, upon the men whom he found convinced of
guilt.   Yet he used to say that it was not to the sense
of guilt he could most powerfully appeal, nor did he
believe that such an appeal was the most suitable to
make to a meeting of young men.   Indeed, the secret
of his large area of power was his recognition of the
enormous variety of religious difficulty and of moral
trouble which beset the young men of his time.   He
took these as he found them, and shaped the beginnings of his gospel to suit their experiences, their
ideals, their lines of study and of recreation.   But the
end was One, and Christ stood at it.   For every man
the thing needful was surrender to Him, and the beginning of a life of service in His Spirit.

These labours and anxieties brought their own
reward.   It came not only in the undiminished meetings, — 'I would not give up my audience in Oddfellows' Hall for anything in the world,' — but in the
more precious acknowledgment by one man after an-

other that he had been turned from evil, lifted to self-control, and was happy in serving Christ.

What sheaves of such tributes he got, and yet so seldom spoke of them! I cannot imagine documents of the kind more honest or reserved.

'I think it my duty to tell you (after my request last week) that I have this week benefited by your address, and feel sure that you have prayed for me. This week has been one of victory and strength unknown to me for years. . . . — Ever gratefully yours,   'A Student.'

'Up till Sunday, and for some time past, I felt myself drifting; but the wonderful things I heard last night, and particularly your words, have done me a great deal of good. I can again enjoy communion with God and my Saviour, and that I know that I work not for myself but for Him fills my heart with joy. I feel assured that last night's meeting has given courage to many. — Yours sincerely,   'L.'

These are like a great number from men whom he did not know, and with whom he had not spoken. But very many others he did know, and, step by step, helped from sin or from doubt to stability of faith and conduct, which so long as he lived he had the joy of seeing unshaken among the real troubles of life, and frequently upon high positions of responsibility and influence.

'Sir, — Some years ago I gave my heart to my Saviour, yet I have not followed Him as I ought. It seemed to me as you spoke as if I had taken it back again, and soiled it with sins unmentionable. But I thank and praise Him that through you I have been enabled by His great unspeakable grace to say "Lord, I come." Will you pray for me that I may be kept from falling, and that I may sit humbly at His feet and learn of Him? God knows, if any ought to be humble I should.'

' DEAR PROFESSOR DRUMMOND, — Though I did not succeed in getting through my " second," I feel it has not been altogether a failure. As a practical result, my getting through three has been more than I expected or deserved; but, apart from that, it has given me more hope for the future, as I look back upon the last two months. It has taught me that I can still do work, if only I apply myself, though it was very difficult at times. (You know of my outbreak.) A very helpful influence to me in my struggle has been yours, sir, and that of Dr. ——. I write to-night to tell you that I thank you from the bottom of my heart for your great kindness to one who was not only a stranger, but even almost a foreigner. I hope and trust that the tide has now turned with me, and that I shall yet be a useful member of society. I begin to realise how nearly I had become a perfect wreck; in a great measure I owe my escape to your personal influence.'

One of the finest features of the movement, however, was the large number of the men affected by it who set themselves, often at great sacrifice, to win their fellow-students for Christ. Here is an instance which Drummond himself told at a students' meeting in America : —

'One night I got a letter from one of the students of the University of Edinburgh, page after page of agnosticism and atheism. I went over to see him, and spent a whole afternoon with him, and did not make the slightest impression. At Edinburgh University we have a Students' Evangelistic Meeting on Sunday nights, at which there are eight hundred or one thousand men present. A few nights after this, I saw that man in the meeting, and next to him sat another man whom I had seen occasionally at the meetings. I did not know his name, but I wanted to find out more about my sceptic, so when the meeting was over, I went up to him and said, " Do you happen

to know ——— ? " — " Yes," he replied, " it is he
that has brought me to Edinburgh." — " Are you
an old friend ? " I asked. — " I am an American,
a graduate of an American University," he said.
" After I had finished there I wanted to take a
post-graduate course, and finally decided to come
to Edinburgh.   In the dissecting-room I happened to be placed next to ———, and I took a
singular liking for him.   I found out that he was
a man of very remarkable ability, though not a
religious man, and I thought I might be able to
do something for him.   A year passed and he
was just where I found him."   He certainly was
blind enough, because it was only two or three
weeks before that that he wrote me that letter.
" I think you said," I resumed, " that you only
came here to take a year of the post-graduate
course." — " Well," he said, " I packed my trunks
to go home, and I thought of this friend, and I
wondered whether a year of my life would be
better spent to go and start in my profession in
America, or to stay in Edinburgh and try to win
that one man for Christ, and I stayed." — " Well,"
I said, " my dear fellow, it will pay you ; you will
get that man."   Two or three months passed, and
it came to the last night of our meetings.   We
have men in Edinburgh from every part of the
world.   Every year, five or six hundred of them
go out never to meet again, and in our religious
work we get very close to one another, and on
the last night of the year we sit down together in
our common hall to the Lord's Supper.   This is
entirely a students' meeting.   On that night we
get in the members of the Theological Faculty,
so that things may be done decently and in order.

Hundreds of men are there, the cream of the youth of the world, sitting down at the Lord's table. Many of them are not members of the Church, but are there for the first time pledging themselves to become members of the Kingdom of God. I saw —— sitting down and handing the communion cup to his American friend. He had got his man. A week after he was back in his own country. I do not know his name; he made no impression in our country, nobody knew him. He was a subject of Christ's kingdom, doing His work in silence and in humility. A few weeks passed and —— came to see me. I said, "What do you come here for?"— He said, "I want to tell you I am going to be a medical missionary." It was worth a year, was it not?'

One of the letters quoted above strikes a note which was a very strong feature of Drummond's mission. He recognised that the first duty of his converts was to the University itself and to their studies. There was an entire exclusion of the romance, the sentimentalism, the vague philanthropies, the short cuts to influence and fame, which often so seriously hurt work among students. The business in hand — the class-work, the examinations, the science or profession for which they were studying — was pressed upon all as their first duty. In this, too, the leaders of the movement, the secretaries, the committee and the most prominent workers, set a noble example. Many of them were the first men of their years. All round, the honours lists showed, as was right, the first-fruits of the mission.

How has it gone since? How have 'Drummond's men' stood the world? In nearly every town of our country, in every British colony, in India, in China, in Japan, converts or disciples of this movement, who gratefully trace to it the beginnings of their moral power, are labouring steadfastly, and often brilliantly, in every profession of life.

If any have grown indifferent, if any have fallen, should the story of those great days come into their hands, may it rouse the memory within them of what they then owned, of what they then found themselves capable of.   And let them be assured, that if sins have fallen on them since, the same Grace which Henry Drummond then pleaded to their hearts is theirs still, if with all their hearts they turn and seek it.

CHAPTER XIII

FOR some years various persons and institutions in America had been inviting Drummond to cross the Atlantic. Mr. Moody was urgent that he should join him in such a general mission as they had accomplished together in 1873–75. But Drummond, as we have seen, was concentrating his energies upon students. About 1885 Mr. Moody, too, began to specialise in the same direction. At Northfield, Massachusetts, he had built a number of institutions for the discipline of young men and women in various forms of Christian service; and in the spring of 1887 he invited Drummond there to a Conference of Students. Drummond agreed to go to Northfield as well as to certain 'summer schools' of Chautauqua and elsewhere. On the 11th of June he sailed from Liverpool, and reached New York on the 18th.

He had scarcely landed before requests for lectures and addresses poured in upon him from all sides. The American Association for the Advancement of Science; the Presidents of many universities and colleges — beginning with Dr. M'Cosh of Princeton, Dr. Dwight of Yale, Dr. Gilman of Johns Hopkins, Dr. Grant of Kingston, and Sir Daniel Wilson of Montreal; scholars like Dr. Bissell of Hartford, and Dr. Rendel Harris of Haverford; literary men like Mr. George Cable; the Christian Associations of many universities; the International Committee of the Young Men's Christian Association; besides the host of 'Lecturing Bureaus,' 'Societies of Inquiry,' 'Institutes of Christian Philosophy,' Women's Clubs, Pastors' Associations, and Societies of Teachers — begged him to give them either single lectures or a series of addresses.

He might have spent a couple of years on the Continent, and made a fortune by lecturing. But he saw the opportunity of extending to the American Colleges the religious movement which he had started among the Edinburgh students, and, with the exception of a couple of visits to 'summer schools,' he resolved to confine himself to this great work. He made arrangements for a strong deputation to come over from Edinburgh and commence a mission to the colleges so soon as these opened in September, and accepted pecuniary engagements only so far as to cover his travelling expenses for the next four months. The few purely scientific lectures which he gave were also undertaken by him solely for the purpose of furthering his influence as a religious teacher.

To the lecturer or preacher from Great Britain, America presents a width of area, an urgency of demand, and a wealth of organisation which are simply amazing after his experience of the insular opportunities and somewhat sluggish conservatism of his own country. It is not only the enormous population — nearly seventy millions — speaking the English language, nor the hunger for knowledge which a young people, hitherto engrossed in the material development of their vast continent, so naturally show, nor the religious freedom which welcomes a strong man for his own sake without asking what denomination he belongs to. But all these lavish opportunities have been as lavishly organised by the present generation of American people.

2 B

The curriculum of the Universities includes opportunity for lectures from 'visiting Professors,' experts
in various sciences and literatures from all parts of
the world.   In every University there are at least a
few, and often many, such lectureships.   'University
Extension,' too, has reached enormous dimensions in
the United States.   Besides the Summer Course which
Chicago University — that never shuts its doors from
one year's end to the other — provides for clergymen,
teachers, and other adult men and women, anxious to
complete an imperfect education, there are the great
summer schools, camp-meetings *in excelsis*, to which
thousands of people gather at some healthy and beautiful spot to attend regular courses of instruction from
experts in all branches of a school and university education.   At Chautauqua, for instance, for two months
every year, a small town of tents, wooden lodging-
houses, and a large hotel is inhabited by seven or eight
thousand people, and you will find among them whole
families, each of the members of which seeks instruction in some subject suited to his or her age; groups
of men and women students from many colleges, a
large number of whom pay for their education by acting as waiters or servants in the hotel and lodging-
houses; and a whole host of teachers, shopkeepers,
tradesmen, and others, who will carry away the good
seed they get from many of the best minds of their
generation, and sow it again in every state and territory
of the Union.   And besides all these concentrations
of intellectual opportunity, there are in every town the
lyceums and lecture associations, which attract a people busy with the practical problems of life, yet alive
to the necessity of culture, to listen in crowds, and
with an eagerness for information that to the lecturer
who is blessed with the privilege of imparting it is one

of the greatest inspirations which life can afford. Of
these things Drummond used to speak with enthusiasm.
It was a frequent saying of his that 'for one man you
can help by lecturing in Great Britain, you can help
twelve or twenty in America.'

'NORTHFIELD, MASS., June 28.

'It is a great chance this Conference — five hundred
    students from over eighty different colleges.'

'July 1.

'I am tearing away here at American speed. Al-
    ready I have been asked to become principal of
    a college, ditto of another college, to write for
    various papers, to lecture in half the states of the
    Union, and otherwise to line my pocket with
    dollars. But I have refused all wiles, and am
    plodding along at Moody's, with lots to do and
    lots to enjoy. The hardest thing is the heat.
    Northfield is like Crieff without the high moun-
    tains, but with a bigger river and more timber.
    It is very beautiful, and Moody is as grand as
    ever. To see him at home is a sight. He is
    simply a farmer, running messages, going for the
    cream and the beefsteak for dinner, and so on.
    Hundreds of students have now come, many in
    tents all over the place. Two are from Cambridge,
    England.'

After his work at Northfield, Drummond spent a
few days at Niagara with Lord and Lady Aberdeen
on their way home from India. Then he went to two
summer schools.

To Lady Aberdeen

'S. FRAMINGHAM, MASS., July 21.

'I hope this will find you safe and well in port once more — very thankful that it has all come to an end. It has been a wonderful episode! Yet how quickly it becomes dreamland again; and one picks up the threads of real life once more just where they were dropped. I cannot believe I really saw you and A. here. It was so short and sudden, and you passed away like a weaver's shuttle. I spent the Sunday at Newport, and often looked over the Atlantic and thought of the service, and hoped and wished all would go well.

'On Monday I came here, and I now write in the open air, while Principal Fairbairn of Oxford is lecturing to two thousand people about Ancient Religions, and imagines I am taking wise notes about Buddha and Confucius while I am scribbling this. Dr. Fairbairn is the only one I know here. I fancy you know some of his books, which are very fresh and able.

'I cannot begin to describe this place. It is one of a dozen Chautauquas, the oldest and biggest of the family, after the great mother which I visit next week. Imagine seventy acres of forest, with a hundred cottages and endless tents buried among the trees, a lake, an orchestra, a vast auditorium, and halls and buildings innumerable. This spot is tenanted for ten days every year by from three to six thousand people, who are all busy educating themselves. The vast majority are young women, especially those of a certain age, but there are many old people, entire families, teachers, clergymen, etc., etc. Their appetite for lectures is insatiable, and from six in the morning till nearly midnight there are meetings all over the grounds, and talks and discussions on every conceivable subject. I have an impromptu meeting each morning at eight for "religious talks," and I have prepared and discharged all the worst bombshells I could think of. There is much heat here, but no light. The Pharisees are down on one of course, but the Barbarians show me no little kindness. On the whole, it is a good thing this Chautauqua, but withal it is a bit of a rabble, and to-morrow I am going to steal away back to Niagara for a quiet Sunday and — a cigarette. On Tuesday I go to the parent Chautauqua for a few days, then back to "call" on Moody, and then to the Science Congress — the American " British Association " — which meets at New York.'

To his Father and Mother

'CHAUTAUQUA, July 28.

' All goes well. I am having lots of work and long, long journeys in the great country. Sabbath last I spent at Niagara alone. This is my third pilgrimage to it, and it gets better every time. Chautauqua is a wonderful place. I think I shall write an article about it, and tell you and the British public how the Americans are trying to educate themselves. I have lectured already to-day to a vast audience, and am " on " in half an hour again ; subject, " Nature and Religion." I have been " interviewed " several times, but some of the accounts I have never seen, and others are so absurd that I have been ashamed to send them to you. . . . My next move will be back to Moody.

He has another big Conference on hand for the first eleven days of August.'

'CLIFTON SPRINGS, N.Y., August 3.

'I had two glorious days at Niagara, then endless meetings for a week at Chautauqua, which is really a fine thing; then a day or two at a vast summer hotel and sanatorium, where also I have been let in for meeting after meeting, and to-night I go back to Moody.

'I do not think I have ever had such meetings in my life as I have had here. Marvellous opportunities have been open on every side, and I never felt so charged with a message. Hundreds of ministers have been coming, some to entangle one in their talk, like the Pharisees, but more to learn what poor things I could give them. I must tell you about it all some day; but the people here never seem to have even heard of Christianity.'

'GREENFIELD, MASS., August 5.

'For two days I have been at a monster hydropathic, "Clifton Springs." I wish father could see how they do things here. There are eight resident doctors all the year round and a chaplain. Some of the baths are very curious; one room is given up to slapping, and rubbing, and pounding done by machinery worked by a steam-engine. What fetched me there was a petition forwarded to Chautauqua, and signed by a great many people of note, including George H. Stuart of Philadelphia. On both nights I lectured on "Nature and Religion," and on leaving I found the folks had raised one hundred dollars to give me. This is the way they do things in America, but I *could* not take their money.   I can charge for science, but not for religion.   I find I could make a fortune here very quickly, and have been offered large sums to lecture, but I have other fish to fry. I charged the Chautauqua Company for what science I gave them, and this will cover all my expenses, along with £20 which I have got for a magazine article.   So I am very well off.   Were it only to break down the universal impression here that all religious work has an equivalent in dollars, I feel it a duty to enter this small protest. But enough about dollars.'

'NEW YORK, Aug. 12.

'I hope my cablegram reached you at dinner-time to-day [1] to act as stuffing to the grouse.   I have come to lecture to the American " British Association," [2] which by some unaccountable ignorance and mistake has given up a whole night to me to discourse on the Geology and Botany of Central Africa.   I am not sorry at heart about this, as I have been riding the other hobby fiercely in America, and need this to balance matters.'

To Lady Aberdeen

'MONTREAL, Aug. 26.

' . . . He [Captain Sinclair] came to Chautauqua,[3] where he found me addressing the mob in the vast amphitheatre.   Greenfield and an Edinburgh doctor, who form part of our College deputation, arrived in Quebec last week, and came straight to Chautauqua also, and we have been all more or less together ever since.   After Chautauqua we

[1] His father's birthday.
[2] The American Association for the Advancement of Science.
[3] Drummond returned there.

went to Niagara,[1] where I went over all the old
ground. After Niagara we did Toronto and the
Thousand Islands, and arrived here last night. . . .
'I enjoyed the American Association greatly. Saw
a good deal of Professor Marsh, who regretted
greatly not seeing you. He had set his heart on
showing you his fossils, which are the most unique
bones in the world. I am going to see them in
September. My lecture to the Association was
mostly about African insects, and I had a magnificent audience, as it was the only evening lecture
of the Association. I was appalled by the responsibility of the occasion, as all the savants of
the country were present, but for the sake of a
certain religious meeting some of us held on the
Sunday I was not sorry to do it. This last meeting went off very well, and even the *New York
Herald* had no fault to find with it. This was
also something to be thankful for, as ―― had
made a coarse attack on religion in his address
two days before.

'At Chautauqua I have been talking at least twice
a day, and this is the only holiday I have had
since you left. I hope to be wandering about
Canada and Nova Scotia with Captain Sinclair
for the next ten days, and we are now making
leisurely for some good fishing ground in the
lower provinces.

'I am in correspondence with half the Colleges of
America about our work, and my mail-bag is
something dreadful.'

'WHITE MOUNTAINS, NEW HAMPSHIRE, Sept. 8.

'I have been having "my holidays" for the last
week, and a very good time I have had. Captain

---

[1] Fourth visit.

S. and I went to Quebec, and had two days' fishing in one of the tributaries of the St. Lawrence. . . . The best scenery here is *nothing* [? in comparison with Switzerland], and everything in that line I have gone to see has been a disappointment. Professor Simpson joins me among the Colleges.'

'Sept. 8.

'My band of guerillas will all be at work by next Sunday — three in New Brunswick, one at Washington, and myself in New England. This division of the forces has been necessary owing to the number of colleges we have to overtake. I hope we shall concentrate by and by, and make the work more effective. I expect to have a very hard spell for the next month or more. Every night of the week will probably be occupied — except those spent in trains.

'We have far more invitations than we can use. Among other things, I am booked for four lectures to one of the theological colleges — the "Something Lectures," which will pay all my expenses, I think. Had this not been a college, I could not have undertaken the work, as I am refusing all paid lectures, our time for the colleges being too short as it is.'

'DARTMOUTH COLLEGE, N.H., Sept. 16.

'You will be glad to know that our College work has opened finely. Last Sunday we had three meetings at Williams,[1] and again on Monday and Tuesday, though we had meant to go on Monday.

'The whole College turned out on Monday night after we had each spoken. To our intense surprise, one of the students rose — one of the very

---

[1] Williams College, Williamstown, Massachusetts.

best and brightest men in the College, whom all knew and admired — and said, "I want to tell you fellows that I've been thinking it's about time I changed my life, and from this time forward I am resolved to follow Christ." You may imagine the effect. All next day we were busy dealing with the wounded; and the work is to be continued among themselves for the rest of the term.

'At Dartmouth the classes are suspended for our visit, and we have already had three meetings. But I have no time to add details. Only all goes well. Professor Greenfield and Dr. G. P. Smith are with me, and we hope to find Professor Simpson at Amherst College to-morrow. Our reception everywhere is most hearty. We generally board with the principals of the Colleges, and have very good quarters and first-rate company. . . . The ground is prepared already by an agent in advance, who has been stirring up all the Colleges by letter about our campaign. The National College Y.M.C.A. Secretary [1] has given up his entire time to us for the next two months.'

Before joining Drummond, Professor Greenfield, Dr. Webster, and Dr. G. P. Smith had been among the New Brunswick Colleges. Professor Simpson went to Washington and Philadelphia.

'HARTFORD, CONN., Sept. 23.

'We are now up to the neck in hard work. . . . We have had really splendid work at the Colleges, far surpassing our expectations. Any one of them would have paid us for crossing the Ocean. We are now all together, — Simpson, Greenfield, and

[1] Mr. C. K. Ober.

Smith, — and Sabbath first will find us at Princeton.'

'HARTFORD, Sept. 30 (? 29).

'Since I last wrote from Hartford I have been to
Princeton and Philadelphia. At Princeton I was
the guest of President M'Cosh, a grand old Scotch-
man whose wife is a niece of Dr. Guthrie's.
Simpson, Greenfield, Webster, and Smith were
all with me, and we had meetings with the students from morning till night all the time. At
all the Colleges we have got the students started
on deputation work, and we hope the movement
will spread all over the country. To-morrow I
go to Yale, and then to Harvard. Unfortunately,
Smith and I have to tackle them single-handed,
as all the others are off on the *Umbria* to-morrow
morning.'

At Yale very careful preparation had been made
for Drummond's mission by students of the University who had met him at the Northfield Conference.
Consequently the work there was very deep, and, in
the testimony of many, permanent.

'YALE COLLEGE, NEW HAVEN, CONN., Sept. 30.

'My life is roaring along like a cataract. I have
not been so busy for years, and have literally not
had an hour to call my own. The Colleges have
given us the most generous reception, and we
have been allowed to hold meetings as often and
at whatever hours we liked. The heads of the
Colleges have given us hospitality, and nothing
has been denied us by the Faculties that could
facilitate our work. The students at the larger
Colleges are a remarkably fine set of men. The

Princeton, Amherst, and Yale men are quite
equal to the English undergraduate on the average, while the best of them will compare well
with the best of our men both in brain-power and
in scholarship.   There is much less antipathy to
Christianity than at home, and many need only
to have the case fairly put to them to win them
over.   It has all been very wonderful and very
delightful.'

'YALE, Oct. 7.

' This has been one of the best and busiest weeks
of my life, but I have not a moment to tell my
tale.   I write in the Yale Graveyard — the only
uninhabited spot I can find; and I have only
twenty minutes for my whole English mail.

The work here has been most wonderful, great
meetings at night, and talks and walks (your kind
of walks) all day long.

' We have got at the very heart and brain of this
College, and I am sure permanent work has been
done which will tell on all the colleges round
when the men start out to work.   They are to
begin the aggressive work on a neighbouring
University on Sunday first, while I go on to
Harvard.   Do not infer that the whole College
is in a state of wild excitement, for it is not so;
nor did we want that.   But the head centres are
reached in every department, and they will do
the rest before the term is many weeks older.

' I had a delightful day at Hartford last Friday after
writing you — called on Mark Twain, Mrs. Harriet Beecher Stowe, and the widow of Horace
Bushnell.   I was wishing A—— had been at the
Mark Twain interview.   He is funnier than any
of his books, and, to my surprise, is a most

respected citizen, devoted to things æsthetic, and the friend of the poor and struggling.'

'UNION LEAGUE CLUB, NEW YORK, Oct. 18.

' All has gone merrily.

' I am now busy among the medical students of New York, a scattered and lawless set, who are housed in colleges all over the city — one for homœopaths, one for allopaths, one for surgeons, and so on — so that they are hard to reach. Harvard College (the college of Lowell, Emerson, Longfellow, Fiske, etc.) is *the* college of the country, and under Unitarian auspices, so that I was told it would be impossible to do anything there, but the work was really better than anywhere. I lived with one of the professors, a Unitarian, but I found no difference between him and myself, and I never saw a more lovely Christian home. I have come away with a new idea of the Unitarians, or at least of some of them. After Harvard I spent a couple of days in the American Girton — Wellesley College. It is the largest and most splendid woman's college in the world, and the standard is as high as Harvard. I was the sole male among six hundred "girl graduates," so you can imagine the terror of the first meetings I had.'

'ALBANY, N.Y., Oct. 21.

' It will be meetings, meetings till the last hour, as we have all the colleges of New York to tackle next week. I am at present on my way to a Convention of Students for the State of New York at a place called Schenectady, but I return to New York on Saturday.'

On the 29th of October Drummond sailed in the *Umbria* for England. The evening after, in Dockstader's Theatre, New York, a meeting of students was held, to hear addresses from members of Yale University and to further the movement among the New York Colleges. The Hon. Chauncey M. Depew was the chairman. The following characteristic report appeared in the *New York World*: —

"Had the chief minstrel attempted to occupy his usual seat on the stage of Dockstader's Theatre last night, he would have found the house packed with a great audience. Had Lew Dockstader himself gone to his usual place in the centre of the circle, he would have seen Chauncey M. Depew there. The end men and the funny men would have seen their places filled with men of brawn and muscle, men who have lowered records, men who can pull an oar with the best, and men who can knock home runs. Athletes, ball-players, runners, and gymnasts, all men of Yale, who had come here to start a new movement among college men, were there. Three years ago some students in the University of Edinburgh formed an association designed to increase Christian influence and Christian teachings among college men. It has borne fruit. Professor Henry Drummond introduced the same organisation at Yale. The men on the stage last night had come to tell their experiences and tell their fellows here that a man can be a Christian and an athlete and be better for being both.

'The theatre was filled with college men: Princeton, Columbia, Dartmouth, Amherst, and the University of New York were all represented. The meeting opened with singing. College men can sing, and the old walls of the theatre had no reason to be ashamed of what they had to echo. Mr. Foster introduced Mr. Depew as the Chairman, who said: —

'"I am here to-night because I am always interested in students and graduates. I don't think much of the man who can't go through life and continue to have the freshness, breeziness, and honesty of the University. The object of this movement is to rescue students from false ideas of life.

To teach a man to live this life and get the best of it.   I
have known one man to ruin a whole class.   Too often I
have seen the pet, the most popular man of his class, a
drunkard, a debauchee, and a depraved man morally, and it is
such examples that have led many a young man to think it
impossible to be a good fellow and a Christian.

 ' "The object of such a meeting as this is to counterbalance
the false ideas and associations of young men.   There has
been too much of the bigotry of creed, and not enough
practical Christianity in this world.   A man must learn that
the largest dividends come from right living.   The only thing
that can save a man from drinking, gambling, and lust is
Christianity.[1]   There are, too, people trying to break the
foundations of society.   Now the checking of all this must
come from the colleges.   We must have Christian men." '

Mr. Depew then introduced some of the leading
students and athletes of Yale University.   They described the work of Professor Drummond, and how he
had enlisted the services of college men.   One told
how he had changed his life for the better.   ' It was
all due,' he said, ' to Professor Drummond.   He talked
to me for an hour one day, and after that I saw my
way clear.'

It was in America as in Scotland.   Hundreds of
men repeated the story of this Yale student about
themselves.   Some from a life of sin, some from an
aggressive hostility to all religion, some from weary
and dark doubts, were won for a clear faith and a
strong life of duty and unselfish service.   The men
did not fail, and the movement did not die.   The
quickened religious life of the American Universities,
the Student Volunteer Missionary Movement, powerful in the United States as in Great Britain,[2] has in

---

[1] I add this sentence from another report.

[2] By 1891 no fewer than six thousand university men pledged themselves to
go to the foreign field if opportunity offered.

a large measure been due to Drummond's mission. The Rev. Charles Fleming of Minneapolis wrote as follows in the *Boston Congregationalist* for 1888 : —

' Sober-mindedness, religious earnestness, Christian aggressiveness, characterise the present generation of college students. These qualities are perhaps more intellectual and less emotional than formerly. They are manifesting themselves less in occasional revivals, and more in regular methods of Christian conduct and service. Religion is, in some colleges, becoming more natural. I know of no college in which this change is greater than in Harvard. A dozen years ago the Harvard student was too much in the mood of the man in Sterne's *Sentimental Journey* whom a mule was about to kick — the attitude of humble apology. The Christian man of Harvard seems to-day to have learned that Christianity has rights which he should be willing to claim and be able to oblige his fellows to respect. It would not have surprised me more, when I was in college, to see Memorial Hall Tower floating on the Charles than to see Harvard students holding public religious services in the Globe Theatre with eminent clergymen as preachers, and the President of the University bestowing the approbation of his presence. Some of the causes which have effected this revolution in Cambridge are at work in other colleges. The influence of Professor Drummond and his associates has been potent. His addresses and his private conversations with students in many colleges have proved to have somewhat of that power which the series of sermons of the elder President Dwight had in expelling infidel opinions from Yale College. His youth, his ease of approach, his ability, his simplicity, his method of satisfying the reason before attempting to arouse the feelings or to move the will — appeal with special persuasiveness to college men. His journeys to the different colleges, and his lectures to students in the Northfield Conferences, have resulted in a revival of personal piety and of Christian service.'

On May 1, 1889, Professor Francis Peabody of Harvard wrote Drummond : —

' I venture to recall myself to you and to report to
you the substantial good that has remained of your
week among us here.   Movements of the deepest interest have sprung from the impulse you gave, and
I date from the beginning of last year a larger sense
of religious responsibility.

' There is a marked and growing interest among us
in work, among the humbler classes, of a University
Settlement or University Extension kind ; and in
order to direct this interest wisely, I think I must
see what has been done both in England and Scotland. . . .   I should very much like to meet you once
more and to tell you how the religious life of our University has been led since your visit to us. . . .   Meantime, pray be sure that a debt of serious obligation
is still felt to you here for your wise and inspiring
counsel.'

2 C

CHAPTER XIV

THE invitation to Australia rose, as we have seen, out of the 'Student Movement.' There are always a number of Australians at Edinburgh University, and many of these had been influenced by Professor Drummond's meetings since 1885. They had sent home reports of his work; some of them had returned with the proof of it in their own characters; and finally news came of how he himself had carried its influence to the American colleges in 1887. In 1889 two hundred and thirty members of Melbourne University invited Professor Drummond to come out to them in the following year. When his promise to do so was known, invitations were pressed upon him from all the Australian colonies. But, faithful to the policy which he had followed in Scotland and America, he refused to go among the churches, or do anything that might distract his mission to students, young men, and boys.[1] He planned to come home by some of the mission stations in the South Seas and China, and to speak to the students of Japan, who had more than once invited him to their country. One other service, which he could not foresee, awaited him in Melbourne. He arrived there in time to watch by the death-bed of his friend, John F. Ewing, and to be the chief mourner at his funeral.

[1] Mr. W. Lucas, F.R.G.S., to whom I am indebted for some details of the Australian visit, informs me that Professor Drummond stipulated that he should be allowed to pay his own travelling expenses.

Drummond left London on the 14th March — the year was 1890 — and embarked on the P. and O. steamer *Carthage* at Brindisi.

'S.S. CARTHAGE, OFF PORT SAID, March 19.

'This is not a voyage, but a trip in the *Columba* in July on the Clyde. Nothing could be more perfect than sky, sea, ship, or weather. It is so glorious that one cannot even read. But I hope to settle to books presently, and even manage "A Death in the Desert"[1] before luncheon to-day.

'I quite forget if you play chess. I have Staunton's book with me, and mean to get up the game scientifically. It is my first love among games, and I have long wanted a week to do homage to it.'

'OFF ADEN, March 24.

'We are just turning in to Aden — memories coming back of the last time I was here on my way to Africa with Bain, whose grave now lies by Lake Nyasa. And Keith Falconer, too, with his mysteriously short life. But one recalls those things only as a tribute to the dead. Nothing could be more living than this ship, or less morbid than its passengers; for we have had the most perfect voyage ever made, and everybody is very happy. . . . The keel has never stirred from the "absolute perpendicular," and for certain the sea will be smooth for the next fortnight. There has been no heat to speak of, and one has felt every day that one could sail on and on like this forever.

'I am at the Captain's table, with five others, a solid yet merry party. My immediate neighbour is an Italian Count on his way, as Ambassador, to China. He is a splendid man, full of sense,

---

[1] He had taken with him all Browning's works for the voyage.

goodness, and wide culture, and we have formed
a friendship.   Indeed, he has given me—by his
personality—quite a new idea of Italy; and such
is my admiration for him that I find myself daily
on the point of asking him whether there are
many more like him in his native land.   We
read Browning aloud together.

'On Sunday we had the usual service in the Saloon.
In the evening I gave an address in the Second
Class Saloon to about sixty or seventy people —
fine young fellows, for the most part, going to
push their way in Australia.

'Last night I followed up with a lecture on "Africa,"
and I hope to get to know some of them presently.'

'NEARING ALBANY, April 12.

'I meant to have written you at Colombo, where
we had the usual day ashore, but some friend
had telegraphed on the passenger list, and I
found at least four deputations waiting to make
life a burden and time a hallucination.   I had to
trot round everywhere, but really that place is too
splendid for this world, and my one regret this
voyage is that Japan has done me out of at least
a fortnight there. . . .

'I think one of the books that has pleased me most
has been George Macdonald's *Robert Falconer.*
Towards the end there are some really fine bits
about work among the poor.'

'April 13, 1890.

'This is my last Sabbath at sea.   Australia is exactly three hundred yards off, and this finds me,
after a voyage of absolute rest, quietness, happiness, and health, the most thankful man under
the Southern Cross.   You know what a miserable

sailor I am, yet all these weeks I have never
missed a meal, and the sea seems to have lost all
its terrors. We judge of it from our own grey,
troubled coast, but to know it, and to know what
climate is, one has to come here. I emphasise
this because you always shiver at the thought of
China, and I would like to try to make the prospect pleasant even if it should never be realised.
Up to Colombo the China route is glorious, and
Ceylon itself is worth the whole voyage.'

'MELBOURNE, April 21.

'Your prediction was right about the interviewers,
who turned up in phalanxes at each port. Happily,
I did not see their lucubrations, as the steamer
always bore me from the scene of trial before the
papers were out.

'A troop of students met me at the pier here on
Saturday morning, and in the evening we met
again to plan the campaign. We begin on
Friday with a reception in the 'Varsity and then
on Sunday.

'To-day is a public holiday, with a workmen's procession to commemorate the Eight Hours'
victory.

'I read Dilke and Seeley on the voyage, according
to instructions, and feel very wise and Imperial-
Federationally.

'We *must* take this jolly child a little nearer its
grey old mother. I am asked to the opening
dinner of Parliament a fortnight hence.

'I did not stop at Adelaide, as Ewing wrote it
would not do to begin there. But I shall return
soon.'

Drummond stayed with John Ewing, his fellow-student, his comrade at Sunderland, and one of 'our Club.' Ewing had built up a large working-class congregation in Dundee; for some years he had held, with great courage, a very difficult post in Glasgow; and in 1887 he was called to the large Presbyterian Church of Toorak, a leading suburb of Melbourne. Physically he was a very strong man. I climbed Monte Rosa and the Matterhorn with him in 1885, and he could then go up hill faster than any guides. But his zeal and unselfishness were even greater than his physical strength, and the way he worked for three and a half years at Toorak wore him out. A week after Drummond landed in Melbourne, Ewing was down with what was thought to be influenza, then raging in Australia. On the 2d of May the doctors pronounced it to be typhoid. He saw his lawyer, and gave Drummond a message for his wife, who had gone on a visit to Scotland. After this he spoke little, slept most of the time for eight days more, his friend by his side, and on May 11th passed quietly away.

To D. M. Ross

'TOORAK MANSE, May 12, 1890.

'MY DEAR ROSS, — I am alone in the Manse. It is very terrible. This is his desk and paper. How can I write you?

'Send this round the Club if you like, for I ought to write each one. After I wrote last he slowly sank; never spoke; no pain. At dusk on Friday he passed away, my hand in his. The nurse said it was the gentlest death she ever saw.

'He never spoke much, and never said farewell. We had four very happy days together, then the

cloud fell, and *he*, the real he, was slowly taken
from my sight. . . .

'Oh, Ross, I cannot go on.   This is the first break
in our ranks, and I never thought it was so big.
We must close up now and work hard.   This is
what I am feeling much these days.   Tell the
men to excuse me writing, as I have all E.'s people to communicate with at length.   For them,
for *her*, how terrible it all is!'

To Lady Aberdeen

'You would hear perhaps of the awful thing that
happened — in the next room.   He passed away,
my hand in his, more gently than a sleeping child.
Strange that I should have been sent across these
seas for this.   For the time it has sobered me.
I feel I must work hard.

'Ewing had some absurd mannerisms, but underneath I never knew a saner, purer, grander soul.
His influence here has been phenomenal.   No
man ever made such an impression on a community in three years and a half.   At his funeral
the church was crowded with weeping people —
from the Premier and the Bishop to the Street
Arabs whom he had saved.   Four of these last
drove in a cab to the grave, and could scarcely
lay down the wreath they had clubbed to buy,
for tears.'

At the memorial service Professor Drummond delivered the address : —

'Six days before the end he asked me to take a sheet
of paper and write a message to his wife.   I think I
betray no trust if to you, his people, I repeat a sen-

tence of what he said. His voice never faltered as
he gave it; his look was grave but calm; he spoke as
one whose mind was made up, as if he expressed a conviction, deliberate, fixed, and fully ripe. " Tell her,"
he said, " that my mind is not very clear, but the one
thing clear in it is *her*, and all this suffering is nothing
if it means going to Christ and getting her after. I
was so robust that I did not feel need of taking special
precaution. Sir James Bain says I should have spared
myself; so I should. But there was nothing to warn
me. I suspect it was God's will."

' There are,' continued Drummond, 'two ways in
which a workman regards his work — as his own or
as his master's. If it is his own, then to leave it in his
prime is a catastrophe, if not a cruel and unfathoma-
ble wrong. But if it is his Master's, one looks not
backwards, but before, putting by the well-worn tools
without a sigh, and expecting elsewhere better work
to do. So he suspected it was in the will of God.
We must try to think so too. Work is given men
not only, nor so much perhaps, because the world
needs it, but because the workman needs it. Men
make work, but work makes men. An office is not
a place for making money, it is a place for making
men. A workshop is not a place for making machinery, it is a place for making souls; for fitting
in the virtues to one's life; for turning out honest,
modest, and good-natured men. So is it with the
work of the State or of the Church. This is why it
never hurries — because it is as much for the worker
as for the work. . . . For Providence cares less for
winning causes than that men, whether losing or winning, should be great and true; cares nothing that
reforms should drag their course from year to year
bewilderingly, but that men and nations, in carrying

them out, should find their education, discipline, unselfishness, and growth in grace. These lessons learned, the workers may be retired — not because the cause is won, but because it is not won; because He has other servants, some at lesser tasks, some half employed or unemployed, whom He must needs call into the field. For one man to do too much for the world is in one sense the whole world's loss. So it may be that God withdraws His workers even when their hands are fullest and their souls most ripe: to fill the vacancies with still growing men, and enrich many with the loss of one. I do not propose this, even as an explanation of the inexplicable phenomenon, which startles the Church from time to time, as one and another of its noblest leaders are cut down in the flower of their strength. But when our thoughts are heavy with questions of the mysterious ways of God, it keeps reason from reeling from its throne to see even a glimpse of light.

' But one diverges into these things mainly because it is easier to say them than to approach any nearer to the man himself. When I think of Mr. Ewing's work and influence here, my soul fills with gratitude and enthusiasm for my friend. His concentration, it is true, was exceptional, his initiative very great, his vitality as exuberant as his hope. It is true — and how wonderful this is — that he never did anything but his work. He had no petty interests. He saw always the main stream of the kingdom of God, all currents in Church or State that make for righteousness, and he threw himself into them. But none of these things could have produced the extraordinary demonstration here on Friday last. Intellectual brilliancy could not have done it, nor ecclesiastical position, nor successful preaching power. What did it was his character, his downright, sterling, pure, strong character. Three and a half years of that — it looks very short. But character knows no calendar, for it alone of all forces is infinitely great, and cannot but do its work. . . .

'Three weeks ago to-day, when he stood here and gave us the last Sunday morning's message of his life, you remember he preached on the "Atonement." He dwelt upon one or two sides of that stupendous theme, and promised to lay before us a further aspect on a future day. I am not sure that that promise is unfulfilled. Perhaps what he meant to tell us was that the principle of the Atonement was a law of Nature . . . that up and down the whole of God's creation the one law of life, the supreme condition of progress, the sole hope of the future is Christ's law of the sacrifice of self. If that were his meaning, his sermon has been surely preached. The corn of wheat, of which he spoke to us that day, has fallen into the ground and died. I, for one, have neglected many a sermon. But for this one never spoken, this mute appeal of a life laid down, this last life-message from one who will never speak again — is there a man among us who will be to-morrow as if that had never been?'

In Melbourne and in Adelaide Drummond held meetings for students, for young men generally, and for boys and girls. As in Edinburgh, he would have nothing but students at his student meetings, and admitted no reporters. Some of the religious papers were very angry at this. 'The newspaper interviewer,' said one editor, 'who can generally draw blood from a stone, can get nothing for a notice out of Professor Drummond.' What he gave the Australian students

was, with suitable variations, what he had been giving
the students of Scotland and America.

'MELBOURNE, April 29.

'The meetings have done well. The students are
turning out splendidly, and I think something
may be effected before long.'

'May 6.

'The students' meetings have gone on. All I will
say is that it has been all I hoped for.'

'May 12.

'I have had a few *good* meetings, and some talks
with the right kind of men. To-morrow I go to
Adelaide for ten days, and back here for nightly
meetings. Thereafter my future is still a blank.
All depends on how the work develops.'

'May 27.

'I have been off to Adelaide and put in a week's hard
work — meetings, meetings, meetings. I can send
you no reports, as I have discovered how to cir-
cumvent the Press, and have succeeded most
effectually everywhere.

'Hobart is not in sight yet. Poor Ewing's illness
has thrown me rather out of my programme. It
is certainly hard to get in anything else when one
is on a mission. Do not be surprised if you hear
that I am off to the South Sea Islands (!) in a few
weeks. It is only a prospect as yet, but some
people here are keen about my going, and I am
at least thinking over it. The point is mainly
political — France wants the New Hebrides, and
Victoria says she shan't get them. They want
me to write the thing up at home. Then there is
a very crucial missionary problem; and the esca-

pade tempts me generally. It would take about
four weeks, leaving Sydney June 17, and returning — cannibals permitting — about July 10th.
But it is only a dream. I mention it in case
there should be a silence presently for about a
month. It would not alter my general plan, as
I am getting quicker through my College work
than I expected. . . .
'Now I must off to the 'Varsity to meet some wild
beasts.'

'SYDNEY, June 7.

'I arrived in How-d'ye-like-our-Harbour a couple of
hours ago, and have just heard that the English
mail starts earlier from here — which is natural.
So I fly to my pen, though I have little or nothing
to report.

'Melbourne has been one round of meetings, sometimes two daily. All were got up quite privately,
and I think there may have been some little good
done. What I liked most was some meetings
with the Young Australian Club men, who gave
me a real chance to speak to them. You will be
disgusted to know that I never had a night for
Government House, though they were most kind
in asking me; but I had every hour of every day
filled with what I came to do.

'On my way here I broke the journey at a Squatter
Station, and had a really happy day in the bush.
I saw heaps of kangaroos, dined on the tails
thereof, and after dinner hunted 'possums in the
moonlight till the Express whizzed up shortly
after midnight. It had been ordered to stop
for me, and when I tumbled out of the bush into
the Pullman I rather surprised Mr. J. L. Toole
(if you don't know who he is, see *The Christian*)

and some of his mates playing roulette, after they
supposed the coast was clear.   I had met Toole
at Melbourne, and he offered me a corner at
rouge-et-noire, which was brotherly.   I cannot get
to Hobart, which is miserable.   Time is the cul-
prit.   I had no idea I should be so busy.   The
New Hebrides look nearer.   I had a long talk
with the Premier of Victoria on the subject.
Every one is very anxious for me to go, as they
have taken into their heads that I can help things
politically.   If I go, it will simply take the time I
should have given to New Zealand.'

'June 9.

'Finished Melbourne.   All very good.   At the last
I had sometimes two or three meetings a day.
Students and others are taking up several bits of
work.   Boys' Brigade launched.'

The following letter to the Rev. John Walker of
Woolahra,[1] who arranged the Sydney meetings, gives
a good idea of our evangelist's aims and methods all
through the last twelve years of his life: —

'AUSTRALIAN CLUB [MELBOURNE], Wednesday.

'If you can manage it, perhaps you will get up a
meeting on Sunday night for better-class young
men, *non-church members* as far as possible.
Everybody goes to the Y.M.C.A. young man ;
I am anxious for a shot at the outsiders.   Last
night a young champion tennis-player got up a
meeting of two hundred splendid young fellows
here, and that is exactly the sort of thing I
should covet.   There were no public advertise-
ments.   He and half-a-dozen young fellows
about the clubs handed cards of admission to

---

[1] Mr. Walker was one of his old fellow-workers in Liverpool in 1875.

their own "set" privately, and we reached a class who never go to church. I should prefer fifty of that class to one thousand of the church-goers. The great problem in these colonies is the young "outsider." I am sure you will know one or two men who will run this quietly through. I suppose seven at night in some *small* central hall would be the best time and place. No *elders* admitted. Parsons, £10 a head. Reporters, £100.

'Lastly, *don't* do this if you don't think it will work.'

'SYDNEY, June 18.

'I was told Sydney was the wickedest place in Oceania. I must say I have nowhere had such a chance. The students have turned out nobly night after night, and they are going to run the meetings henceforth every Sunday night themselves. The most influential undergraduates are leading the movement, and the two most liked and most brilliant among the professors will second them in every way.

'On Sunday I had one of the most curious gatherings I ever faced. Some doctors asked me to address "the Sydney doctors," of whom it seems only four or so go to church. They got the Royal Society's rooms, and the President thereof took the chair. There were exactly one hundred and forty present, *all* doctors. I spoke from the standpoint of Evolution; and they were so much interested that next day twenty of them agreed to pay £50 a year each to "start a Church for doctors" on the spot, and get out a man from home at, at least, £1000 a year. Many of them are extremely able men, and several medical professors have joined since. The "Conversion" is somewhat "sudden," but something will certainly come of it.

'Yesterday I was honoured by a Sydney magistrate with a Picnic on the Harbour. A steamer was chartered, and about one hundred and fifty guests invited. We sailed about all day, and had luncheon and afternoon tea on board. I talked for seven hours without a comma, and saw very little of the Harbour, but I hope for a more private inspection on my return.

'It is now two in the morning, and in eight hours I start for the New Hebrides. The ship is good, the sea smooth, the cannibals fairly fed at present, and all looks well for a happy voyage. The wretch who led me on the ice (a politician), who was to go with me, telegraphed me from Melbourne, a few hours ago, that he could not come. It seems my fate to be a solitary traveller. A special ship is to call for me at one of the groups and land me here about July 10th. . . .'

On his return from the New Hebrides, Drummond 'found the Sydney students running their Sunday evening meeting bravely, and all going splendidly.' From Melbourne he had 'also good news.'

What else can be said about his Australian mission, except that it evoked the usual number of personal appeals, which met him wherever his books had come or he himself spoken. To every platform on which he appeared, there came a rush of questions, and many hours a day were filled with private interviews. His addresses to students must have taken the line of his *Ascent of Man*, for the questions which he kept relate to the reconciliation of the doctrines of evolution with the statements of the Bible as to man's creation.   Among the letters he received are a number from men praying for the appearance of a broader and more rational Christianity, and expressing the sense that it is at least 'in the air.'   As if to emphasise the need of this, there are letters of a kind which met Drummond wherever he went in Britain, America, or Australia—letters which reveal Christian faith wrecked and Christian energies dissipated by the doctrine of verbal inspiration.[1]   In remote corners of our great colony, Drummond came across men who still knew only of the older orthodoxy and the easy triumphs which certain infidel writers had obtained over its beliefs in the equal and absolute inspiration of every part of the Bible.   To read the letters of such men is to understand how many earnest and pure spirits in our day have been forced to give up Christianity because they have ignorantly thought that it is identified with everything in both the Testaments.   And it was no small part of Drummond's mission in Australia, as in Great Britain and America, to bring home to such 'forwandered' souls the new possibilities of faith which lie in the rational and discriminating criticism of the Old Testament, to which Christ Himself has shown us the way in the Sermon on the Mount.

But difficulties of faith are not the subject of all the letters Drummond received in Australia.[2]   Some men and women write to ask his prayers for their recovery from long disease; they are convinced that God must grant what he asks.   And, as usual, there are petitions

---

[1] A note by Drummond on a character projected for a story by a friend runs thus: 'No. I.'s fundamental mistake is verbal inspiration.   This prevents him thinking.   The paralysing and stunting effect of anything which interferes with the legitimate exercise of human faculty.'

[2] At one place in Victoria a 'Drummond Club' of men was formed for the regular study of his writings.

from men with grievances, with unrecognised inventions, or with patents overlooked by Government. One curious letter, which he received after his return to Scotland, intimates that the writer, a resident in some far-away station, has ideas for which the world is hungering; that he is afraid to communicate them to Drummond lest the latter should unconsciously appropriate them; but that he will send them in a sealed envelope, to be opened on the author's death, and published with his name. And a still more pathetic epistle comes from an old man, who has spent his life in vainly trying to get expression for a 'system' of philosophy he has perfected, and who wishes to name Drummond as his successor and its prophet.

For wherever he came, men both old and young had new hope, and the weary were refreshed by his sympathy.

2 D

CHAPTER XV

*Coral Islands and Volcanoes; the Last of the Canni-
bals; Civilisation and Christian Missions*

In a letter, quoted above,[1] Drummond gives his
reasons for going to the New Hebrides. He had not
included them in his Australian plans; but after his
arrival at Melbourne, several leading colonists pressed
upon him the importance of making himself acquainted
with the political problems on these islands, from which
our Australian colonies were then suffering no small
anxiety. The New Hebrides lie some fifteen hundred
miles east from the coast of Queensland; to the south
is the French convict settlement of New Caledonia, to
the south-east the British Fiji Islands. Discovered by
the Portuguese in 1606, but first explored by Captain
Cook in 1773, they were found to be inhabited by cannibals of the lowest type. Every one knows their
strangely mingled history since they came into touch
with Europe. The trade for sandalwood, cocoanuts,
and arrowroot; the exportation of the natives to labour
in Queensland; and the work of the English and
Scottish missions — none of these has happened without bloodshed and cruelty. After long toil and many
martyrdoms, the missionaries have civilised the southern islands, the labour traffic has been regulated by the
Australian governments, but politically the islands
remain, so to speak, in the air. Before 1890 Great

---

[1] P. 395.

Britain claimed them, but had done nothing to annex
them.   France claimed them, but our Australian
colonies resented the claims of France, and baffled
more than one attempt to make these good.   By a
Convention both Powers have since agreed to respect
their independence.

It was in order to bear testimony at home on this
critical state of affairs that leading men in Australia
pressed Drummond to visit the islands.   He was also
attracted by the prospect of seeing the effects of
Christian missions upon a savage people; the mission
in Aneityum was of his own Church, and he would be
her first direct visitor to it.   Moreover, as a geologist
he would have the opportunity of studying islands at
once of volcanic and of coral formation.   On all these
lines the bright promise was fulfilled.   Drummond
made a close and most exciting inspection of the crater
of a volcano in full activity.   He conversed with sheer
savages, and with his own eyes saw their customs.   He
obtained a clear view of the political situation.   But,
above all, he came home from his visit to the missions
with a new belief in the power of Christianity, and in
the heroism of his fellow-churchmen upon those lonely
and barbarian edges of the world.

He left Sydney on June 19th, and by way of Noumea,
the capital of New Caledonia, he reached Aneityum.
He attended the Synod of the New Hebrides Mission,
and heard it pass a resolution calling on the British
Government, *first*, to encourage British settlers on the
group and provide for the secure tenure of the lands
they purchased; *secondly*, either to extend the prohibi-
tion of the sale of firearms, which was enforced only
on British subjects, to men of all nations, or to rescind
it altogether; and, *thirdly*, to abolish the foreign labour
traffic, 'the more especially as settlers on this group

will have need of at least all the available labour which
it can afford.'

'ANEITYUM, June 25.

'All the missionaries are gathered here for the
General Assembly.[1] I represent the Free Church
there to-night. What a change!'

He left Aneityum next day, and now we follow his
diary.

'June 27.

'At dawn skirting Futuna. The volcano of Tanna
very much in evidence all night. Usually a narrow
pillar of red, neither dull nor glowing; a red-hot
colour, very large, occasionally a brilliant display.
This was at a distance of over forty miles.

'Futuna, one huge block of rock covered completely
green, like Aneityum: caused by grasses, herbs, and
wildflowers, patches of forest here and there, and a
dense fringe of cocoanuts along the coast. Cocoanut
trees in quantity do not help a landscape much. It
is *one* against the sky that stirs your soul with the
wonder of its grace and beauty. But any kind of
tree will beat them as foliage. The form is not fine;
shadows are wanting. There is a stiff, metallic look,
and the green is dingy and tarnished with decaying
fronds, the shreds of fibrous cloth, and even the
bunches of brown . . . [?] which hold the cocoanuts.
Green to water's edge. Roughly terraced; only here
and there bare rock visible.

'Very like Table Mountain.

'Geologically one would say at once "a truncated
cone." One or two baby volcanoes. On landing all
is coral. It extends upwards at least one thousand
feet. Dip upwards, ////. This dip *towards* a supposed

[1] Administrative Synod.

crater is found all round. The top is a plateau. Is
any basalt visible? I think not. It looks all the
same, coral to the very top. Basalt, water-worn stones
gathered from shore are arranged round the Manse
garden, and I was told there was volcanic rock " on
the other side." The small hill on shore line, where
the " geological photograph " was taken by Dr. Gunn,
seems from his description to be like the Giant's
Causeway.

' Glorious colour of the sea — bluest blue.

' Off in whale-boat to land Dr. Gunn. Coral growing everywhere. Ashore on human-back. Small crowd
of natives. Real article this time. Some clothed
women; with grass kilts and shell necklaces; huge
earrings made of tortoiseshell look like a bunch of
keys. Bushy hair of the aureole type. Some women
had this covered with a green banana leaf decoratively
arranged thus: wound once round head after being
cut into four or five " liths," and then gathered on the
top of the head and tied in a knot. The appearance
is most picturesque, looks as if each had a crown on
her head.

' Many shook hands. Offered bags for sale made
of neatly plaited pandanus leaf. Some offered rare
shells of great beauty and a flint axe, which I bought
for a stick of tobacco. Another offered four eggs.

' Clambered up rugged path, winding up coral. Introduced to Mrs. Gunn. She has not been off the
island, except to Aneityum for short time, for eight
years. Only had ship calling once in six months.
" I suppose I cannot ask you if it is ever dull ? " —
" We prove that," said Dr. Gunn, " by taking furlough
every twelve years instead of every ten." But this is
phenomenal. This couple on this Rock for eight
years. For six years saw absolutely no visible result.

Now just beginning. New mission-house finely situated on a terrace of coral shrined in palms as usual.
Old house destroyed by hurricane lately. Cocoanut
grove behind house, walk six yards, behold, a native
village! The houses are like the thatched cover of a
bullock waggon, without windows of course, and door
at end.'

'TANNA, June 27.

'7.30. — Steamer steamed at its best to reach Tanna
in time for volcano visit. Close under the island almost
two o'clock. Spot was Port Resolution. Captain
Cook's eye (he had a genius for seeing these things:
any ordinary navigator would have passed the place
as a mere shallow irregularity on the coast-line), saw
here an anchorage, and called it after his ship the
Resolution.

'This was the scene of Mr. Paton's struggles. Not
a sign of life, the usual type of Hebrides island —
mountainous, sloping gently towards sea, the belt of
tropical vegetation terminating below in the usual
fringe of cocoanut, above in light-green underwood, and wooded to the top. The volcano is not
centrally situated, so much so that from a distance it
almost seems a low island separate from the large
mountainous masses of the interior. The coast here
to the far-away side has a very strange look to the
geological eye. It has a *new* look. A low cliff of
unswathed rock runs all along the coast, quite unbroken by the sea. This was the result of an upheaval
in 1878. *Instantaneous.* Seen by Mr. Neilson the
missionary. Accompanied by tidal wave. A trader
man woke up next morning, things so changed,
thought he had *delirium tremens.* Half the harbour
quite shallow now. Largest ships cannot enter.
The elevation was thirty-two feet. Later a further

elevation of sixteen. Quite local, affecting only as far as Sulphur Bay, say one and a half miles, the end quite distinct where the normal beach resumes, *i.e.* only one and a half miles disturbed: no appearance of fault.

'In Tongoa nation, native tradition has it that Api and all the Shepherd group formed one island (Tongoa, Tongariki, Buninga, Ewose, Valla, Api, and two small islets, Laika, Tevata, and a small rock), which was depressed during a volcanic disturbance. All life was destroyed. Island reinhabited for upwards of eight generations. One man was saved inside a native drum. This is a well-known tradition. The missionary has used the drum in his preaching as a symbol of Christ. There are no indications in these islands of elevation. Tradition also of a large island existing called Buleiwo, to the west of Emae, where Cook's reef is now situated.

'Evidence of elevation very distinct in other islands, especially at Nguna Bay in Efaté, and at Eromanga and at Dillon's Bay, also Havannah Harbour. Few feet of tide, five or four feet.

'Ashore in whale-boat. No sign of life. Then dusky figures gathered one by one, stood motionless, each with his gun, no women or children. Very threatening crowd of savages, say forty or fifty, ranged on open beach. Mr. Gray went to bow, stood up, waved hat. "Missionary from Wassesi." Magical effect, guns laid down, women came out from the trees. Men advanced, pulled boat over breakers, helped us ashore.

'The Pure Savage. Men naked with three-quarters inch band of leather or grass. Women with voluminous short skirts in tiers. Some painted red or blue. Hair in threads, tied behind in a thick bunch. Fierce,

furtive look.   One noseless, another with forehead
battered in.   Earrings, Breech-loaders, Sniders, half-
cock, loaded.

'Walk through tropical vegetation, especially Pandanus.   After half hour of gentle ascent reached great
crater, many miles round, with lake in centre, on left
the active cone rising some seven or eight hundred
feet higher.   Total, eleven hundred feet.   Ash cone,
pure fine ash dotted with lumps of scoria, one side
quite free from these stones, pure ash.   Climbed up a
shallow ravine to a Solfatara, much sulphur about, bad
smell, very fatiguing, natives trod with bare feet the
rough scoria, very cutting.   Peles'-hair scattered in
threads over every inch: some eighteen inches long,
of a pale horny, gamboge colour; very fine, sometimes
in wisps or bundles.

'Then to left up crater rim, with unequal edges,
sometimes rising to a point, then dipping to rise again,
about a mile and a half round, one mass of steam and
pale blue vapour.   Explosions nearly every two or
three minutes, like powder in a quarry.   At long intervals there were very severe, tremendous explosions
without warning, a "bang" only louder than loudest
thunder, with trembling earth.   Superb display of red-
hot stones and splashes, shooting to an incredible
height, and clattering down in hundreds.   Shaped like
bombs, carcases of sheep, boomerangs, shreds and
patches, roots of trees, etc., etc. — indescribable forms.

'Greeted with one of these when within twenty
yards of crater lips — pelted with stone.   They were
most alarming — made one spring back, then watch
overhead to dodge.   Dust like rolling smoke exactly.
Brown.   After some hundreds of yards' walk, steam
rolling all about, came to a clear glimpse, lurid fire.
Watched, saw something like a fountain spouting, also

a boiling pond at the side, a smaller one spouting
some yards off; but the vision closed tantalisingly just
when you thought you had made out something.
Then further on a perfect view from an ash cornice,
lower down, at just over the focus.   Very precarious
standpoint.   But what a spectacle!   The fountain
resolved itself into a dome of fire (shape of a bell-jar
or cathedral dome) of streaming lava, almost white
heat, changing immediately into a lurid red, boiling up
and exploding every few seconds, bespattering the
walls of the funnel with red-hot lava.   These did not
trickle down like water.   They *stuck* as they fell, very
curious, as if it was putty, never budged, cooled black
almost immediately.   Occasionally they fell back into
the pot, but the *form* did not alter.

'At one side of this fountain was a seething linn of
swirling fire — all colours of red writhing about.   Surmounted with steam.   Some distance back another
little pot spouting away.   Beyond that three-fourths
of the area of the funnel was shrouded in steam and
blue vapour.   No sulphurous colouring as at Etna.
Probably whole crater is full of lava, with septal
between, a series of funnels.

'A great spectacle!   The suddenness of it.   You
come up smiling — awe-stricken in two minutes.   A
surprise.   You are totally taken aback by what you
see.   Not the extent of it: the fierceness of it, the
wickedness of it, the instantaneousness of it.   It lives.
Wonderful — this unwatched thing working away
there.   *Royalist* officers agree that crater, where lava
swam, was two or three hundred feet deep.   This would
give a hundred feet for height of dome.   Stones flew
up as high again, certainly say five hundred feet.
Surely *this* at least is not exaggerated.

'While peering over this cornice Mr. . . . [?] pho-

tographed the scene. Asked two others and myself
to sit down while he took us. Position taken. " Don't
look back," he said, " or move for anything less than
the size of a brick. I will warn you if anything bigger
comes." Photo over, we had scarcely risen when there
was a terrifying report, and a bewildering shower of
molten projectiles rained around us. One block the
size and shape of a small sheep descended with a
sullen thud on the *very spot* where a minute ago I had
sat. It was not *near* the spot, but across the very
mark in the soft ashes. I took my revenge by lighting my cigar at it.

' Very fine panorama as we mounted the top again
to descend on the other side. Circle of wooded
mountains. Sun slanting over the lake below. Descent like coming down a snow mountain on the Alps.
The natural slope of fine dust. As we passed along
(far below) the direction of the wind, had to put up
sun umbrellas to shield ourselves from the volcanic
dust which rattled like fierce hail upon us.

' Here our guides sped off to their village, frightened
to go farther, paid in tobacco sticks. Left volcano
about 4.30. Moonlight walk through tropical vegetation, very thick; footpath; the feature, tree-ferns.
Those require moonlight, and *overhead*, as it then
was. Like gigantic ostrich feathers, translucent fronds.
" Log " passed along line, " Hole," " Overhead," " Snag."
Here and there a luminous fungus. Size of a large
button, vividly phosphorescent, like a small velvet
button soft and flexible to the touch. When travelling at night, missionaries stick one on a native's back,
who goes on in front.

' Came to a native village about eight o'clock, first
a magnificent Platz — oval sward surrounded with
enormous spreading banyan-trees, where dances and

feasts are held. Then reed-cane fence, three feet high, to keep out pigs; same reeds as are used for arrows, quite straight, yellow. Women came out, dogs barked, children trooped round. No men. Where? Away drinking kava, *i.e.* "at the public-house." Women brought cocoanut milk, most refreshing [with?] water.

'Ten minutes farther met men drinking. Some stupid with kava.

'. . . [?] very rugged and almost dangerous path with abrupt descents, reached shore. Went aboard.'

'June 28.

'Not under way till 4.30. Eromanga reached about twelve. Coasted. Coral plateau, tier above tier, covered with vegetation — no special feature. Coral cliffs met at an obtuse angle. Bit of beach, creek, expanded mouth of good brook or stream. Ashore after dinner at one. Crossed in boat, pulled and pioneered by two natives, one the son of the murderer of Williams, and the leading elder! Two other brothers also about station, both members now.'

'Sunday, June 29.

'After very nasty night, heavy sea and rain, arrived at Fili Harbour.[1] A wide bay, then an inner bay, like Sydney Harbour. Islands. Lagoon running up six miles across nearest neck. All elevated coral reef — typical.

'After breakfast, went off to island, Fila, for service. Mr. and Mrs. Michelsen tried to Christianise this some years ago. Couldn't even live on the island, but made their home on small island adjoining. No success. Now the whole island is Christian, an out-station of Mr. Mackenzie. We found a fine church.

---

[1] On Efaté or Sandwich.

Service just over. Warm reception on the beach.
Held another service. Native hymn, then a native
read and prayed at length. English hymn, and then
I spoke twenty minutes, 2 Cor. iii. 18. Mr. Macdonald
translated afterwards. Very attentive. After service
went to mission-house. Natives brought puddings of
yams; ditto taro (*cooked on Saturday*); both very
good. Also cocoanuts. Charming spot. Great
drums in a cluster, like Stonehenge, in manse garden.
These had been carved and painted: sounding-board
worn thin with use, now going to decay. Small ban-
yan taken root on top of one of them. Heathenism
will soon be forgotten.

'Site of Franceville here. A commune. On paper
a fine city, with municipal buildings, and streets all
planned and named. From the sea a single one-story
house is visible on the whole expanse of forest. I
believe another exists, but did not see it. The first
house is a store, the second a doctor's house. For
the patients I looked in vain. The Commune collapsed. One after another withdrew. But there are
one or two planters about here who grow coffee, etc.
Plantation young yet, but prospect fair. Planters are
French; one is Portuguese.

'Rowed back to steamer to lunch. After, accompanied by Mr. Fraser, to visit Mr. Mackenzie's mission-
station. Were rowed (four native crew, splendid men)
ashore. Walked through French and Portuguese
plantations, cocoanut. Saw the *nut sprout*. Reached
lagoon, like a still river of emerald green, two hundred
yards broad, white coral sand, tumult of green creep-
ers rushing down into it from lofty branches of trees.
Bastard cotton-tree with its Padella lights of flowers,
as large as saucers, lemon-yellow, little brown candle
rising from centre.'

'Monday, June 30.

' Left at ten for Havannah Harbour.   Temperature
at H. H., never rises above 92°.   There are never
mosquitoes.   Mr. D. does not use curtains in his
house.   Almost none of the missionaries do.   None
complain of heat.'

'Tuesday, July 1.

' Left at seven for Tongoa.   Flying-fish common,
sometimes seen walking about on surface. Occasional
shark ; few birds.   On the whole, *life* is scarce.

' Tongoa, Tongariki, and the neighbouring islands
are probably the tops of a large submerged island.
They are all like tops of hills.   Contain almost no
flat acres.   Very healthy in consequence.   Fever little
known on Tongoa.

' Earthquakes very frequent in all the islands.   On
Tongoa counted seventeen in one day.   Can *see* them
— see the banyan-trees twisting and shaking.'

' TONGOA, July 2.

' Arrived about three.   Worst anchorage in group.
A beautiful island, black sand showing its volcanic
nature, apart from the rounded cones and waving lines
of the craters, and richest possible foliage.   Cones and
craters always manage to depart from the conventional
type, and never announce themselves as volcanic.
Great assemblage of natives on beach, red cloth pre-
dominating ; very picturesque ; fires smoking.   Every
man different.   Some had red handkerchiefs loosely
knotted round neck, a turban of same, with two waving
feathers over his neck or in his ears.   One woman
wisp of yellow pigs' bristles tied in each ear.   Wood
for Mr. Smaill's house lying on beach.   Each man
seized a block or sheet of iron — each boy and woman
— and carried down to boats for shipment.   Animated

scene, all done for nothing, being for *missi*. Bought
a club for a shilling from an old savage. Stroll up
with Mr. Michelsen, steep pull, hot, ferns, flowers,
stones, stopped us at every yard. Mission-house on
flattish ridge, facing the sea, dipping down on other
side into a large shallow depression, like [a] crater.

'Scene on beach next morning (July 3d) waiting for
steamer. One handsome damsel in red gown picking
her teeth vigorously with a carving-knife; rim of
strawberry basket on head, one or two wildflowers
stuck in it; hair, close cut, except island on top,
which the basket fringed like a coral-reef.

'One group in a canoe. Tallest savage on
island, white vest open, bedecked with new red handkerchief, trying to count 5*d*. and three halfpennies,
very dirty, to see if he could make out a shilling from
them; several helping the arithmetic; deep problem.
Fine figure; hair bushy, swelling all round in a ring;
coloured white with coral lime; on top of this a red
handkerchief crown, twined round with a tender spray
of convolvulus. Very striking figure. *N.B.* — The
ornamentation is never overdone. If a flower is stuck
anywhere, it is the size of a button, never a showy
flower, though there are myriads everywhere. Sometimes a fern stuck in the ear, or two white cock's
feathers. Many a comb or scratcher. No sameness.
Most men have shirts and a loin cloth, red, over
them. Women have either skirts of calico, spotted
and striped, or a nightgown. Several men have old
slouch hats; most uncovered. Bracelets made of a
creeper's stem, or boar's tusks; no anklets. Many
chewing sugar-cane, held in both hands, most monkey-
like. Many women carry neat native baskets woven
with pandanus.

'Tongoa small, especially luxuriant even for the

Pacific.   Remarkable variety of foliage conspicuous
on all islands, but especially here.   Every shade of
green, wooded to the top of highest hills.   Natives
very kind and quiet, in spite of the butcher's knife
most of them carry.   One half-naked fellow followed
us up path with two feet of cold steel in his hands.
They use these for clearing their way through the
bush.   House four hundred feet; grand view of sea
and island.   Mr. Michelsen's station a model of neatness.   Trim, terraced garden, glowing with balsam,
roses, and golden egg-plant.   All buildings very
roomy, built with his own hand.   Has poultry, pea-
cock, ducks, goats, even horses; teacher's premises —
perfect.   Most unassuming of men, simple Norwegian.
Sat down opposite bread-fruit tree.   Asked native to
taste.   Went to adjoining hut; brought one out from
oven, like dough of very French rolls.   My favourite
native food.   At supper tasted it again, also queen-
cakes made from arrowroot (native) and cocoanut
milk; very delicious.   Taro mashed like potatoes;
great improvement, as the hard texture is the chief
distinction; white like potatoes.   A dish of native
mushroom, a fungus which grows mostly on the ban-
yan-tree, stewed in cocoanut juice, a great delicacy.
Saw the luminous centipede, $1\frac{1}{2}$ inches long, a wrig-
gling yellow packthread, luminous in spots along the
body, at least as I saw it, rather than glowing as a
whole.   The chief effect comes when it is crushed,
when everything is phosphorescent. . . .   The great
trumpet-shell, now rare, with smaller shell patched in
for mouthpiece, probably the origin of the trumpet.
Sound very similar, and not unvaried.   Talking of
music, an old fellow on the beach had a pan-pipe, on
which he ran down the scale.   Mr. Atkinson bought
it for me.

'Mr. M. has been eleven years on Tongoa. All Christian. Three years ago the last cannibal feast. Going up hill was introduced to a man who had been at it, the "*pièce de résistance*" being his own half-brother. At Tongoa, in the moonlight, on the verandah, heard evening song going up from hut after hut on this side and on that. Less than four years ago the missionary had seen from this same verandah the smoke ascending from roasting human flesh.

'While I was eating my bread-fruit, word was passed round that I was a purchaser of clubs, etc. All that afternoon things were brought to me. Was offered several bundles of arrows, carefully tied up at the points with black feathers and matting (small lancet-like heads, very slender and fine). I wondered why. Asked were these poisoned? Yes. Again and again they were brought me.

'"Where you get him you put along arrow?" "No savez." "You get him on tree?" "No savez." "Get him on ground?" "Ei, no." "Where you get him?" "Put him along man he finish"—*i.e.* thrust it into a dead body. Blood-poisoning. Strange fact; a body with the life gone out of it is one of the acutest poisons known.

'On Tongoa causes of decrease of population: early marriages, destroying function; abortion; suckling children till three or four years old; young bloods going off to labour traffic, leaving only old men and children at home; foreign diseases only to a very small extent. On Api infanticide is common to save bother.

'The bountifulness of these islands — on Tongoa natives are very well off. Far better than the Africans. Yam, taro, banana, cocoanut, bread-fruit, are staple diet. Better off than the crofters in the Highlands. Fish, shell-fish, fungi.

'Left Tongoa about 11.30 [July 2d] for Api. Crossed open water for an hour, with two shreds of rock in mid-channel. The water is very shallow here, bearing out the submergence tradition. No coral reef on Tongoa; all volcanic. Api at first volcanic, then reef growing along shore, finally elevated reef visible on terrace inland. The out-station of Mr. Fraser.

'Coasting along Api, approaching Borumba, Mr. Fraser's station — two sea . . . three miles apart, very gentle curve, like an unstrung bow; land rising as usual, but more gradual, and much tumbled about; neither hills in the immediate foreground nor plateau, but broken hilly country, with many valleys and depressions, all timbered. Fever here and mosquitoes. Five different languages, not dialects, make work very difficult.'

'July 3.

' Planting new station for Mr. Smaill. Bad anchorage about ten. Two sweeping bays; high point between is the site. Coral-reef with foam upon it. To land, wade over coral-reef with shoes on; delicate branches, antlers, cauliflower, almost sacrilege to walk on them. Blue star-fish like guttapercha. Walk along sand. Halt under tree. Native women brought fourteen young cocoanuts. Stiff climb, and crawl to proposed site. Poor Mrs. Smaill, what a home! She was with us, with Mr. and Mrs. Annand, Mr. and Mrs. Michelsen, and their two little girls (five and six), and Mr. Atkinson from Ceylon. More cocoanuts; roasted plantains whole on fire. Return to lunch on beach. Table landed, captain sent ashore victuals; more cocoanuts for water. Awful crowd of savages surrounded us as we ate. Never saw white ladies before, probably, nor plates, knives, and forks.

2 E

Every man (fifty at least) stark naked, except for infinitesimal strip between legs, turned into a belt of bark, back and front.   Women wear a scant loin-cloth of bark.   All armed, mostly rifles, cocked.   Several had bows, with sheafs of poisoned arrows.   One face painted vermilion.   ·Little tattooing.   Necklace of white small bead-like shells on a few.   Many armlets, beads or bark, with a pipe stuck in.   Some with coral, a sprig of leaves, bracelet of tortoiseshell.   Many with diseases of the leg, bones soft.   This is common all over group.   Men kept gathering from far and near all afternoon to watch the show, especially to see stores landed.   Immense curiosity as each article was carried (wading) across the shallow strips where the ship's boats stuck.   Cane deck-chair very exciting, as it was in their line; use undreamt of till I sat down in it amid great laughter.

' No cloth here; everything native except guns. None of us knew this language.   Mr. M. had one native with him who knew the language, and whom he could speak to in another lingo, so a little communication was possible.

' Volcano of Lofevi in full foreground, a superb volcanic cone of great grace rising out of the sea, with a single momentary change of slope at one side, and a piece of rockwork to balance it at other.   Slight abrupt tilting of whole from the abrupt straight line of base when seen against horizon.

' Landing of goods eagerly watched.   Climax reached when two native women, teachers' wives, stepped ashore in full dress, *i.e.* nightgowns, their babies slung with calico.   Immense sensation.   Pots and pans much criticised, especially frying-pans.   Iron water-tank painted red much discussed.   Great drumming on it. Packet of native bows and arrows from Eromanga greeted with lively gesticulation. No one would touch it at first, then picked up gingerly with one finger and thumb by one brave, and hastily laid ashore. Probably frightened for poison, as arrows were very delicate.

' Two tents pitched, two huts also made from roofing-iron. Each native got three sticks tobacco for his day's work. Full moon at night, surf roaring, glorious scene, perfect temperature.

' Confab on beach. " Now Missi come; no more war; all change now. Sing-song to-morrow, kill pig, dance." Celebrate the end of heathenism, and arrival of missionary. Real object is to make an end of war. One thing they all know, that when he comes there is peace. On Mr. Annand's island the canoes from Malokolo had not visited for a generation. Now they come constantly. Life is safe. On other islands, where the peace-making power of the missionary is unknown, no doubt they receive him for what they think they will get out of him. In these cases at first they will be friendly, but when they see what he has really come for, after he can speak to them, the trouble begins. They had not counted the cost; now will not pay it. For it means renunciation of heathen customs and immorality.

' Holothuria examined. He was choke full of coral. No doubt he chews up vast quantities. Helps denudation of reef, and makes sand. Possibly these pieces which strew the beach like inches of white slate-pencil have passed through the bodies of worms.

' Induction soirée in house made of four window-sashes, two doors for roof, iron for sides; tea, bread, butter, cheese.

' Many murders on this beach and cannibal feasts. Notorious district. All cannibals here, and armed.

Land next year, and probably there will not be a weapon on the shore.'

'Friday, July 4.

'Got on board by breakfast, and steamed off for Sandwich Harbour, Port Sandwich, Malokolo, at nine o'clock. Malokolo has the worst reputation of any in the group. The missionaries make little headway.

'Passed Lofevi. Passed along Ambrym. Volcano on inconspicuous part of a central ridge composed of several hills; not prominent. Through telescope seemed to be steaming distinctly, but may have been cloud.

'At three entered Port Sandwich, another noble harbour, quite landlocked. One buoy here — only one I have seen on the group. "Is the *Royalist* there?" "There she is," said Captain King, with his glass. Went on board with Lieutenant, who had called for mails. Captain Davis.'

'Saturday, July 5.

'Jogged along, mostly under sail, reaching Havannah Harbour, Efaté, about eleven morning. Mr. Macdonald, with Mr. and Mrs. Macdonald (elect of Santo), and Mr. Lindt, boarded us, and took me off for day's picnic to Island of . . . ? (See Mr. Macdonald's *Oceania*.) Heathen village; man spearing fish. Folks all off on mainland, clearing plantations. Few idlers about. One, seven years in New Zealand, spoke pretty fair English. Stroll to caves. Immense, finely shaped dome, very lofty, scooped [out of] calcareous sandy hill by sea action; probably a current struck it at this point. Rude inscriptions on walls, made by natives ///////////// °₀°₀°₀₀. These lines (notches), they say, represent lives of men. The spirits notch them each time a man dies. Idea, perhaps, taken from their dreams. Three [?] are notched each

time a great man dies. Only on one side. Lindt
photo'd these with magnesium light. Drums in village, obscene; thirty or forty in cluster, longest group
I have seen.   Immense labour to cut these with stone
adzes in former generation.   Celebrations for dead
last a year or two; most elaborate customs.   Dance.
Drummer in centre, then men advance in pairs, with
spears; face each other, dance, others join.   Then all
join hands and dance round and round the drums.
Women by themselves dancing.'

'HAVANNAH, Sunday, July 6.

'Grow anything, no manuring for eight or nine
years — on coffee.   Unsifted, sun-dried article, £70
per ton, value at 2000 lbs. to the ton, say £75.   Pep-
per, allspice, cocoa, rice, sugar-cane; three crops of
Indian corn per annum = Tella flint [?] variety.   Two
kinds of soil, volcanic centre, coral lime round it,
equally suit different crops.   Good coffee land everywhere, but not near water in many cases.   Water
needed for pulping, etc.   But spices would do everywhere.   Plenty of rain; safely 100 inches per annum.
Rain every week the year round.   Never flood, never
drought, the rainfall is so distributed.

'Labourers from adjoining islands; thirty of these.
Feed themselves.   £4, 4s. per year is paid in wages
for labour per man; and £10 for the recruiter who
finds the men in his cutter.   The £4, 4s. is not paid
to the natives until the three years' engagement is up.

'First year make a nursery of coffee plants, then
clean land.   Next year you are a year on your way,
having the nursery.   In three years you have your
first crop.   There is no disease, no manure is needed.
Almost the sole risk is a hurricane, which may blow
off the flowers, or at the drying season a showery day

may interfere.   But artificial drying here, as elsewhere, will be introduced in time.   The natives eat yams and bananas with cocoanuts and taro.   When they run out, a boat-load can be bought for a few sticks of to-bacco, so that a few extra shillings, scarcely pounds, are enough to keep all in abundance.

'Owing to the slopes there is choice of land for dif-ferent kinds of planting; one kind grown on shore, another higher up.   Bananas alone would pay splen-didly.   Three and a half days nearer to Sydney than Fiji.   All the year steamers with bananas run from Fiji to Sydney.   The three and a half days sooner would deliver the fruit in prime condition and avoid the heavy depreciation at present existing.

'Fever not serious anywhere, and most islands quite free from it.   Havannah Harbour has a bad reputa-tion, but all much exaggerated.   Ships of war met in group, *Dart* and *Royalist* had seven per cent. on sick list, all slight cases.

'French population, adult males, on group may number sixty in all.   English, perhaps ten, excluding missionaries.   Land may be bought for almost noth-ing.   A couple of old muskets and a bag of tobacco will buy an estate.   A good deal of land has been "chapped" already, especially by French, who have bits on most islands, never touched of course.   No one ever comes near them.   Boundaries are very dubious.   Sometimes a stone mark is used.   Natives are very fair about these purchases, and respect them loyally, provided the right owner or owners have been treated with in the first instance.   Natives have often professed to sell land as theirs; when the real owner turns up months or years later, a row is inevitable. Some of the missionaries have paid for their land to one "owner" after another.   Unavoidable, for there is no tribunal. *The* desideratum is an authentic means of conveyance and registration of titles.

'English skies in New Hebrides, not blistering, burnished skies. White clouds as at home, and even dull days. Constant light winds (trades) blow.

'Quite true about the gayfish, red, striped, barred, box-shaped, etc. One exquisite thing, a dart of brilliant blue or purple. A pure-blue starfish. But the scenic effect is not quite what one had expected, any more than parrots make a great feature on an Australian landscape. They are really inconspicuous in the woods, and fly so fast you only see a general dark form.

'Few seaweeds. I question if our seaweedy pools are not more lovely. White coral sand does give brilliancy to the water, but there is much coral island without any.

'Corals individually are exquisite, but do not expect to see them like what they are at Kensington. Shells, ditto. The nacreous shells are all covered with membrane. The speckled ones are all right, but the majority are swathed. The corals are swathed in gelatine, coloured slime. Like a clump of cauliflowers half withered. Like large fungi or mushrooms. Faint purple or pinkish. Red coralinus grows in deep water. I am speaking of what you can see in a boat. Irregular bottom is a feature. Like sailing over a submerged flower and shrub garden. When the tide is out it is not beautiful. The colour is dirty-brown or black, as if smoked with a torch. Rough and uneven, like a field frost-bound — very hard to walk on with bare feet. "Still lagoons" you see generally roughened with wind. "Calm retreats" are not common.

'White ants [1] on all the islands; furniture destroyed.

---

[1] This and the following paragraphs taken from stray notes.

Some make tunnels in the trees; small hills not so large as in New South Wales.

'In Tongoa there is a native turkey; black bird, long legs and neck; red wattles, scarcely size of common hen, lays eggs, one above another, sometimes to the number of ten. The birds leave them to hatch there, but from time to time change the order, digging up the deeper ones, which have most heat, and placing them on the top. These birds are also found in Efaté. In Tongoa they lay in the neighbourhood of the Fumarole. This is some acres in extent, faintly steaming. There are two such places in Tongoa.

'*Ascendency of the English Language.*— Formerly chief's sons and the leading bloods were sent for a year to another island to learn the language for trade purposes. This is now stopped, owing to the rapid rise of pigeon-English. All trade is done in that language; French labour boats have to use it. Remember the convict at Noumea speaking to the native prisoners in English: "Do not like wee-wee man." [1]

'*Process of Evangelising an Island.*— Missionary settles in a village often by request of natives. Either (1) they want a "missi," as he will see justice done between them and passing trader — a court of appeal: he is known as always on the side of the natives; (2) the islanders may have shot so many boats' crews that they want him as a guarantee of good behaviour; (3) labour men returned may have been influenced in Queensland and want a teacher; or (4) they know that Christianity will abolish sorcery, which is the cause of all death and war. They *do* want to stop war, and therefore ask missionary. Christianised natives never carry firearms, but go unarmed.

'Sometimes the missionary comes on a bare con-

---

[1] A sketch of the political situation is not inserted here, as it is now out of date.

sent, extracted from the people, after much discussion on their part.   This permission will be given, and followed by repeated hints, and even requests, to leave. But he sticks to it.

'*Programme.*—He settles, builds on bought site. Never wanders one hundred yards from door, learns language.   For a year he may be almost a prisoner. Then he extends his walks gradually till he compasses all.   Sometimes the nearest village is hostile, the next friendly.   He may have to go round by open sea, or be fired at.   At Eromanga, Mr. . . . [?] was always attacked at "the point," unless he kept out to sea till he reached the further villages.

'*The Missionaries have made the Islands Habitable.* —On several (Tongoa, Mai, etc.) for long not even a missionary could land.   Christianising *comes before* civilising, say the missionaries.   Thus, a native from a heathen village goes to Queensland, comes back with box of clothes.   Will sell them for two sticks of tobacco, and return to savagedom.   They have *never been civilised*.   Their heathen customs make it impossible.   Only Christianity can make them give up their heathenism.   Must be made gentle men.'

Drummond's regular diary closes with Sunday 6th at Havannah Harbour.   He left it for Eromanga, and on Monday left Eromanga for Noumea, the French capital of New Caledonia, where he arrived on Wednesday.   He has one note upon the place: 'Amphitheatre of really fine hills; tawdry boulevard of one- and two-story houses, each different; a central square or place; flamboyant trees, most of their growth still to come; a semaphore station.   Government House (£1500 a year).   Lives = convicts.'

'SYDNEY, July 21.

' Just stepped off steamer. Have had a wonderful
time among New Hebrides. I do not think I
ever had such an interesting tour in my life. I
was on Mr. Paton's Tanna, and saw all his painted
cannibals. But for the missionary with me, I
should now be—inside them. No grander missionary work was ever done than by these N. H.
missionaries. Every man is a king.'

Having seen one end of the labour traffic in the
New Hebrides, Drummond went on a tour in Queensland to find out about the other. His companion was
Professor Rentoul, of Melbourne, and they not only
investigated the facts about the importation of the
Kanakas to the sugar plantations, but inquired as
well into the condition of the Queensland aborigines.
What opinions Drummond formed were stated by
him to a representative of the *Pall Mall Gazette*, and
published in that paper on the 18th May, 1892. He
corrected the proof himself.

' " Below the surface of this question there lies a
story with a world of interest. It has its deep pathos,
and it has also its bright side. But the question of
continuing the labour traffic with Polynesia is an
anthropological rather than an economic question.
Here you have hundreds of islands inhabited mainly
by cannibals. They are utterly uncivilised. Except
for a handful of heroic missionaries, a white man
hardly ever steps ashore among them. There they
are, doing no work, sitting all day long under their
palm-trees, and living the life of savages and cannibals, except in the few cases where the patient labours
of the missionaries have had some civilising and soft-
ening influence. They know nothing of the outside

world.   No vessel, possibly, has ever touched their
shores, and the only white man's face they have ever
seen is that of their missionary.   Then, one day, a
vessel arrives, and a boat is lowered filled with armed
men and steers for the island.   These armed men are
the traders who have come to engage labour.   It also
lands a Government agent, whose duty it is to see that
matters are arranged humanely and on fair terms.
This boat is followed by another carrying a further
bodyguard, armed to the teeth, and covering the first
boat with their rifles at a short distance.   The Kanaka
is easily persuaded to engage to accompany the trader
for a term of years, when a few sticks of tobacco, a
gun, or some other toy is put into his hands as a present.   When, a few days later on, the vessel leaves the
island, it carries the flower of the population away
with it.   There are, happily, a good many islands on
which the unwearied work of the missionaries has
borne fruit, where the natives are docile and indus-
trious; but there are many others on which this is not
the case.   For an unarmed man to land would be
certain death."

   ' " Have they a common language ? " — " No ; the
dialects are innumerable on these island groups, and
it is, indeed, not infrequently the case that several
almost distinct languages are spoken on the same
island.   Each dialect differs widely from the rest, and
each is only understood by a handful of natives.   On
the island of Eromanga, which I visited the year before last, the first missionary who came was murdered
by the natives ten minutes after he went ashore.   The
second also was murdered, and several after him.   But
the work was not, therefore, given up, for the missionaries will not be kept back, and now the missionary
whom I found there has been at his post for thirteen

years. There is a church on the island, and the Kanakas live peacefully together. Can you wonder at the
missionaries protesting when some day they wake up
to find that the pick of their young men have left their
island and gone to the sugar plantations in Queensland?"

'"Then, Professor Drummond, do I understand that
you sympathise with the outcry against the importation of the Kanakas into Queensland?"—"Not exactly; I am with the *Pall Mall's* reasoning in Monday's
leading article. At the same time, it is a question on
which there is so much to be said on both sides that
I should not like to speak too definitely. What I have
told you is a matter of information, not of opinion. On
the whole, this is not a problem peculiar to the Pacific.
Wherever the white man comes into contact with the
black, wherever the product of civilisation has to deal
with the child of nature, the same class of difficulties
arises. To keep these happy children to their own
coral islands and cut them off from the contaminations
of civilisation may be a pardonable ideal to the missionary. But it is a question whether such a state of
things is possible, or possible long. Sooner or later
the breath of the outer world must reach them. In
too many cases it has reached them already. They
must brace themselves for the contact. The drafting
of successive bands of natives to a civilised country for
a term of years and then shipping them back again to
their own islands — as the labour-employer is bound
to do — might become an important factor in the progress of these races. Everything would depend on the
treatment they received and the moral atmosphere
which surrounded them. The Queensland Government has certainly left no stone unturned to secure
that, so far as legal enactments can protect an inferior

race, the Kanakas are safe on Australian soil from any possible tyranny, violence, or even physical discomfort. If it could also secure that the planter would do his duty, and feel an adequate moral responsibility with regard to his employees, there would be no righteous opposition to the labour traffic. The question, therefore, reduces itself to the universal moral problem. Given the ideal employer, the man who will protect his people from moral contamination, who will seek their good and interest as well as his own, and return them to their country wiser and better men, and with some rational equivalent for the labour they have given — then this traffic can do nothing but good. Nor is it idle to hope that one day this ideal may be partially realised. . . .

'" If it is inevitable that this human stream from the Pacific should continue to discharge itself upon Australian soil, one very practical thing remains for those who have raised their voices against it — to turn every energy to secure henceforth the righteous fulfilment of the conditions under which the Kanaka is engaged, and especially to ameliorate his lot, and give to it that educational and moral value which humanity and Christianity demand. More than ever it must be made certain that the Government agent on board the labour schooner will resist the temptation to play into the hands of the employers, and make it certain that in each individual case the terms of the contract are fully understood by the natives whose services are enlisted. The plantations themselves must be protected from the illicit drink-seller; and educational and missionary work among the colonies of workers ought to be everywhere introduced. If this were done, and done effectually, the return of the Kanaka to his island home would mean something vital in social and

moral influence for his race. At present, though the
Kanakas are thoroughly well treated by their masters,
— on the mere ground of economy this is necessary,
Kanaka labour being far too costly to be trifled with, —
it is questionable whether they gain anything by their
absence either morally or materially.   Their hard-
earned wages they cannot take back with them in
coin, since money is almost unknown in Polynesia.
What they do take back is usually a lot of rubbish,
purchased in Brisbane at fancy prices, to be distributed
among their brother savages as presents.   This, it must
be confessed, is a poor show for three or four years'
work among the cane-brakes.

' " On thinking over this whole question it is impossible not to compare the action of the Queensland
Government, where the Kanakas are concerned, with
their treatment of their own natives.   The comparison
is all in favour of the Kanakas.   The Queensland
natives are treated as veritable outcasts.   They are
not employed; they are driven away from the towns
and settlements, and their lives in certain districts are
freely taken on the smallest provocation, and no questions asked." '

From Australia Drummond voyaged slowly by Java,
to Singapore.   He had two days among the Anamese
at Saigon, and came round to Hong Kong and Shanghai, where he saw the missions.

At Shanghai he addressed a native meeting as follows : —

' I know just one word of Chinese, and that is " Foh "
(happiness); the missionaries come to China to give
the people happiness, and there is nothing in the world
can give the people happiness except the teaching of
Jesus Christ.   I have been all over the world, and have

just come from Australia. Away among the South
Sea Islands I saw men who feed on human flesh; a
few miles off the islanders ten years ago were cannibals
too; why not now? Because the missionaries of Jesus
Christ have been among them; and these people gave
me their spears and bows, which I have now in the
ship — "because," they said, "we do not need them
any more."

'When Jesus came into this world to give happiness,
He said His religion was to be three things to men, —
salt and *light* and *leaven*.

'What is the use of salt? It is the salt in the sea
that keeps it fresh. It is the salt on the fish that keeps
it from going rotten. The people of Christ are the
salt of the earth. Every country will become rotten
if there are no Christians in it. Nothing can prevent
men turning rotten and bad but the Gospel.

'Christ is light. The world is dark. It needs a
heavenly teacher to tell men what is truth. If one
man tells me this or that is true, another tells me it is
not true; whom am I to believe? If I go to an idol,
it cannot tell me anything, true or false.

'Christ is the Light of men, and we know His Word
to be truth beyond all doubt or dispute. There may
be only two or three men in this great congregation who
want to know what is truth. They have only to read
the New Testament, and they will see that Jesus Christ
is the Light of the world.

'I suppose you know what leaven is; it is that which
raises up. It is the religion of Christ that uplifts men.
It makes them higher and nobler and nearer God; and
if we come to Jesus Christ and learn of Him, He will
lift up first one, then another of you who hear me now,
then this city of Shanghai, and then this great country;
but if we reject Him we must sink lower and lower.

' I understand too little of what passes in your minds, stranger and foreigner as I am, to say more to you this evening. But I leave with you these simple thoughts — Jesus Christ is Light, Leaven, and Salt — and if we learn from Him, learn what He is, and what He says, we shall be made light and salt and leaven to those among whom we dwell.'

From China he went on to Japan, and at Tokio was able to answer the invitation sent him a year before by a large number of students. He addressed about five hundred of them. From Japan he came home through Canada.

In November he opened the College Session with an address upon Missions, which he repeated on several occasions during the next month or two. As it was not only fresh and full of information, but raised some controversy, it seems desirable to give at least a summary of it : —

He begins by saying that 'there are two ways in which men who offer their lives to their fellow-men may regard the world. They mean the same thing in the end, but you will not misunderstand me if I express the apparent distinction in the boldest terms. The first view is that the world is lost, and must be saved ; the second, that the world is sunken, and must be raised. . . . The first preaches mainly justification ; the second mainly regeneration. The first is the standpoint of the popular evangelism ; the second is the view of evolution. The danger of the first is to save the souls of men, and there leave them ; the danger of the second is to ignore the soul altogether. As I shall now speak from the last standpoint, I point out its danger at once, and meet it by adding to its watchword Evolution the qualifying term Christian. This alone takes account of the whole nature of man, of sin and guilt, of the future and of the past, and recognises the Christian facts and forces as alone adequate to deal with them.'

He then emphasises the complexity of the missionary

problem, and the amazing variety of the work required in different fields. 'Nothing ought to be kept more persistently before the minds of those who are open to sense as missionaries. . . . It is just as absurd for a man to choose in general terms "the foreign field" and go abroad to rescue "heathen," as for a planter to go anywhere abroad in the hope of sowing general seed and producing general coffee. . . . It is irrational for the missionary to carry the same *form* of message to every land, or to think that the thought which told to-day will tell to-morrow; he must rotate his crops as God through the centuries rotates the social soil on which they are to grow. . . . Above all, when he reaches his field, his duty is to find out what God has sown there already; for there is no field in this world where the Great Husbandman has not sown something. Instead of uprooting his Maker's work, and clearing the field of all the plants that found no place in his small European herbarium, he will rather water the growths already there, and continue the work at the point where the Spirit of God is already moving.'[1]

He next illustrates, from the fields he had visited, 'the necessity for specialisation in missions.' 'In Australia the missionary problem is to deal with a civilised people undergoing abnormally rapid development. . . . It is what a biologist would call an organic mass of the highest possible mobility, of almost perilous sensitiveness to prevailing impressions, with feeble safeguards to conserve its solid gains, and few boundary lines either to shape or limit other growths. . . . The chief problem of Christianity is to keep pace with the continued growth; the immediate peril is that it may be wholly ignored in the pressure of competing growths.

'The South Sea Islands lie at the opposite end of the scale. Growth has not even begun. . . . The first step in evolution, aggregation, has not taken place. These people are still at zero; they are the amœbæ of the human world. There is no complication here from immigration, but the opposite difficulty — depletion due to emigration and other causes.'

---

[1] 'A hasty critic, when these sentences were spoken, construed them into a plea for building Christianity upon heathenism. The words are: "What God has sown there," and "Where the Spirit of God is already moving." '—H. D., in a later edition of this address.

China stands midway between the Australian colonies and the South Sea Islands, 'an instance of arrested development. On the fair way to become a vertebrate, it has stopped short at the crustacean. The capacity for change is almost non-existent, and there is a powerful religion already in possession.'

Japan, in turn, is an almost perfect contrast to China. 'It has broken its "cake of custom." It is the insect emerging from the chrysalis. From a Christian standpoint the case is unique in history. Its own religion was abandoned a few years ago, and the country is at present looking for another.'

If the variety illustrated in this rough classification were present, in the degree it ought to be, to the imagination of the Christian churches, 'the missionary staff would be differentiated with more exactness than at present. Each man would make his choice, and, equipping himself along certain lines, would become a specialist. In the second place, it would become possible for some men to be missionaries, and these among the best men entering the universities, who see no room for them at present in the foreign field.' . . . They 'would find, in a service which they had looked upon as perhaps somewhat limited and narrow, something which, when looked upon in all its length and breadth, was large enough and rich enough in practical possibilities to make them offer to it the whole-hearted work of their lives. To-day, certainly, some of the best men do go to the foreign field, but the reason why more do not go is uncertainty as to whether they are exactly the type of men wanted, *i.e.* in plain language, uncertainty as to whether the cut of their theology quite qualifies them to be the successors of Carey or Williams. . . . Now, this feeling is very real, but I am convinced it is very ignorant — ignorant of the changed standpoint from which scores of our missionaries are even now doing their work, ignorant of the world's real needs, ignorant of the hospitality which they would receive from many at least of the officials of most of the Mission Boards.' Not that he counts these altogether guiltless in this matter. 'I do not think the Mission Committees of the world have ever worded their advertisement for men in language modern enough to

include the class of whom I speak. I am not arguing for
free-lances, or budding sceptics, or rationalists being turned
loose on our mission-fields, but for young men — and our
colleges were never richer in them than at this moment —
who combine with all modern culture the consecrated spirit
and Christlike life. . . . It ought at least to be understood
that what qualifies to-day for the leading churches at home
ought not to disqualify for the work of Christ abroad, but that
there is for Christian men of the highest originality and power
a career in the foreign field at least as great and rational as
that at home. . . . I am sure the committees at least of some
of the churches not only want these men but scarcely want
anything else.'

He then describes the different classes needed — ' first, the
old missionary pioneer of the Sunday-school picture-books,
who stands with his Bible under the stereotyped palm-tree,
exhorting the crowd of impossible blacks. . . .   Their work
must still and always continue.   Next, we have these same
men in settled charges . . . carrying on the whole evangelical work of the Christian Church.   But next, among these,
and gathered from these, and in addition to these, we require
a further class, not wholly absorbed with specific charges, or
ecclesiastical progress, or the inculcation of Western Creeds,
but whose outlook goes forth to the nation as a whole — men
who, in many ways not directly on the programme of the
Missionary Society, will help on its education, its morality,
and its healthy progress in all that makes for righteousness.
This man, besides being the missionary, is the Christian
politician, the apostle of a new social order, the moulder and
consolidator of the state.   He places the accent, — if such an
extreme expression of a distinction may be allowed, — not on
the progress of a church, but on the coming of the kingdom
of God.   He is not the herald, but the prophet, of the Cross.'

Of course, he says, every missionary acquires some general
idea of this, but ' what is needed is more than a general idea.
The Christianising of a nation like China or Japan is an
intricate, ethical, philosophical, and social, as well as Christian,
problem ; the serious taking of every new country, indeed, is
not to be done by casual sharp-shooters bringing down their

man here and there, but by a carefully thought-out attack upon central points, or by patient siege planned with all a military tactician's knowledge. . . .'

He then describes the fields he has seen, and begins with the New Hebrides and their slowly dying populations. The mission there, he says, has no place in the evolutionary branch of missions, and cannot attract the class of minds he has been describing. 'It belongs to the order of the Good Samaritan. It is a mission of pure benevolence. Its parallel is the mission of Father Damien on the Leper Island.' He follows with a eulogy of the missionaries, and of the martyrs who preceded them. 'I have no words to express my admiration for these men . . . and their even more heroic wives; they are perfect missionaries; their toil has paid a hundred times, and I count it one of the privileges of my life to have been one of the few eyewitnesses of their work.' But, he adds, the missionaries themselves do not ask for more workers here.

On China he offers a 'surface impression of little worth.' 'Small congregations are springing up everywhere. The industry and devotion of the workers is beyond all praise. . . . But they possess no common programme or consistent method; there is waste and confusion — the sin not of the missionaries, but of Christendom. A reconsideration of methods is needed in face of the fact that the educated classes are not being reached. The best missionaries themselves are crying for this.' But he warns his hearers against the criticism of missions which one gets from ninety per cent. of commercial men who after a time in China return to this country. 'As a rule, these critics have never had ten minutes' serious talk with a missionary in their lives. If they had, they would find two things — first, that there were some missionaries a thousand times worse in folly and incompetence than they had ever imagined; and, second, that there were others, and these by far the majority, than whom no wiser, saner, more practical could be found in any of the business houses in the world. It is men of this latter class who are calling for more scientific work and more rational methods in the mission-field.'

'. . . It is the deliberate opinion of many men who know China intimately, who are missionaries themselves, that half of the preaching, and especially the itinerating preaching, carried on throughout the empire, is absolutely useless. I cannot verify this criticism ; I merely record it. But at a time when the loud cry for hundreds of more laymen to pour into China is sounding over this land, the warning ought at least to be heard. I go further. This call is frequently uttered in such terms as to take almost an unfair advantage of a certain class of Christians — uttered with a harrowing importunity and sensationalism of appeal, which, when it falls upon a tender conscience or an excited mind, makes it seem blasphemy to decline. The kind of missionary secured by this process, to say the least, is neither the wisest nor the best ; and China not only needs to be protected from these men, but they need to be protected from themselves and from those who, in genuine but unbalanced zeal, appeal to them — protected by sober statements from sober men, who love the work of God and souls of men not less, but who understand both better.'

He passes to Japan, 'where the situation is still more delicate,' 'the most interesting country in the world at this moment,' 'the past has never witnessed the birth of a civilised nation so remarkable, so orderly, so sudden.' 'The Japanese have set themselves up with all the material and machinery of an advanced and rising civilised state — all the materials except one.' 'They are in the unique position of prospecting for a religion.'

He describes the competition for Japan by the various sections of Christendom, the chance for all, the 'mood and malleability of the nation.' 'If there be here one prophet, or half a prophet, or even the making of half a prophet, let me assure him there is no field in the world to-day where, so far as man can judge, his best years could be lived to so great a purpose.' 'You are aware the work of the missionaries has been so successful that there are already thousands upon thousands of Christian converts, very many as perfectly read in European literature and as cultured as the picked men in our universities ! A leader of thought among these said to me : " We have got our Christianity almost exclusively from the missionaries, especially the American missionaries, and

we can never thank them enough.   But after a little we began
to look at it for ourselves, and we made a discovery.   We
found that Christianity was a greater and a richer thing than
the missionaries told us. . . .   We want Christianity, not perhaps necessarily a Western Christianity. . . ."   In justice to
the missionaries, it ought to be said that all were agreed that
the Japanese Church could not yet be left to stand alone. . . .
In Tokio I had the privilege of addressing some thirty or forty
Japanese Christian pastors.   At the close I asked them if
they had any message they would like me to take home to the
churches here or in America.   They appointed a spokesman,
who stood up and told me in their name that there were two
things they would like me to say.   The one was, " Tell them
to send us one six thousand dollar missionary rather than ten
two thousand dollar missionaries."   But the second request
went deeper.   I again give the exact words : " Tell them," he
said, "that we want them to send us no more doctrines.
Japan wants Christ. . . ."   To judge from the Japanese converts I met, I would question whether any mission work in the
world had ever produced fruit of so fine a quality.   How deep
it is, how permanent, remains for the test of time to declare ;
but the immediate outlook, though disheartening possibly to
individual missionaries, seems to me one of the richest
promise.'

On the whole mission-field which he had visited, Drummond said : —

> ' If one saw a single navvy trying to remove a
> mountain, the desolation of the situation would
> be sufficiently appalling.   Most of us have seen
> a man or two, or a hundred or two — ministers,
> missionaries, Christian laymen — at work upon
> the higher evolution of the world ; but it is when
> one sees them by the thousand in every land, and
> in every tongue, and the mountain honeycombed,
> and slowly crumbling on each of its frowning
> sides, that the majesty of the missionary work
> fills and inspires the mind.'

CHAPTER XVI

1891–1894

THE LAST LAP — CONTROVERSIES AND ATTACKS — THE DEATH
OF ROBERT BARBOUR — LIFE AND WORK IN GLASGOW — VISIT
TO AMERICA — THE LOWELL INSTITUTE LECTURES — NORTH-
FIELD — CANADA — CHICAGO — LAST ADDRESSES TO EDIN-
BURGH STUDENTS

WE have now reached the last lap of Henry Drummond's race: the point at which he had but three
years and a half of work left to him. These years,
with their many interests in Glasgow, their controversies, the visit to America in 1893, and the preparation of the *Ascent of Man*, will occupy this chapter.

He was hardly back from the South Seas when he
was attacked from many quarters for what his critics,
friendly and unfriendly, called the defects of his teaching. The trouble started from the address, with which
he opened the winter session, on the 'Christian Evolution of the World.'[1] We have seen with what admiration the missionaries inspired him. He once said
that what he saw in the New Hebrides of the life of
the missionaries helped him to understand the Incarnation. His address, too, had other tributes of the
same kind. Yet his critics fastened upon those portions of it in which he stated the still unsolved
problems of the mission-field, and urged upon the
churches a wider policy in meeting them, and a more
elastic choice of men. The perusal of the letters with
which he was bombarded reveals on the part of his

[1] This address is summarised above in the end of last chapter.

439

assailants a genuine alarm and an honest zeal to put down error. But the astonishing thing is that Christian men should have so little sense as to base such charges upon a necessarily brief report in a newspaper. Also, it is still more grievous that when this has been pointed out to them, they should not express regret at having misrepresented a fellow-Christian, nor seem to appreciate the pain it gives him to have his opinions travestied to the public. On that line the morality of the religious among us has not a little to make up. Drummond's letters of this date are full of pain, and, for the first time in his life, of warm indignation on his own behalf. He calls his traducers 'assassins of character.' But there is no use going into the details of what was an utterly unnecessary controversy.

'Nov. 20, 1890.

' I am catching it for my " attack on missionaries " — all the result of a one-sided newspaper report.

' The redeeming feature is that when I redelivered the address last Sunday night in Edinburgh, it bagged several really first-rate men for the mission-field.'

The attacks, however, scattered from the Address on Missions to the little books which for nine years Drummond had published before Christmas, and they were specially virulent upon the last of them, *Pax Vobiscum*. All that need now be told of the temper in which he met these criticisms, or of the substance of his replies to them, is contained in the following letters to his uncle, Mr. David Drummond of Dublin, and to Mr. Sankey.

On January 4, 1891, his uncle wrote him a very kind letter, expressing his disappointment at finding that in 'all your writings and addresses you all but ignore the Atonement,' and deploring this ' in view of the great influence you exert over young men.' To this Drummond replied : —

'3, Park Circus, Glasgow, Jan. 6, 1891.

' My dear Uncle, — Your letter has just this moment been handed to me, and I sit down to answer it at once. I am very glad you have written me, and thank you most sincerely. It is surely the only fair as well as the only Christian thing to do in such circumstances, and not to harbour dark suspicion and mistrust, as some of my enemies do. I think you will find the straight answer to your question in the little book [1] which I enclose, if you will kindly look at the last two or three pages. This will not only show you my belief in the doctrine you refer to, but partly explain my attitude towards it.

' The two little booklets lately issued were not evangelistic addresses, but simple talks to Christian people, and beyond these I have no other " published writings " from which people can judge my views.

' It passes my comprehension how people should venture to " judge " at all — much less on the ground of two half-hour addresses — and say the fierce things that are said of me without any basis. Therefore it is that I am grateful to you for asking the question before sharing in my condemnation.

' A man's only right to publish an address is that he thinks the thing said there *is not being said* otherwise. Now, ninety per cent. of the evangelical literature of the day is *expressly devoted* to enforcing what I am accused of not enforcing, *i.e.* the

[1] *An Address to Workers* at Dollis Hill.

fundamentals of Christianity.   But if a doctor
treats a patient for nerve-disease, or writes a
book upon it, no one would accuse him of not
believing in heart disease?   He writes his book
because nerve-diseases are not being treated by
others, while half the profession is busy over
heart-disease.

'Of course, you may think I make an error of judgment in my reading of the popular pulse, and in
   not writing books on the fundamentals.

'But there seem to me very many more books on
   those aspects of Christ's work than on the others,
   and I must give the message that, *in addition*,
   seems to me to be needed.   While saying this, I
   repeat, I may be making an error of judgment.
   But one can only judge by the facts around him
   and act for the best, as it seems to him, with such
   dim light as he has.

'I am afraid I shall have to trouble you to return
   the little booklet accompanying this, — say within
   a month, — as I have only a copy or two left, and
   I believe it is out of print.   It is not expressed so
   fully or clearly as I would like, for it was spoken
   in a field, without more than ten minutes' notice,
   and I had no idea a reporter was present. — I remain, your affectionate nephew,
                         'HENRY DRUMMOND.'

His uncle's reply is so kind and true, that it is well
to give it: —

                                        'Jan. 16, 1891.

'MY DEAR HENRY, — I had yours of the 6th inst.,
with enclosure, and your frank, open explanation has
greatly delighted me, and removed from my mind an
anxiety I confess pressed heavily on me.   You have

quite satisfied aunt and me, and we both express how
pleased we are at the kind way you took my letter;
but, indeed, I knew you so well, I need not have had
any anxiety on that score. Now that you show in
your *Address at Dollis Hill* how clear your views are
on the Atonement, notwithstanding all that is written
and said to the contrary, I have every expectation that
in some of your future writings you will take your own
way of making it clear; and you have such a hold of
the public through the immense sale of your publica-
tions, it is quite incalculable the power you can wield,
and, therefore, I repeat, I hope you will yet give out,
by no uncertain sound, your belief on a matter of such
vast importance. I admit that as you have the blood
of the clan in your veins, like myself, you may be "a
wee thrawn," and won't be drilled as I see certain
writers are trying to do; hence my reason for saying
that I have no doubt but that by and by you will take
your own way of speaking out on the subject, only
asking the "Sure Guide" to direct you. . . . — Ever
your old uncle, D. DRUMMOND.'

The other letter on this subject is of later date, 1892.
It was written in reply to Mr. Sankey, who was then
in Scotland, upon his and Mr. Moody's last mission
to the country. Mr. Sankey had come across the extract quoted on page 8 of this volume, and wrote
Drummond asking if the words were really his.
Drummond's reply came next day. 'On his last visit
to America in 1893,' says Mr. Sankey, 'I showed him
this letter and the "extract," and asked him if he had
any objection to their publication if occasion should
arise. After reading them over, he replied: "Certainly not; you have my hearty permission to use
them in any way you think best."'

'3, PARK CIRCUS, GLASGOW, April 3, 1892.

'MY DEAR MR. SANKEY, — Would that all, calling themselves by the sacred name of Christian, had your charity; knew the meaning, as you and Mr. Moody do, of "judge not," and afforded a man at least a frank trial before convicting him.

'These *are* my words, and there has never been an hour when the thoughts which they represent were not among my deepest convictions. Nor, so far as I know, have I ever given any one ground to believe otherwise, nor is there any one of my writings where these same ideas will not be found either expressed or understood.

'If you ask me why I do not write whole books on these themes, I reply that I believe one's only excuse for writing a book is that he has something to say *that is not being said.*

'These things are being said. Hundreds of books and millions of tracts are saying them afresh every month and year. I therefore feel no call to enter literature on that ground. My message lies among the forgotten truths, the false emphasis, and the wrong accent. To every man his work.

'Let me thank you most heartily for your kindness in writing. The way to spoil souls, to make them hard and bitter and revengeful, is to treat them as many treat me. If I have escaped this terrible fate, it is because there are others like yourself who "think no evil."

'But tell your friends that they know not what they do, or what solemn interest they imperil when they judge. — Yours very sincerely,

'HENRY DRUMMOND.'

The session of 1890–91 was spent in his college work, his weekly visits, after the New Year, to the Edinburgh students, and a multitude of other duties. In April came a call to the sick-bed of his friend Robert Barbour, who had been carried, on a vain quest for health, to the Riviera. In the beginning of May, Barbour was taken to Aix-les-Bains, from which Drummond writes : —

'HOTEL SPLENDIDE, AIX-LES-BAINS, May 6, 1891.

'I have had a very anxious and doleful time and much heavy nursing, as Barbour all last week would allow no one near but his wife and myself. No one can predict when the curtain may fall, but I feel he has already left us. This day last year I was standing by Ewing as the sand ran low in the glass.'

This vigil lasted for three weeks, Barbour not caring to have Drummond out of sight, and loving to hold him by the hand. He read, cheered, and tended the dying man, and wrote to the friends daily letters full of those details which we all love to hear about our dear ones when they hover between life and death and we are far away. Barbour died on May 27.

To Lord Aberdeen

'June 18, 1891.

'Your letter much more than pleased — it touched me. It is much, in this busy life, through whatever silences and separations, always to be able to count on the true beat of a heart. Friendship can yield but little more, and nothing more that is greater.

'So, many real thanks.

'It was hard to watch Barbour die. The impression
of his life is cropping up from many sides just now,
and it is very wonderful. His peculiar characteristic was saintliness, an element in life which one
is apt to think either superfluous or morbid, but
which is after all a vital ingredient. When one
thinks of it, it is the unworldly people who have
really helped us most.'

Drummond spent July and August in Sutherlandshire, fishing at Loch Stack, and driving about the
country. All September he worked steadily at home,
was at Haddo House, fishing and holding services for
part of October, and in the end of the month, after
the publication of his new booklet, *The Programme
of Christianity*, he began the winter session.

Perhaps this is the most convenient point at which
to attempt to express Drummond's feelings towards
the city of his winter residence, and to describe the
place he took in her life. From 1885 he lived in
No. 3, Park Circus, above the West End Park, on the
summit of one of the range of low hills that run
parallel to the Clyde, and is covered by the north side
of Glasgow. It is a large house, and he could not use
the whole of it, but he worked best when there was
space about him, and the house afforded a noble study,
with a long view northwards across some suburbs to
the Campsie hills. The house was furnished, as he
himself put it, 'with dead hobbies,' one of which, however, was not dead, for till the end he added to his
store of beautiful cabinets, and of pictures of which
accuracy obliges one to say that they were of more or
less ambiguous value. The hall had a few spoils of
travel — javelins, arrows, and curious candlesticks.
The large dining-room contained a carved sideboard,

which friends averred, but which he would never allow,
had been part of an altar; on the walls were pictures
of the glories of the Yellowstone Valley, and some
European landscapes, one by Thomson of Dudding-
ston. The study contained a large library, scientific,
theological, and literary, a table of new books, and the
aforesaid cabinets, an etching of Millet's *Angelus*, and
several portraits of friends. At the writing-table
against one of the windows Drummond wrote only
letters. All his other work was done in a chair with
his back to the light, and a large blotter on his knee.

His working day began after a half-past eight o'clock
breakfast. He read or wrote till his lecture at twelve,
lunched at one, and generally went out to walk or to
business till half-past four or five. After tea he settled
down, if he was permitted, to a long spell of work till
ten, when he supped, and so to bed usually by midnight. But his evenings were often broken by visitors.
Sometimes there would be a constant stream of these,
most of them with errands that required his close
attention. For a few years after 1886, the interests
that poured into his study were largely political; men
came to consult him about Liberal prospects in the
neighbouring constituencies. The philanthropic societies of Glasgow are innumerable; equally so are the
associations in need of lectures and addresses; and
gradually, as the years went on, he became personally
engaged in movements like the University Settlement,
the Boys' Brigade, and the Pleasant Sunday Afternoons at the Canal Boatmen's Institute. On behalf
of these he was constantly receiving visitors. But in
addition there drifted upon him from the vast population, in which he occupied so conspicuous a position,
all sorts of individuals, representing only themselves:
students with mental difficulties, unacknowledged

poets, artisans with a gift for writing, a host of 'cranks,' and more than one actual madman.　Yet even their visits, frequent and prolonged as they could be, were exceeded by the letters which came in showers, chiefly after his lectures in America and Australia.　Those who blamed him for not answering all his letters ought to have seen his daily post.　Much of his correspondence, of course, deserved no answer; but, with his other work, it was impossible for him to overtake even that portion which had a real claim on his attention. He had no staff of clerks, like a business man, nor a secretary.

His interest in more than one 'settlement' brought him the acquaintance of a number of artisans; and his knowledge of their life was increased by his habit, already described, of contracting for the printing and binding of his books himself.　It must have been out of this that the following call came, soon after his return to town in the autumn of 1891 : —

To Lady Aberdeen

'3, PARK CIRCUS, GLASGOW, NOV. 25.

'. . . I am off to settle a strike, positively sole arbiter.　*Printers.*　How A. would envy me — and how I wish he had to do it!'

The winter passed in the usual change of labours between his class and other interests in Glasgow, and his meetings with students on Sunday evenings in Edinburgh.　The latter were continued for a few Sundays during the summer session of 1892, and it was at this time that an Edinburgh journal raised that cry against the meetings which has been referred to in a previous chapter.

The summer of 1892 brought another General Election, which carried Mr. Gladstone into power with a small majority. Drummond took a smaller part in this Election than in the previous one. The following are the only notes I can find with regard to it:—

'June 12.

'I had a call from John Burns and Cunninghame Graham, mourning over their lost cause. The latter will lose his seat *certain*. The labour people are a serious threat this time.'

'July 11.

'We [Captain Sinclair and H. D.] go to speak at Helensburgh to-night. We sleep there, and go all over the county [Dumbarton] from dawn to dark to-morrow visiting the polling-booths.'

During September he took a fishing at Banchory-Ternan, on the Dee. Then, and for the rest of the autumn, he was hard at work on the *Ascent of Man*.

In November I joined the Glasgow College, and lived for the first month of the session with Drummond. It was then I became aware of the big correspondence and large number of daily visits to which he was subject, and learned to admire his constant patience, and the leisure he made for those who had the least claim upon him, although at the time he was preparing his American lectures. A number of the letters he used to get were very amusing. Some admirers wrote him regularly, I think every day, but at least every day or two. Other letters brought the penalties of his American fame. Unscrupulous persons in the United States had put his name on the title-page of pamphlets and of poems with which he

2 G

had nothing to do.   One day there came a letter in a
feminine hand —

'DEAR SIR, — I am a widow with one boy of twelve
years of age.   He promises well, and, I think, could
be secured for the Kingdom if you would send him an
autograph copy of your sweet hymn, "Are they safe
with Him?"'

One day he said: 'You are a decent fellow.   You
never ask a man "whom he sits under," or "whether
he has been at church to-day?"'   Now, it has been
commonly supposed that he hung loose to church life,
and very seldom of a Sunday worshipped with his
fellow-Christians; and this idea has been strengthened
by a mistaken reading of his booklet *The City Without a Church*, which was published that autumn in
1892.   I can only say that during all the winters I
worked by his side in Glasgow I never knew him to
miss attending church on Sunday; and a more hearty
and reverent worshipper it would be hard to find.[1]
During the week he very seldom went to any dinner-
party, 'At Home,' or evening amusement.   He had
not the time for them, or he had a friend staying with
him.   But he made an exception for the social meetings of students.   There his gaiety was always infec-
tious, and he joined in every chorus.   On Saturday
afternoons he was always found watching football —
either one of the great League matches, or a match
between two companies of the Boys' Brigade.

By the end of the session of 1892–93 he had written
his lectures on the *Ascent of Man*, and on March 22nd
sailed on the *Teutonic* for America.

Drummond went to America to give at Boston

---

[1] Compare what he says about church-going in his Addresses to Students, Nos.
I. and VI., given in the Appendix to this volume.

the Lowell Institute Lectures, founded by Mr. John Lowell, Jun., in 1839, and delivered from year to year by a series of famous scholars, artists, and literary and scientific authorities. But before he started he received, even more numerously than on his visit in 1887, invitations from other institutes and societies, and from nearly all the leading universities of the States. The Chicago Exhibition was about to open, Lord and Lady Aberdeen were in Canada, and his friend, Mr. W. E. Dodge of New York, had asked him to go on a fishing expedition up one of the Canadian rivers. He left England, therefore, to spend all the summer and autumn vacation in America. Even if the material existed for doing so, it would be impossible, for reasons of space, to follow his work and his wanderings in detail. There is room only for a few salient points.

In Boston, one of the most intellectual cities in the world, the Lowell Institute Lectures of 1893 aroused the most vivid interest.[1] They were practically his volume on the *Ascent of Man*. 'For every one who received a ticket of admission to them, there were ten turned away.' 'Standing room is at a premium, and scores are turned away every evening.' On Wednesday and Saturday afternoons, therefore, Drummond repeated the lecture of the previous evening. But, the strain of this notwithstanding, he remembered other interests which were dear to him, and gave a number of addresses upon the Boys' Brigade, and to the students of Harvard University. One of the latter in Appleton Chapel, by which he said he desired to reach those who were not Christians, concluded with the characteristic words: 'Above all things, do not touch Chris-

[1] For information as to this, I am indebted to Mr. Howard A. Bridgman, one of the editors of the *Boston Congregationalist*.

tianity unless you are willing to seek the kingdom of heaven first. I promise you a miserable existence if you seek it second.'

In May he spoke to the students of Amherst University[1] upon Temptation, and delivered addresses in other places. In the end of the month he went to Chicago, to see the 'World's Columbian Exposition,' and in particular the Irish village, which formed part of it, and the existence of which was mainly due to Lady Aberdeen. There he gave lectures on Evolution, and addresses in connection with the Boys' Brigade at Minneapolis and Duluth. In the former of these towns he had a curious adventure. At the close of his lecture he was denounced by a well-known citizen as 'a fraud and imitator of the real Professor Drummond, whom the speaker had heard elsewhere, and knew.' In July he repeated his Boston lectures at Chautauqua, and went on to a Conference, under Mr. Moody, at Northfield. Here he delivered the three addresses — 'A Life for a Life,' 'Lessons from the *Angelus*,' and 'The Ideal Man,'[2] — and it was here that he encountered the inevitable attack upon his teaching. Drummond told me that the reporter of one of the leading English religious papers said to him, that he had orders not to report a word of what Drummond said; and the story goes that a deputation of the usual adherents of the Northfield Conference waited on Mr. Moody and urged him not to allow Drummond to speak. Mr. Moody asked a day to think over the matter; and when the deputation returned, informed them that he had 'laid it before the Lord, and the Lord had shown him that Drummond

---

[1] It was Amherst which gave him the only degree he possessed, LL.D.

[2] Published with an introduction from Mr. Moody by the Fleming H. Revell Co., New York, Chicago, and Toronto, 1897.

was a better man than himself; so he was to go on!'
This, if true, was like the man who penned the tribute
to Drummond, given in the first chapter of this volume, and who once said to the writer, ' There's nothing I ever read of Henry Drummond's, or heard him
say, that I didn't agree with.' What Drummond himself felt about his Northfield visit appears in the following lines, written some days afterwards : —

> ' At Northfield I felt a good deal out of it, and many
> fell upon and rent me. Before the close of the
> Conference, I struck an orthodox vein and re-
> trieved myself a little. But it was not a happy
> time.'

In the end of July he went on holiday into Canada.

To Lord Aberdeen

'RESTIGOUCHE SALMON CLUB, METAPEDIA, QUEBEC,
July 27, 1893.

' MY DEAR A., — You will see by the above heading
that I am at present not only one of your loyal
subjects, but that in spite of the *contretemps* with
the Cascapedia, I am permitted the indulgence of
my besetting sin. This river is perhaps the next
best to the Cascapedia, and as I know several of
the members of the Club, my deplorable instincts
are more than satisfied. . . .
' One goes up the river in a house-boat (primitive)
with a fleet of Indians and canoes for the actual
fishing, and sleeps either in the boat or in the
clubhouses at the various pools. Salmon abound,
and I have had my share, though the river has
been very low, and barely fishable these last few
days. A man sitting opposite me as I write,

along with a friend, captured ninety-two salmon
in five days — a phenomenal score, however, even
for Canada — at the beginning of the season.
Pardon all this fish-talk.   Your thoughts must be
in better and graver directions at present.'

To Lady Aberdeen

From the same address, July 31.

' Here is the last of this poor old Monkey[1] — sent
in shame and confusion of face for writing such
stuff, and especially for *not* writing it months
ago.   How ever did you get me to make such a
fool of myself I can't imagine.   But you are an
angelic editor not to worry your contributors for
return-of-post copy, and how you have let me off
the scolding I deserve I can't fathom.   Cannot I
make atonement by doing something else to help
on *anything* after you are gone from us?   I shall
really try, if you will commit some untied knot
end to me.

' At the moment, fishing being over, I am trying to
write a few papers for Chicago and elsewhere.
But the beauty of this river, absolute solitude,
and an extra good box of cigars are somewhat
against work.   All the fishermen have gone home,
and I am camped in a snug farm a few miles from
the clubhouse.

' A humming-bird passed the verandah a moment
ago.

' A week hence, if I succeed in doing any work, I
shall pay a visit to Bar Harbour.'

[1] The end of his story, *The Monkey that wouldn't Kill*, published first in *Wee
Willie Winkie*, and separately, in 1898, by Messrs. Hodder and Stoughton.

In September he stayed with their Excellencies the Governor-General of Canada and Lady Aberdeen at the Citadel, Quebec; and it was here, on the great rock above the St. Lawrence, one Sunday afternoon, that he gave his beautiful address from the text, ' There is a River.'

In the first week of October he was back in Chicago for the opening of the University. It was the beginning of the second year of that wonderful institution — wonderful in its great and sudden endowments; wonderful in the broad and complex organisation which President Harper and his colleagues had already achieved; and wonderful in the way in which the classes go on all the year round. Drummond often said how large and open he found the life to be there, and how strongly it roused the best that was in him. On the first Sunday of October he gave his religious address on Millet's *Angelus* and two days later the Convocation Lecture on ' Some Higher Aspects of Evolution.' Outside the University was the Great Exposition, about whose beauty and vastness he could hardly cease talking when he came home. Drummond addressed the Congress of the Evangelical Alliance under the presidency of his friend Mr. W. E. Dodge. On his way home, in New York, he addressed another meeting for the Boys' Brigade.

Drummond's American visit was accompanied and followed by the usual showers of letters, which fell wherever he spoke for any length of time. They recall the results of his earlier missions. It is astonishing how his words touched the hearts of men and women who, brought up to religion, had suddenly found it mere routine, and had slipped away from faith, and often from all hope. Their grateful letters justify the jealousy with which, at the risk of offending

the orthodox, he adapted his teaching to such cases.
He knew that these existed in crowds, unsought, un-
cared for; and in numbers they responded to his
efforts to reach them. 'All the old hopelessness is
gone,' says one; 'you sent it away.'—'Your words
last night gave me back again the faith I had lost, and
this morning I woke for the first time for long a happy
and a hopeful man.' And so on. Of course, with
these came the customary appeals from the simple and
from the twisted; the young man who wrote, 'I like
your style of speaking so much, I venture to ask you
how you acquired it,' and the 'recipient of marvellous
revelations,' 'Heaven's vice-gerent on earth' (as he
styled himself), who 'has been commanded to publish
the Gospel that the Coming Man is a Woman!' 'I
think,' said Drummond once, 'they do breed more
cranks in America than we do here; yet we run them
hard.'

On Drummond himself the energy and hopefulness
of the people — and all the more that upon this visit
he had seen it concentrated in the colossal exposition
at Chicago — had produced the effect which never
failed him on his journeys to America. From the
States he always came back, he said, as from 'a bath
of life'; and America and the Americans remained to
the end one of his great enthusiasms.

> 'I do think they are the most wonderful people un-
> der the sun. A nation in its *youth* is a stirring
> spectacle.'

Physically, however, this visit to America tried him
greatly, notwithstanding the short rest he got while
fishing, and he came home looking much older. The
preparation of the Lowell Lectures had been a strain;

he said that after he saw his audience at the first of them he had practically to rewrite the rest.[1]

The winter session of 1893–94 was passed in work harder than usual. He was preparing his Boston discourses for the press. He gave a number of lectures outside the College, and on February 5th began his last series of addresses to the Edinburgh students. About this time he was offered the Principalship of M'Gill University, Montreal, and he did not refuse it till after long consideration. The summer was spent in fishing-holidays, hardly enjoyed under the first pains of his last illness, in addressing various clubs, and in writing some articles, among them two for *M'Clure's Magazine*, on Mr. Moody. One of his visits in June was to a boys' club in Edinburgh. He asked them to put questions to him, and he was so struck and amused by those put, that he kept a list of them. Here they are: (1) How can we find happiness? (2) What is the bottomless pit? (3) What is the camel through a needle's eye? (4) What do you think of gambling? (5) What do you think of strikes? (6) Is it offensive to God to smoke a pipe? (7) Who is God? (8) Why do monkeys not become human? (9) What is the use of going to church?

In May the *Ascent of Man* was published.

[1] From a note by Mr. James Drummond.

CHAPTER XVII

THE *ASCENT OF MAN*

THE Lowell Lecturer for 1893 did not intend to publish his lectures in a volume for some years. He had secured an American copyright,[1] and Messrs. J. Pott and Co. of New York were announced in the literary journals as the American publishers. But no date was fixed for the publication, and Drummond looked forward to a long revision of his material. Before he left America, however, he heard that a Philadelphian publisher was about to issue a volume entitled ' The Evolution of Man, being the Lowell Lectures delivered at Boston, Massachusetts, April, 1893, by Professor Henry Drummond,' and claiming to be made up from a contemporary report of the lectures recently delivered by Professor Drummond in the Boston Institute, which ' reports,' the introduction further stated, ' have been carefully collated and presented to the reader with the certainty that they will prove of value.' The reports were said to be taken from the *British Weekly* of April and May, 1893, in which the first lecture had appeared almost in full, but the rest in gradually dwindling summaries, up to the eighth, when they ceased. They were, therefore, partial reports, and besides, in

---

[1] To do this all that is necessary is to print or typewrite a title-page with name, date, and ' copyrighted by So-and-So' printed on the back, and enclose a registration fee of a dollar. It is not even necessary that the book be written. ' Twelve copies must be exposed for sale,' but at what time is not explicitly stated. An account of the whole case appeared in *The Bookman* for July, 1894, and I have verified the facts given there from the copy of the original papers, which Drummond had preserved.

the volume they were modified; 'edited' was the term used.

Drummond wrote to the enterprising publisher, who answered that, though not legally bound to do so, he would suppress the edition if all his expenses were paid. As the edition consisted of some ten thousand copies already printed, Drummond refused, and the case was carried into Court — the Circuit Court of the United States for the eastern district of Pennsylvania, to the judges of which it was presented by the plaintiff's agents 'in equity.' In pronouncing judgment, Judge Dallas remarked that

'The subject of copyright is not directly involved in the case. The complainant does not base his claim to relief upon the statute but upon his right, quite distinct from any conferred by copyright, to protection against having any literary matter published as his work which is not actually his creation, and, incidentally, to prevent fraud upon purchasers. . . . The defendant's book is founded on the matter which has appeared in the *British Weekly;* and if that matter had been literally copied, and so as not to misrepresent its character and extent, the plaintiff would be without remedy; but the fatal weakness in the defendant's position is that, under colour of editing the author's work, he has represented a part of it as the whole, and even as to the portion published has materially departed from the reports which he set up in justification. . . . A most important circumstance in this connection is that the defendant, while precisely adopting his title from the headlines of the reports, has so altered their text as to make it appear, contrary to the whole tenor of the reports themselves, that what his book contains is the precise language of the author of the lectures, although, as has been said, it contains only some of the lectures, not all of them, and presents none of them fully or correctly. The complainant's right has been fully made out, and the case shown is manifestly one which calls for the interposition of the Court at this stage.'

Decree was accordingly given,[1] temporarily restraining the precipitous publisher from selling his edition. The injunction was afterwards made permanent; the edition, ten thousand copies, with the stereotype plates, was ordered to be destroyed, and Drummond got his costs. It is said to have been 'the first case in which a favourable judgment was given to an alien in such a matter.'

But Drummond was obliged to hasten his own publication of the lectures, and after being able, to his chagrin, to spend only the leisure of one busy winter in revising them, he sent them to press in the spring of 1894, and they were published in May of that year.

The *Ascent of Man* was looked for with the interest and the curiosity which await the works only of the most popular writers in literature or science. But immediate and universal as was the recognition which it received, its author could not have expected so unanimous a chorus of praise as had greeted the appearance of his *Natural Law*. The men who had at first been carried away by the latter remembered, and were on their guard. The author was not now a new writer; he had some enemies and many jealous critics in the camps both of religion and of science. Moreover, the reports of his lectures had already excited the suspicion of some and the full-armed hostility of others. On the whole, the criticism of the reviewers when it came was worthy and without ulterior motives. One daily paper, indeed, sought persistently to stir up ill-blood in the author's church by its insinuations upon his adhesion to the doctrines of Evolution; one scientific critic wrote in a bad temper that betrayed him into scientific error more grave than any with which he charged the book; and Mrs. Lynn

[1] This judgment was given at the October Sessions, 1893.

Linton[1] made a furious onslaught on what she alleged to be Drummond's 'pseudo-science' and 'plagiarisms,' overlooking, as her critics pointed out, his acknowledgments of indebtedness to Herbert Spencer and other writers on the very points with reference to which she made her serious charges.[2]　But these were almost the only exceptions in the adverse criticism which the book encountered.　The fairness of his reviewers Drummond himself heartily acknowledged.

The book, as the critics confessed, had all the external qualities of his previous works — the lucid style, the power and charm of illustration, and the many happy phrases.　Nor had it any less of the youthful courage and enthusiasm which made *Natural Law* so famous.　It disarmed, too, a large number of

[1] In the *Fortnightly* for September, 1894.

[2] A very trenchant reply to the good lady, whose zeal on this occasion outran her knowledge, will be found in an author who has no sympathy with Drummond's religion, but, as an Agnostic, attacks this strenuously — Mr. George Shoorbridge Carr, M.A., in *Social Evolution and the Evolution of Socialism : A Critical Essay.* London: W. Stewart and Co., 1895. It is an able and candid essay, but very much mistaken in its conception of what Christianity is.　Mr. Carr says of Mrs. Lynn Linton's sentence, that Drummond 'brings his subject, which only the educated can rightly understand, down to the level of the ignorant,' that it ought to run: 'He brings his subject, which only the specially educated can rightly understand, down to the level of ordinary minds,' and adds: 'This is true, and it is to his everlasting praise that he does it.'　As to her charge of 'pseudo-science,' he points out that she has given no instance, and he claims that in the main the science is correct; as to her statement that 'the philosophy is inadequate and shallow,' he says that her 'attempt to prove it by the single instance adduced of what she is pleased to call "clap-trap" about the fission in the cell, is unfortunate, for it involves her chosen authority, Herbert Spencer, in the same accusation.'　And he continues: 'Professor Drummond's vocation and object are quite different from those of Herbert Spencer.　No comparison need be instituted.　If Mrs. Linton prefers the philosophic diction of the latter, that fact does not abstract one iota from the value of the Professor's eloquent, ingenious, and masterly argumentation.　Thus in no instance does Mrs. Linton make good her sweeping assertions, and she may be hoisted with her own petard.　It is this wholesale, indiscriminating, exaggerated criticism, so easy in the writing, but not pleasant in the reading, that 'lets slip truth,' that is 'inadequate and shallow,' that is 'false, strained, and inconclusive.'　These furious onslaughts . . . are mischievous, for they tend to make a byword of criticism and a laughing-stock of the reviewer' (pp. 46 f.).

the most severe critics of *Natural Law*, and won their praise by a line of argument and by conclusions, set in an opposite direction from those which had provoked their condemnation of the earlier volume. In *Natural Law* Drummond had attempted to carry physical processes into the region of the moral and the spiritual; in the *Ascent of Man* he essayed the converse task, and succeeded in showing the ethical at work in regions of life generally supposed to be given over to purely physical laws — or at least he succeeded in exhibiting among the lower stages of the evolution of life bases and opportunities suitable for the action of moral feelings and for the formation of moral habits. In the opinion of the same critics, there was another improvement in his philosophic attitude which was akin to the one just described. *Natural Law* had drawn a very hard and fast line through the universe; it had divided human experience on either side of the new birth into two kinds of existence, the lower of which was emphasised as without capacity for, or prophecy of, the higher. Drummond had favoured by his argument an opposition between all man's natural qualities and powers on the one side, and religion on the other; in the feelings and the reason of the natural man he had said there was nothing of grace nor the power of the Spirit. He had, in fact, excommunicated Nature, and, without intending it, had given his support to a dualism prevalent not only in some of the churches, but in certain of the philosophic schools, of our day, a dualism which emphasises the opposition between human reason and (according to the temper of the writer) either revelation, or grace, or religious authority. Between 1883 and 1893 Drummond had seen this dualism develop, and had recognised its falseness

with a start which swung him free of his own entangle-
ments in some of its premises. How free may be
seen from the following statements in the *Ascent of
Man* : —

> ' Nothing can ever be gained by setting one-half of
> Nature against the other, or the rational against
> the ultra-rational. To affirm that Altruism is a
> peculiar product of religion is to excommunicate
> nature from the moral order, and religion from
> the rational order.' [1]

And again—

> ' If Nature is the Garment of God, it is woven with-
> out seam throughout; if a revelation of God, it is
> the same yesterday, to-day, and forever; if the
> expression of His Will, there is in it no variable-
> ness nor shadow of turning. Those who see
> great gulfs fixed — and perhaps we have all
> begun by seeing them — end by seeing them
> filled up. Were these gulfs essential to any
> theory of the universe or of man, even the estab-
> lishment of the unity of Nature were a dear price
> to pay for obliterating them. But the apparent
> loss is only gain, and the seeming gain were in-
> finite loss. For to break up Nature is to break
> up Reason, and with it God and Man.'

There could not be a more complete recantation of
the principal philosophic heresy of *Natural Law*, and
for such a recantation the *Ascent of Man* received a
warm welcome from the most severe of the philosophic
critics of its predecessor. Nor was it in this respect
any less welcome to the theologian. For the book
vindicated Nature, as also the sphere of the God of

[1] *Ascent of Man*, p. 72.

Love, and sought to prove the presence of the characteristic forces of Christianity—sympathy and self-sacrifice—upon the lower stages of the evolution of man. It might almost be said that Drummond expressed, in the language and with the information of his own time, the vision which the ancient seer saw of the *Lamb slain from the foundation of the world.*

But having passed these tests, the *Ascent of Man* had next to undergo the examination of scientific authorities as to the methods by which its author sought to prove his great principles. The book covers the evolution of man both as an animal, a rational being, and a member of society. It draws its proofs and illustrations from biology, the sciences of language and of the origin of mind, as well as from that new and interesting department of modern research which deals with sex and the beginnings of the human family. In all these departments Drummond made use of the thoughts of many thinkers. His book would never have been written without inspiration derived (not to speak of the great authorities of our time in physical science) from the investigations and arguments of Herbert Spencer, Fiske, Westermarck, and others, and from the brilliant suggestions of Martineau. Drummond has spoken of his main thesis, the influence upon the evolution of man of the struggle for the life of others, as 'the missing factor in current theories,' and as if it were a new discovery. But no one who reads his frequent references to other thinkers can honestly believe that he intended to take the glory of this discovery to himself; and he has certainly expounded and emphasised the appearances of Altruism, or the provocations to Altruism, which are present in the earlier stages of evolution, as these had never been illustrated, or impressed upon the public

mind by any previous writer.[1]   Mr. Carr makes one
criticism, which I have not found elsewhere.   It is
with reference to the distinction which Drummond
draws between ' The Struggle for Life ' and ' The
Struggle for the Life of Others,' and the charge
which Drummond makes against Darwin, of omit-
ting all notice of the latter while expounding the
former.   Mr. Carr points out that when Darwin spoke
of the ' struggle for life,' and consequent ' survival of
the fittest,' he had in view the struggle of the *species*.
The ' struggle for life,' therefore, included two aspects
— the struggle for self and the struggle for others ; in
the latter category the struggle for the preservation of
offspring being absolutely necessary for the continuance of the species. . . .   Professor Drummond at-
taches to the phrase the false, restricted meaning of
the struggle of the individual for its own life, and then
scores his point by opposing to this, in strong antithesis, and with much rhetoric, the ' Struggle for the
Life of Others.'[2]

By some critics the *Ascent of Man* was charged
with containing a number of errors in the domain of
physical science.   On such a point the present writer
is incapable of offering an opinion, but here are the
criticisms of two authorities on the subject — Professor
M'Kendrick, of the Chair of Physiology in the University of Glasgow, and Professor Alexander Macalister,
of the Chair of Anatomy in the University of Cambridge.[3]

Professor M'Kendrick calls the first chapter an excellent
account of the *Ascent of the Body*, but takes exception to the

[1] Compare Mr. Carr's remarks quoted above, p. 461, n. 2.
[2] *Social Evolution*, pp. 36, 37.
[3] The latter reviewed the *Ascent of Man* in *The Bookman* for June, 1894;
the former reviewed it in the *Critical Review* for October of the same year.

statement on p. 79 that the ova of different animals are practically identical. . . . 'Certainly the highest microscopic powers can observe no marked distinction, although recently progress has been made in this direction, and we may be assured that physical differences exist.' Of the same chapter Professor Macalister says that 'once or twice his love for analogy betrays [the author] into trivial misconceptions, as on p. 86, and as a lecturer he only deals with what may be regarded as the sensational points of his subject.' Both authorities think he has been hardly just to the place of the ape in the ancestry of man. In Chapter II. Dr. M'Kendrick thinks it 'dangerous to reason as to habits supposed to have been derived from ancestors,' e.g. to infer that the clutching power of a new-born child is derived from the arboreal habits of animal progenitors. Both Professors reckon the statements in Chapter III. on 'The Arrest of the Body' to be in need of qualification.[1] Dr. M'Kendrick says, 'How unthinkable is the proposition that "the slumbering animal brain broke into intelligence": Professor Drummond cuts this knot with a hatchet'; and finds otherwise on this point 'some confusion of language.' In Chapter IV., on 'The Origin of Mind,' Dr. M'Kendrick thinks that the account of Mr. Wallace's opinion, in opposition to Mr. Darwin's, is hardly accurate; and that the illustration, which Drummond gives from the sensitive plant, 'is not cogent, as few naturalists would admit the mimosa possesses sensation. Mere movement is no proof of the psychological condition termed a sensation.' Nor does this critic think the evidence adduced from the writings of George J. Romanes trustworthy 'regarding the correspondence as to order in the evolution of the emotions in the animal series and in the development of the same emotions in a child, because of the great difficulty in the interpretation of the motor phenomena accompanying these emotions. . . . Unintentionally, we interpret the movements by reading our own thoughts or emotional states into the creatures we happen to be watching. Mr. Romanes was an excellent observer, but his work in the direction indicated

---

[1] Dr. Macalister says 'it would be enough for his purpose to show that physical endowment could not progress at the same pace as psychical growth.'

was tentative, and it is hazardous to treat these observations as if they were on a par with the facts of comparative anatomy.[1]

With one exception, to be presently noticed, these are all the defects which those two great authorities find in the natural science of the volume. And it cannot be denied that they give some grounds for the charges of hasty inference and exaggeration of the emphasis on certain points, which seem favourable to the author's main thesis. Such charges were chiefly fastened by many critics upon that part of the chapter on ' The Struggle for the Life of Others' which discovers the appearance of altruism in the self-multiplying cell. On this Dr. Macalister says: ' The multiplying cell may be the potential, but can scarcely be called the actual exponent [of the ethical element in life], for in its origination cell division is really selfish, and solely for self-interest, as far as this language of moral import can be applied to a biological process. . . . The physiological mechanism of cell reproduction has its ultimate base in the necessity for small size with relatively large surface, or else the cell cannot be properly fed. If the division be regarded as an act of self-sacrifice, it is one which is submitted to for a purely selfish end.' Similarly Dr. M'Kendrick, who adds, ' One cannot help feeling that in not a few of the illustrations Professor Drummond reads into the phenomena of nature some of his own mental moods.'

In his account of evolution Professor Drummond, Dr. M'Kendrick hints, has emphasised disproportionately the favourable features, and this was also the

---

[1] Dr. M'Kendrick does not think that the illustration drawn, in the last chapter, from the Sigillaria and the Stigmaria is quite apt. Their relation is not a true analogy. He thinks that Professor Drummond lays too great an emphasis on environment, and is guilty of some confusion of thought in endeavouring to blend the physical with the spiritual.

opinion of a critic who approached the book from the standpoint of philosophy. Professor Iverach, in a review which called forth from Drummond a warm acknowledgment of its justice,[1] pointed out that the argument of the book avoided such difficult questions as are raised 'by the stumbling and the failures of evolution, and the persistency of lower forms of life alongside the higher.' In answer to this, it might be urged that Drummond had set himself to emphasise aspects of evolution, which, though mentioned by others, had not had full justice done them; and it might be added that the book is the work of a poetic translator of the science of his time rather than of an original scientific thinker.[2] Still, if this were granted, others might justly urge that in imputing ethical character to some of the lower processes of life, Drummond sinned also in art, by overdoing his case, and rendering it open to ridicule.

It would not be fair to give these adverse criticisms upon points in the *Ascent of Man* without adding from the two distinguished critics who have been quoted their appreciations of the volume as a whole. Professor Macalister says of it : —

'The problems which Professor Drummond has dealt with are perplexing and complex, and there will probably be much difference of opinion as to the degree of success with which he has applied the biological method to their solution; but the candid reader cannot lay down the book without feeling that it is an honest and manly attempt to grapple in a rev-

[1] The review appeared in the *British Weekly* for May 24, 1894. On May 25th Drummond wrote to his critic : 'I wish I had had your own volume sooner, for it would have made me wiser. It has already helped me, and it will do much more in the future. Your criticisms are just. I did not like the "self-sacrifice" passage myself, but let it pass, thinking the qualifications strewn through the book *ad nauseam* might save it. But it is not good.'

[2] 'Not so much science as the poetry of science.' — Mr. Benjamin Kidd, in his appreciative review of the volume in the *Expositor* for June, 1894.

erential spirit with these difficulties, and that it constitutes a seasonable contribution to the literature of the fundamental department of sociology.'

And Professor M'Kendrick says : —

'Towards the close, Professor Drummond indicates that the appearance of Christianity is a part of the evolutionary process. "What is Evolution? A method of creation. What is its object? To make more perfect living beings. What is Christianity? A method of creation. What is its object? To make more perfect living beings. Through what does Evolution work? Through Love. Through what does Christianity work? Through Love. Evolution and Christianity have the same Author, the same end, the same spirit." This is the grand conclusion. Still one is inclined to ask, Does Evolution really work through Love? We wish it were proven to be the case, but facts seem to be against it.

'We have not entered on the consideration of the *Introduction*, because we thought it better to let the lectures speak for themselves. The Introduction is an excellent account of the position of the author towards the Evolution view, and it emphasises the contribution that the author has added to the discussion, namely, the recognition of the great principle of the *struggle for others* as a factor in Evolution. There can be no question that this is a substantial contribution to the philosophy of the subject, and it has never been put forward with such force and fulness as by Professor Drummond. Apart from the general literary excellence of the book, this is the part that will live in literature, and this is the portion that will awaken thought in many minds, and lead them to look again at Nature. At present we feel bound to say we are not convinced, although, as we have hinted, nothing would be more delightful than to be able to look at the struggle going on in Nature through Professor Drummond's spectacles.

'As a contribution to the discussion of the great theme of Man's relation to the evolutionary process, the book must be regarded as tentative. The time has not yet come for anything like a final statement. The gaps that science has yet to fill up are far too great to allow us to frame a consistent scheme, as has been attempted in this book. The adoption of such a scheme will not ultimately weaken faith, although it will necessitate change of view. We doubt if Professor Drummond himself fully realises the tremendous consequences that must flow from a complete acceptance of the theory of Evolution as applied to man (body, mind, soul, religion, sin, death, the future) *as we are at present advised.* A thorough-going evolutionary view demands a new theology, and such fundamental questions as the origin of sin, human responsibility, the taking of our nature by the Son of God (as implied in the doctrine of the Trinity), the possibility of miracle, the possibility of a future life for the individual, will all need to be restated and to receive fresh answers. No one could attempt such a task at the present stage of the world's history, as the data are still far too insufficient. The last word has not yet been spoken by science as to the evolution of life from dead matter, or the evolution of animal forms, still less as to the evolution of all that is included in psychology and morals. Even physical science is only struggling to the light, and cannot yet explain Energy, Light, Electricity, Gravitation, Matter. More light will come, but it may take years, hundreds of years, before it will pierce the darkness of our present ignorance, and enable us to see things in their just proportions. In the mean time, Professor Drummond deserves credit for the courage with which he has applied the evolutionary hypothesis to current views, for his attempt to form a consistent cosmology, for the clear-sightedness with which he sees that all must ultimately be explained by the application of one great Law or Principle representing the Mind of God working out the Harmony of His Universe, and for the beautiful account he has given of the story of Evolution, a story that reads like a fairy tale.'

In addition we may quote the following opinion by Dr. Gairdner, F.R.S., Professor of Medicine in the University of Glasgow[1]: —

[1] Now Sir William Gairdner, K.C.B. The opinion was expressed in a letter to Dr. Stalker immediately after H. D.'s death; it is quoted in an article

'The earlier book,[1] while full of suggestive and finely
expressed thought, did not convince me nor appear to me a
permanent forward step in the Eirenicon between Religion
and Science.   The latter book has, to my mind, a far wider
sweep, and a much more permanent value in its marvellously
lucid and at the same time profound exposition of the root
principles of altruism, as evolved in the wide field of nature.
Nothing that I have read on the subject of ethical theory has
appeared to me to go so deep or to be so convincing as this,
which makes it a fundamental part of God's universe from
the beginnings, at all events, of sexual life therein.'

And finally, we may take, along with the views of
these scientific authorities, the following expression of
opinion from a philosophical standpoint.   It is by the
Rev. D. M. Ross, one of Drummond's oldest and
closest friends, whose criticism of the main thesis of
Natural Law had been adverse : —

'If *Natural Law in the Spiritual World* was an apologetic
for his early individualism, no less is the *Ascent of Man* an
apologetic for his later socialism. The *Ascent of Man*, whether
we have regard to its literary style or its intellectual power, is
unquestionably his greatest book.   Here again, for the study
of his religious teaching, the chief interest of the book is not
in its proofs, but in what it seeks to prove — that love, or the
struggle for the life of others, is a law deeply embedded in the
whole life of the universe.   Love, service, sympathy, sacrifice,
co-operation, brotherhood — these were dominant thoughts in
his own "wider outlook and social ideal."   One may question
whether it is necessary to appeal to "nature" for a sanction
to the law of love in our social life, and one may question
whether the author is successful in obtaining from "nature"
the sanction of which he is in search ; but no one can read
this brilliant volume without being impressed by the social
enthusiasm which lies behind its reasoning and eloquence.

by Dr. Stalker, 'Henry Drummond,' in the *Expositor*, Fifth Series, vol. v. p.
293.
[1] *Natural Law.*

'It has been said that Professor Drummond had already given the world the best work he was likely to achieve before he was struck down in the prime of his manhood. It seems to me that there are indications in the *Ascent of Man* that, had he been spared, he would have given us work of a still higher quality. The concluding chapter on Involution shows an appreciation of the import of an idealistic philosophy which is a new feature in his thinking. "Are we even quite sure that what we call a physical world is, after all, a physical world? . . . The very term 'material world,' we are told, is a misnomer, that the world is a spiritual world, merely employing 'matter' for its manifestations." "Evolution is not progress in matter. Matter cannot progress. It is a progress in spirit, in that which is limitless, in that which is at once most human, most rational, most divine." "Evolution is Advolution; better, it is revelation — the phenomenal expression of the divine, the progressive realisation of the ideal, the ascent of Love." I cannot help feeling that Professor Drummond hampered himself needlessly by seeking arguments for the laws of the spiritual world in Nature. The sentences I have quoted show how he was beginning to work himself free of this hampering influence by recognising that spirit is the prius of matter, that nature is itself only interpretable through the mind of man, or (to use his own phrase) the spiritual world. No one could have adopted a more hospitable attitude towards new truth. Had he lived to follow out the hints contained in the last chapter of the *Ascent of Man*, he had it in him to do work as an Evangelist to the scientific and cultured classes for which the great work he has already done would have seemed but a preparation.'

CHAPTER XVIII

BOYS AND THE BOYS' BRIGADE

Not only did Henry Drummond preserve the memory of his boyhood, as the pure do, but to the end he remained a boy, happy, whole-hearted and unspoiled. None could be fuller of the love of sport or of the spirit of fun than he. He would have confessed that his chief liking was for a fire, a launch, or a football match. He had climbed to the height of experience and success; he was on familiar terms with the greatest men of his generation; but some angel had blessed him with the fortunate gift of still being able to look out on life from the level of a boy's eyes, and nothing in him was more attractive than his wonder at a new engine, or his awe of every great man whom he encountered for the first time. Many men, when in all sincerity they 'humble themselves and become as little children,' do so awkwardly and with a clatter; they tumble down to the children's level, and are childlike only by being boisterous. But he had never left that level. I always think of him as the fulfilment of the broken dream of which Mr. Wendell Holmes tells us so prettily in one of his poems: Drummond had the secret of being a boy without leaving his manhood behind him.

This brought him great influence with boys, and he won their love without difficulty. To us who were his contemporaries, nothing gave more pleasure than to discover, when we had boys of our own, all the way from seven to seventeen, how quickly they too became his friends. He was amazingly fertile in surprising their wishes. Every new book a boy could love, every new game or puzzle, on these he was our trusted adviser. A children's party was sure to go off well if he was there. When boys were at school or parents from home, his visits to those, his letters to these, were things to be remembered for many a day. In deeper things it was the same. He read a boy's heart, understood his temptations, and knew on what side religion touched him. Lads who shirked religious meetings did not shirk those which Drummond held after they had heard him once. His services for boys in Edinburgh were happy and unforced. In style (it almost goes without saying) his addresses had nothing about them of the conventional or condescending — the ' my-dear-young-friends ' attitude. In substance they were true to his maxim that 'a boy's religion must be his own, and ought not to be his grandmother's or his aunt's.' What he counted such a religion to be, may be found in *First !* printed for the Boys' Brigade, or in *Baxter's Second Innings.* Here we may give a few of his letters only to show how happy he was with boys, and what trouble he took to be kind to them. The first is in anticipation of a visit that some brothers were about to pay him in Glasgow. It is to their mother.

'Feb. 28 [year not given].

'. . . The boys will swagger in later. *Private.* — Can you indicate anything in the wide world which I could buy, borrow, or steal which could make them happy: anything edible, drinkable, scentable, seeable, or feelable which could give them delight. Perhaps there is nothing; but most boys have a particular brand of chocolate or something.'

He sent *Baxter's Second Innings* to a young friend
before he published it.

'3, PARK CIRCUS, GLASGOW, Oct. 8, 1891.

' Boys are so terribly cute that I must have an old
boy's opinion before I can venture to print this !
You will notice there is a minimum of direct
religion, but that is designed.'

To another who wrote asking if he might pay a
visit there came on a card this reply : —

MR. H. DRUMMOND
very much
AT HOME
on
Friday, March 1st
From 6 P.M.
till
All Hours.

Come and bring a friend

All seats free

No Irish need apply.

The Hippodrome,
Feb. 28, 1889.

To the same boys, in 1889, he sent examination
papers.   Here are some of the questions : —

' HISTORY

' 1. Give a short life of Piggott.
' 2. Where was Major Whittle born ? contrast him briefly
with Wellington, Napoleon, General Booth, General Tom
Thumb, and the General Supply Stores.
' 3. Who was Lord Fauntleroy, and what were his chief
battles ?
' 4. How long did it take Dante to " climb the mountain " ?
and what is the shortest time it has ever been done in ?   Who
first beat Dante's record ?
' 5. Are you a Home-Ruler ?   If so, why not ?

'Domestic Economy

' 1. What is the retail price of sausages?

' 2. Name the two best brands of shortbread. What is longbread, and how does it differ from high-bred?

' 3. Discuss the following : " Has the Discoverer of Chloroform or of Beanbags done the most for humanity ? "

' 4. How would you spend 2*d*. if you got it? Subtract ½*d*. from 2*d*., and parse the remainder.

'Physiology

' 1. Define the term "Get-your-hair-cut," and say if Red Hair is Hair-red-itary.

' 2. Where was your face before it was washed?'

When he was at Dax, in the Pyrenees, in 1895, one of the same brothers wrote him that he had discovered a skeleton in the gravels of the river Garrie in Perthshire. The skull had two 'clours' in the back of it, signs that it had belonged to some fugitive from the battle of Killiecrankie, caught from behind as he fled south. Drummond wrote this reply, while he was lying on his back, racked with the pains of his last illness. The '*fama*' is a reference to the attacks made upon his *Ascent of Man* by some Highland Presbyteries. The card is undated : —

' Monsieur, — Honoured as I am by any communication from you, I cannot but be aware of the motive which has induced you to acquaint me with your disgusting discoveries. No, Sir, *I* did not kill that man. Doubtless he was fishing with worm, and therefore was worthy of Death; but if you judge my hand did this deed, the suggestion is the product of a disordered intelligence, and I have witnesses to prove an *Alibi*. I beg, Sir, that this *fama clamosa* — which, as

I am credibly informed, has, to my grievous
hurt, already spread to Dingwall and the borders
thereof — be immediately arrested, and that you
will cease to trouble the short nights and lingering days of a Poor Invalid with Base Suspicions.
— Your obedient servant,

'H(und) D(ax).'

But it was not only the sons of his friends whom
Drummond loved.   He studied, for he loved, the Boy,
wherever he found him.   In Glasgow, message and
telegraph boys, the urchins that play football behind
the policeman's back, and the little ragamuffin bands
which used some years ago to parade the streets with
penny whistles and tin pails, — these were his constant entertainment.   He was always stopping you
to watch some of them.   Here is a picture he drew
from his own windows : —

'What are these creatures shambling up the cres-
cent?   These are two message-boys.   And who
is that troglodyte roosting on the railing?   That
is Drake's boy, waiting on Peel's boy and Smellie's
boy.   Why does he wait?   Because he never
travels alone; secondly, because he has infinite
time.   Do they shake hands when they meet?
No: Drake's boy puts out his foot and trips up
Peel's boy.   What does Peel's boy do?   He
rises in haste and smites him with a leg of
mutton.   Are they now enemies?   No; these
are proofs of attachment.   After burnishing the
leg of mutton, they sit down to discuss the universe — *i.e.* the street, the pantomime, and one
Kidd, a pirate.
'Why does Smellie's boy go off by himself and
yell?   If he did not do that, he would burst.   He

does not know he is yelling. Why does he lay down his basket and dance? Hush! do not betray him. All boys do that when they are alone. Does he look ashamed if you see him? No; boys never look anything. Will he come to, if you leave him? Yes; he will whistle presently, and calm down. How much does he get for this? Four-and-sixpence a-week.'[1]

Since the days when he taught in the Sunday-schools of the Edinburgh Cowgate, he had been face to face with the religious problem of our city-boys; when he came to Glasgow he felt its urgency still more; and in addition, there were pressed upon his observation one or two painful facts concerning, in particular, message-boys, and still more, message-girls. I do not know whether the evil continues, but some years ago it was not uncommon for boys and girls to be sent from shops with baskets or parcels far too heavy for them. Drummond tested some of the weights himself, while helping these poor children along the street, and found them cruelly overladen. In some cases, the constant carriage of a heavy basket on the elbow drew round the shoulder-blade and rendered the child slightly deformed for life. Drummond saw the folly of using a child's elbow to hook on to a great burden, and he had baskets made to strap over the shoulders and rest on the back like a knapsack. Several tradesmen in Glasgow adopted these, and we used to see them in use on the streets. I have not seen any for several years.

But the moral problem of the city-boy was a much harder one, and there was nothing in existence which had quite solved it. In many Sunday-schools the

[1] From article in *Good Words* printed by the Boys' Brigade.

discipline was genuine; and here and there teachers of rough boys not only interested them on Sunday, but kept in touch with them through the rest of the week. To this extent Drummond's wholesale criticism of Sunday-schools, which we shall presently quote, needs qualification, as indeed he himself hints. But of a very large proportion of Sunday-schools, whether in the rougher or more respectable parts of our cities, every word he says is true. The discipline was fitful, and often secured only by threats of exclusion from the winter soirée and summer trip, for the sake of which many children would attend two or three schools in the course of one Sunday. Beyond an occasional visit to the homes of their boys, or having them once a year at their own houses, the teachers did nothing to control or refine the life of their pupils. The crisis was becoming desperate, for a large number of teachers annually deserted a work of which they recognised the futility, and for which they knew of no other methods.

To one teacher who had felt all this the happy inspiration came of bringing down upon the older boys the methods of military discipline. Mr. W. A. Smith was a Glasgow merchant, a lieutenant in the 1st Lanarkshire Rifle Volunteers, and a Sunday-school teacher, with good business capacity, soldierly efficiency, a sound judgment, and a real love for boys. On October 4, 1883, Mr. Smith formed thirty of the pupils of his own school—the Mission School of College Free Church—into a company, and tried upon them the effects of regular drill. This was the first company of the now famous Boys' Brigade. The experiment succeeded so well that it was imitated in some other schools; the movement won the confidence of several men of position in Glasgow and other Scottish towns; and at last, in January, 1885, the Brigade was formally constituted as a national organisation. The movement rapidly spread, companies were formed in every part of the kingdom, and in connection with nearly every branch of the Christian Church.

The object of the Brigade was defined as 'The advancement of Christ's kingdom among boys and the promotion of habits of obedience, reverence, discipline, self-respect, and all that tends towards a true Christian manliness.' The Brigade seeks 'to secure this object through the agency of military drill and discipline, as a means whereby boys are attracted, held together, and brought into a receptive attitude for the religious teaching and guiding, which is the main work of the Brigade.'[1] Each company is attached to some Church or other Christian organisation, which is held responsible for everything connected with the formation of the company, for the nomination of suitable officers, and for the religious teaching of the Boys. The management of the Brigade is committed to an executive of fifteen members, elected annually by the council, which represents every company in the Brigade. The headquarters are in Glasgow,[2] but the annual gatherings of the council and the periodical meetings of the executive are held in different large cities throughout the kingdom. The patron is H.R.H. the Duke of York, the vice-patron His Grace the Archbishop of Canterbury, and the honorary president, the Earl of Aberdeen. In 1883 there was the single company with three officers and thirty boys. On May 31, 1898, the returns for the United Kingdom were 786 companies, with 2828 officers and 34,209 boys.

---

[1] From a Memorandum by Mr. J. Carfrae Alston of Glasgow, the Brigade President, to which I am indebted for most of what follows.

[2] Full information may be procured from Mr. W. A. Smith, the Secretary, at 162, Buchanan Street, Glasgow.

The district battalions are inspected annually at their
centres by military officers. Among those who have
acted as inspectors, and have expressed high com-
mendation of the discipline and efficiency of the battalions they have reviewed, have been Field-Marshals
Lord Wolseley, Lord Roberts, and Sir Donald Stewart,
General Chapman commanding Her Majesty's Forces
in Scotland, and other distinguished soldiers. From
Great Britain the movement has spread to the United
States, Canada, the West Indies, South Africa, Australia, New Zealand, and India. The numbers in these
countries, when added to the Home Brigade, made a
grand total of 1550 companies, 5400 officers, and
67,500 boys.

The Brigade is neither Presbyterian nor bound to
any other denomination. Nor is it confined either to
the Churches established by law or to Dissent. The
Church of England and the Episcopal Church of
Ireland are largely represented on its strength, and
throughout the kingdom most of the other Christian
organisations give it full support. The Roman
Catholic Church in Ireland and elsewhere has adopted
the methods of the Brigade; and the Jewish community in London has found that these can be adapted
to the religious training which they give their boys.

The movement had to make its way at first in
face of hostile criticism, chiefly from those who were
alarmed at its military side, and were ignorant of what
was behind. But the sound sense of its promoters, the
sincerity of the religious aims of the officers, and the
manifest effect upon the conduct and character of all
the schools in which companies were formed, very
speedily silenced objectors, and the Brigade has become established as one of the unquestioned religious
forces of our time.

21

The distinguishing feature of the organisation is that it has two sides — the military and religious — which are not separate, but closely interwoven. The first is the letter of the movement, the language, the means, the discipline; the second is the spirit, the significance, the power, the final aim and purpose. By the first, the methods of which have caught their fancy to a quite remarkable extent, the boys have been brought under a control rarely, if ever, attained by the methods common to most Sunday-schools. They take the Brigade seriously, perform the duties with alacrity, and obey the restrictions which it imposes upon them. A boy takes readily to drill because he enjoys it. And it is this liking that first brings him within range of the good influences by which he is to be surrounded in his company. Then there grow upon him the feelings of strength in union, of joint responsibility, and of the dependence of the boys upon each other, — all of which by themselves produce within him acquiescence in that wonderful pressure of discipline that is calculated to bring important and permanent changes upon his character. Those in charge of the movement, however, have been very careful that its military side shall not be carried further than is necessary. While the formation of companies involves the appointment of officers, aping of the style of a military force is avoided. The uniform is limited to a cap, belt, and haversack, added to the ordinary clothing of the boys. A cross-belt and chevron distinguish the sergeants, and the officers wear a suitable cap and carry a cane. This simplicity does not prevent the drill being of the very best quality. It is the Army Drill laid down by the War Office in the Official 'Red-Book,' and in many instances it has been brought to a remarkable perfection.

But while this external evidence of the Brigade is that which is most conspicuous to the public, the deeper and the principal operations of the movement are upon the religious side. The personal dealing with each boy in relation to religion, to his home, to his companions and his amusements, is not a thing to be paraded, but it is here that the strength of the Brigade lies; and just in proportion as this inner work has been genuine, the movement has earned its great success. The Brigade is not a conglomeration of drill-classes. Religion permeates it in every department. The religion of the Company Bible-class is the same as that of the drill-meeting, the recreation-room, and the club for cricket, football, or athletics, which is attached to the company. It is sought to make the boys realise that religion is for the whole life of a boy, and not merely for one day in the week.

From this it will be seen how much depends on the company officers. A company officer not only maintains discipline, gives orders, and brings the drill up to a high standard. He is the friend and guide of his boys, the home visitor, the superintendent of sports, and the Bible-class teacher. He conducts the short service at drill and gives the tone to the whole life of the company. If he be the right man, he can so mould the boyhood of our land that Christ's kingdom shall be truly advanced. Now, one of the successes of the movement has been to secure a supply of able and devoted young men to act as company officers. When Lord Roberts came to inspect the Glasgow battalion, he was satisfied with the discipline and drill of the boys; but more than once he expressed his admiration that so many young men of the requisite skill and earnestness should have been found to act as officers, and he repeatedly praised their diligence in a cause so unselfish and so practical. They have their reward. There is nowhere at the present day such a field for young men who desire to work for the community in the spirit of Christ.

I have thus fully described the Boys' Brigade, because from the first the movement won Henry Drummond's heart, and secured his hearty and deliberate co-operation. He was consulted by its promoters, entered its councils, became an Honorary Vice-President, frequently addressed its members, wrote books for them, and pleaded for them before the public both on platforms and by articles. He started the movement in Australia, and laboured for it strenuously in the United States and Canada. Next to his own work among the Edinburgh students, there was no institution of our time to which he gave more thought in the last ten years of his life, or of which he used to speak up to the very end with more satisfaction and more hope. I have quoted[1] the opening of his article in *Good Words*. Here are some more extracts:—

'The boy is accounted for by the Evolution Theory. His father was the Primitive Man. It is only his being in a town and his mispronunciation that make you think he is not a savage. What he represents is Capacity; he is clay, dough, putty. This boy cannot as yet walk straight, or dress better, or brush his hair. He is not good. He is not bad. He has no soul. He has not even soap. He is simply Boy, pure, unwashed, unregenerate Boy. Can anything be done for him? Yes, a very great invention has appeared; it is known to the initiated as the " B.B." Until the " B.B." was discovered, scarcely any one knew

[1] See above, p. 477 f.

how to make a man, a gentleman, and a Christian out of a message-boy. The thing had happened, perhaps, as a chance or sport, but there was no steady machinery for it. Specimens could be turned out at the rate of a score or two in a year, but under the New Process you have them by the battalion. The message-boy of the close of the nineteenth century, in fact, will soon become a tradition. All that will remain of him will be a basket and a woollen comforter.

'Like all really great inventions, the New Process is very simple. It rises naturally out of a process already in use, or rather in uselessness, for the Old Process rarely effected anything. Let us suppose you have gathered a Sunday-class of boys, and treat them at first on the old or time-dishonoured plan. Infinite trouble and infinite bribery have brought these creatures together; and as they come solely to amuse themselves, your whole effort is spent in keeping order — in quelling riots, subduing irrelevant remarks, minimising attacks upon the person, and protecting your Sunday hat from destruction. No boy, you know perfectly, has yet succeeded in listening to you for two consecutive minutes. They have learned nothing whatever. Respect is unknown, obedience a jest. Even the minor virtues of regularity, punctuality, and courtesy have not yet dawned upon their virgin minds.

'What is wrong is that they have no motive, no interest, and you have not tried to find these for them. They are street-boys, and you have treated them as if they had the motives and interests of domestic boys. The real boy-nature in them has never been consulted. You may be a very re-

markable man, but it is not their kind of remark-
ableness, so you are a person of no authority in
their eyes. You may be a walking biblical
cyclopædia, but they have no interest even in a
stationary biblical cyclopædia. They believe you
to be a thoroughly good fellow in your way, only
it is an earth's diameter from their way; and that
you should know precisely what their way is they
guilelessly give you opportunity of learning every
single second you spend among them.

'One night, after the usual *émeute*, you retire from
the place of torture vowing to attempt some
change. Next morning you betake yourself to
the Headquarters of the New Process and determine to explore its secret. The whole art and
mystery of making Boys is explained to you; the
whole process of cleaning, restoring, renovating
them; of clothing them and putting them into a
right mind, of giving them a sound body and a
reasonable soul. And at your preparation-hour
the following Saturday night, instead of trying to
find out whether the Israelites crossed the Red
Sea by the shoals at Suez or went round, "as
some say," by Wady Tawarik, you read up the
literature of the " B.B.," and learn how the children of your own city can be led across the more
difficult sea of life's temptations.

'When you faced your Boys the next night, the New
Process bursting within you, they discerned at a
glance that something was going to happen. To
be sure a carefully planned mutiny was to come
off that night on their part, but the look of you
arrests them, and they delay hostilities to give you
one more chance. You confide to them that next
Thursday evening you are going to secure a hall,

and if they will meet you there at eight o'clock they will spend the most wonderful night of their lives. Yourself and a friend who is an Officer in the Volunteers are going to tell them all about Drill and teach them exactly how it is to be done. You promise, moreover, by and by, to bring caps and belts, which they may have for the price of a few *Sons of Britannia*, and hint that in time a haversack may be entertained, and a band, and stripes, and prizes, and even a rifle, which, though warranted not to go off, will yet be a weapon of no mean calibre. After a few other details of an equally enticing nature, the mine is fairly sprung, and with a very brief postscript on the Israelites you bring to a triumphant close the first successful class-meeting in your experience.

' Next Thursday, strange contrast to all Sunday precedents, every Boy is on the spot at the hour. Instead of the wandering, bored look, every eye is transfixed on the brown-paper parcel which, with newly acquired cunning, you have labelled " Accoutrements " — not that they know the word, but they feel sure it is something military. After capping and belting them, — though this is not lawful at this early stage, — and standing them up in a row, you proceed to business. You do not start off with the old injured Sunday air, " Now, Boys, behave yourselves." There are no Boys in the room. These are privates, full privates. You do not cringe before them and beg and implore attention. You pull yourself together and shout out that last word, " 'Tenshun," like an explosion, and the very change of accent to the last syllable paralyses the whole row into rigid statues. Following up this sudden advantage you keep them

moving — marching, halting, marking time, and
doubling, till they are dropping with fatigue.
What liberties you take this blessed night! No
lion-king making his wild beasts jump through
hoops could be prouder of himself. You order
them about like an emperor. You criticise their
hands, their faces, their feet — even their boots —
without a murmur of dissent. Number Five's
hair is pilloried before the whole company, and
he actually takes it as a compliment. Eleven's
coat has a tear across the breast which is denounced as unmilitary, and he is ordered to have
it repaired on penalty of the guardroom. If Three
of the rear rank again kicks Two of the front rank
he will be put into a dungeon. Any private absent
from drill next Thursday will be branded as a
deserter, while unwashed hands will be a case for
a court-martial.

'Amazing and preposterous illusion! Call these
Boys, *Boys*, which they are, and ask them to sit
up in a Sunday-class, and no power on earth will
make them do it; but put a fivepenny cap on them
and call them soldiers, which they are not, and you
can order them about till midnight. The genius
who discovered this astounding and inexplicable
psychological fact ought to rank with Sir Isaac
Newton. Talk of what can be got out of coal-tar
or waste-paper! Why, you take your boy, your
troglodyte, your Arab, your *gamin*, on this principle, and there is no limit to what you can extract
from him or do with him. Look at this quondam
class, which is to-night a Company. As class it
was confusion, depression, demoralisation, chaos.
As Company, it is respect, self-respect, enthusiasm, happiness, peace. The beauty of the change

is that it is spontaneous, secured without heart-
burn, maintained without compulsion.   The Boy's
own nature rises to it with a bound ; and the live-
lier the specimen, the greater its hold upon him.'

He then gives the history of the movement and the
details of organisation.   After stating that the Brigade
takes boys between twelve and seventeen, being 'designed to operate on a Boy only during a specific part
of his development,' and then hand him over to the
Y.M.C.A., or Church Guilds, or the like, he continues : —

' The Brigade, in fact, is meant to supply the missing link between these institutions and the ordinary Sunday-school.   As soon as a Boy becomes
a wage-earner, and breathes the free air of street
or workshop, the Sunday-school ceases to hold
him, and without something to bridge the interval
between school life and the educative and religious associations for young men, he would either
be lost or spoiled before these could throw their
meshes round him.   It is in this respect more
perhaps than in any other that the Boys' Brigade
is to be welcomed to a place among the staple
institutions of the country.   If those higher institutions are not large enough or elastic enough or
attractive enough to receive and hold the veterans
who pass out of the ranks of the Boys' Brigade,
they must either do better or give place to some
organisation which will.'

Then follows an emphasis on the fact that every
Company must be connected with a ' Church, Mission,
or other Christian organisation.'

'For it cannot be too emphatically said that the
Boys' Brigade is a religious movement. Everything is subsidiary to this idea. It may not
always be brandished before the eyes of the Boys
themselves in so many words, and it would not be
wholly true to the type of boy-religion to over-
advertise it, but at bottom the Boys' Brigade
exists for this, and it is never afraid to confess it.
On the forefront of its earliest documents stand
these words: " The Object of the Boys' Brigade
is the advancement of Christ's Kingdom among
Boys, and the promotion of habits of reverence,
discipline, self-respect, and all that tends towards
a true Christian manliness." That flag has never
been taken down. "A true Christian manliness"
— that is its motto; and the emphasis upon the
manly rather than upon the mawkish presentation
of Christianity has been its stronghold from the
first.

'Contrary to a somewhat natural impression, the
Boys' Brigade does not teach the "Art of War,"
nor does it foster or encourage the war-spirit. It
simply employs military organisation, drill, and
discipline, as the most stimulating and interesting
means of securing the attention of a volatile class
and of promoting self-respect, chivalry, courtesy,
esprit de corps, and a host of kindred virtues. To
these more personal results the military organisation is but an aid, and this fact is continually
kept before the Officers by means of the magazine
which is issued periodically from Headquarters, as
well as by the official Constitution of the organisation. With the Officers, saturated as they are with
the deeper meaning of their work, feeling as they
do the greatness and responsibility of their com-

mission, it is an idle fear that any should so far
betray his trust as to conceal the end in the means.
As to the retort that the end can never justify such
means, it is simply to be said that the "means"
are not what they are supposed.   To teach drill
is not to teach the "Art of War," nor is the drill-
spirit a war-spirit.   Firemen are drilled, policemen
are drilled; and though it is true the cap and belt
of the Boys are the regalia of another order, it
may be doubted whether drill is any more to them
than to these other sons of peace.   That the war-
spirit exists at all among the Boys of any single
Company of the Brigade would certainly be news
to the Officers, and if it did arise it would as certainly be checked.   One has even known Volunteers whose souls were not consumed by enmity,
hatred, and revenge; and it is whispered that there
are actually privates in Her Majesty's Service who
do not breathe out blood and fire.   Besides this,
what is known in the "Army Red Book" as
Physical Drill is more and more coming to play
a leading part in Brigade work, and the governing body may be trusted to reduce the merely
military machinery to the lowest possible minimum

'The true aspiration and teaching of the Brigade
could not be better summarised than in this further quotation from its official literature:—

'"Our Boys are full of earnest desire to be brave, true
men; and if we want to make them brave, true, *Christian*
men, we must direct this desire into the right channel, and
show them that in the service of Christ they will find the
bravest, truest life that it is possible for a man to live.   We
laid the foundations of the Boys' Brigade on this idea, and
determined to try to win the Boys for Christ, by presenting

to them that view of Christianity to which we knew their
natures would most readily respond, being fully conscious
how much more there was to show them after they had been
won."

'There are at least two points where religious teaching directly comes in. The first is the Company
Bible-class. Every Company being connected
with some existing Christian organisation, the
Boys are urged to attend whatever Bible-class
exists, and in most cases they do so. But wherever no existing interest is interfered with, the
Captains usually provide a class of their own.
These special Company classes now number
about two hundred, with an average attendance
of over four thousand Boys; and that this side
of the work is receiving special impulse is plain
from the fact that last year saw the birth of over
fifty new classes.[1]

'In addition to these Sunday-classes, nearly every
Company reports an address given at drill on
the week-night, with more or less regularity; and
each parade is opened and closed with prayer,
or with a short religious service. Once a year
also it is becoming an increasing custom for the
Companies in populous centres to have a united
Church parade, where they attend Divine Service in "uniform," and hear a special sermon
from some distinguished preacher.

'But though this is the foundation of the Brigade,
it is by no means the whole superstructure. The
Brigade has almost as many departments of activity as a Boy has needs. It is clear, for instance,
that, in dealing with Boys, supreme importance

---

[1] The report for 1898 gives 473 Bible-classes, with an average attendance
of 12,819 boys.

must be attached to maintaining a right attitude towards athletics. And here the Brigade has taken the bull by the horns, and formed a special department to deal with amusements — a department whose express object is to guide and elevate sport, and, by unobtrusive methods, to get even recreation to pay its toll to the disciplining of character.

' One or more clubs for football, cricket, gymnastics, or swimming have been formed in connection with almost every Company, and the honour of the Brigade, both physical and moral, is held up as an inspiration to the Boys in all they do. The Captains are not so much above the Boys in years as to have lost either their love or knowledge of sports, and a frequent sight now on a Saturday afternoon is to witness a football match between rival Companies, with the Lieutenant or Captain officiating as umpire. At practice during the week also he will act as coach, and the effect of this both upon the sports themselves and on his personal influence with the Boys, is obvious. The wise Officer, the humane and sensible Officer, in short, makes as much use of play for higher purposes as of the parades, and possibly more. The key to a Boy's life in the present generation lies in athletics. Sport commands his whole leisure, and governs his thoughts and ambitions even in working hours. And so striking has been this development in recent years, and especially among the young men of the larger towns, that the time has come to decide whether athletics are to become a curse to the country or a blessing. That issue is now, and in an almost acute form, directly before society. And the

decision, so far as some of us can see, depends
mainly upon such work as the Boys' Brigade is
doing through its athletic department. Were it
for this alone — the elevation of athletics, the
making moral of what, in the eyes of those who
really know, is fast becoming a most immoral
and degrading institution — the existence of the
Boys' Brigade is justified a hundred times.'

The article then describes the Summer Camps and
other organisations for working-lads' holidays — which
when Drummond wrote (in 1892) had not reached a
tithe of the development to which, with vast benefit
to the health and morale of the boys, they have now
attained — the ambulance classes, musical bands, and
reading-rooms — and it closes with these remarks on
the Officers : —

' Behind all lies the supreme moulding force — the
personal influence, example, and instruction of
the Officers — manifesting itself in directions and
in ways innumerable and varied, and in results
which can never be tabulated. There is no limit
to what a good Officer can do for his Boys. He
is not only their guide, philosopher, and friend,
but their brother. In distress, in sickness, they
can count upon him. If they are out of work, or
wish to better themselves in life, they know at
least one man in the world to whom their future
career is a living interest. In short, throughout
life they have some one to lean upon, to be ac-
countable to, to live up to. He, on his part, has
something to live for. He is the Pastor of Boys;
and, if he is the right man, of their homes. Great
and splendid is this conception — that every Boy

should have a brother, that every home a friend;
not missionary, not ministering spirit, not even
woman, but man, a young man, himself in the
thick of the fight and helping others, not because
he is above them, but because the same powder-
smoke envelops both.

'Many of the prime movers in this new cause are
men who have been almost strangers to such
work before. But they saw here something definite, practical, human; something that they could
begin upon without committing themselves to
positions which they had not quite thought out;
something which could utilise the manlier elements in them, and give them a useful life-in-
terest outside themselves. Thus through the
instrumentality of the Brigade not only have
multitudes of Boys in town and country been
brought under a *régime*, morally and physically
educative, but numbers of influential young men,
including a great many Volunteers, have found
themselves for the first time enlisted in the cause
of social and religious progress. For a real field
of honest usefulness, a field where the tools required are simply the stronger and better elements in Christian manhood, there is probably
nothing open just now to laymen which has in it
anything like the same substance and promise as
this.'

CHAPTER XIX

THE END

THE first touches of the disease which ultimately killed him, were felt by Drummond in the spring of 1894 — on the back of a winter of hard work. Our club meeting, the last which he attended, was held in the beginning of May at St. Mary's Loch, and we noticed that of an evening he would sit in the warm sitting-room with his topcoat on. He had an easy summer, and spent several weeks fishing on Loch Stack, on the River Beauly, and elsewhere. But I am told he was sometimes so stiff that he could hardly cast a line. When he returned to college in November, his face looked worn, and he would shield himself from cold in a way we had never seen him do before. In December he had some sharp attacks of sickness, but he held to his college work without complaint, spoke in November at a meeting of the Glasgow University Settlement, presided in December over the gathering of the West of Scotland Ramblers' Alliance, of which he was President, and even arranged, with some trouble to himself, for the opening of a new line of work, to which for many years he had been looking forward.

This was the establishment of a 'Pleasant Sunday Afternoon,' for the men of that district of Glasgow known as Port Dundas, round the terminus of the Edinburgh and Glasgow Canal. Some citizens of Glasgow had founded here the Canal Boatmen's Insti-

tute,[1] in a fine building with a hall, library, and club-
rooms.   In the early part of January the missionary,
Mr. Gilbert, distributed a large number of circulars
calling the men of the district to a preliminary meeting
on Sunday, January 20th, at which Professor Drummond and Bailie Bilsland were to be present; and it
was intimated that they were prepared, if the movement went on, to give short addresses on subsequent
Sunday afternoons.   The meeting was full and hearty.
A large number of members was enrolled, and the
services were continued.   Drummond had at first an
exaggerated idea of the dislike of the men for whom
the meetings were planned to the forms of religion,
and he intended that there should be almost no
prayers.   This idea, however, was abandoned, and a
small service was printed; good music was provided,
and besides pieces from visitors, two or three hymns
were sung by the whole gathering.   Drummond grew
too ill to take his promised share of the work, but till
the last his heart was in it.   I do not think he sufficiently realised the danger, which the P.S.A. movement involves, of leading its members away from the
family aspects of religion; yet it is certain that, as in
other places, so here, the meetings attracted a large
number of men, who would otherwise not have attended
a religious service, and in his helplessness during the
next two years he was cheered by news of the progress
and the undoubted benefits of the work.

He intended to go to Edinburgh as usual for some
of the student meetings in February and March.   But
at last he had to write as follows: —

---

[1] In connection with the Canal Boatmen's Friend Society of Scotland.   President, Leonard Gow, Esq.; Vice-Presidents, Major Allan and Bailie Bilsland.

2 K

To Professor Simpson

'3, PARK CIRCUS, GLASGOW, Feb. 5, 1895.

'MY DEAR DR. SIMPSON, — I am very loath to write this letter, and have put off doing so from week to week, in the strong hope that it would not be necessary. But I see now the inevitable must be faced, and I wish to say that I must abandon the idea of coming to the Oddfellows' Hall this winter. I have had a second breakdown in health since Christmas; and though not at the moment actually ill or unfit for daily duty, I feel it would be wrong to attempt Edinburgh in my present condition.

'What you and the "Committee" will do in the circumstances I do not know, nor dare I suggest; but I know how well my place will be filled by others. Those who have come to our platform all these years have each their message, and one which will be fresher and weightier to the students than mine. I should stand aside with a very much lighter heart than I now do if I thought *they* would fill the breach. . . . I shall add nothing as to the disappointment all this means to me.'

It was grievous to watch him during these days at the work to which he clung in spite of all his pain and our remonstrances. When he came to his daily lecture the straight, lithe figure that used to bring brightness into our sombre college, crossed the vestibule bent and stiff. We found he was not sleeping at night, and his face grew pinched. So he struggled on till just a few days before the end of the session, when his doctors peremptorily forbade more lectures. He stayed in Glasgow a week or two, dissipating our

fears — all the more gloomy that fear for him was so
unusual — by his brightness between the attacks of
heavy sickness. Then for change of air and relief
from the constant siege of interests which his house
endured while he was in it, he left Glasgow — left it
for the last time. His work was done.

His work was done, yet one of the great services of
his life remained to be rendered. Looking back upon
the two years of weakness which ensued, we can clearly
see that as it had been given to him to prove how
fame, prosperity, and wealth of brilliant gifts may be
borne with unselfishness, so now he was strengthened
to show us how to suffer pain uncomplaining, endure
long illness, thinking more of others than of himself,
and at last face death, not only without fear, but without even a strained or hectic consciousness of his
fate. His disease, though this was not known till
afterwards, was produced by a malignant growth of
the bones, that caused him intense agony. As the
months passed, and his hair whitened with the pain,
it deprived him of all power to move, and made him
so brittle that he could not endure even the grasp of a
friend's hand. Except for some moments of wandering — and these only during the last weeks — his mind
was unclouded. He retained unabated the vigour,
and even the brilliance, of his intellect. He took an
eager interest in politics and in literature, remembered
in an astonishing way what absent friends were doing,
surprised them with telegrams of congratulation or
sympathy, planned the entertainment of those who
came to see him, and used to pose them with puzzles
and problems which he invented as he lay. The only
game he could play was chess, and he often won a
hard match. His sense of humour never left him,
and his room became a kind of 'pool' for new stories

which were brought him by his friends, and passed on
by him to others. He greeted you in his old way with
a flash of welcome, had a score of questions to ask
about your work, chaffed you, and chaffed himself,
too, in droll descriptions of his helpless state. His
weakness reaped the harvest of the love he had so
richly sown in the years of his strength. No man had
such friends or more devoted physicians. Some of
the former, and his brother, were always within hail
of him; the latter gave weeks out of their busy lives
to watch beside his bed. And so he sank slowly down
a long slope to the last edge, racked with pain, and
unable to move, but in clearness and peace of mind,
with faith and love and humour undiminished, and
with his friends about him to the last.

The stages of the journey were these. He was
taken from Glasgow to Edinburgh in the end of
March, 1895. In April he travelled to the south of
France for sunshine and the hot baths of Dax. In
May he removed to Biarritz. When these changes
failed to ease him, he was brought back to London
in July for further medical advice. From London he
was taken to Tunbridge Wells, where he lay under
the care of an old friend, Dr. Claude Wilson, his Scottish doctors visiting him from time to time. There
was always some talk of taking him south again, but
he was never fit for the long journey, and at Tunbridge Wells he remained from September, 1895, till
the end, in March, 1897. At first he was able to go
about in a bath chair, and even to walk a few steps in
the open air. But as winter came on he moved only
between his bed and the dining-room. Soon he
ceased to sit up, and his couch was wheeled from the
one room to the other. Sometimes he was unable
even for this.

I have tried to put together some of the relics of
those days — the wise and humorous words with which
he charmed us to the last; his kind judgments of the
men who were prosecuting him before the courts of his
Church; his pencilled letters about the lands which
some of his friends were visiting; his amusing telegrams; the fresh stories he told; his jokes and his
puzzles; his sane criticism of books and men; his helpful counsels — but they won't come into print. He
spoke often of the 'stupidity of being ill,' and twice or
thrice he said: 'Ah, you can't think how horrid I feel.
I have been giving all my life, and now it seems to me
positively indecent to be only getting. Well, perhaps
there's a lesson in that too.' Every good work of
which he heard still roused his interest, and sometimes
he longed to be up again for his share of it. 'I would
like to give a shove in there, if only with a catapult.'
Nor would he cease to plan what fishing he would
take for the next season. He did not speak of religion
more than he had done in the days of his strength;
yet you felt it was there, as natural and unforced in
the face of death as it had been in the fulness of life.
Sometimes he asked us to pray and to read the New
Testament. 'That is the book one always comes back
to.' And sometimes he asked for music: 'Oh, anything you like — a hymn for preference, or a Scotch
song;' and once he named 'The Land o' the Leal'
and 'Crossing the Bar.'

He was not without hopes of recovery, but it was
always difficult to know whether he really felt these,
or uttered them for our sakes. Yet from August, 1896,
his general health improved considerably; he put on
flesh. Towards the end of the year his pains abated,
and when his mother paid him at that time one of
her frequent visits, she could leave him without ap-

prehension.   To a friend who was leaving after a visit
at Christmas he said, 'You may see little difference
upon me in a week, but in three months I shall be
another man.'   This was not to be in the sense in
which he uttered it.   The cessation of pain was due to
the progress of the disease, and only showed how nearly
this had finished its work.   The constant strain was
telling upon his heart; and we now know that when,
on New Year's Day, he spoke so brightly, and ex-
changed telegrams of congratulation with his colleague, Professor Candlish, who, like him, had been
bedridden for months, the end for both was only
a matter of days.   Through February they grew
weaker, and when Dr. Candlish passed away on Sunday, the 7th of March, Drummond lay feeble and
languid.   In the afternoon Dr. Barbour played to him
the music of the hymn, 'Art thou weary, art thou languid?' and other hymn tunes, with no response.   Then
he tried the old Scots melody of 'Martyrdom,' to which
Drummond beat time with his hand, and joined in the
words : —

> ' I'm not ashamed to own my Lord,
>   Or to defend His cause,
>   Maintain the glory of His cross,
>   And honour all His laws.'

When the hymn was done, he said, ' There's nothing
to beat that, Hugh.'   It is a paraphrase of the words
of Paul: *I know whom I have believed, and am persuaded that He is able to keep that which I have committed unto Him, against that day.*

On Monday he rallied, but on Tuesday he was
weaker again, and his brother James and Dr. Greenfield were summoned.   His mind wandered upon
old themes.   He talked, half-dreaming, about John's
Gospel.

On Thursday morning he was very low. He murmured a message to his mother, became unconscious, and passed away very quietly about eleven o'clock.

The news came to us in Glasgow, by a tragic coincidence, as we were gathering to the funeral of his colleague, Professor Candlish. Upon the following Monday we went to Stirling to lay his body beside his father's, on the Castle Rock, in the shadow of the old Greyfriars' Church. This was not the only mourning for him. On that day, or upon one of the Sundays on either side of it, services were held in many towns of the kingdom; also in Princeton University, at Ottawa, at Adelaide, at Singapore, and I know not where else. Telegrams, public and private, with many later letters, proved that there was hardly a country on earth in which he was not being mourned. Yet at Stirling it seemed as if all were represented. The day was a wild one of sleet and rain, the steep town black with wet under heavy clouds, the surrounding hills white with snow. To lay him to rest there, upon the playground of his boyhood wrapped in gloom, there gathered mourners from every stage of the life that thence had started on its brief but brilliant way: his own people, the magistrates of the town, his mates at school and college, his fellow-workers in every cause for which he had laboured; but chiefly a crowd of young men, students in Edinburgh and Glasgow, yet from all parts of the empire, and from lands beyond, whose fresh faces shone through the dark church, not with the light of memory only, but with the bright assurance that for at least another generation Henry Drummond's work on earth would not cease.

APPENDIX I

THE reports from which these have been transcribed by me were
taken down, with Professor Drummond's permission, by Mr. George
Newman.[1] I have abridged or summarised them where they repeat any part of his published works. The audiences to which they
were given were of students, graduates, and professors only. They
were spoken from notes, for the most part very meagre notes, which
I have collated, so far as they are extant, with Mr. Newman's reports. The reader will keep in mind that these are mere reports;
and that, while the substance of the addresses is given in them, and
also, so far as they go, Henry Drummond's very words, yet they are
not complete, and cannot reflect, except in a broken way, the ease,
the vividness, and the grace of his style.   G. A. S.

I. EVOLUTION AND RELIGION

(January 26, 1890. Chairman: The EARL OF ABERDEEN.)

After illustrating Evolution as the method both of Nature and
History, the lecture takes up those aspects of it which concern the
Individual — (1) The Evolution of the Body, (2) The Arrest of the
Body, the Arrest of the Animal, amply described in the *Ascent of
Man*, Chaps. I.–III. The lecture continues: —
'Henceforth the *man* must rule, the body serve. Marcus Aurelius
tells us that the body is to be considered nowhere, and Paul says,
Reckon ye yourselves dead. This,. gentlemen, is one of the most
radical and subtle utterances ever spoken. But it does not mean
that the body may be treated in any way. Nay! Neglect your
body, and it immediately comes from "under arrest" and cries
aloud. But this speaks and aims straight at the *Temperance* of the

[1] See above, p. 353.

505

Body,' which the lecture then illustrates in a homely fashion by 'the effects of a "third pipe," indolence,' etc.

He continues: —

'Religion is not negative; it consists in spending life and time for the man, *i.e.* the spirit — to evolve. Give this a chance, and it will evolve. Hence, *crucify the flesh, take no thought for the morrow*, but *seek first the kingdom of God and His righteousness*. The moment a man allows his body to rule — this is sin, against God and against Nature. . . . Men say as justification that sin is natural, and man must sin. Aye, aye, gentlemen, he will do it naturally if the body is supreme; but if the spirit is noble and ruling, sin is not only not natural, but repugnant. One night some years ago in a University town there was a meeting of the White Cross Society. The meeting was over, one of the members had argued that sin was not natural, and at the close one of the medical professors, gathering a group of students around him, said, "That's gammon! The sin you have heard of to-night IS natural," and the students to a man hissed him out of the room. It was not in Edinburgh. What I say is this. I answer you, and I answer the world. It is *not* natural to be inverted, *not* natural for the man to be dead and the body to rule.

'"Sin is the subordination of the higher nature to the lower" (Martineau). It is, as I say, the subordination of the man to the beast. But, remember, the Body is the Temple of the Holy Ghost, and a violation of this Temple will be punished by certain death — nothing else, simply and purely *death*. Cell by cell, molecule by molecule, the magnificent fabric will tumble to pieces. The rule of the Body over the man is death. You (say, for example) are allowing your body to rule; project your life imaginatively a decade, and I say, *tremble* as you think. Death here, now and forever. Religion gammon? Gammon, when it tells you that the Body shall grovel to the man? I tell you, this is by far the grandest thing in the wide world. . . .

'Temptation is music to all ears. What is it that makes this vast throng of men feel to-night like brothers? Temptation. You know the man sitting next you is tempted like as you are. We are all tempted, *and we thus grow*. The man grows as "the man" wins. It is the brotherhood of temptation, a new and real tenderness, which binds man to man, not body to body.

'Why is it that student life is critical? Because the body has grown through all these ages, and we are thus full-grown "men-bodies," so to speak, whereas that man in us, that good spirit in us, is but a child, at the very most perhaps a score of years old. Train that boy to beat down the "man," the young spirit to beat down the old body. How? By a Power not his own, a Power which is greater than the power of evil.

'Religion, etymologically, is that which binds — binds a man to something higher, nobler, and better than himself, and binds man to man. All the accessories of Religion are merely auxiliaries. Prayer and church and reading your Bible are not Religion itself; they are auxiliaries. They help to *bind* you to a Perfect Man, and that Man is Jesus Christ, from whom can issue power to beat the Body. You must be associated with something stronger and higher, as the pure love of a sister or a faithful companion. You must be bound to Jesus Christ, and this will help you *to withstand, and having done all to stand*, that is, to rule.

'*Without Me ye can do nothing*. That is, without something higher and nobler than yourself you will do nothing good. You must have an aim to evolve yourself to. This is an imperceptible and a natural thing. You do not *think* about breathing. It is natural. Your mother has thrown a sacredness over your life. Her name brings to you purity and love in their highest forms; you are bound to something higher, and through her you are bound to Christ. Thus naturally you are evolved into the Perfect Man. You reflect Him everywhere; in other words, gentlemen, you are growing like Him. A man at college who reflects Christ is a man who is bound to Christ, and *thus* the "man" in him rules his life. You must bind yourselves to Christ to get it at first hand; you must become acquainted with the Lord Jesus Christ as your best Friend.

'Gentlemen, my object has been to bring into relief the great line running across Nature. On which side will you live? I call for decision. No man can serve two masters. Religion is what meets you on the upper side of the line, and carries you upward to live the life of the Spirit. Henceforth there is a dividing line in your lives between dead (the body) and living (the man); between temporal and eternal; between bad and good. I have one word to utter to you — *Choose*.

'Gentlemen, choose! If you choose life and good, you choose "the man"; something which can evolve and go on from better to better, even to the Image of the Perfect Man, backed up as you will be by evolution and nature. Grace and strength come from the Power to which you bind yourself. *Remember*, you cannot live on meetings. This impetus will only last a day or two. Go home to your knees and your Bible. Lay hold of Christ. You are a child in Christ to-night; wait and trust Him, and you will evolve — if once

you are in connection with Christ. *Reckon ye yourselves dead —
seek first the kingdom of God and His righteousness, and all things
shall be added.*

'May God bless the men of this University, and evolve in His
grace and power "perfect men," noble and upright and pure, that
they may go forth in their lives to bless and to heal, to purify and
to sanctify the world.'

II. EVOLUTION AND CHRISTIANITY

(February 2.   Chairman : Sir WILLIAM MUIR, K.C.S.I., D.C.L., Principal and
Vice-Chancellor of the University.)

Professor Drummond began by speaking of Love upon the same
lines as he has expounded it in *The Ascent of Man :* —

'Love is the greatest evolutionary force the world has ever seen.
All opposing forces fall at the sight of it.   The animal power in
life yields to it.   The power of war is broken by that which formed
the power of war at the first. . . .   This has been a long story, but
its application, I trust, will not be so long.   Last Sunday it was
Evolution and Religion.   To-night it is Evolution and Christianity.

'For what is this great ascent of power rising out of mere grega-
riousness into sympathy, into love, into sacrifice — what, I say, is
this, if not the dawn of Christianity before Christ comes? . . .
Christianity is as old as the dawn of life itself.   It began in the
nooks and crannies, far away down there in the past, built in to the
very foundation of the world. . . .

'A man came to my house last week, and said he wanted to talk
over religion, for he was in a muddle.   I asked him in, and we set
to.   He was not a Christian, he said.   He found Kings very difficult to understand.   He knew a man who called himself a Christian,
and did not seem to live by the Bible truth.   He thought the
commas in the Bible uninspired, for he could not make things tally.
I thought, Is it possible that this is a "man" before me?   Has all
this absurdity anything in the world to do with Religion?   Not understand Kings!   Nor the "six days" of Genesis!   A few days
before I had been thinking about this most glorious scheme of Christianity, and here before me stood a man whose whole religion I
could put in a pill-box!   And yet I say to you that there are men
listening to my voice now who will not accept Christ because they
do not understand the Old Testament nor see how Jonah could live
in a fish's belly. — Oh, gentlemen, look for one moment at the

magnificence and sublimity of Christianity from the standpoint of evolution. Look at the sublime age — from the earliest dawn of life! Look at the size — illimitable! Look at the beauty! Could anything be more perfect than the greatest thing in the world: any force so irresistible as the greatest evolutionary power, Love! I say, stand back if you can. A man with the faintest touch of reason sees something before which everything else fades. He cannot help reaching forward and grasping the most splendid treasure in the universe.

'All this fits in perfectly with Science. . . . A Christian is a man who furthers the evolution of the world according to the purposes of Jesus Christ. I do not see how men can resist religion if they have the most elementary views of evolution. . . . But has everything occurred by its own evolutionary power? I answer definitely and distinctly, No. As there is a force pushing cell to cell, or a cell onwards alone through life, so precisely in the course of nations, God is behind all. The love of God pushes on society, pouring itself into the hearts of men. What is the outcome then to you sitting before me to-night, looking forwards to your lives and professions? It is this in a word: Choose that life and profession in which you can work alongside this evolutionary force for the redemption of the world. Work with God!

'Work with this love of God. An iota short of that you are lost and useless, but this power will last to the end, till all else has passed away. It is for you and me simply to *choose*. Oh, for a new poet to place in a religious poem the power of this evolutionary force!

'Gentlemen, it is nothing sudden or capricious, nothing vague. It has come now in perfect order, not a day too late, and it could not have come sooner. By the revelation of God in Christ Jesus it is yours; and how does it affect us to-night? This-wise, that if you and I agree now to cast in our lives with His scheme, we shall be different men to-morrow morning from what we are to-day. To-morrow in this University there will be a new evolutionary force of Brotherliness to stimulate our actions. . . . Every word you utter, every thought you think, every action you do, will be said, thought, and done by Christ Jesus in this power of the love of God. . . .

'There was a medical student a year or two ago, who was half way through his course, when it dawned upon him that he had lived for himself, and he decided to change and go and see if he could find any one to help. And he found an old chum who had gone to the dogs. He had fallen to pieces, given up his work, and his exams., and was living aloof from other students and drinking hard.

No. 1 went and found him lying on the floor drunk. He paid his debts and took him to his own rooms, gave him supper, and put him to bed. On the next day he had a talk with him. He produced a piece of paper, and they made a contract to keep them both straight: —

'(1) Neither of us to go out alone.

'(2) Twenty minutes only to be allowed to go to the college and return: overtime to be accounted for.

'(3) One hour every night to be given over to reading other than studies.

'(4) That byegones be byegones.

'Both men put their names to this, and for weeks they lived, No. 1 praying and doing all he could to help No. 2. After a time No. 2 saw that the odd evening hour was spent by No. 1 in reading his Bible. No. 1 never spoke to him about it; he simply sat and read. Aye, gentlemen, I tell you that was a fine sermon. He never spoke *about* Religion; but he spoke Religion. He was teaching the brotherhood of man and the life of Christ. Now No. 2 was learning unconsciously to know God. Why? Because God is Love — No. 1 loved him; and Christ is Sacrifice — No. 1 sacrificed his life for him. Not a word was said. At last No. 2 changed. What he changed to I need not say. The last I heard of them was this. No. 1 is filling an appointment of great importance in London. No. 2 passed his exams. that year with the highest University distinction, and is now in private practice.

'Gentlemen, you have that opportunity of doing good. You have asked me here to-night. I have come, and you have brought on yourselves this responsibility. I lay it upon you. Gentlemen, you are not doing a small and silly thing when you follow Christ. That man was a Christian. Take up the cross of Christ to-night and follow Him this week, for it is the most reasonable and natural thing for you to do. Band yourselves together as consecrated men in the Divine struggle of the world. It will bring you happiness of which you have never dreamt. Arise as men in Christ to-night, and give yourselves altogether to this supremest duty!'

III. SIN

(February 9. Chairman: Professor T. GRAINGER STEWART, M.D., LL.D., etc., President of the Royal College of Physicians.)

'For two evenings, gentlemen, I have tried to speak to your Reason[1] . . . but this is only one part of your existence, and to-night I want to open the Book of Human Nature. As your Principal has said, the great thing is your life: we do not want your theories and your knowledge, but your life. Religion is not to be *proved*, but to be lived, and every man among us to-night is trying the experiment of how best to conduct his life. You must remember that this life of yours is an original creation. Each life is a fresh gift from God, for usefulness or uselessness. How can I use this precious gift to the best ends?

'To-night I would like to say a few words on the deepest thing in Human Nature — that which is called in theological language *Sin*. We may view this subject in three different aspects. (1) There is the *guilt* of Sin. (2) There is the *power* of Sin. (3) There is the *stain* of Sin. It is to this last I wish you to look — to the consequences of Sin — that something which you and I cannot turn our backs upon and let alone. It is a stain. . . .

'Sin is a living thing. The idea which I had as a child, and which probably many of you had as well, was that our sins were like bad marks put opposite our names. They were placed against us in the Book, and then Some One would come and wash away the whole lot, and we should be fit for the Kingdom. Our page would be white and clean, and therefore the little things one added to the list mattered little, because it all would be washed away and made clean.

'There is no more disastrous view that you can possibly take.

'Once when I was at Sunday-school I heard this story: In the East there was a man lying in his prison cell for murder. A friend came to see him, and in their conversation they spoke of the murder. I should have said that between the cells there was only a curtain, so that one on the other side could hear all that was being said. Well, the man told his friend all about his life, and then came the story of the murder, when, in the middle of it, he suddenly pulled up startled, and stopped. Why? Because he heard through the curtain the scratch of a pen. So he remained silent; the interview ended, and his friend went. The man was afraid lest his words should be noted against him. So I used to think that a Recording

---

[1] Here follows a summary of the last two lectures.

Angel stood by me and noted down all I did or said.   This, gentlemen, is an erroneous view to take of Sin.   God does not play the
detective with us.   That would make men dislike God, not Sin, and
they would attempt forthwith to forget Him and live without Him.
They would have no hatred for Sin.   Since then I have found out that
there is, after all, a Recording Angel.   She is yourself, and her
name is Nature.   And her pen never scratches, and you never hear it.
It is silent, for it is great.   Year by year, moment by moment, all is
taken down, but in complete silence.   The pen never ceases to write.
It works in the body, aye, in the very nerves and tissues of the soul;
and all you have ever said or done, or left undone, is registered
forever in your own nature.

'*Whatsoever a man soweth* THAT *shall he reap.*   Mind you, he
shall not only see it grow and see it ripen, but he shall *reap.*   And
everything you sow shall grow, and you, and you only, shall most
certainly reap.   *Be sure your sin will find you out.*   It won't perhaps be found out.   But, I say, it will find *you* out.   It will grow
and grow and eat out your life.   It will run you to earth a doomed
man.   For the end of these things is Death.

'And you will reap in many directions.   You may not know the
seed or the ground you sow, but *sow* and you will *reap.*   You will
soon know what harvest when you reap.   Men know thistles from
oats.   You sow and sow, and then you hope God will forgive and
your page be clean.   I answer you, Nay.   Sow thistles, and thistles
will come up.   Sow oats, and thistles will not come up, oats will
come up.   "Sow thistles," you say, "and then sow good oats,
and thus clear the thistles."   No, the harvest will be thistles and
oats. . . .

' Physiologists tell us that men never forget — that the memory is
independent of the will, and that our memories will follow us, will
live to the end, and will go down with us to the grave.[1] . . .

' Students' sins are special sins.   Every class of man is tempted
in its own special way.   You are not tempted to avarice, stealing,
murder.   No.   You are tempted to dishonesty; and though it is
not spoken of in sermons, it is, all the same, as big a sin as drunk-
enness and lust.   Nay, more so.   Why?   Because it is a sin of the
higher nature, and sins of the higher nature are blacker than sins of
the lower nature.   If there is a man in this University who is doing
evil things; if he is scamping his work, he will *reap.* . . .   In the
church, in law, in commerce, in medicine, scamp your work, cheat
your examiners, and you maim your lives.   I say the consequences

---

[1] Here follow some cases of cheating at examinations.

of Sin are living and real, and a man has not done with them at the moment. He may have done with them, but they have not done with him. He will reap in his memory, in his conscience. Remorse is the most awful thing that can haunt a man's life. It is, in a word, a stain.

'And the stain spreads to those around him. . . .

'The whole of a man's nature is built up, I might say, of cells. One after another, good and bad, all things have become part of him. His sins have made *sin* a part of him. That unkind thing you say or do makes you an unkind character. That selfish thing you do makes you selfish, pure and holy and noble thoughts are turned out, and you become an animal. Paul says, *Wretched man that I am, who shall deliver me from this dead body?* Chained as they were in those dark dungeons of the East, if one prisoner died he was left chained to the man next him. . . . *This dead body* — it was Sin. But, gentlemen, we are making dead bodies with our own hands and lives: cell by cell we become dead. Sin is a part of one, and the end of these things is death, and all of a sudden some morning we awake and say, *Wretched man that I am, who shall deliver me from this dead body?*

'Sin finds men out in the form of Temptation. Temptation is the result of constantly yielding. A constant doing passing into a habit — it really comes to be a predisposition to do what we have done before over again, and this is temptation. We have built up the muscle-fibre of temptation by constantly using it. Some day Tennyson's lines will be true, that our character is a part of all we have met. Look at the brain. It is made up, as you know, of countless cells and processes. If an intellectual process runs through our brain once, it leaves comparatively no effect. But say it over a hundred times, and a foot-path is worn through the brain; the hundred and first time will be easy. Say it a thousand times, and lo! through all the cellular structure of the brain there is forever laid a thoroughfare upon this one intellectual idea, and temptations and sins march to and fro in endless procession along the beaten track. Men do not commit two different kinds of sin. You have your own favourite sin, and I have mine, and as it grows the trick is intensified, the path more beaten still, and the end is Death. One thing kills a man, and if you are guilty of one sin, your doom is sealed. Therefore guard against making a thoroughfare. Decide once for all to close the thoroughfare by gates which shall last forever. Let that evil thought never pass that way again.

2 L

'Some say and will tell you that religion has the power to take away the punishment of Sin. I think not. You and I shall bear the punishment of the sins we commit, for whatsoever we sow we shall reap. But what is taken away is the guilt. The guilt of Sin is forever swept away from us by one thing only, and that is the death of the Lord Jesus Christ.

'If you are drinking hard, don't think religion will give you a new body. No; you must go back and undo it. Your religion will not uproot it [the old body], however much it may change you. But I believe, gentlemen, that if a man goes back, the grace of God will overpower and minimise his sin, but it must be paid for. In other words, you shall reap.

'Now, what am I to say to the man who wakes up to-night from the past and looks back, and wants now to change. I say three things, and the first is a hard saying.

'It is Restitution. If it be possible to go back along the trodden road, find the place where you fell, and undo the mischief. . . . God can give you courage to go through fire and water for His sake, and He will do it now and here for any man who hears my voice in this silence.

'I knew a man who led a woman astray. He was fast and evil then, but a year or two after he was changed, and became what he is — one of the most prominent men in the religious world. But through all his success and apparent blessings there was the stain and the shadow of that woman's life upon him. Only three people ever knew about it, and it was twenty years ago. He preached all through England and Scotland and Ireland in the hope, I fervently believe, that that woman might hear him and be saved. Every prayer he prayed, he prayed for her. Not long ago I was in London at a meeting which he was addressing, and after the meeting a woman walked up to him with bent head, weeping. I saw them alone as they stood. That was the woman he had searched for in the restitution of twenty years. That man's sin was finding him out, and God will help and stand by you if you will make a manly and heroic effort to turn back and undo the past.

'The second, gentlemen, is Resolution. Be decided for Christ. Don't just come here and go away again and forget. Don't let it be any passing emotion. Go away home across the Meadows to your rooms, and stand alone in the silence of the night before God, and decide, and be prepared to pay the cost.

'And the third is Religion. It is cruelty to tell a man to give something up if you don't give him something in its place. Nature abhors a vacuum. He must not say, "Yes; I will arise and be this, that, or the other;" but it must be, *I will arise and go to my Father;* and in that Father's presence, love, and power, he will find a new life, a new love, a new power — aye, something that will change him and restore him to the image of his Maker. Put off the past, but in putting off the old, put on the new. Emerson says that the great crises in men's lives are not marriages, deaths, or great occasions, but some afternoon at the turn of the road you find new thoughts and new impulses fill your breast. You are *con*-verted to something. Your life is changed, and you henceforth live for that new and higher impulse. As you sit to-night alone, before your Maker and your God, is there no new impulse fills your heart? Something which sweeps the past away? Something which wins you; something which is the perfection of loveliness; something peaceful? Do not fear it, but listen, and in the stillness there comes the voice of Jesus: "*Come unto Me, all ye that labour and are heavy-laden, and I will give you rest.*"'

IV. TEMPTATION

(February 16. Chairman: Professor CALDERWOOD, LL.D., represented by Dr. C. W. CATHCART.)

'Gentlemen, I must ask the forbearance of the men here to-night who are in intellectual difficulties if I speak to the men who are in moral degradation. It has come to my knowledge through the week, from a bundle of letters from men now sitting in this room, that there are a large number with their backs to the wall. They are dead beat, and I shall consider their cases first.

'I want to say a few words on the subject of Temptation from an evolutionary point of view, and I shall begin by planting one ray of hope in the heart of the man who listens to my voice at this moment who is in utter despair, for this is the most brotherly thing I can possibly do for him. He says his best resolutions for years have been broken, and his prayers apparently unanswered, so that all his hope for the future is gone down in the struggle for his life.

'It was said once that the Duke of Wellington was in a foreign country trying to get his soldiers to a place of safety, and between him and this hoped-for safety there was a deep and rapid river, neither bridge nor ford could be seen, and it was a hostile country; he sent his men up and down the side of the river to hunt for a bridge or ford, but they found none. So the Duke went to the top of a hill near by and looked through his telescope, and far away down the river side he saw a town, and on the other side of the river he saw a straggling village, and he said, "Now, between that town and that village there must be a ford or a bridge." So when night came he sent his soldiers in the darkness and silence to see, and they returned and said, "Yes, there is a ford." He passed his army over in the night, and the next day they were found in the land of safety. Gentlemen, many men have been in dangers as great and greater than you, and have found a ford. So I say to that man and to you all — Don't despair!

'You can do nothing when you are in despair. The very first thing to do in this, as in everything else, is to believe in *possibility*. All things, you remember, are possible to a certain class of men.

'There may be some here to-night who were here some years ago when these meetings had their first beginning, and you may remember me reading a letter which was characterised by some of you as "A Letter from Hell." You remember, it was a frightful revelation of a tortured, sunken, lost human soul. It was anonymous, and signed "Thanatos."[1] Years have gone by, and I have not forgotten that man; and if ever I thought a man was hopelessly, irretrievably lost, it was that man. He was an intellectual, physical, and moral wreck. I thought that case an impossibility. Gentlemen, I have in my pocket to-night a letter from "Thanatos," which he sent me this week, and he says he is at last a changed man — a new creature in Christ Jesus. He says the new life has choked the old, and that he is now in a position of responsibility and usefulness in this country.'

The address then proceeds to 'view the whole subject of Temptation from an evolutionary standpoint.' 'Temptation is this man enticing that man,[2] flesh *versus* spirit. . . . Temptation is not sin, and not only not sin, but it has a high evolutionary value. *Count it all joy when you fall into divers temptations.* It is an opportunity for virtue; it stimulates us to a higher and nobler life; it is the test of a "man." . . . Now comes the practical teaching. To-day I asked one of your professors: "What do you tell a man will help him to resist temptation?" He said: "I tell him that the best thing by far is to ignore it." Do you hear that, gentlemen? — "Ignore it." Don't think he meant "take no thought of it, or don't think it of any consequence." But it is to be ignored. *Reckon ye yourselves dead.* . . . Give it no quarter, and the moment you do that a great natural force comes at once to your rescue, and the most wonderful principle of nature backs you up — "*vis a tergo*" —

[1] Θάνατος = Death. [2] See above, in the first address.

Degeneration, that great power which removes everything that is not used — the great lopper off, the Scavenger. For some time, however, the temptation will appeal to you. It will ask to be heard again, or for the last time. It has [too] a habit of hibernating. . . . I say to you — Trust in Nature and trust in God, and Degeneration will do its perfect work.

'That is the negative, and now I turn to the positive, and would like to express it to you in Scriptural formula: *Walk in the Spirit.* Expand and enrich that higher life. In all ways and in every way expand. In music, in the arts, in literature, in poetry, in religion — anything which is stimulating to the man. And I would mention another way which is foremost for us, and that is, Work, good hard work, nothing can keep the devil out so well. . . . But let me add, don't work too hard. In the interests of physiology and the physiological relations to temptation, don't work to excess.'

Then follow some wise counsels about food and exercise; some counsels taken from *The Mental Diseases* (p. 490), by Dr. Clouston, the lecturer on Insanity in Edinburgh University; and a beautiful parable. The address closes: —

'Now I have only two words to say. The first is, Begin thoroughly. It is a thousand times easier to live altogether for Christ than half for Christ. Don't be an amphibian, half in one world, half in another. Be men, through and through, men in Christ Jesus. Come to Jesus now, and come altogether. — And the other thing is: Every man will only finally succeed in gaining the victory in himself so that it includes others. A man this week was in difficulty about these things, and I said, "Have you ever helped any one?" He said, "No." So I said, "Well, go *now* and help somebody. I don't care how or when you do it. Simply do it. Go and help somebody."'

V. THE NEW NATURE

(February 23. Chairman: Professor A. R. SIMPSON, M.D.)

'I think, gentlemen, I can get to the position at which we left off last Sunday night if I tell you a story about an Indian officer.

'A certain Indian officer lived in a bungalow in India, and this bungalow was elevated on the top of a mound. One season the whole country was inundated with a flood; water was everywhere; but there was just a speck of land which was left, and it was the mound with the official bungalow upon it. And upon this mound was gathered together a motley crowd of natives, some wild beasts, insects, and birds, all having gone there for safety. And after a while, to the consternation of the company, they observed a large, fine Bengal tiger swimming to the island. It reached it, clambered up on the bank, and lay down close to the edge in fear and quietness. It lay like a dog, and did not know what to do. What made that tiger be like that, so quiet? What made it forget its natural and ordinary fierceness? It was the expulsive power of a new emotion. It was *Fear:* the fierceness and wild nature were gone, and it lay perfectly still because it was afraid. But the officer knew that shortly that fear would pass away, and the fierceness would return, so he took his gun and walked close up to the tiger, and put the muzzle of the gun into the tiger's ear and *shot;* and the great beast rolled over *dead.* You say that was cruel. Maybe, but it was the wisest thing to do. I tell you that because it brings out a point of great importance. It shows the power of a new emotion, and it also shows its transitoriness. What would you and I not give, I would like to know, to shoot dead in us the tiger? Some men here have for the last five weeks been slowly killing it. I ask you to *shoot.* Shoot it *dead.*

'Last Sunday we tried to see how to deal with the animal. To-night I want to show, if I can, what is to be done for the Development of this New Nature when we have ceased to live the animal life after our own nature. But I need scarcely tell you that the new nature, the new life, may fade away and pass off as an emotion would fade. If the officer could have *kept* that tiger in great fear, there would have been no need to shoot. The tiger would have been *domesticated.* The secret of all taming of animals is by a process of fear and subduing nature. If you and I could keep up the new nature of ourselves, we should go on aright to the end of the chapter. But to keep in the new life and to keep out of the old animal is the great problem of religious life. How can we be brought into the new life, that the new life may stand by us to the end, not for a session or two, but be something which will build its foundation into our deepest nature, that we may be ready for the struggle of life which is before us?

'How is the ship tested? When it is in mid-ocean, in the middle of a cyclone? No; the ship is tested with its ropes down, its masts not yet fixed, and the last rivets not driven. It is tested first, and then it goes out to sea. Shortly, gentlemen, you will be out at sea, and I must ask you, Is your building stable? Is the helm adjusted? Because if it is not thoroughly made, it will not overcome in this world of temptation.

'The question of Evolution, as you know, is divisible into two factors: (1) The Nature of the Organism; (2) The Nature of the Environment. We have learned in the past something of being evolved. There are two compartments — one the animal, the other the spirit. That is a correct classification; but, to be exact, split the higher into two or more parts, because men must not only stand above the animal nature, but between him and the animal nature a long, weary series of years, during which our ancestors existed, has welded a force into our nature, and we must deal with both. Many of you are not troubled with flesh temptations, but you are troubled with temptations of the disposition, so I divide temptations into two classes — from the Beast and from the Savage.

'The question to-night is, How to evolve, how to pass from the Savage. We have already learned of the Passage from the Beast. We know we must reckon ourselves *dead*, our animal nature dead. We simply let it alone and evolve past it. But what is to be done with this savage disposition?

'In this disposition we have one fact, the organism, and a second fact, the environment. There is no organism that is self-supporting or self-sufficient. Nothing can do for itself. It must of necessity be helped by its environment.[1] . . . Now of all created beings man is the most sensitive to his environment. . . . God has provided environments for all other constituents of man's nature. . . . It is inconceivable that He has provided nothing for the highest of these. What has He done for the environment of the soul? He has done the most natural thing conceivable. What is it you want to be in the Spiritual Life? I say, you want to play the MAN. We want to be above the Savage, not below. The Savage state is selfishness, love of approbation, absence of sympathy ; these are the marks of the Savage. We have the same savage in us. He has come to us through our ancestors, and he is in every one of us. We must find somewhere a larger mind, a sweeter disposition. Now, what God has done is to place before you and me an absolutely Perfect Man, with whom, as we are in contact, we shall rise. He is to be our environment, and we shall slowly change till we are like Him. Can a man be born when he is old? Not so easily, I grant you, as when he is young. But still he may be born when he is old ; it is not impossible, and this new birth is a change in a man's nature, as he is in contact with the perfect spirit and the perfect nature of the Lord Jesus Christ. I am not talking any false religion or cant. It is perfectly natural that a man's nature may be changed by

[1] Here follow several illustrations from the physical sphere.

the spirit and nature of another man. God sent Newton to teach physics, Kepler astronomy, Darwin biology. And God sent Christ to teach humanity. I do not put Christ on the same level as Newton or Darwin. I am speaking of analogue, not of homologue. As Christ was a perfect representation of God Himself, by so much more was He greater than Newton, Kepler, or Darwin. But just as these men were provided by God for the times, and each taught and perfected his own science to his best ability, so Christ was provided as an environment of thought and nature for the spirit and nature of man. In a word, He was divine. But that does not remove Him from the rational and intelligent, for it is by taking Christ as a man that we understand the power of His life. There's the principle, and it is demonstrable by science. Nothing can evolve of itself. . . . There is something without which you cannot possibly grow. *Without Me ye can do nothing.* Get into contact with the perfect life of Christ, and leave the rest to nature. But how is this to be done?'

There follows a passage on the real and full manhood of Christ, and the absence of mawkishness, sanctimoniousness, and effeminacy from true Christianity.

'Find out the people who are the friends of Christ. Read books about Him. Find how He spoke, how He lived, what He lived for, how He died, and what He died for. Faith cometh by hearing, and you will find as certainly as anything that an irresistible passion will rise within you. . . . You say to me, "Give me details about Him." I cannot do that, for time is passing. Read Ullmann, read *Ecce Homo*, read any of the recent great biographies of Christ. Can you not spend thirty minutes of your life in getting to know the Perfect Man? Go home and take up the best of all the lives, the exquisite biographies by simple, honest men, the authors of the New Testament. Begin with Matthew; and if you don't run aground before the end of the fifth chapter, I shall be astonished. You cannot help yourselves, gentlemen. You read a few verses, and you fall hopelessly in love with a Man you have so far neglected. Slowly the knowledge changes into character, and that is changed in turn into the same Image. . . . Then you lisp, "My Lord and my God"; then you know His Divinity.

'This is not a sudden change. . . . You won't find this life in Christ in these meetings; no sensation revival and sweep and all done. To-day and to-morrow will be the same, generally speaking, because the evolution of a life is a gradual process. *Start* in a moment. Be born *now;* but grow like unto Him, and be changed in time into His image, for *the kingdom of God cometh without observation.*

WHAT COMING TO CHRIST MEANS

' There will be two more meetings only, and I want to say a very few words to those who are really anxious for these things. I want to be practical, and so I am going to ask those of you who would like to stay for ten minutes to keep your seats while we sing a hymn. You will be asked no questions; you'll not even be called to come forward. You may remain in the seats you occupy. We want new lives and consecration to Christ. Now I hope all the rest will go out quietly as we sing the last verse of the hymn.'

Some two dozen men left. ' The rest,' eight hundred or nine hundred, remained for the ten minutes.

' Gentlemen, I proposed this because, unless I am wrong, there are men in the hall to-night who have seriously made up their minds to live for Christ. And there is another set of men, more numerous still perhaps, who do not know whether or not they are Christians. There is a certain value in decision on our own parts; not that the change from the old to the new life is marked by any decisive periods, but it is help to many following Christ and to many hanging back to have definite epochs of encouragement or choice.

' I want to ask you one or two questions in the secret chambers of your hearts.

' Why do you come to Christ? What do you want? Is there a sense of need? Do you want the unholy part to be blotted out forever? If so, you have come to the right place, for God for the sake of Jesus forgives sin.

' Have you a sense of the power of sin that nothing you know of can break? Do you believe Christ is stronger than the Devil? If so, again you have come to the right place, for that is true.

'Are you longing to live a better, nobler, truer life? If so, again you have come to the right place, because Christ alone can give you this. Remember, *Blessed are they that hunger and thirst after righteousness.*

'Another question is, Have you counted the cost? Have you made up your mind to throw in your lot with the people of Christ? I don't ask you to be identified with all that is done in the name of Religion. Religion is a popular thing, and many things are done in its name which will make you revolt; but I do insist that you shall not be ashamed to be identified with Christian men and join them in their work for the world. Gentlemen, count the cost.

Have you made up your mind to say good-by to the world, the flesh, and the devil? If your answer is, Yes, I have to say that you are eligible candidates for the kingdom of God, for of such is the kingdom made. And I have further to add, that you are not only eligible, but invited; *that* on the authority of Chirst. It is not presumption on your part. You are to come just as you are. Little as you have and are, you are requested to bring it all for the service of the Master. Otherwise, otherwise you are not wanted. He says, *Come unto Me; Give Me* thine *heart*, thine all; and, *Him that cometh unto Me, I will in no wise cast out.* It is Recruits Wanted! A personal invitation. Christ has set His heart on you here and now; and now and here invites you to enter into His life.

'What steps must you take? Different are the aspects, different the ways all leading unto Him. We are told in the last chapter but one in Revelation that the twelve gates of the city were twelve pearls. You may come in by any of them: some of you will come by one, some by another. Don't think you *must* go in by the way your friend went. Go your own way. *Every single gate was of one pearl.* Spurgeon goes in by one; Robertson of Brighton by another; you by a third. Go just as you are in your own nature. You must get near to Christ and close to Him. The emphasis is on the *object*, not the *action* of faith; and that which is in us showing us the way *is* Christ Himself holding out His hand to help us.

' There are one or two different aspects in the New Testament of the Christian Life — a Race, a Fight, and Fellowship (John's aspect). . . . They are all the same, and include one another.[1] . . .

' You are before God now. Just tell Him all about it. Tell Him your need. Consecrate your life and talents to His service; and if you will listen, you will hear Him say, *Him that cometh, him that cometh I will not cast out.*

'I cannot guarantee that the stars will shine brighter when you leave this hall to-night, or that when you wake to-morrow a new world will open before you. But I do guarantee that *Christ will keep that which you have committed to Him.* He will keep His promise, and you will find something real and dependable to rely on and lead you away from documental evidence to Him who speaks to you in your hearts at this moment.

'Gentlemen, He will be youı leader, He will be your guide, He will be your highest ideal. He has asked you for your life, and He will make you just as you are at this moment His — entirely His.'

---

[1] Here follows what he said in 1885 about matriculating in the school of Christ.

VI. WHAT IT IS TO BE A CHRISTIAN

(March 2. Chairman: The Rev. Professor FLINT, D.D., LL.D.)

'Gentlemen, I do not feel at all anxious to continue the somewhat formal set of addresses which I have given to you. Not only because this is one of the last, and we are near the end, but because we cannot possibly go on to-night as if nothing had happened last Sunday evening. You remember that at the end of the meeting I expressed a wish that those who desired to come to the point and know what were the first steps into the Christian life should wait behind the others for ten minutes; and, as you know, several hundred men remained; and therefore, gentlemen, it is impossible to go on as usual. You remember that I asked you to count the cost. Have you done so? I asked you if you felt a sense of need, and I put Christianity before you in the form of four metaphors, which I chose from Scripture, in which I explained to you the beginning of the Christian life.'

Professor Drummond then summarised his second address of the previous evening, and added:—

'Decide once for all, and have no more coquetting with the world, the flesh, and the devil. You cannot serve two masters. Make up your mind, gentlemen, what you are going to do.

'When a man begins to be a Christian, he does not commit himself to a great many things which some people think necessary. The antithesis is not whether good or bad, but the choice between temporal and eternal. Christianity is not to make men behave themselves — all men should do that. Paul did it before his conversion. . . . *Christianity is to be something more than good.*

'I need not tell you, of course, that it is not *necessary* for Christians to go to church. Thousands of Christians never go, and thousands go who are not Christians. . . . But I qualify the statement by saying that every right-minded man will go to church, because it is advisable and expedient. Not only as a personal matter, but for the sake of the community, *associate yourselves with the people* of God. A Christian can do without church, but it weakens himself not to go. To go to church is to be taught how to do without church, and, though I say this, I also say that if he goes he will be fed. He will be helped, and he will have a better chance of survival in the higher life. However much you like to despise such institutions, if you give them up you will get lost; because they prevent Reversion. A domesticated animal cannot go back to the wild state — it will die. All Christians should make that an impossibility by building up around them a fortress.

'In the next place, to be a Christian does not mean that you must believe in all the various doctrines. All doctrines are not Christianity. Many a man with no doctrine is a Christian. . . . Christianity is not a thing to be proved, but a life to be lived. But I qualify this also. You men will be wise indeed to find out and study the great doctrines of Christianity. There are doctrines in Christianity as much as in medicine. The authorities are as scientific in method as the most learned scientific observer here. You must search theology as you do other subjects. Go to the experts, not to the penny magazines. From tracts men get depraved and distorted views of the great Christian doctrines, as, for example, the Incarnation and Atonement. Take your stimulus from wherever you like, but for doctrines you must go to authorities as trustworthy and confident as you go to in any other subject.

'I do not say that to be a Christian you must have no doubts. Doubts show interest and zeal, and I pity the man here to-night who is cocksure of everything in Christianity. It is not all plain as a pikestaff. . . . Doubt is one of the most blessed states a man can be in. It is the purifier of thought. Until he has doubted and then thought, faith to a man is merely credulity. . . . No man can live in this nineteenth century and not have doubts. . . . All great truths are doubtable. I don't say doubtful, but doubtable. The instrument through which a doubter looks is broken more or less, and it must be corrected for achromatism or distortion. Men don't understand, and when they don't understand they doubt. There was no class of men with whom Christ was more sympathetic than those who doubted. He liked to get away from the Pharisees and the men who were cocksure, the men who "knew it all," and to walk with the humble, true-hearted, loving spirit. . . . Christ was not hard on those who were not sure. He was not narrow, like so many Christians to-day. There was no speculation about His teaching. He taught truth which men might lay their hands upon and grasp. He said to them all: I don't speak truth, or about truth either, but I am truth. I am truth — the truth of life, of conscience, of righteousness. . . .

'Well, all these things, gentlemen, are non-essential; and there are one or two minor things which men must not hold back for. I am often told by men here in Edinburgh that they don't come to Christ because they are told that it is setting themselves up. This is a charge made against every man, and I acknowledge the possibility that self may wrongly get set up. But so far from a man feeling set up by accepting Christ, he feels like a brand plucked from the burning, and it is the grace of God which is holding him up by the skin of his teeth — the grace of God which has pulled him out of the mire of his temptations.

'Others come and say they don't like to begin, because they are afraid they will go back. This is remedied completely by making a decided step and stand for Christ. Be a Christian, and let men know it.

'Everything in Christianity, I always think, should be in the superlative degree. The best men are the men Christ wants. The best mentally, the best morally, the best socially.'

Then he pointed out the high places in the honours list of medicine which were gained by men foremost in the Christian life of the University, and also how some of the latter were members of the University Fifteen.

'I have said all this, gentlemen, because there are men who delay because they expect some marked epoch in their lives to usher them into the Christian life. They are waiting for some catastrophe to begin the new life. I tell you, it is a mistake. Nature does not work by bangs, catastrophes, and great events, Nature works silently, Nature glides; and I solemnly say that I know of nothing in the wide world more natural than Christianity, for the *Kingdom of God cometh without observation.*'

He then stated the case of the Metazoa, and illustrated metamorphoses taking place after birth, from the caterpillar and butterfly. ' So is it,' he said, 'with man. No wonder that Christ said *Marvel not.*' Here follow the heads and much of the matter of his own sermon on 'Marvel Not' in the *Ideal Life.*

'And now I have told you the negative side of the question with which we started, and the positive is, *Help on the evolution of the world.* Although Christ allows us to be indefinite about our beliefs [? doctrines], still He has expressed this duty in the plainest possible way. Look all through the New Testament, and the important facts of Christ are marked by *Verily.* To those you must be consistent, for He has asserted His purpose to carry on the evolution of the world. But He uses a figure of speech, *The Kingdom of God.* This is evolution. It begins, He says, in the grain, then the blade, then the ear, then the full corn in the ear. What do you want more? Is not that a precise evolutionary statement? . . . The man who joins the Christian Life finds security and something which, as a Law of the World, will evolve the animal into the perfect man.

'Let me choose three words which Christ used to make His teachings plain,— Salt, Leaven, Light.

'What use is Salt? It is to keep things from going rotten. . . . It is Christ that keeps this University from going rotten. It is the followers of Christ in this city that keep Edinburgh from going rotten. . . . Without Christ this world would fall to pieces. There is nothing in Nature which can hold together without the salt of Truth, Honour, and Righteousness.

'What does Leaven do? It raises. Why is it that education follows Christ round the world? Because Christ is the elevating and raising force of the world.

'And, gentlemen, Christ is the Light of the World. The moral Light and the mental Light. Half of the great problems are unsolved, because they are without Christ and without light. Increase your knowledge, and you will increase your sorrow. It will trouble you. You will be weary of it, and there will be no end. But hear this from Christ: *Learn of Me, and ye shall find rest.* The more you think and know, so much the more will you find in Christ.

'Christ wants you to join Him in His work: this is the *motif* of God through all the ages. Is it not worthy to accompany Him in the evolution of the world? There is no higher life than helping others. And the only way it is to be done is by men's lives. . . . I solemnly say, *God wants you.* As you came along the street to-night you heard a man preaching the gospel of the Lord Jesus. You heard the bare, narrow, stern religion, and as you passed, a smile crossed your lips. Why? Because you know of something which is broad and lovely, infinitely loving and beautiful. I say, don't laugh till you have done better; for these men are the evangelisers of the world. So don't sneer at them, but, gentlemen, cast in your lot with them, go forth, stand under the lamp-posts, and tell out to the world the grand old story of Jesus and His Love.

'The first thing is to carry that story into the world in your lives. Every man here to-night who names the name of Christ is to create round him an environment of Christ, so that men shall see the kingdom of God, and grow up like Christ. Give them the social position to serve Him; give them legislation, give them wages, give them houses; to keep, to spend, to live in for His sake and service.

'And, gentlemen, to you, some of you, who will go out to your village and be the doctor of the neighbourhood, to you I say: Create the environment of Christ. Be some one to remind the people of Jesus. Be some one to represent Christ in the district. Do what He would do; say what He would say; live as He would live, just as if He were the Doctor of the neighbourhood. Live the life, and reproduce the life of Christ.

'To those of you who have in the past few weeks learned the rudiments of following Him, I offer my sincere congratulations, because this will grow. Be decided for Him. I am more and more convinced of the fact that what the world wants now is not more men of the ordinary type of Christian, but better men and finer men: men consecrated to Christ, men out and out for Christ, whose one life's ambition is not to get rich or achieve a great name, but to learn of Him, and to seek *first the kingdom of God and His righteousness.*

VII. ADDRESS BEFORE COMMUNION

THE BREAD OF LIFE

(March 9. Chairman: Rev. Professor CHARTERIS, D.D., who afterwards presided at the Communion Service and dispensed the Sacrament. There also assisted Principal Sir William Muir, the Rev. Principal Cairns, Professor Calderwood, Professor Crum-Brown, Drs. Coldstream, Barbour, etc.)

'Gentlemen, I am glad that this series of meetings is to close by our sitting down together at the Lord's Supper. Because it is one of the many things that bring into our memories the necessity of living upon Christ. It teaches you and me, in the first place, that man may be hungry, and it shows us that Christ is the Bread of Life. And, secondly, the presence of the actual bread is an object lesson to us which will emphasise the essential things that we are to carry away with us. I was talking last Sunday to a man who said that though he could live for Christ at the close of the meetings, or could even for a month or so keep straight, yet after that his new life went down and was lost. Now, gentlemen, this proves two things. It proves the possibility of a man living for Christ and keeping straight under suitable conditions, and it proves also that if a man tries living without the Bread he will flag and die. You can't live on air. You can't live on one another. You can't live on what I say; but, gentlemen, you can live on the Bread of Life, which is Jesus Christ.

'Now the great question which we must ask ourselves is this, Have we ourselves, *at first hand,* learned to draw our nourishment and strength from Christ? I want you to settle now and forever, Is He the heart and kernel and spring of your life, or is He not? If He is not, then all these meetings are of no avail, all this talk of no use; but if He is, then, gentlemen, you need nothing else, for He is the Bread of Life.

'Your holidays are coming to some of you, and to some of you your examinations. Now I warn you the hour will come when hunger will assert itself, and I tell you to-night that Christ is the Bread at that hour. The time will come when temptation will knock at the door, and it will be something then to know that Jesus Christ is the Bread. Perhaps during the summer you will meet another beggar, and you will hear his piteous cry, and you will see his condition, and you will want to feed him. It will be something *then* to know that Christ is the Bread of Life and can keep a man from starvation. Keep from starvation? Aye, and not only that, but give happiness and fulness to life.

'The problem of Nutrition is the fundamental problem of physiology, the fundamental problem of living beings. So exactly is it the fundamental problem of the Christian life.'

He then drew a long analogy between physical and spiritual nutrition in the terms of physiology.

'But the closest parallel I can draw is that which we see in life and read of in tales, where one man is the sustenance and life of another, or more often where a woman is the sustenance and help of a man. Something which is very pure, which is fresh, which is high and lofty — why, it throws an influence around the base life which elevates and ennobles that miserable life to the level of its own. Not in a day. Not in a year. But in a long continuous process which works unseen. How is it done? By abiding in the presence of that which is pure and noble. One life affects the other, and the weak becomes stimulated and roused; *there* are the elements of growth. So a man who abides in the presence of Jesus Christ in some mystical way appropriates, unconsciously and unavoidably, the life and character of Christ, so that he is built up like Him. That is the whole process. It is perfectly simple and perfectly natural. The point of importance is this, that it is quite impossible to go on at all in the spiritual life without living in the immediate presence and fellowship of Christ. This, gentlemen, is to reach the Supreme. This is to be nourished and strengthened for life, not showing just a leaf or two of the fruits, not something that will last only to the end of the session; but something that will last *from day to day*. You know of people who have fasted thirty days. Don't try that in your own spiritual lives. You cannot do it. *Give us this day our daily bread*. And, gentlemen, I warn you in all affection and humility that if we try living on ourselves, it will fail. Why? Because Jesus has said, *Without Me ye can do nothing*. Nothing at all, so don't try it. Our spiritual lives will dry up; our characters become poor, our faculties atrophied. You may have ill-health and a breakdown in your spiritual, as in your natural, lives. It is just as simple, just as natural. Eat bad food, or no food, and it will tell in a fortnight. Your nourishment must be pure, noble, lovely, and of good report, or else you will lose your appetite. These meetings may come again, but you will not be there. The Christian men will know you not, and you will not be found with them, because you have lost the taste of better food. This I say: Let us keep ourselves in Christ as we are now; live day by day; and be renewed day by day into the image of Christ Himself. Surely that is simple to understand, and perfectly natural.

'But, gentlemen, you need something more than bare life, I tell you. Christ expects from men like you more than mere life. He wants the fulness and richness of Himself impressed for ever upon you. He wants from you the Christian graces in their fullest and utmost perfection. We hear that as long as men have the *roots* of these things they are all right, and never mind about the graces. I answer, What do you imagine a garden like full of roots only? Beautiful soil yet — nothing but roots! What do you say to a garden full of sour apples? What is the difference between a sour apple and a sweet pippin? The gardener will tell you it is a difference mainly of nutrition. Transplant that sour apple, give it your best soil, give it fresh air and sunshine, and lo! it becomes larger, and then it changes and becomes sweet, and then luscious and juicy. Take only average food, and you will have average life; but good nourishment will bring forth a strong and beautiful character.

'You will find in your Bibles a lovely phrase which I like very much. It is this: The Beauty of Holiness. The Beauty! The perfection of the Christian character; not simply things done after a good style, but things done with beauty and with grace. Look for a moment at the exquisite loveliness, beauty, and grace which characterised all the actions of Jesus. There is a marvellous *grace* about each and all; there is an attractive peculiarity which calls forth unbidden our deepest love and admiration. What is it? Gentlemen, it is the Beauty of Holiness.

'There are a great many graces which go to form our religion. Religion does not just consist in stopping this sin and stopping that, and fleeing this temptation or that, but it consists in growing — not perfection, but growth — growing into the likeness of Christ. If a man's ideal is simply to stop sinning, his Christian life becomes monotonous. The man here who knows how to play the violin goes to hear R—— play, and it dawns upon him that it will take at least

2 M

another twenty years before he can play at all. The artist goes through the Turner gallery, and he finds it will take him a lifetime to copy the major points from Turner. The man who will sit down for twenty minutes in his room and look at the character of Jesus Christ, feels his longest life not long enough; nay, that eternity itself is not long enough to approach the surpassing and infinite glory of that Figure. Then, gentlemen, a new sensation comes. He rises and — what? Lo! He is hungry and thirsty. He hungers and thirsts to live like *that*, or see in himself and in others the mind which was in Christ Jesus. The spiritual life becomes stale and uninteresting when the man has lost sight of his Ideal. He has forgotten his life's work. He perishes morally, just as he would do in his physical nature by ceasing to take nourishment.

'But we are told by some that beauty in character is a matter of birth; that it is a matter of temperament whether you and I have a bad temper or not; whether we have patience, gentleness, meekness, and that therefore we need not trouble about them. These may have been affected by predisposition — they are, I grant you, influenced more or less by heredity — but I say, these are fitted into men's lives. Any man in this hall who covets any single virtue or grace can have it, if he sets about getting it in the right way. Let me try and indicate some of these graces.

'I remember well how I used to pray for joy. I was told that a Christian must be joyful. I prayed and prayed, and I must say I did not get it. Why not? Because it does not come by prayer alone. It may come that way, but not alone. I used to think that joy was kept in lumps — packets which were stored up and then doled out — or injected like morphia — and that if I prayed a lump would come. This is a material conception that many hold. They want virtues and graces, and they set to and pray. They pray for rest, peace, love, joy, and they hope these will drop from heaven and stay with them forever. But these are *Fruits*. How can you have *Fruits* without *Branches*? Where are your branches to bear fruit, where is your blossom to precede it? What's the use of a lump of joy if there are no branches? Now, gentlemen, look up in your Bibles and find out how to get joy; find the *cause* of joy. Work by the law you know of as "cause and effect." Joy is an effect, find the cause. There is one, just as surely as you have a cause for toothache. Turn to the fifteenth of John, and there you will read the parable of the Vine in the words of Jesus. He tells His disciples about the tree and its branches, and then He tells them the "why" of these things: *These things have I spoken unto you, that*

My joy might remain in you, and that your joy might be full. That is the end of the parable — the cause of joy, something of which the effect is joy. Joy comes of a great law. But what is the condition? Go home and look and see. *It is to do good.* Abide in Christ and bring forth fruit, then comes the joy, and you can't help yourself. You don't make the joy. It simply follows after a certain cause, and I defy any man in this hall to go off and do something for somebody, comfort them, help them, any one whom you may meet — I say, I defy him to do that and not come back happier and full of joy. This is cause and effect, and any one can get joy in this way. Abide in Christ, be in His presence, and you shall certainly have fulness of joy. *These things have I spoken unto you that your joy may be full.* Find out these things, and the joy *must* follow.'

Then follows a paragraph or two on the same thought, applied to the gift of Rest — as in *Pax Vobiscum.*

'All this is simple, and it comes to a Christian. By living on the Bread of Life we get the form and the functions of the Christian. Those things *follow* . . . and make your lives fair and lovely, which is the Beauty of Holiness.

' You know how healthy and full of vigour you feel after a walk or exercise. So it is after spiritual exercise, doing good to those around you, that you have the fulness of spiritual health and vigour. But while each grace and virtue has a cause, of which it is the effect, yet to secure them we must go back to the source — which is Christ. As you know, all power in the mechanical world is from the sun. It is the source of all energy. . . . So also all the energy of the Spiritual Life comes from the Bread of Life, which is Christ Jesus. God is our Sun.

' There are a few other things I would wish to say. No man liveth or worketh for himself. Live for others. Work for others. Work unitedly as members of His body. This at once brings me to the social character of the members of Christ. Let there be among you Christian Solidarity. The man who goes away from the world and shuts himself up in his rooms and won't come and join you in the social life of his time is useless, and useless things die. Don't, gentlemen, don't live for yourselves. The finger is not useless. Cut it off and place it on the table, and it is not only useless, but ugly. But you are living; you must be useful and lovely. Take away any member from the body, and it becomes ugly. *Apart from Christ* — you may say what you will — you are ugly, and you are useless, and you will die. Watch these men on the street finishing those figures to adorn that building. How foolish the pieces look until they are put together in the building, until they become part of the building. A solitary Christian life is an anomaly. You are to be social, joyful, beautiful, and fresh for His sake. For the body has for its Head Jesus Christ. That changes life, and man has a new tie to the man next him, because they are both members of one body . . . each in its own place with its own work to do for the body. And *the hand is not to say to the foot, I have no need of thee; nor the ear to say it has no need of the eye.* . . . There is nothing, I think, of more comfort than that we are all, as members of the body of Jesus Christ, of some use; and made by Him especially for His work in the world. If you have not discovered your function, depend upon it, that is something out of the ordinary. . . . There is an endless variety of things in the Christian life. One says: No, I have nothing to do. I say, let that man believe he has something very definite to do as a member of the Body. Because the Head expects it, and will show him what it is.

'Gentlemen, you will not live long before you find your work for Him. Do it with all your might. *Seek first the kingdom of God and His righteousness.* I have said it so often, I am almost ashamed to repeat, but I must. It is this. Do your seeking thoroughly. Be out and out for Christ. It is far away easier. I have the most supreme pity for the man who is an amphibian, a sort of Dr. Jekyl and Mr. Hyde — at church to-day, to-morrow with the world — a constant struggle to get back the life. Some men think it is easier to do so. But they will, I hope, live to discover that it is a thousand times easier to be out and out for Him. Go in for His service thoroughly. Be soldiers of the Cross. Be completely consecrated, as you have sung in that hymn —

> "Take my life, and let it be
> Consecrated, Lord, to Thee!"

Reversion to the old man and his life will be impossible. Not until each of you has consecrated his whole and his all will he have any chance of usefulness or joy in the Christian life.

'You will remember what is said in Revelation of the lukewarm, the amphibian — *Because thou art neither cold nor hot, I will spue thee out of my mouth.* This is the only passage in which words of disgust are written from the lips of Christ. A last love, a dying man, a sacrifice because of the half-hearted! *I would thou wert cold,* for thy sake, but especially for the world's. Why? Because He says that tepid Christians bring the world's contempt upon Jesus Christ. They crucify Him.

' Resolve to-night at the Table of the Lord. Make an oath before Him to consecrate your lives to Him—a living sacrifice, holy, acceptable unto God which is your reasonable service. You, come to minister, not to be ministered unto. *For me to live is Christ.* Don't, oh, gentlemen, I beg you, don't go out at that door to-night without Christ, without God, without hope in the world. Leave the past, forget it, and come to Him now: men consecrated entirely to Christ.

' The harvest is past, the winter is gone, and yet you are not saved. You will look back over years to this night, and you will see you missed your chance. Have no fear, for *perfect love casteth out fear.* Jesus loves you, loves you all with an everlasting love. If you are the chiefest among sinners, come now to Him, just as you are, and He will receive you gladly and cleanse you from all unrighteousness!

' May God bless and elevate this University! May He purify it by His followers! May He bind together a band of men who shall go forth to the ends of the earth to spend their lives and be spent in His service.'

APPENDIX II

ADDENDA

Since the larger part of this biography was in print, papers of Henry Drummond, and recollections of him by others, have continued to reach me. They contradict nothing that has been recorded; for the most part, they only corroborate this; but a few report some facts which I have overlooked, and which appear important enough to demand notice. I give them here, with references to the relative pages.

Pages 82, 91. For Dr. Dale's opinion of Moody and Sankey's Mission, see his biography, just issued.

Page 120, line 8 from bottom, read 'in the Free Church of Ayr.'

Pages 137 ff. Henry Drummond did see Holmes after all — on his third visit to America in 1893. To his delight, the old man, who was then eighty-four, talked 'straight on for an hour and a quarter, then apologised that no one that day had previously called to "run off the electricity." He says he usually gets ladies to call first and "go into the water like the horses to take the electricity off the electric eels before the men come." He talked of all the Immortals of New England.'

Pages 147 ff.   Henry Drummond has left notes for a new Preface to *Natural Law in the Spiritual World*.   These make it clear that he meant not to rewrite the Book, but in the Preface to qualify a number of its absolute statements.   He restates more guardedly the physical law of Biogenesis.   And in the spiritual sphere he says that 'any suggestion of spiritual birth as an isolated phenomenon or unrelated effect is to be taken with reserve.'   Cf. pp. 157 and 463 (the quoted paragraph).

Pages 190 f.   It should have been stated here that the United Presbyterian Church has a share in the Livingstonia Mission of the Free Church of Scotland.   Dr. Laws, the head of the Mission, was a member of the former Church, and is supported by it.

Page 224.   Here, or on some other page of the chapter on Henry Drummond's African journey, it should have been stated that the natives called him by a name which signifies 'He who looks' or 'gazes'; whether because of his careful scrutiny of minerals, insects, etc., or because of the keenness of his eyes when he looked into another man's face, is unknown.

Page 237.   It is a remarkable fact that Mr. Campbell Finlayson's very able reply to *Natural Law* reached in 1895 a third (a posthumous) edition: London, James Clarke and Co.

Page 380.   Yale University, Oct. 3, 1887.

'I spent half-an-hour with Mark Twain at his own house [Hartford, Connecticut].   He turned on the gun at once, and is really a very droll creature.   He speaks just like his books.   He let off several jokes which would have printed on the spot.   He has a reputation for great kindness to all who need help.

'Next door to him I found Mrs. Harriet Beecher Stowe — a wonderfully agile old lady, as fresh as a squirrel still, but with a face and air like a lion's.   I have not been so taken with any one on this side the Atlantic.'

INDEX